Fields of Sense

Speculative Realism

Series Editor: Graham Harman

Since its first appearance at a London colloquium in 2007, the Speculative Realism movement has taken continental philosophy by storm. Opposing the formerly ubiquitous modern dogma that philosophy can speak only of the human-world relation rather than the world itself, Speculative Realism defends the autonomy of the world from human access, but in a spirit of imaginative audacity.

Editorial Advisory Board

Jane Bennett
Nathan Brown
Levi Bryant
Patricia Clough
Mark Fisher
Iain Hamilton Grant
Myra Hird
Adrian Johnston
Eileen A. Joy

Books available

Quentin Meillassoux: Philosophy in the Making Second Edition by Graham Harman
Onto-Cartography: An Ontology of Machines and Media by Levi R. Bryant
Form and Object: A Treatise on Things by Tristan Garcia, translated by Mark Allan Ohm and John Cogburn
Adventures in Transcendental Materialism: Dialogues with Contemporary Thinkers by Adrian Johnston
Form and Object: A Treatise on Things by Tristan Garcia, translated by Mark Allan Ohm and John Cogburn
The End of Phenomenology: Metaphysics and the New Realism by Tom Sparrow
Fields of Sense: A New Realist Ontology by Markus Gabriel

Forthcoming series titles

Romantic Realities: Speculative Realism and British Romanticism by Evan Gottlieb
After Quietism: Analytic Philosophies of Immanence and the New Metaphysics by John Cogburn
Infrastructure by Graham Harman

Visit the Speculative Realism website at www.euppublishing.com/series/specr

Fields of Sense

A New Realist Ontology

Markus Gabriel

EDINBURGH
University Press

© Markus Gabriel, 2015

Edinburgh University Press Ltd
The Tun – Holyrood Road
12 (2f) Jackson's Entry
Edinburgh EH8 8PJ
www.euppublishing.com

Typeset in 11/13 Adobe Sabon by
Servis Filmsetting Ltd, Stockport, Cheshire,
and printed and bound in Great Britain by
CPI Group (UK) Ltd, Croydon CR0 4YY

A CIP record for this book is available from the British Library

ISBN 978 0 7486 9288 0 (hardback)
ISBN 978 0 7486 9290 3 (webready PDF)
ISBN 978 0 7486 9289 7 (paperback)
ISBN 978 0 7486 9291 0 (epub)

The right of Markus Gabriel
to be identified as Author of this work
has been asserted in accordance with
the Copyright, Designs and Patents Act 1988,
and the Copyright and Related Rights
Regulations 2003 (SI No. 2498).

Contents

Series Editor's Preface

As of this writing, Markus Gabriel is probably still best known to Anglophone readers of continental philosophy as a prominent interpreter of German Idealism. His 2009 book *Mythology, Madness, and Laughter*, co-authored with no less a figure than Slavoj Žižek, is a fascinating work in this subfield.[1] Gabriel's solo-authored 2013 book *Transcendental Ontology* is another study that uses German Idealism as a speculative launching pad, and one in which Gabriel's own philosophical voice edges more towards the forefront.[2] In Germany itself, Gabriel's best-known work is the astonishing bestseller *Warum es die Welt nicht gibt* (*Why There is No World*), which has made him a German media presence like perhaps no other philosopher since Peter Sloterdijk.[3]

This is not to say that Gabriel was previously unknown in Germany, a country that reveres its philosophers at least as much as France. He was born on 6 April 1980 in Remagen, a twenty-minute drive south of Bonn: in the shadow of the castles of Siegfried and Roland, and close enough to the student fraternity of Friedrich Nietzsche. The reason for evoking this history of the Rhineland is that Gabriel has already written himself into that history in at least one respect. Namely, in 2009 he became the youngest holder of a full professorship of philosophy in Germany, younger even than the prodigious F. W. J. Schelling. While this would make him only an academic curio in the English-speaking world, in Germany it has led to a certain degree of public acclaim. While Gabriel's unusually warm and commanding personality has made him the centre of increasingly visible activity in Bonn, his uncanny talent for foreign languages has allowed him to function almost ubiquitously on the world philosophy scene. Name a country in the developed world, in either hemisphere, and it is likely that Gabriel has already appeared there in some capacity.

More formal arrangements have made him a visiting professor in Lisbon, Berkeley, New York, Naples, Venice, Fortaleza, Porto Alegre, Rio de Janeiro, Toulouse and Aarhus, lecturing always in the local language of these places. And now China appears to be next on his list.

At least two other things make Gabriel a unique figure in contemporary continental philosophy (despite his distaste for this term). The first is his nationality. Following the Second World War, the epicentre of the continental tradition shifted from Germany to France; Paris has been the leading factory of new continental theory for the past seventy years. Other than the special devotees of Jürgen Habermas and the late Hans-Georg Gadamer, most Anglophone continental philosophy students travelling to Germany have done so for scholarly purposes rather than to roll the dice on the future of philosophy. Those wishing the latter have generally steered toward the *Quartier latin* of Paris. But now Gabriel, well connected and with seemingly boundless energy, is quickly developing Bonn into an alternate centre of activity. If Germany re-emerges as a leading site of new continental philosophy, as history suggests it will, it seems likely that Gabriel will play a role in this development. His influential Summer School in Bonn consistently draws the most promising students in the field, and his impressive parade of invited speakers in Bonn sets a standard that is hard to match.

Second, it is difficult to imagine that anyone stands in the midst of more currents in present-day philosophy than Gabriel. The appearance of the present book in the Speculative Realism series bears witness to his serious engagement with this recent school, which he alone has brought into contact with the Italian New Realism of Maurizio Ferraris, that renegade former heir of Gianni Vattimo. But as the present book will demonstrate, Gabriel is also thoroughly conversant with analytic philosophy, devouring the works of Kripke and Putnam, Sellars and Searle, as ravenously as those of Badiou and Žižek. Indeed, many continentally-inclined readers might have the first impression that *Fields of Sense* is primarily a work of analytic philosophy. But the diverse character of Gabriel's references, his convincing way of weaving together different traditions, is a probable early signal that the analytic/continental divide (whose end has often been prematurely declared) may *actually* end in our own lifetimes.

I will end this Preface with only a brief overview of *Fields of Sense*, since Gabriel is his own best explicator. Gabriel is himself a realist: a standpoint that has been deeply unpopular in continental philosophy since long before Husserl and Heidegger. Yet Gabriel also rejects what he calls the 'old' or 'metaphysical' realism. One problem with the old realism is that it cannot account for the grain of truth in relativism: the fact that the existence of entities such as mountains seems to require some individuating work on the part of human-sized beings for whom certain bumps on the surface of the earth are more relevant than others, and who make certain arbitrary decisions about where the bumps end or begin. Another problem is that at least some versions of the old realism insist on mind-independence in such an extreme fashion that they automatically exclude minds from existence, in an attempt to turn everything into just a third-person description of what it is. Gabriel is no eliminativist; he insists that philosophy must come to grips even with the sheer illusions that occur in consciousness, rather than exterminating all naïve 'folk' descriptions of reality as the price of doing philosophical business. Gabriel's position, which he calls New Ontological Realism, is that the constructivism of individual perspectives must be grounded in a reality that is itself not necessarily constructed. As he puts it in his helpful Introduction: 'The fact that Mount Etna looks like a mountain to me and like a valley to the Martian are relational facts involving Mount Etna itself and not just facts involving me or the Martian'.[4] Or more generally, 'metaphysical (old) realism is exclusively interested in the world without spectators whereas constructivism is exclusively interested in the world of the spectators ... New ontological realism accordingly occupies middle ground by recognizing the existence of perspectives and constructions as world-involving relations'.[5]

This is why Gabriel abandons the anti-realist connotations of the word 'perspectives' and replaces it with the Frege-inspired term 'senses'. While perspectives are generally taken to be a matter of how humans look at objects, Gabriel takes senses to be properties of objects themselves. This explains how a book called *Fields of Sense* can be realist in spirit, rather than defending an epistemology of the senses that things have for human speakers and observers. Unlike object-oriented philosophy, which speaks of a gaping chasm between real objects and their sensual counterparts, Gabriel acknowledges no such gap, and instead treats concepts and objects as cut from the same cloth. In the terms of analytic philosophy, this leads Gabriel to defend a descriptivist theory of reference even in the face of Kripke's powerful objections to any such theory. The argument of Kripke is that we can easily refer to objects despite using bad descriptions (such as 'Columbus is the one who discovered America' or 'Einstein invented the atomic bomb'), and therefore that we can refer 'rigidly' to Columbus or Einstein even if all of our descriptions of them turn out to be utterly false. But Gabriel counters boldly:

> all this proves is that we can refer to objects with bad descriptions, which does not amount to an argument that objects can exist independently of all the descriptions that indeed hold good of them. The claim that there are no objects below the threshold of senses (ontological descriptivism) is not in conflict with Kripke's insight for a theory of reference.[6]

Gabriel shows how an entire system of philosophy follows from his initial insight into the uniform status of concepts and objects. Gabriel's intriguing fusion of realism with descriptivism also helps explain how he can simultaneously defend both realism and German Idealism, an unlikely two-step that he performs quite differently from other contemporary authors. On that note, I leave the reader to enjoy the lucid argumentation of Gabriel's *Fields of Sense*.

Graham Harman
Cairo
June 2014

Notes

1. Markus Gabriel and Slavoj Žižek, *Mythology, Madness, and Laughter: Subjectivity in German Idealism* (London: Continuum, 2009).
2. Markus Gabriel, *Transcendental Ontology: Essays in German Idealism* (London: Bloomsbury, 2013).
3. Markus Gabriel, *Warum es die Welt nicht gibt* (Berlin: Ullstein Verlag, 2013).
4. p. 10.
5. p. 11.
6. p. 12.

Author's Preface

Luckily, there are many people I have to thank for having contributed in different ways to the publication of this book. There are so many of them, in fact, that I am not able to mention everybody to the extent they deserve. This book was mostly written during my visiting professorship at UC Berkeley in the spring semester of 2013. During that time I had various occasions to talk with colleagues in the department of philosophy, occasions from which I highly profited. I would like to thank Hans Sluga for making my visit possible, for pushing me on many details in epistemology, and for improving my understanding of Wittgenstein. Many thanks to John Searle, who regularly formulated important objections to some of the ideas presented here in his notoriously and profoundly clear manner. It was great to be his office neighbour. I would like to thank the department for inviting me, and all the students who influenced me. Most particularly, I owe a lot to discussions with Umrao Sethi, who was kind enough to provide me with very detailed critical comments on an earlier draft of the manuscript.

I have presented the ideas that led to this book in various seminars in Bonn, Naples, Beijing, Porto Alegre and Palermo, as well as in lectures in many other places. I tried to accommodate as many of the insights that I was able to bring home from these trips as possible. Many thanks also to my home institution, the University of Bonn, with its International Centre for Philosophy and the Käte Hamburger Kolleg 'Law as Culture', which generously granted me a series of sabbaticals.

I also learned a lot from the International Summer School on 'The Ontological Turn' hosted at Bonn in July 2012, where I profited from very open-minded and lively discussions with Graham Harman, Iain Grant and Ray Brassier. In Bonn, my thanks go to Wolfram Hogrebe, Michael Forster and my research team Jens

Rometsch, Abby Rutherford, Marin Geier, Dorothee Schmitt and Max Kötter. They all regularly presented me with objections and forced me to clarify my views. Regular discussions on the topics of this book took place in conversations with other graduate students as well. Special thanks go to Marius Bartmann and Conrad Baetzel. Special thanks also to Abby Rutherford for reading so many different drafts of this manuscript, for correcting the language, and for pushing me to acknowledge that metaphysics is still a meaningful practice even if we divorce it from the – in my view – misguided idea that there is such a thing as the fundamental nature of reality.

The final version of the manuscript was written during my stay at the Freiburg Institute for Advanced Studies in the winter semester 2013/2014. I thank the Institute and the University of Freiburg for the invitation and all the colleagues who discussed some of the ideas presented here at the Freiburg philosophical colloquium at FRIAS and during private meetings. I am thinking in particular of Günter Figal, David Espinet, James Conant, Anton Koch, Tobias Keiling and Nikola Mirkovic.

This book also contains repercussions of my time as a DAAD post-doc at New York University, where Thomas Nagel (who was then writing *Mind and Cosmos*) and Paul Boghossian (who was then writing *Fear of Knowledge*) convinced me of the one-sidedness of relativist and constructivist tendencies in my earlier way of thinking about knowledge and justification. I also owe a lot to Crispin Wright and his work in epistemology. This influence crystallised in my book *An den Grenzen der Erkenntnistheorie*, in which I first spelled out the idea that the recent discussion of sceptical paradoxes is substantially related to the German Idealist discussion of the problem of the existence of the world (though not of the external world, which is an entirely different topic!). My ideas about the degree of relevance of German Idealism for contemporary epistemology, ontology and philosophy of mind have also been shaped by recent discussions with James Conant, Robert Pippin, Jonathan Lear, Manfred Frank and Sebastian Rödl.

This book is the much more detailed counterpart to my introduction to the topics discussed here in my *Why the World does not Exist*. Together with Meillassoux' *After Finitude*, Nagel's *Mind and Cosmos*, Boghossian's *Fear of Knowledge* and the work of Maurizio Ferraris from *Goodbye, Kant!*, *Why the World does not Exist* has lead to a renewal of the realism debate in German contemporary philosophy under the heading of a 'new realism'. In this context, I would express my gratitude to Maurizio Ferraris, who suggested thinking of the sea-change in contemporary philosophy as it is practiced in Italy, France and Germany in terms of a new realism. Many thanks to all the participants in the international conference on *Prospects for a New Realism*, which was hosted at the International Centre for Philosophy at the University of Bonn in 2012, and which brought renowned philosophers from the USA, Italy and Germany together in an effort to spell out the consequences of the failure of the exaggerated forms of constructivism that have haunted the humanities for decades.

This might be the right place to emphasise that I reject the idea that there are such entities as analytic and continental philosophy. If 'analytic philosophy' means a commitment to clearly expressed arguments and the willingness to revise arguments and give up beliefs in light of better counter-arguments, all philosophy is analytic, and what is not is mere rhetoric or metaphor-mongering. Where it means anything more (such as the famous respect for 'science', or for 'common sense'), it usually is just a form of dogmatism or scientistic distortion of the activity traditionally called philosophy. If 'continental' philosophy means 'philosophy' as it is practiced in continental Europe, there is no continental philosophy, as philosophy in continental Europe is just like philosophy anywhere else: an attempt to deal with concepts fundamental to our self-description as rational animals under the condition that we are able to articulate them in more concise and coherent ways than they are often used loosely in everyday life and in the other sciences. Like a 'continental' breakfast you cannot find 'continental' philosophy in Europe, just as there is no such thing as a unified 'Anglo-American analytic' philosophy. If there were such specific national practices, it would undermine the claim to universal rationality and the willingness to revise arguments in light of better arguments regardless of who presents them. In short, the categories of analytic and continental philosophy are often merely used in order to prevent bad philosophy from being criticised by people who do not belong to the group of those sharing a particular set of beliefs or parochial standards of justification.

It seems to me that there is a climate change in global academia away from the constructivist or relativist idea that somehow our thinking is radically shaped by our various group memberships to the genuinely universalist idea that philosophy can only be practiced if we believe in the overall unity of reason or rationality, which corresponds to Habermas' famous phrase of the 'unity of reason in the diversity of its voices'. Such a commitment to the universality of reason should have repercussions for our thinking about the unity of philosophy as such, and my hope is that the realism-label might lead to a broader acceptance of both: 1. that thinkers somehow stem from local traditions and that this, 2. does not mean that they have to make an irrational or unintelligible leap when confronted with people who were brought up in different circles of philosophers.

Having said that, my own way of approaching the topics presented in this book was shaped during my Heidelberg upbringing as a graduate student. There is a sense in which this book comes from the tradition of German philosophy, where this just means that I am used to taking philosophers such as Fichte, Schelling, Hegel, Gadamer or Husserl seriously. I neither grant privilege to the living nor to the dead, as long as they can teach me how to enhance my views about the role played by the concepts we traditionally deem central in theoretical philosophy, such as knowledge, being and its modalities, justification or the mind.

Introduction

According to common wisdom, ontology concerns what there is, or rather, what there really is. In one breath, it is often supposed to be concerned with the problem of how reality is regardless of our preconceived opinions regarding its composition. Against this background, it is no surprise that ontology since its very beginnings from the Eleatics onwards is infamous for flying in the face of common sense. The answer to the question of what 'being' means is originally presented as a sort of superhuman insight that transcends the mere opinions of mortals who are confounded by illusions such as that some bodies move, that there are mesoscopic stable bodies, or even with the illusion that there are manifold things or objects. Instead, we are told, ontologists get to the bottom of things, they dig out the 'fundamental nature of reality' behind the appearances. In this picture, ontology and metaphysics are combined, and ontology is introduced not just as an answer to the question of what it means for something to be or for something to exist (and more precariously not to be or not to exist), but rather as deeply concerned with the opposition of reality and appearance. Since then, ontology and metaphysics have regularly been identified. In the current literature, they are often used interchangeably as names for the investigation into the fundamental nature of reality, where 'reality' seems to contrast with 'appearance'. What is more, reality is treated as a unified domain that goes by the common name of 'the world'.

Ontology – the investigation concerned with being – in this somewhat unclear division of labour is ancillary to metaphysics, or the investigation concerned with (unified) reality insofar as it contrasts with appearance. Moreover, metaphysics is seen as the most substantive investigation into the very concept of substance, an enterprise that began with the Presocratics and is still with us today. The manifold twists and turns of ancient metaphysics indeed all hinge on the notion that there is a fundamental distinction between 'how things really are' (in one word: being, ὄν, ἐόν), on the one hand, and how our presence among these things potentially distorts them so as to give rise to illusory appearances. Metaphysics and ontology are thereby treated as dealing with the same domain of objects, with what there really is.

Despite prominent efforts over the last two hundred years of philosophy to alter this propensity to think of philosophy in terms of a strict dichotomy of unified reality (a.k.a. the world) and appearance (a.k.a. the mind), from Kant's dissociation of epistemology from metaphysics to the critique of metaphysics in Heidegger, Carnap, Wittgenstein, Rorty and Derrida (to name but a few milestones in this history), contemporary ontology has returned to mostly materialist variations of Presocratic metaphysics with a hint of Plato and Aristotle. In contemporary ontology/metaphysics 'the fundamental nature of reality' is a constantly recurring formulation. Russell perhaps set the tone with his definition of 'reality' as 'everything you would have to mention in a complete description of the world'.[1] Of course, the methods and the degree of logical sophistication underpinning recent metaphysical arguments significantly differ from the era of Democritus. Yet, the world picture we are expected to accept from the outset uncannily resembles the age-old idea of 'atoms in the void' aided by the projection of quantificational structure onto the raw physical and in itself neatly individuated material.[2] A good deal of the work that has triggered recent debates – most prominently the ontological and meta-ontological debates found in Carnap, Quine and David Lewis – is premised on the materialist idea that what there (fundamentally) is is adequately defined by physics, such that we now only need to subtract human projections from what there (fundamentally) is in order to unmask reality. *Reality seems to be everything but the illusion that it is more than what physics tells us.* Of course, claims of this sort need a lot of additional support, in particular, because they will always be forced to accept the reality of the illusions themselves while unmasking them.

The tendency to look for reality on this side of the illusion also explains the ongoing debate about mereological composition, that is, the debate about the question of whether reality in itself consists of any possible composition of chunks of matter including temporal parts of four-dimensional objects. Here the idea is that if reality is fundamentally physical reality and if the latter is four-dimensional space-time, then there seems to be a sense in which my table right now is only a temporal part of my overall table, which would be a four-dimensional object stretching through time in the same sense in which it is extended in space.[3] As a lover says in a recent novel by Ferdinand von Schirach, 'You are never entirely there. There is always only a part of you, but another part of you is not there.'[4]

There are various diagnoses as to what has gone wrong for this discussion to take place. Whereas G. E. Moore substantially changed philosophy by referring to his hands, making it sober up from its metaphysical torpor, contemporary ontologists seriously debate whether in addition to hands there are also fists, or whether fists are really nothing but hands arranged fist-wise. Sebastian Rödl has made an interesting case to the effect that the underlying confusion in such debates results from a misguided conception of the nature of time.[5] Others, such as Eli Hirsch, argue that the distinction between *descriptive* and *revisionary metaphysics* should be applied to contemporary ontology as well so that we can safeguard trivial common-sense existential assertions from onto-logical destruction.[6] Hirsch, however, continues to treat ontology and metaphysics as the same investigation, maybe seen from different angles (the one, ontology, as primarily concerned with existence; the other, metaphysics, as primarily concerned with the difference between reality and appearance, say). Object-oriented philosophers, most particularly Graham Harman, make use of Heidegger's insistence that we must not ontologically undermine 'the thing', that is, the real things presented to us in meaning-ful interaction with the world.[7] Interestingly, Harman adds that besides undermining in the form of the search for a miniscule fundamental reality, traditionally there are also manoeuvres of 'overmining' mesoscopic things by grounding them top-down in overall general eidetic structures such as transcendental conscious-ness or what have you.[8]

It is remarkable how many terms Jonathan Schaffer uses to refer to the big integrated single substance: cosmos, reality, the world as a whole, the universe as a whole, the whole material universe (= the cosmos). 'The existence of such a thing claims intuitive and empirical support.'[9] Here he refers to 'the whole material universe'. I have no idea what the intuitive support for this would be. In a footnote Schaffer gives his 'reasons' for this: '"cosmos" derives from the Greek "κόσμος" for order, and served as a title of a 1980s public television series featuring Carl Sagan'.[10] As Schaffer thereby acknowledges, the Greek word does not refer to the whole material universe, but to a certain conception of order. This leaves us with his second argument for the intuitiveness of the notion: the existence of a 1980s public television series. This argument deserves no comment and almost certainly is intended as irony (or so I hope).

He also briefly tells us what the 'empirical support' is supposed to be: 'Empirically, the cosmos is an entity posited in physics, and indeed the subject of cosmology.'[11] However, if an entity is posited by some investigation, this certainly does not entail that we thereby have empirical evidence for it. Witches are posited by the investigation called 'witch hunting', which does not entail that we have empirical evidence for witches. Lastly, Schaffer hints at a genuine argument when he writes: 'Only the most radical views of mereological composition, contravening both intuition and science, could refuse the cosmos.'[12] He has not provided any valid argument to the effect that intuition or science require the kind of thing he posits as a meta-physician, so all his arguments must hinge on the claim that only certain or even 'the most radical views of mereological composition' might be able to 'refuse the cosmos'. But even granted that we can make reasonable metaphysical sense of the almost maximally unclear term 'the cosmos' – which I regard as the expression of our 'oceanic' feeling of unity with an alleged whole – this still leaves it open to think of the cosmos as only one domain among many, which would come close to the view defended in this book.[13]

On the scale of the investigation associated with metaphysical micro-fundamentalism, or generally the search for 'fundamental reality', many issues in contemporary ontology turn on decisions regarding the reality of 'moderate sized specimens of dry goods',[14] as Austin famously put it. In a different vein, but with roughly the same intention, Stanley Cavell speaks of the 'generic object',[15] whose nature and independent reality has been discussed in philosophy from the ancient towers and bent sticks to the modern apples, tables and chairs. Yet, as Cavell has reminded us, we should not generalise on the basis of these examples such that in the end bubble chambers, governments, or love affairs somehow begin to look ontologically defective to us.

The terrain of ontology is huge, both in its historical and its contemporary ramifications. Many new disciplines have entered the scene, designed in order to establish common methodological ground, such as meta-metaphysics and metaontology.[16] Be that as it may, I believe that many assumptions underlying all of the discussions hinted at in the previous paragraphs are fundamentally flawed beyond repair. Against this background, this book is an attempt to shed new light on the questions traditionally dealt with under the heading of 'ontology' and 'metaphysics' by giving up two ideas: first, the association of ontology and metaphysics, and second, the idea that there is or ought to be a unified totality of what there is, whether you call it 'the world', 'being', or 'reality'. In order to begin the actual work of this book, it is crucial that I present you with a preliminary understanding of the terms I will use throughout.

Ontology is the systematic investigation into the meaning of 'existence', or rather the investigation of existence itself aided by insight into the meaning of 'existence'. Of course, there are traditional problems deriving from the concept of 'being', and my understanding of ontology as primarily concerned with existence will not solve all of the issues raised in these debates. However, 'being' is notoriously affected with ambiguities, such as its different uses in existential and identity statements, not to mention the problem of the copula. Even worse, the distinction between 'being' and 'existence' is traditionally associated with the modalities 'possibility' and 'actuality', such that possible objects have at least being, but not existence, which was supposed to help explain God's capacity for creating new objects or objects at all. These associations, however, are already part of what I reject by dissociating ontology from metaphysics. I give up the concept of being on the ground that it is a philosophical invention designed to account for the quasi-existence of *possibilia*, *impossibilia*, the future, intentional inexistence, or other candidates to be treated as evidence in favour of Meinongianism. I accept the objection most clearly articulated by Kant that 'being' is not only said in manifold ways, but that 'being' in the existential sense, 'being' in the sense of the copula and 'being' in the identity sense of '*x* is *y*', do not jointly make up a category of 'being', let alone being as the most universal concept, kind, or genus. In this regard, there is no question of being just as there is no question of banks. Whether you mean by 'bank' the bank of a river or the Bank of America, they are not different manifestations of the same thing. Nevertheless, there are successor problems to the ancient riddle of being, problems I will cast in terms of existence.

Metaphysics is a combination of (a) an account of reality versus appearance, and (b) a theory of totality, a theory I also refer to as the investigation of the world as world. There are many forms this can take.[17] Metaphysics can understand totality as an overall entity, for instance, the universe in the sense of a maximally spatio-temporarily extended thing, or it can understand it as some more complicated substance (as we see in Spinoza). It can also understand totality as the totality of facts. It is important to bear in mind that the idea that totality is projected as a regulative idea by our conceptualisation of it (Kant), or that it is an ultimate horizon (Husserl), or that it is a discursive presupposition of successful communication (Habermas) is as metaphysical as the more straightforward idea that totality is independent of us and any of our discursive practices or conditions of awareness. Roughly, metaphysics originates in the desire to uncover reality as it is in itself, where this means reality independently of what we add to it by thinking about it. This typically turns reality into the totality of what is the case anyway, an idea Bernard Williams has summed up as 'the absolute conception of reality'.[18] Even if totality is not always the explicit topic in the attempt to say what reality is in opposition to appearance, the idea will always be that reality is unified, for instance, by being what it is 'regardless of the activities, if any, of knowing and acting subjects'.[19] In this understanding, we have to deal with a dualism of reality and appearance, where the first is unified by being in itself and the second by how it appears to us.

This gives rise to all sorts of familiar manoeuvres either for bridging this gap or for arguing that it does no further harm to theory-building. Nevertheless, even if one tries to retain a dualism of reality in itself and its appearance for us, there will be a further question regarding the domain unifying the two into the overall domain of what there is. Unless one wants to eliminate the appearances by claiming that they do not really exist, one has to accommodate them into a larger world-picture as long as one operates within the metaphysical project.

Metaphysics takes many shapes, but all metaphysical theories arguably agree that there is a unified overall reality, the world, which is at least unified by the fact that everything that exists co-exists in that domain. Depending on further theoretical choices often relating to our preferred answer to the question of how reality is defined in opposition to appearance, there will be a variety of ways of spelling out what it means for objects to co-exist in the world. A bit more technically, the postulated domain of unified total overall reality corresponds to the idea of unrestricted quantification. One familiar methodological idea in contemporary metaphysics is to think of the world in terms of quantification. Then one might say that the appearances are generated by contextually defined, perhaps vague and messy, levels of restricted quantification.[20] For instance, if one identifies the range of unrestricted (metaphysical) quantifiers with the objects in the domain of the universe and the latter with whatever is studied by microphysics, fridges and beer will turn out to be appearances. They are not real or not really real. However, it makes sense to speak of them in a restricted way. 'Fridge' might be shorthand for a complicated description of a space-time region not mentioning fridges. On the adequate metaphysical picture, there really are no fridges, as fridges only turn out to be random mereological sums of the micro-particles they are composed of, such that fridges are not sufficiently different from any old merely disjunctive entity. If we say that there are fridges, we are supposed to say that there are fridges in a way analogous to the way in which we say that there is beer. If we say that there is beer, we usually say that there is beer somewhere, for instance, in the fridge. The question, 'Is there any beer?' in common parlance most of the time does not mean, 'Does beer exist at all?' but only wonders whether there is any beer in the fridge or, say, close enough to the party location so that someone can go and fetch it.

Unrestricted quantification, on the contrary, is supposed to satisfy the metaphysical desire; it asks after some object or other's real or ultimate existence by asking whether it or its kind exists – full stop, regardless of the contextual parameters we impose upon that reality by being interested in there being things such as beer and fridges. According to this analysis restricted quantification (the appearances) is contrasted with existence (period!) where the latter corresponds to the notion of ultimate or fundamental reality.

In this book, I defend *meta-metaphysical nihilism*, that is, the view that metaphysics literally talks about nothing, that there is no object or domain it refers to. I will also call this the *no-world-view*, that is, the view that the world does not exist. Of course, I do not mean that nothing exists, which would be metaphysical nihilism, and which according to some readings is still a metaphysical view (whatever it might mean to hold it). I also do not intend to deny that there are meaningful ways in which we can draw a distinction between a reality and mere appearances. Yet, this distinction does not necessitate acceptance of the further claim that all realities are unified by some overall feature (existence or real existence) such that we can draw a clear enough line between how things really are and how we generally represent them.

Depending on your preferred concrete conception of what metaphysics does and studies, you will hear my negative existential assertion – that the world does not exist – differently. For some, I will deny that there is a unified entity, which goes by the names of 'the world', 'reality', or maybe even 'nature'.[21] For others, I will deny that there is a unified domain of facts, the single all-encompassing 'sphere of objects' unified by some conceptual operation or other.[22] For yet another group, I will deny that there is absolutely unrestricted quantification or that the stipulation of an absolutely unrestricted universal quantifier has any meaning. For the latter group, I will give somewhat detailed arguments to that effect, which vary in scope and impact, as I do not only deny that there is unrestricted quantification full stop, but more particularly argue that even if there were unrestricted quantification in some sense, this would not lead to any increase of knowledge in either metaphysics or ontology. I do not believe that existence is relevantly tied to quantification at all. I reject the idea that the meaning of 'existence' can be fully or relevantly captured by the language of quantification. I also reject the idea that existence is relevantly bound up with the concepts we use in order to understand or practice set theory. Existence is just not a particularly mathematical or logical concept, as there are vague and messy objects of all kinds, and also incomplete objects, like half a cake, that do not immediately fit the bill of the idea of discretely individuated objects spread out in a domain independent of any human activity. Why understand 'half a cake' as 'one half-cake'? The idea that '1/2' is unified so as to be individuated as this-rather-than-that-number certainly does not require the *mathematical* concept of '1'. Individuating unification is not *per se* related to the mathematical concept of '1'.

Despite the fact that I am a meta-metaphysical nihilist and that I will make use of arguments somewhat similar to those sometimes deployed by Hilary Putnam in his fight against metaphysical realism, I am a fully-fledged ontological realist. As a matter of fact, in this book I will lay out a new realist ontology. The originality of the approach can be brought out with a very simple example. Let us say that we are standing in front of a particular volcano, perhaps Mount Etna in Sicily. To make things simple, follow me in granting that there are volcanoes. Metaphysical (that is, old) realism about volcanoes would traditionally claim that there really is a volcano in this particular space-time region regardless of how we might relate to this fact. This would mean that there is exactly one somewhat complicated description fully individuating the volcano, a story about the volcano that essentially does not involve our ways of individuating it by our sense organs or by anything we add to the mountain in its sheer mountainhood in the semantically cold universe. To be a realist in the old sense is to associate realism with a reality in any sense independent of how we think of it, or even worse, to associate a commitment to realism with commitment to mind-independence. Accordingly, anti-realism about this volcano would insist that we somehow create the volcano by individuating it.

One line of argument for anti-realism about volcanoes could base itself on a general anti-realism about mountains and valleys. Evidently, when we divide a region up into a mountain and a valley, we approach it from a particular perspective, namely from the perspective of creatures standing on planet earth. But what if some Martian came to earth who had evolved in such a way that it walks on its left hand and can defy gravity in unexpected ways. From this spatial perspective, it sometimes will seem as if it walks down a mountain when it approaches what we call 'the mountain' from what we call 'the valley'. This argument is supposed to establish that 'mountain' and 'valley' are interest relative, essentially perspectival concepts. One of the protagonists in Ferdinand von Schirach's novel *Tabu* interestingly makes a case to the effect that Switzerland is almost as big as Argentina. His argument is quite simple: If you stretch the mountains in Switzerland, you would see that its surface is much bigger than its somewhat compact manifestation would make you believe.[23] From this perspective, the mountains dissolve in the concept of the overall surface occupied by a country. They become, as it were, mere modes of a more encompassing substance, Switzerland; they look like bumps in Switzerland without sufficient ontological independence. If realism is tied to maximal mind-independence, one can use arguments from Martians or general ethnological speculation in order to undermine quite a few categories. In the most extreme case, this amounts to radical constructivism in the sense that we create all things by individuating them (although perhaps out of the prime matter of which they are made).[24] I take it that anti-realism has a point, but that there is a realist interpretation of that point that does not turn acceptance of mountains, governments, love affairs and electrons into a matter of convention, as Putnam claims. By this I mean that a complete understanding of the existence of mountains and love affairs need not mention any convention according to which we agree that the term 'object' can be made to cover these affairs. There is no potentially hidden act of constitution, convention or decision reference to which puts us into a better position to understand the very existence of mountains and love affairs.

There are many reasons why old realism fails. Another important one is that it rules out the reality of the mind by its criterion of reality as the domain of everything that is metaphysically objective, meaning accessible from the third-person perspective alone. But why would the mind be less real than proteins or electrons just because it is evidently mind-dependent in some sense? Why would we even engage in the business of reducing the mind by trying to get rid of the word in our vocabulary designed to give an account of the stock of reality unless we have already decided to treat as real only that which is mind-independent in any sense of the term?[25] In addition to the fact that subjectivity exists and the fact that it also harbours illusions whose real existence we should not deny, but rather study for the sake of self-knowledge, minds bring with them the fact of conceptual relativity in Hilary Putnam's sense. The fact that we can describe situations in different ways depending on what we count as an object, as real, or as really existing, needs to be accounted for and old (metaphysical) realism has a hard time allowing for the claim that there is anything conventional or theory-laden in the acceptance of the existence of the denizens of reality.

New ontological realism claims that any perspective on Mount Etna is as real and 'out there' as Mount Etna itself. The fact that Mount Etna looks like a mountain to me and like a valley to the Martian are relational facts involving Mount Etna itself and not just facts involving me or the Martian. New realism, then, is the idea that in order to be a realist there is no need to introduce the idea of mind-, or more generally, perspective-independent reality. In my view, then, realism fundamentally contrasts with constructivism, as the fact that we bring forth (construct) criteria of the identity of objects should be taken as evidence that the objects themselves need not be subject to these criteria. The language of construction serves to introduce a distinction between what we contribute to experience and what the objects or things in themselves contribute. But this overlooks the option that our constructions serve to individuate objects that are not necessarily themselves constructions.

For the sake of an introduction to the view defended in this book, one could simplify further and say that metaphysical (old) realism is exclusively interested in the world without spectators, whereas constructivism is exclusively interested in the world of the spectators (oscillating between phenomenologically bracketing the world without spectators and its outright denial). New ontological realism accordingly occupies middle ground by recognising the existence of perspectives and constructions as world-involving relations.

Of course, the no-world-view ultimately makes it impossible for me to put things as simply as that, given that I reject the idea that there is a world on the one hand and a mind on the other hand from the outset. I do not believe that mind and world can be sufficiently unified each on their own so as to give rise to their even potential duality. This will be defended in this book under the headings of ontological and epistemological pluralism respectively, where these chapters claim that there is neither a unified domain of perspective-independent existence nor a unified domain of (human) knowledge as such. Just as I am not a metaphysical nihilist, I am also not a sceptic. To claim that there is no unified object, which goes by the name of '(human) knowledge as such' need not be to claim that no one knows anything. More precisely, I will argue that the unification of forms of knowledge can at the very least not be achieved via its overall relation to the world, where different forms of knowledge would correspond to different sectors of the world or reality. There are further reasons why knowledge cannot be unified, some of which will be discussed in Chapters 12 and 13, but the main thrust of the argument remains tied to the no-world-view. In my view, epistemological pluralism is a liberal stance in that it allows for a plurality of forms of (propositional) knowledge not unified by any such thing as the method for finding out how things are and of justifying our findings in a privileged discursive practice (in 'science').

While fleshing all of this out, I will replace some traditional vocabulary with a suitable ontologically realist counterpart. For instance, instead of 'perspectives' I will talk of 'senses'. The relevant concept of sense derives from a certain (admittedly contentious) reading of Frege. In this reading, first, senses are objective modes of presentation associated with objects, no matter what kind of object is in question. Second, and more contentiously, senses are properties of objects and not ways of looking at them. In my reading, even in Frege the theory of sense is located primarily in ontology and belongs to a reconstruction of the meaning of existence. It is only derivatively part of a theory of knowledge- or information-acquisition, namely insofar as sense also plays a role in our understanding of linguistic meaning, which, however, is not the central function of the concept.[26] Roughly, my idea is that Frege argues that there are no objects on this side of their manifold modes of presentation given that for him, first, to exist is to fall under a concept and, second, concepts are individuated by their senses. Concepts are just more objects. In this reading there is no category gap between senses and objects. We thereby avoid the assumption that there should be a realm of mere extension (the objects merely falling under concepts) below the threshold of modes of presentation. Senses therefore are properties, or 'features', of objects, as Mark Johnston has also recently suggested.[27] In this light, Frege disagrees with logical atomism in its Russellian version, as he does not need to postulate individuals or objects (*Gegenstände*) whose individuation remains a mystery and who only enter thought by being named, an idea already rejected in Plato's *Theaetetus* for similar reasons.[28]

In this context, I will defend an ontological variety of descriptivism and defend it against Kripke's basic objection. Kripke has convincingly pointed out that unqualified descriptivism cannot be the best theory of reference, as we are able to refer to objects in our environment with bad descriptions, that is, with descriptions that do not hold good of the objects, but that nevertheless put us in contact with them. Once contact is established, we can revise the description, which seems like evidence for there being an objective (to some extent merely causal) contact with objects not mediated by our descriptive conceptions of them. However, all this proves is that we can refer to objects with bad descriptions, which does not amount to an argument that objects can exist independently of all the descriptions that indeed hold good of them. The claim that there are no objects below the threshold of senses (ontological descriptivism) is not in conflict with Kripke's insight for a theory of reference. I will argue that the difference between objects and concepts, or rather objects and senses, is functional and not substantive, which means that senses are objects, too, depending on the function they fulfil. If objects are not generally considered to be linguistic entities, why should senses be if they individuate the objects? Kripke argues against descriptivism in the domain of the theory of linguistic meaning, whereas ontological descriptivism is an account of object-identity (regardless of how we manage to refer to objects). However, Kripke himself infers from his correct insight that there are natural kinds, which is part of his explanation of his insight. I reject this part of his explanation as unwarranted given that no objection against ontological descriptivism can be based on considerations from the theory of reference without further ado. At least, there is a gap in the argument. Of course, I do not intend to maintain that there are no objects independent of the linguistically articulated descriptions we use to pick out objects. Rather, my position is that objects are individuated by descriptions that objectively hold good of them regardless of whether anyone is apprehending the facts about the objects. Loosely speaking, senses are part of the furniture of reality, which is why reality can appear to us without thereby somehow being distorted. That the star looks like a tiny speck from here under our neurobiological earth-bound standard conditions tells us something about how things really are and not just something about how they seem to us. This is why there can be objective optical laws, and why we can study the sensory equipment of other species without having to make a leap of faith into 'alien subjectivity'.

Instead of domains of objects I will talk of fields of sense, where a field is supposed to lay out structures for objects to appear within independent of our projections of criteria of identity. When we talk of 'domains of objects' or 'sets', there often remains a tendency to think of the actual demarcations of the domains of the sets in terms of predicates we make up or construct in order to make discoveries about what holds good in certain domains or of sets. Given that I believe that domain-like field-structures are laid out independent of how we settle the criteria for identifying them, and that this also holds in areas where we explicitly refer to our ways of thinking about what there is, I believe that the view defended in this book deserves the label of 'ontological realism'.

More particularly, the new realism I am presenting here is ontological to the extent that it derives from an analysis of the concept
of existence.

However, I also defend a form of epistemological realism in
line with this ontological realism. Here, another sense of 'realism'
also plays a role, namely the sense in which we are accustomed to
thinking of realism as a commitment to an unhampered access to
what there is, which in the best or paradigmatic cases amounts
to knowledge. To some extent I agree with an old phenomenological argument according to which even if we are somehow struck by
a deep illusion, such as a fairly global hallucination of a Cartesian
kind, we are nevertheless confronted with a world to which we
have immediate access.[29] Any explanation according to which
there are epistemic intermediaries between us and how things
really are needs to account for our access to the alleged interface
(whatever the specific nature of the interface: sense-data, neural
states, or mental representations). Given that the interface is part
of how things really are – after all, it is a structure uncovered by
the critical or sceptical analysis – even in the sceptical scenario of a
fairly global hallucination we are granted immediate access to how
things really are. All that interface scepticism is ever able to show
is that we mistake immediate access to the interface with immediate access to something else. It can never show that we do not have
immediate access to anything.

The very point about introducing sceptical scenarios of the hallucination kind is to offer an alternative explanation to the one we
prefer, an explanation we cannot rule out by simply insisting on
our prior explanation or its superiority in terms of an inference
to the best explanation. The reason for this is quite simple: the
best explanation is the one which is true to the facts, and if we are
struck by a global hallucination of a Cartesian kind, then the best
explanation for why such-and-so seems to be the case to us is via
facts involving an account explicitly mentioning the global hallucination. Yet, this is not at all good reason for a sceptical retreat, as
it is rather evidence for an overall trust in our capacity to find out
what is the case by being immediately confronted with it.

My argument laid out in detail in Chapter 12 is of the following
form: given that there is as much reality to be accounted for in
the case of a hallucination as in the case of veridical experience,
there is no specific epistemological threat to genuine openness to
reality in the veridical case. The hallucinatory case is, thus, as open

to reality as any other case, with the difference that the subject involved in the hallucination might not be aware of this and draw misguided conclusions on this basis. But this does not show that hallucinations are not open to reality, as long as we do not define 'reality' in a specific way so as to rule out the reality of hallucinations by stipulation.

Let me just briefly illustrate this point with the help of Laura, the perfect futuristic neuroscientist. Laura knows everything there is to know about hallucinations on the basis of her knowledge of the brain. However, poor Laura regularly suffers from a condition that causes her to hallucinate about Mary, the mother of God. In her hallucinations, Mary always wears a blue dress and a golden crown. Now, given Laura's knowledge, she does not conclude that she sees Mary with her blue dress and golden crown. She is a radical atheist and does not believe in Mary in that sense. However, thanks to her neuroscientific knowledge, Laura is in a position to know something about highly specific events in her brain by being aware of Mary's blue dress. For Laura, Mary's blue dress is direct evidence of neural event E or of a cluster of such events C. She is not 'taken in' by the hallucination. Her case is, thus, similar to our veridical case where we know that there is a star very far away from where we stand by identifying a speck in the night sky as a star. Why would either of the cases be interpreted as constituting evidence for interface scepticism rather than for direct openness?

In other words, global hallucination scenarios do not really go beyond pointing out our fallibility with respect to what is the case; they do not establish that there might be epistemic intermediaries all the way up such that we are never able to make sense of 'unproblematic openness'.[30]

Let us call the upshot of this the *argument from facticity*, versions of which I see at work both in Quentin Meillassoux' revival of speculative philosophy and in Paul Boghossian's major attack on the very intelligibility of constructivism.[31] The argument maintains that in any explanation designed to sever any given representational system from what it is supposed to represent (with the aim of establishing that the system might be radically isolated from any kind of environment), we will sooner or later assume that the system has immediate access to some stratum of information or other. All we might hope to show, therefore, is that the nature of the information available to the representational system (be it language, consciousness, thought, cognition, knowledge, justifiable belief-formation or what have you) might differ from the expectations inherent in the operation of the system. I might believe that my computer appears alongside my table in my subjective visual field because there is exactly a computer and a table causally interacting with my sensory capacities relevant to determining such scenes. However, the real explanation for the representational state I am in will in any event be extremely complicated, even if we look for the most straightforward naturalistic account of how I am in touch with these things, as even this account potentially involves virtually infinite (well, billions of) nerve cells as well as a very long physical and evolutionary story of how some such representational system could ever come into existence. Of course, a full account would also include a history of modern technology based on increased human knowledge, and so on. Thus, any explanation will be more complicated than the phenomenological findings, but that neither undermines their reliability nor even their accuracy given the task at hand.

As I will argue in Chapters 12 and 13, there is no way of unifying human knowledge into the concept of (human) knowledge as such that could then be undermined by some sceptical procedure so as to ground constructivist or more straightforward idealist epistemologies. There is no sense in which we can justifiably come to the conclusion that we are really 'sealed off from the world'.[32] For one thing, I will have argued that there is no such thing or unified domain as 'the world', but more importantly this also counterbalances the force of epistemological unification. The concept of maximally unified knowledge is the epistemological counterpart to the metaphysical attempt to unify reality.

It is hard to do ontology without speaking about the modalities. Accepting this challenge, in Chapters 10 and 11 I offer a new account of the modalities in line with the concept of existence defended in the first part of the book, in particular the no-world-view. As you can imagine, I reject the very idea of possible worlds as a remnant of metaphysics. In a certain sense I replace the language of possible worlds with something like a plurality of actual worlds, which I call fields of sense. They coexist, but they do not jointly make up one world of which they would be part or to which they would relate like descriptions to a description-free 'flat' world of facts. My fields of sense, therefore, are neither identical with nor fully translatable into Nelson Goodman's worlds, nor do they serve the function of many equally good descriptions of an underlying domain, as is the case in Eli Hirsch's picture of the relation between quantifier variance and realism.[33] Formulations such as that of 'our ability – or apparent ability – to conceive of different ways of breaking the world up into objects'[34] are misleading to the extent to which they suggest that there is a unified domain, the world, whose order we try to trace with our ways of thinking about it. This would then create worries about the adequacy or truth-aptitude of our epistemic activities. In the view defended in this book, such worries are unfounded, as any epistemic activity in any event would have to be part of the domain traditionally called 'the world' and even more traditionally 'the absolute'.[35] Here I provisionally agree with Hilary Putnam's ironic remark that 'mind and world jointly make up mind and world'.[36] Yet, any such remark has to be further qualified as long as it still makes use of the idea of the world without even bothering to articulate whether there is such a thing or such a domain and what it would mean, for instance, to say of it that it is any kind of totality.[37]

One way of looking at the problem is via the *argument from the list*. Although the argument is ultimately less accurate than the ones presented in Chapter 7 where I spell out some of the arguments for the no-world-view, it can serve as a first approximation to the point. Let us imagine that there are exactly three objects: x, y, z. Now let a *fact* be something that is true of something.[38] For instance, it might be true of x that it is a bear and of y that it is a rabbit, whereas it could be true of z that it is a forest. There might be further facts in that world, such as the fact that the bear and the rabbit live in the forest, or that the bear regularly tries to kill the rabbit or the other way around (depending on the kind of rabbit you choose). For the sake of simplicity, let us say that there are finitely many facts about the x-y-z-world: F_1, F_2, ..., F_n. Now we decide to write a list including all the facts in this world in which all the objects are embedded. This list would be a representation of the totality of facts, a world-picture. The problem is that the world-picture would have to be part of the world if the world really is the all-encompassing domain and not just a restricted totality such as all the beer in my fridge. In this case, then, the fact that there is a list changes the world quite drastically; it adds more objects (the writer or thinker of the list) as well as more facts involving the fact that there is a list of the totality of facts. There will always be another list we can write in order to achieve a world-picture and any list will (slightly) change the world by adding facts and objects to it. This incompleteness is not a property of our descriptions of the world, something we could neglect when believing that there has to be a totality of facts for some reason, as this very belief implicitly draws on the idea of a list (a world-picture). Of course, we could say that the world was complete and total before we started thinking about it and our ways of thinking about it at the same time. But that would be an ad hoc change in the meaning of 'the world', as we would start conceiving of 'the world' as the world before someone tried to describe it antecedent to her description of it. But why in the world rule out the capacity to describe the world from the world in order to regain its integrity? From an ontological point of view this seems to be an arbitrary sense of reality, where 'reality' is understood as everything that would have been the case had no one ever been around to notice that we notice things. Why would the epistemic and semantically cold universe be a better way for the world to be itself (namely a totality of facts) than the world described by some of its inhabitants?

My suspicion is that behind the idea that reality should be conceived as something absolutely neutral so that we can be good realists lies a decision to treat the appearance of how things are to be thought of as ontologically ephemeral. Thought with its manifold ramifications sees itself as a minor side-effect of a process it is able to describe after a long 'history', or rather after a long in itself meaningless biological time of evolution. But this decision is unwarranted. The fact that for all we know there is no good reason for the universe evolving thinking animals (by underlying teleology, say) is irrelevant for the question of ontology.

I call the idea that understanding being is understanding life and death *zoontology* (see Chapter 1). Zoontology seems to underpin our evolutionary hard-wired sense of reality. I do not mean to deny that human beings are, among other things, interested in the problem of life and its relation to our epistemic activities. However, these matters are just not central to the question of ontology. It is just a parochial feature of what there is that some objects are alive and even that some objects are engaged in ontology. Nevertheless, it is true on various levels that our human form of life shapes our understanding of what is going on by providing our logical bare bones of describing facts with concretely coloured flesh.

By this I mean the following: Facts can essentially be described as things being such-and-so. More technically, a *fact* is a constellation of objects held together by a description that holds good of the objects. 'It is a fact that $7+5=12$' means that it holds good of 7 and 5 that they jointly add up to 12 given certain semantic restrictions on the meaning of 'add up' articulated by the laws of basic arithmetic (that are themselves grounded at a more fundamental level depending on the chosen philosophy of mathematics). Another way of saying that a certain description holds good of 7 and 5 is to say that it is true of them, which is a sense of 'truth' below the threshold of any representational conception of truth. Facts are truths articulated by descriptions involving objects. Now, many descriptions we gain access to are articulated via our specific sensory or otherwise information-processing equipment. For instance, our visual descriptions of a scene in the objective visual field, that is, in the field defined by what can be seen by average individuals of our species, unfold in coloured and specifically temporalised ways. That objects are presented in just this way at this moment in time is how we visually describe them: a visual description is a logical and not a linguistic entity, as words certainly are not literally coloured, but trees and paintings really are. Just imagine, as Herman Melville does in his description of what it is like to be a whale, a different scopic situation, one in which the objective visual field significantly differs by being more panoramic.[39] Or even more radically, imagine you had eyes on four sides of your head such that the image made possible by this equipment would always be a panoramic shot of your surroundings. In addition to the visual possibilities (and actualities given the manifold perceptual systems realised on our planet), there are different temporal possibilities and actualities due to the different life spans of animals. As Michael Theunissen has argued in his seminal book about early Greek poetry, the first articulated conception of time (prior to its philosophical fixation as physical time in Aristotle) was in terms of the life span of the human life form.[40] The perceptual descriptions involved in being a fly differ from ours also along the lines of their temporalisation. I am referring to these differences only as an example of how the abstract descriptions we use in order to individuate facts come to us in specific sensory forms associated with the differentiation of our ecological niche. However, this does not make our access to an independent reality hopelessly perspectival, as we dispose of abstract descriptions of our sensory perspectives. The descriptions I am giving of our sensory equipment are not themselves sensory, or more precisely, they belong to a different level of sense, the one associated with thinking (on this see Chapter 13). In one word, I suggest that we generally think of sensation and accordingly of perception as having the form of descriptions. In case these descriptions hold good of the objects they refer to as being a certain way, the descriptions are true of these objects and accordingly true *simpliciter*. Thus, I treat a true thought (including a true visual description of something, say as a green meadow) as a fact. True thoughts are facts, which is not to say that all facts are true thoughts. Many or most (if one could count them) facts are not exactly thoughts, but just truths, that is to say, objective mind- and representation-independent descriptions of objects. That the moon is smaller than the earth is true of moon and earth regardless of whether anyone thinks so. It would have been true of earth and moon had no one ever noticed. A thought becomes a fact by being true of earth and moon. This means that there is no more space to think of true thought (including apt sensory descriptions) as excluded from the manifold domains of what there is. On this construal, the difference between true and false thought is that true thought holds good of its object(s) whereas false thought is in part or entirely dissociated from its object(s) by not holding good of it. A true thought is a fact whereas for any false thought there is a fact to the effect that it is a false thought. A false thought is a fact only by accident, that is, by the further fact that it is a false thought. A true thought immediately is a fact; it is a property of its object(s), whereas a false thought is only a fact despite itself. One might even claim that a true thought is subject-less, which is why we can share it by transparently just referring to what it is about. A false thought, on the contrary, constitutes a subject, someone who is the object of a true thought that consists in an account as to how that subject got it wrong. This is why it is easier to communicate true thoughts, because they are essentially already shared, whereas we need a more complicated account for the emergence of false thoughts involving a theory of subjectivity.

In this book, in the epistemological chapters I will mostly focus on a description of true thought. I agree with the methodology at work in McDowell and subsequent work to the extent to which he sets out from a description of true thought in order to 'exorcize skepticism' rather than from a description of true-or-false thought, which might then turn into evidence for sceptical manoeuvres.[41] Further justification for this methodological stepping-stone could be gathered from the consideration that even false thought is embedded in facts that describe it as false thought. For any false thought or perspectivally distorted sensory description there is a possible true thought to the effect that the false thought is false because of —— . The description '——' is a placeholder for whatever makes a thought false. What we still lack is a theory of false thought that does justice to the pluralism of the categories of the false, such as ideology, illusions, hallucination, and so on. Maybe there is room for a revival of psychoanalysis within contemporary theoretical philosophy if we start thinking of psychoanalysis not as an instrument of debunking true thought (which has often been criticised under the heading of 'psychologism'), but rather as an instrument typically deployed in the service of descriptions of the realm of false thought. The same holds for other forms of 'critical theory' directed at an articulation of the manifold pathologies of human thought. Something similar might also hold for phenomenology, which would thereby restore the eighteenth and nineteenth-century meaning of the term, where 'phenomenology' was introduced as a name for an overall theory of error and its manifold forms. However, any such revival must live up to the standards of contemporary epistemology, which first and foremost means that it has to be re-described in terms of the achievements of realism. Staring into the abyss of false thought (and its manifold manifestations) should not lead us to the false thought that thought as such somehow tends to falsify itself or to ground itself in opposition to reality.

It is fair to say that the upshot of twentieth-century philosophy is an overall realist turn uniting all traditions of (Western) philosophy. In particular, the constructivist 'orgies' of constant sceptical self-denial of truth, deferral of commitment, meta-reflexivity, higher-order *epochê*, or language game relativism turned out to be misguided, as they could not accommodate the argument from facticity. If there will always be a point where we have to stop digging deeper or climbing higher, any methodology which presupposes that we could in principle always ask another question is not an option anymore.

Elisabeth Anscombe pithily remarked that we need to draw a distinction between the fact that there is always a point where we have to stop asking from the fact that we always have to stop at the same point.

Ancient and medieval philosophers – or some of them at any rate – regarded it as evident, demonstrable, that human beings must always act with some end in view, and even with some one end in view. The argument for this strikes us as rather strange. Can't a man just do what he does, a great deal of the time? He may or may not have a reason or a purpose; and if he has a reason or purpose, it in turn may just be what he happens to want; why demand a reason or purpose for it? And why must we at last arrive at some one purpose that has an intrinsic finality about it? The old arguments were designed to show that the chain could not go on forever; they pass us by, because we are not inclined to think it must even begin; and it can surely stop where it stops, no need for it to stop at a purpose that looks intrinsically final, one and the same for all actions. In fact there appears to be an illicit transition in Aristotle, from 'all chains must stop somewhere' to 'there is somewhere where all chains must stop.'[42]

There is no overall point where we have to stop or even where we typically stop. In a more classical language, we can say that there is no ἀνυπόθετος ἀρχή, which is what Plato and Aristotle were looking for. In this sense, the ontology defended in this book is a form of anarchical realism, realism without an overall principle that organises everything, unless you want to call the no-world-view a (methodological?) principle. This might be fair to say to the extent that it defines a limited space of orientation by claiming that no move is permissible that leads to or is grounded in a world-picture.

Let me stress in conclusion that I deem it important that we not forget Heidegger's well-justified reminder that we need to overcome ontotheology. In my understanding, *ontotheology* is the association of metaphysics (theory of unrestricted totality, of the world as world) with ontology (the systematic investigation into the meaning of 'existence'). Thus, ontotheology is very much with us today, as it underlies many arguments in ontology and metaphysics that are often not separated but almost treated as synonyms. I take it that the critique of metaphysics in Heidegger and post-Heideggerian French philosophy was right to the degree to which it was explicitly directed against ontotheology and false where it turned into 'postmodernist' constructivist hyperbole. I leave it open whether any alleged French protagonist of 'postmodernism' in philosophy (such as Lyotard, Lacan, or Derrida) really ever was a postmodernist in this critical sense, whereas it seems rather obvious that, at least, Richard Rorty had his fully-fledged postmodernist moments. In that sense, it seems to me that post-modernism really was an American invention, if it ever took place at all. Maybe it was just a fleeting simulacrum apparently claiming that everything is a fleeting simulacrum.

Be that as it may, Heidegger and in his wake Hans Blumenberg were right in pointing out that ontotheology still shapes our current world-pictures in virtue of the very fact that they are world-pictures.[43] Like Wittgenstein, who made similar observations in his discussion of world-pictures and their relation to mythology, they came to the conclusion that philosophy should not be presented as a series of arguments or as a theory. Here I disagree. Being informed about the failure of ontotheology presupposes insight into fallacies involved in the formation of ontotheology. Overcoming ontotheology just means giving different arguments in the regions opened by ontotheology. We need to replace metaphysics by relevant successor disciplines, such as ontology, as metaphysics does not only affect philosophy. It largely structures our overall ways of looking at things by suggesting that there has to be a good world-picture out there. As long as we think that there are two competing ways of explaining the world, that of science and that of religion, there will always be a struggle between the two, which is both a misguided philosophy of science and even more so of religion. I am not making a relativist point of equal validity here; I am saying that neither science nor religion can amount to world-pictures. If they were essentially tied to the possibility of world-pictures (which I do not believe), we would have to consider them as erroneous and replace them with different practices.

In this book, I will leave open how we have to think about more specific ways of grasping facts assembled under the heading of 'science', 'art', or 'religion'.[44] I will only deal with ontology and some parts of epistemology in order to sketch the outlines of a new realist ontology, the ontology of fields of sense. Some arguments and trains of thought presented in this book will most likely turn out to be defective or not sufficiently laid out, but the book has not been written under the presumption that every single word is in its right place and that every single argument is a knock-down of its actual or potential opponents. No book, philosophical or otherwise, can achieve this, which is part of the argument of this very book. The spirit in which I think of the relation between my interlocutors and me (including future temporal parts of me) is rather the mode of the opening of an actual dialogue, as I do not claim to have exhausted the field of ontology itself. As Schelling nicely writes towards the end of his *Freedom Essay*, which despite its romantic and somewhat inaccessible format is still among the most important works in the history of ontology:

> In the future, he will also maintain the course that he has taken in the present treatise where, even if the external form of a dialogue is lacking, everything arises as a sort of dialogue. Many things here could have been more sharply defined and treated less casually, many protected more explicitly from misinterpretation. The author has refrained from doing so partially on purpose. Whoever will and cannot accept it from him thus, should accept nothing from him at all and seek other sources.[45]

Of course, I claim knowledge by putting forward theses and analyses of philosophical concepts. This presupposes that I define their meaning to a certain degree, where the degree is determined by contextual parameters of clarity. There is no absolute clarity. As Leibniz nicely spelled out in his *Meditations on Knowledge, Truth, and Ideas*, there is no absolute clarity, as this would presuppose adequate intuitive knowledge of all semantic atoms articulated in the definition of the philosophical concepts we use in our analysis of other concepts.[46] Given the impossibility of this ideal, it cannot be our driving idea of what philosophy, or any other science for that matter, is. Each philosophical argument and each philosophical train of thought is and remains one path through the indefinite jungle of possibilities. Its plausibility derives from the clarity we achieve by going through it in light of the possibility of change of entrenched but harmful ways of thinking.

I thoroughly believe that the era of world-pictures that has followed us since the axial age is governed by harmful habits of thinking that we need to overcome in the same way in which we overcame other forms of dogmatism and blindness so as to achieve a 'progress in our consciousness of freedom'.[47] This book provokes objections, and objections are needed in order to clarify the terrain laid out by my account.

Notes

1. Russell, 'Philosophy of Logical Atomism', p. 224.
2. See, for example, Sider, *Four-Dimensionalism*, in particular pp. 209–36.
3. Cf. Sider, *Four-Dimensionalism*, pp. 87–92.
4. von Schirach, *Tabu*, p. 88.
5. Rödl, *Categories of the Temporal*.
6. Cf. Hirsch, 'Against Revisionary Ontology', pp. 96–123. See, of course, also Strawson, *Individuals*, pp. 9ff.
7. Harman, 'On the Undermining of Objects', p. 25.
8. Harman, 'On the Undermining of Objects', pp. 24–5. Ben Caplan explicitly assumes 'that the microphysical is the fundamental', a view he calls '*micro-fundamentalism*' in 'Ontological Superpluralism', p. 108. He opposes this view to Jonathan Schaffer's view, who holds that 'it is the whole cosmos itself that is fundamental'. On this see Schaffer, 'Monism', 'Fundamental Reality'. This discussion of 'fundamentality' is a nice example of the Scylla of undermining (micro-fundamentalism) and the Charybdis of overmining (metaphysical holism). Both aim at unmasking the illusion of us mortals that some ordinary things are as fundamental as need be.
9. Schaffer, 'The Action of the Whole', p. 74.
10. Ibid., p. 74, fn. 12.
11. Ibid., p. 74.
12. Ibid., p. 74.
13. Let it be noted in passing that Schaffer's constant reference to Spinoza's concept of substance is misguided given that Spinoza's concept of substance is not at all identical with any such thing as the whole material universe. If anything, the material universe for Spinoza would be an attribute of the substance, not the substance itself. In other passages, Schaffer points out that his views about the cosmos are based on the ontologically neutral conception of his priority monism. 'The claim that whole is prior to part is only a claim about the dependence ordering amongst concrete objects, and is neutral on how concrete objects stand with respect to further entities such as properties and abstract objects' ('The Internal Relatedness of All Things', p. 344). For him, this leaves room for different instances of priority monism. But why opt for monism if the arguments do not hinge on the conception of the cosmos as the entire material universe? Schaffer's arguments make use of mereological considerations, and it is not clear what it would mean to apply mereological

considerations to the composition of a poem or a nightmare. It seems to me that his arguments already presuppose what he calls 'thick particularism', that is, the view that concrete things come first in any metaphysical explanation.

14. Austin, *Sense and Sensibilia*, p. 8.

15. Cavell, *Claim of Reason*, p. 52.

16. See, for example, Chalmers et al., *Metametaphysics*, and van Inwagen, 'Meta-Ontology'.

17. Of course, there are many other conceptions of metaphysics out there. The most minimal one is to think of it in terms of an 'acceptance of a more than-physical – that is, transcendental – significance in a large number of thin sheets of wood-pulp covered with black marks such as are now before you' (Schrödinger, *My View of the World*, p. 3). In this minimal sense, this book is an exercise in metaphysics, nay, a defence of metaphysics against physicalism. I also accept a number of versions of a reality/appearance distinction. In this sense, I am also a metaphysician. However, I wholeheartedly reject any attempt to develop a 'view of the world'. Given that the totality assumption or belief in the existence of the world is probably the focal point of metaphysical theorising, I prefer to regard the discipline to which I want to contribute with this book as that of ontology as opposed to metaphysics.

18. Williams, *Descartes*, p. 49. See also A. W. Moore's discussion of Williams' idea in Moore, *Points of View*, in particular pp. 61–77.

19. Brandom, *Tales of the Mighty Dead*, p. 208: 'The *thought* [my emphasis, M. G.] that that world is always already there anyway, regardless of the activities, if any, of knowing and acting subjects, has always stood as the most fundamental objection to any sort of idealism.'

20. This is suggested by Eli Hirsch. See, for instance, his *Quantifier Variance and Realism*, p. 138: 'Our common-sense selection function [meaning: our ordinary criteria of identity for objects, M. G.], as far as one can make it out, seems to be an amorphous and intractably complex mess, containing in all likelihood disjunctive conditions and grue-like expressions.'

21. As you will see later, I do not intend to imply that nature does not exist. In my view, nature is a local domain unified by being the domain of objects investigated by whatever is the best natural science or set of natural sciences, depending on how one thinks of the unification of physics, chemistry, biology, and so on. I leave this open in this book. For an interesting defence of nihilism about nature, see Hampe, *Tunguska oder das Ende der Natur*.

22. Carnap talks about the 'unity of the object domain' in Carnap, *Logical Structure of the World*, p. 9.

23. von Schirach, *Tabu*, p. 20.

24. For an attempt to defend radical constructivism see Luhmann, 'Erkenntnis als Konstruktion'.

25. On this see also John Searle's arguments against both materialism and dualism in *The Rediscovery of the Mind*.

26. I evidently disagree here with the tradition of reading Frege most prominently defended by Michael Dummett in Dummett, *Frege*. One of Dummett's achievements was that he closed the gap between Frege and Wittgenstein to the extent that he was able to see Frege as being interested in the conditions of asserting and acquiring knowledge even on the level of his semantic analysis. This reading makes him look much less like a Platonist in an objectionable sense. However, any such reading tends to be in conflict with Frege's realist commitments. His insistence that the criterion of good thought is that all senses are anchored in what there is (that they refer in his sense of 'Bedeutung') was directed against the very possibility of creating the idea of thought as fundamentally different from what is the case. It is unclear to me if there really is a straight road from these commitments to untenable assumptions in our theory of meaning.

27. Cf. Johnston, 'Objective Minds and the Objectivity of Our Minds', p. 256: 'But modes of presentation are not mental; they are objective, in that they come with the objects themselves as the very features of those objects that make them available for demonstration, thought and talk. And they are individuated by the objects they present.' See also Johnston, *Saving God*, chapter 10.

28. Markus Gabriel, *Die Erkenntnis der Welt*, Ch. 2.1, pp. 45–64. For a discussion of similar issues see Gilbert Ryle's paper on this, 'Logical Atomism in Plato's Theaetetus'.

29. For a recent version of this argument, see McDowell, *Mind and World*. However, McDowell's version of the argument differs in that McDowell further derives from it reason to deny the possibility of us ever suffering from a global hallucination. This seems to be a decisive point of difference between McDowell's disjunctivism and Husserlian phenomenology. See John McDowell, 'The Disjunctive Conception of Experience as Material for a Transcendental Argument'. However, one might attempt to read Husserl's concept of 'evidence' in *Formal and Transcendental Logic* along those lines. If I understand McDowell correctly, one step in his argument is that any understanding of the very objective purport

of experience must come to terms with the possibility that we sometimes achieve direct access to objective reality. Husserlian 'evidence'
is premised on this feature of McDowell's disjunctivism and the
notion that repeated confirmation of the structure of a given appearance speaks in favour of objective purport really being intended.
In this light, Husserl secures a basis for the kind of transcendental
argument McDowell envisages, a basis he takes for granted in his
paper (as he believes that it can be ascribed to the sceptic herself). See
McDowell, 'The Disjunctive Conception of Experience as Material
for a Transcendental Argument', p. 380f.

30. McDowell, *Mind and World*, p. 155: 'So languages and traditions
can figure not as *"tertia"* that would threaten to make our grip on
the world philosophically problematic, but as constitutive of our
unproblematic openness to the world.' On this see Gabriel, *An den
Grenzen der Erkenntnistheorie*, §11, pp. 297–314.

31. Meillassoux, *After Finitude*; Boghossian, *Fear of Knowledge*; and
my afterword to the German edition of Paul's book in Boghossian,
Angst vor der Wahrheit, pp. 135–56. See also Gabriel, *Der Neue
Realismus*.

32. Cavell, *Claim of Reason*, p. 144.

33. Hirsch himself introduces the 'doctrine of quantifier variance' as the
claim 'that there is no uniquely best ontological language with which
to describe the world' (*Quantifier Variance and Realism*, p. xii).
This formulation serves the function of distinguishing his view from
the view 'that language creates reality' (p. xvi), which he ascribes
to 'some post-modernists' (p. xvi) he does not bother to mention
by name. Against any such position he maintains: 'What varies in
quantifier variantism is only the language; everything else remains
the same' (p. xvi).

34. Hirsch, *Quantifier Variance and Realism*, p. 132.

35. On this see Gabriel, *Transcendental Ontology*, pp. 8–21.

36. Putnam, *Reason, Truth and History*, p. XI.

37. Remarkably, McDowell only mentions his understanding of 'the
world' in passing. All he tells us about the world in his book on *Mind
and World* is that it 'is everything that is the case' (p. 27). It remains
unclear what exactly he believes about the totality-structure of the
world involved in this formulation, as he is only interested in secur-
ing access to those facts by arguing that 'there is no distance from the
world implicit in the very idea of thought' (p. 27).

38. Umrao Sethi has remarked that this definition makes it look as if
mere properties were already facts on my construal. Yet, the differ-

ence is that we think of mere properties as contingently instantiated. The property of being a blue cube is contingently instantiated. It need not be true of anything. If it is instantiated, however, it is indeed a fact.

39. See Melville, *Moby-Dick*, Ch. LXXIV. For an actual biological account of the species-relativity of time-experience see Healy et al., 'Metabolic Rate and Body Size are Linked with Perception of Temporal Information'. Thanks to Abby Rutherford for pointing this out to me.

40. Theunissen, *Pindar*.

41. McDowell, *Mind and World*, p. xxii: 'I have tried to make it plausible that the anxieties I aim to exorcize issue from the thought – often no doubt only inchoate – that the structure of the logical space of reasons is *sui generis*, as compared with the logical framework in which natural-scientific understanding is achieved.' See also, Rödl, *Self-Consciousness* and Rödl, *Categories of the Temporal*.

42. Anscombe, *Intention*, pp. 33–4.

43. Heidegger, 'The Age of World Picture'; Blumenberg, *Work on Myth*; Blumenberg, *Paradigms for a Metaphorology*; Blumenberg, *Höhlenausgänge*. For a different elaboration of their point see my contribution to the volume with Slavoj Žižek, *Mythology, Madness and Laughter*; Gabriel, *Der Mensch im Mythos*; Gabriel, *Warum es die Welt nicht gibt* (English translation forthcoming with Polity Press as *Why the World Does Not Exist*).

44. For a sketch of my overall approach to these areas see the chapters on science, art, and religion in *Warum es die Welt nicht gibt*.

45. Cf. Schelling, *Philosophical Investigations into the Essence of Human Freedom*, p. 71 (SW VII 409).

46. Leibniz, 'Meditations on Knowledge, Truth and Ideas', pp. 23–7.

47. Hegel, *Lectures on the Philosophy of World History*, p. 88.

Part I

Negative Ontology

Zoontology

Let us begin with a simple thought experiment. Imagine you go into the kitchen. As you enter, you notice a strange object in the middle of the room. It looks like a fuzzy cloud with a left arm randomly attached to it. The cloud constantly changes colour, and all the colours look utterly unfamiliar. Just as soon as you actually figure out that there is something like a cloud with a hand attached to it in front of you, the cloud unexpectedly changes into a giraffe with car tyres instead of a head, and as you even so much as begin to wonder at this, half of the giraffe is now occupied by the cloud, this time with a right arm attached to it. Things are actually worse: you are hardly able to finish any of the thoughts about the strange 'scene' in front of you. The utterly strange and rapidly altering 'object' in front of you makes it impossible for you to ever satisfactorily determine any of the stages of change and to pin whatever it is that you are observing down as some individual object hovering, standing, moving or changing in front of you.

The situation might even be more confusing if we add that your occurring thoughts about this whole event change as fast and unexpectedly as the 'object' in question. Nothing in your stream of consciousness, your progression of articulated thoughts or in the scene of your visual field comes with any clue regarding the definite identity of any individual. There are only absolute processes, processes without anything being processed, mere becomings, not becomings of anything, but just becomings, change without anything changing.

The term 'individual' is introduced in order to account for the fact that we are not in a situation of radical change or pure processes. We always experience substances, rather than pure processes, and there really are no pure processes if we mean by this something that someone could possibly refer to. And surely they are not introduced as sceptical scenarios. Even at the level of quantum mechanics we are not constantly confronted with pure processes in Sellars' sense, where pure processes contrast with individuals or substances. Muons and gluons are just more (even if in some sense strange) individuals. No identifiable change is radical enough to amount to a pure process.[1]

At this stage of the argument, it is sufficient to understand *individuals* as satisfactorily determined objects. The degree of explicit individuation and therefore of satisfactory determination for many individuals varies relatively to the interest invested in the individual. The timetable of most New York subway lines is satisfactorily determined by the fact that a train is pretty much almost about to arrive, whereas the Sunday timetable of a bus line in a small village is only satisfactorily determined by an actual timetable in written form.

In order for there to be individuals, even in this *interest-relative* sense, some *interest-independent* conditions have to be met. Given that we are knowers of a biological species, trivially some of these conditions are physical, or rather neurobiological. We are ourselves interest-independent individuals to the extent to which we belong to a species to which we can ascribe interest-relative (species-dependent) ways of 'carving up' given situations into discrete objects. Given that our biological species still only contains knowers belonging to historically produced communities, further historical and sociological conditions have to be satisfied as well. 'Zoontology' generally is the ontology of life, and it contains considerations regarding what has to have happened in order for there to be knowers of the kind we are most interested in, namely ourselves. We are still so interested in ourselves as knowers that only a few epistemologists are willing to grant knowledge to the other species so far discovered.[2]

Yet, zoontology comes with a number of traps to be avoided. The *first trap* is that we might overestimate our position as special knowers in our planet 'zoo'. The *second trap* is what I call 'zoontological optimism'. By this I mean that the wrong kind of emphasis on zoontology leads to thinking that ontology is generally somehow constrained or governed by features of human development or rationality – a position wrongly attributed to Hegel (most notably to his philosophy of history). In this light, zoontology can lead to a kind of anti-realism according to which the existence of 'the world' is interpreted as depending on our existence – a position wrongly attributed to Heidegger on the ground that he understands 'the world' to be the way things appear to human beings. He does not, however, claim that there is a totality ('the world') whose existence depends on our existence, as he explicitly draws a distinction between 'nature' and 'the world', where only the latter is *Dasein*-dependent. The *third trap* is 'zoontological pessimism', that is, the view that our interests and their relation to our interest-independent belonging to nature do not really matter in ontology. What matters is how things would have been had we never come into existence as well as what will be the case after our extinction. Zoontological pessimism takes the shape of what I will call 'scientistic naturalism', which is different from scientific naturalism. The difference is that scientistic naturalism is not itself a scientific stance; it does not abide by the criteria of the scientific methods we call 'empirical', but rather amounts to a metaphysical position. This leaves room for naturalism as an actual research programme that would not be based on a priori rejections of any kind of entity from the sphere of an alleged 'fundamental reality'.

It is thus first and foremost important not to lose sight of the fact that humans are just part of the zoo, even though we are currently in the lucky position to be on the very top of the food-chain, a fact the comedian Louis C. K. in his ground-breaking HBO-special *Oh My God!* recently used in order to fight the depressed view of the meaninglessness of our lives: at least we are not part of the food-chain![3] To be more precise, we are, of course, part of it insofar as we are on top of it. We are part of the overall zoo. There is a sense in which Woody Allen was right when he pointed out that earth is a huge restaurant where everything eats everything.[4] But why would any of this matter for ontology, the matter under investigation in this book? Why would the meaning of 'being' or 'existence' be a matter of life and death? And yet, contemporary folk metaphysics with its fundamental idea that there is nothing but the physical universe with its unbendable laws that blindly generated life at some point, which in turn has become intelligent in some of its manifestations, also penetrates ontology.

Many philosophers from various traditions believe that the most fundamental problem of ontology should be phrased in terms of an investigation of life, an idea to some degree grounded in the Platonic and Neo-Platonic tradition reaching as far back as Plato's *Sophist* and culminating in Hegel.[5] This leads me to another trap of zoontology, zoontological optimism. To be precise, what this tradition was really talking about was not biographical life, βίος, but rather ζωή, whose fundamental ontological significance derives from the idea that rational animals can move themselves by having a conception of what they are doing. Most prominently, Hegel has turned this basic Platonic claim into the notion that fully-fledged thinkers who are able to describe thought-processes as governed by the norm of truth or by the laws of being-true observe the fact that thought itself has the form of life in this sense. The famous 'movement of the concept'[6] ultimately boils down to the idea that inference patterns are valid because they correspond to how things really are. We do not project inferential relations onto an inferentially blank reality, as if things existed unrelated prior to the additional existence of our conceptual nets we throw over them. Articulated thought that moves from one individual to the next and is able to bridge spatio-temporal distances of almost any kind according to Hegel cuts nature, or rather logical space, at its joints. We are able to formulate the laws of nature in formal languages precisely because they are apt to being thus described (whatever this aptness involves). 'Life' for Hegel, then, is nothing more than an anti-sceptical commitment to the validity of our most successful inferentially explicit theories. It is not part of a theory of biological life, a wild claim to the effect that by some metaphysical necessity there are teleological laws driving the universe from quantum fluctuations to humanoid incorporation.

Traditional anthropology is based on an evident fallacy: philosophers have said that human beings are rational animals and concluded that, therefore, there is a difference between animals and human beings. This is a one-step fallacy: Human beings are rational animals. Therefore, they are not animals. This is like claiming that pigs are not animals because pigs are grunting animals. Being rational is perhaps a defining feature of our species, and perhaps it is exactly this feature that has made us the queens and kings of the food chain. But this is neither evidence for us not being animals nor (and much less so) for us being ontologically special.

Unfortunately, even Heidegger is still prone to the fallacy when he argues that human beings (well, he famously made up a special term for them: *Dasein*) are different from other animals and objects by being aware of the question what 'being' means. We are, he maintained, ontic-ontological: We both exist and wonder what this means, which is our specific mode of existence he calls

'Existenz'. This is true and trivial and should never mislead us into thinking that nothing would exist had no one been around with a special self-referential awareness of this fact.[7]

Of course, Heidegger can be read in a different light. In my view, what he is driving at with *Being and Time* is an understanding of the activity of philosophy as continuous with ordinary activities. For him, our activities are ours insofar as they are ultimately driven by *Sorge*, by our concern with what it means for each and every one of us to be around. The fact that we have to understand ourselves as someone who does this is a condition of the possibility of ontology. We care about the meaning of 'existence' (in the broader sense) because we exist in a specific way (as *Existenz*) that tells us something about the disclosure of reality. Be that as it may, Heidegger's specific and interesting account of the roots of the theoretical enterprise called 'ontology' in everyday life and its hermeneutic conditions should not motivate any form of ontological anti-realism. At best, Heidegger tells us how we can be interested in the interest-independent conditions of human interest without thereby committing the error of believing that ultimately nothing is interest-relative (a view he will later call *Gestell*).

In my view, an excessive focus on zoontology underpins the project Kant already criticised under the heading of 'ontotheology'. As a matter of fact, they have been closely related since Plato's desire to bring being and life together.[8] Yet, ontology should not be a particular study of human existence, but primarily a study of existence full stop. Ontology should neither primarily, let alone exclusively, be designed to give an account of how intelligent life through a long chain of evolutionary intermediaries eventually emerged from inanimate matter. It should also not primarily address how intelligent life fits into an allegedly in itself meaningless universe. First and foremost ontology has to address the question of what the meaning of 'being', or rather (as I will argue) 'existence', is regardless of the fact that human beings have certain cognitive interests and needs. The desire to know what 'existence' is should not be conceptually driven by the desire to understand ourselves. We can only gain a better understanding of what we humans are if we understand that we are precisely able to abstract from our interests and human-all-too-human conceptual schemes on some of the most fundamental levels of thinking traditionally associated with ontology, logics and other domains (maybe even including ethics, but I leave that open for now).

Metaphysics has always been haunted by the fact that there are animals insofar as it first sets out from the axiom that existence is not identical with life, and then wonders how life fits into an essentially inanimate world.[9] Yet, the fact that the concept of existence and the concept of life do not characterise the same individuals (as not everything that exists is also alive) it must not follow that nothing that exists is alive (or thinks, refers or is otherwise conscious). I believe that the 'mystery' of how thought or consciousness fits into the inanimate universe is an illusion generated by both a bad ontology and an even worse form of metaphysics. In part, this book is written to undermine the impression that leads to the formulation of this mystery so that we can gain a fresh look at the very nature of the domains we currently tend to analyse as illusions, such as the overall domain of human spirit or subjectivity. We lost subjectivity on our way to abstracting from ourselves in our description of the meaningless universe without noticing that the very idea of an in itself meaningless universe of extended inanimate gunk is largely an inflated objectified human nightmare.

This leads me to the third trap of zoontology, namely zoontological pessimism. *Scientistic (not scientific) naturalism* is the idea that 'nature' primarily designates a domain of bare particulars extended in space and time (including the entirety of space-time itself as a noticeable and potentially paradox-generating exception, as it is not extended within itself). It is a hidden form of zoontology as it defines nature by ruling out our existence in it as relevant to our understanding of nature. It assumes that any properly objective understanding of how things really are or of what the actual facts are has to be couched in terms compatible with the assumption that our traditional self-descriptions in terms of subjectivity are ultimately meaningless fantasies, mere folk psychology. To really understand ourselves objectively would be to think of us in terms of highly complex biochemical arrangements that give rise to illusions such as that of a self precisely because any properly objective understanding abstracts from the meaningless possibility that fully-fledged meaning is found and not made up. Heidegger nicely calls this idea of ourselves as highly complex biochemical arrangements 'the atomic age (*Atomzeitalter*)'.[10] Heidegger takes the German expression literally and understands it as 'the era of atomic time', which for him is a way of looking at reality in terms of meaningless time-slices, atoms of time. His diagnosis is that behind this really lies an illusory self-description, the fantasy of a reality never inhabited by us. He argues that this is essentially an ill-conceived attempt to construe an overall metaphysical realism. This attempt is ill-conceived because it simply loses sight of itself as something that needs to be explained as part of the reality it aims to describe. In my reading this is what Heidegger meant when he claimed that 'science does not think'.[11]

I believe that scientistic naturalism is bad science and that it does not think, indeed. It is based on various metaphysical premises behind which it is not hard to see an alienated form of subjectivity: Modernity is still in the habit of trying to describe itself as an anonymous process, as something which merely happens and is not made by us. It seems that many people would rather believe that our brain is responsible for the ecological crisis or for the problems of industrialisation still with us today than accept that these problems are really our problems, the problems of fully responsible morally autonomous agents who are essentially the outcome of large-scale socio-historical processes and ongoing political struggles. Our history begins where it emancipates itself from its biological conditions to the extent that what we do is not identical anymore to what happens to us.

In order to return to the subject, that is, in order to overcome a contemporary version of radical alienation or nihilism from subjectivity, it is important to give up the misguided idea that to exist is to be part of the universe, and to be part of the universe essentially is to be an inanimate chunk of extended stuff. Space-time is just not that central in ontology, which does not mean that we could live without it. But the question under which biological conditions humans can breathe and therefore think, albeit interesting in itself, should not be put centre stage in our understanding of what it is to understand something. Thus, we should overcome zoontology to the extent to which it is supposed to lay at the (methodological) heart of ontology.

It does not make sense to unify reality by identifying it with nature as governed by the laws of nature. Our capacity to think about thinking simply does not follow the laws of nature, but the norm of truth and the laws of being-true. If I think the true thought that I am currently writing this sentence on my computer, the stability of the thought cannot be identical with the fact that some parts of my body are in a particular state. My computer is as important for the truth of the thought that it happens to be in front of me right now as the biological conditions enabling me to write it down (including my properly functioning hands and my sufficient expertise at typing).

Of course, zoontology is not identical with the human standpoint. It is not explicitly anthropomorphic because it largely contains interest-independent conditions and, therefore, interest-independent facts. Our interests are rooted in a domain of facts independent of our interests. This should not mislead us into believing that there are only interest-relative facts or only interest-independent facts. The first mistake culminates in what Quentin Meillassoux has called 'correlationism', that is, roughly in the view that we can only ever know how facts appear to us and never how they are in themselves, that we can only access the world through our conditions of accessing it, and can never transcend these conditions.[12] The second mistake culminates in the 'absolute conception of reality', according to which reality fundamentally consists of the facts that would have been the case had no one been around so that our account of what it is to be around has to be given in accordance with the allegedly fairly negligible fact that we are around as conscious intelligent beings.[13]

Both are equally extreme and unmotivated mistakes. 'Reality' is neither generally of our own making (the *world of the spectators*, as I called it elsewhere), nor is it generally the unobserved or even in principle unobservable conceptually 'spooky' in-itself (the *world without spectators*).[14] The interest-relativity of the individuals observable by our species neither entails that there are no interest-independent facts, nor that there are only interest-independent facts. Nor does it entail that the world is our home, that is, was created for observation, nor that it is just a gunk of pure processes some of which suffer from the delusional notion of there being stable individuals. Where correlationism is a form of zoontological optimism essentially tying our species-relative survival conditions to how things really are, scientistic naturalism is a form of zoontological pessimism. The first is fascinated by the origins of life, the latter by its extinction.[15] Yet, I believe that neither the origin of life nor its possible or actual extinction should be put centre stage in ontology. Zoontology is at best a regional inquiry. It is a very interesting enterprise for beings essentially interested in their survival. Don't get me wrong, I am as interested as anyone in survival, but the answer to the ontological question of the meaning of 'existence' bears no essential relation to the fact that there are living organisms asking this question. We do not create the meaning of 'existence', that is, existence.

Notes

1. Cf. Sellars, 'Foundations for a Metaphysics of Pure Process', in particular Part III: 'Is Consciousness Physical?': 'The underlying truth is that the *ongoingness* of absolute process requires the idea of *continuous* coming to be and ceasing to be' (p. 59). Cf. also Seibt, *Properties as Processes*; Seibt, 'Pure Processes and Projective Metaphysics'; Rescher, *Process Metaphysics: An Introduction to Process Philosophy*.
2. Sosa, *Virtue Epistemology*, in particular chapter 2: 'A Virtue Epistemology', pp. 24, 32–6, 42–3.
3. However, it seems that this standard non-scientific view of our position in the food chain is actually false. See: www.smithsonian-mag.com/science-nature/where-do-humans-really-rank-on-the-food-chain-180948053. Thanks to Abby Rutherford for pointing this out to me.
4. Allen, *Love and Death*.
5. Cf. Thompson, 'The Living Individual and its Kind'; Thompson, *Life and Action*, in particular Part One, pp. 25–84.
6. See, for instance, Hegel, *The Science of Logic*, p. 180 (GA 21.206).
7. Cf. Heidegger, *Being and Time*, § 4, p. 11. In my reading Heidegger later tried to counterbalance the anti-realist penchant of *Being and Time* with the 'Kehre'. He realised that philosophical theorising about the relation between our ways of understanding how things are on the one hand and how things actually are on the other hand at some point or other has to commit to modally robust facts. A 'modally robust fact' is something that would have been the case had no one ever been around to notice it. For an extensive discussion and justification of this reading of Heidegger see Gabriel, 'Ist die Kehre ein realistischer Entwurf'.
8. Plato, *Sophist*, 248e7–249a2.
9. Markus Wild recently made me aware of the fact that this is the upshot of Jacques Derrida, *The Animal That Therefore I Am*.
10. Heidegger, *Das Argument gegen den Brauch*, p. 65.
11. Martin Heidegger, *What is Called Thinking?*, p. 8.
12. Meillassoux, *After Finitude*, p. 5.
13. Cf. Williams, *Descartes*, pp. 64–8, 211–12, 239, 245–9, 300–3 and

Ethics and the Limits of Philosophy, pp. 138–40; Moore, *Points of View*, pp. 61–77.

14. On this see Markus Gabriel, *Warum es die Welt nicht gibt*, p. 15.
15. Cf. Ray Brassier, *Nihil Unbound*.

2

Existence is Not a Proper Property

In this chapter I will explore some versions of the claim that existence is not what I call a 'proper property'. By that term I understand a property reference to which puts one in a position to distinguish an object in a domain from another or from some other objects in the domain. In my view, modern ontology at least since Kant sets out from what I call the 'ontological motive'. This motive has the following form:

(P1) Existence is not a proper property.
(P2) Existence is a property.
(P3) All properties are either proper, metaphysical, or logical.
(C) Existence is either a metaphysical or a logical property.

In this chapter I will explore the background that motivates this common theme. In the next chapter I will take a closer look at two champions of modern ontology, Kant and Frege, whose views are indeed similar, even though they greatly differ in important details.

The ontological motive rests on a number of assumptions about the relation between objects, facts and the world. In particular, modern ontology usually makes implicit use of the idea that a proper property first and foremost has to be distinguished from a metaphysical property. A *metaphysical property* is a property anything has to have in order to belong to the world. In this context, the term 'individual' plays a role in the sense that individuals are considered to be the elements of which the world is made up. Given that there might accordingly be objects that are not individuals, such as imaginary objects like unicorns, we can derive a further contrast between *metaphysical* and *logical properties*. In contradistinction to a metaphysical one a *logical property* is a property anything has to have in order to be an object at all. This motivates the idea that objects are essentially related to truth-apt thoughts and assertions given that they are supposed to be organised in light of the norms of truth that can be regarded as the cornerstones of logical space. In this picture, the world consists of all the individuals, where these are specific kinds of objects, whereas logical space consists of all the objects including all the individuals. Traditionally, the concept of individuals is tied to some criterion of complete determination. In modern philosophy, most explicitly in Kant, this becomes associated with the further claim that for individuals to be completely determined in the relevant sense, they have to belong to totality, that is, to the world. The idea of the nomological, specifically causal closure of the physical universe is one version of such a claim to completeness, even though the actual metaphysical topic is more general.

I will explore this territory in order to arrive at the position that existence, after all, is a property, but that it is neither a proper, nor a metaphysical, nor a logical property in the traditional sense. It should not be too surprising that it is the *ontological property par excellence*. As a first approach to a fuller understanding of this claim we can understand existence as a very thin property, namely as the property of belonging to any of the several domains. To exist is to appear in specific fields of sense where the fields of sense characterise what exactly it is for something to appear in them. When I say 'appearance', I do not refer to the appearance/reality-distinction. I use the term technically in order to avoid 'belonging' or 'being part of', as this might invite the set-theoretical or mereological conceptions I am avoiding throughout this book.

My approach to the topic of the ontological motive is in light of the question of realism, as an anti-realist or even idealist penchant tends to drive the accounts of modern ontology. To the extent to which they make the attribution of existence and even existence itself a fact whose obtaining depends on propositional functions to be sometimes true, concepts to have extensions, things to be experienceable, or bound variables to have values, they invite anti-realist and even idealist interpretations. My aim is to avoid this penchant and to find a way of thinking of existence within a realist setting while acknowledging that it is not a proper property.[1]

We saw how zoontology had to admit that there are some interest-independent facts grounding our specific interests. Both Meillassoux and Boghossian have recently made a compelling case that no position in ontology or epistemology can avoid acknowledging absolute facts: Something is the case regardless of whether we acknowledge it or not, for even if almost all facts were interest-relative, this fact itself would not be interest-relative.[2] We could not change the fact that almost all facts are interest-relative by deciding to be interested in them not being interest-relative. Therefore, in order to get a firm grip on ontological realism on this level it is important to present a realist conception of facts.[3]

By 'fact' I refer to anything that is true of something. It is true of my left hand that it is right now typing this sentence. This fact is not identical with my left hand. My left hand and the facts within which it is embedded are different at least in that my left hand is embedded in many facts without therefore being many left hands. My mug stands on a saucer. This is a fact. That my mug stands on a saucer is neither my mug nor my saucer, but the fact that they are related in a certain way, that they stand in the relation of one standing on top of the other. It is a fact that $7+5=12$ in that it is true of 7 and 5 that when they stand in the relevant relation of addition, they are equal to 12, that is, that a certain three-place relation holds between 7, 5 and 12.

This conception of facts differs from the traditional Russellian conception in many respects, most notably in that it attributes truth to the facts and not to a relation between facts and propositions. I refrain from the idea that facts are truth-makers such that they make some propositions true and some false.[4] A true thought about an object that it is such and so is a fact as much as it is a fact that London is north of Italy, or that Mount Vesuvius is a volcano. The true thought that Mount Vesuvius is a volcano differs from the fact that Mount Vesuvius is a volcano, as Mount Vesuvius would have been a volcano had no one ever thought so. Nevertheless, true thoughts do not only become facts by being thought about and, therefore, by making thoughts about them true or false; they are already facts by themselves in just the same sense in which it is a fact by itself that Vesuvius is a volcano. I accordingly give up on the idea that truth-aptitude, that is some system's property of being at least either determinately true or false, is primarily a matter of that system being a representation of facts. Truth is not identical with an accurate representation of facts, even though there are instances of truth where this partly holds, such as when I truly believe on a perceptual basis that I stand in front of Big Ben.

Truth in my view rather is the glue holding facts together insofar as there only are facts if something is true of an object.[5]

There are facts only if something or other is true of an object. Russell thinks that facts are independent from truth to the extent to which they allow for something to be true of an object (for propositions to be true or false). They make propositions true or false, but they are not themselves true or false. My view is that truth is not primarily a property of propositions, let alone articulated thoughts (thoughts someone has). Of course, some thoughts are true, but this does not make it the case that thoughts and only thoughts (or any other representational system) can be true. Facts are truths in our ordinary way of speaking about them.

As I will argue in more detail later, this preserves another valuable insight from Russell, namely his claim that no object just exists by itself. He famously makes an interesting case that 'o exists' is meaningless.[6] One of his arguments is that every individual which has any properties whatsoever has to exist, so that denial of existence becomes pointless, as we can never deny the existence of a given individual. He believes that existence, therefore, is not a predicate in the ordinary sense, which is why he offers an alternative revisionary ontology. However, this opening move is problematic given that existence might still be a property that simply holds good of all objects. Why claim that there cannot be any properties that all objects necessarily have even though assertions in which this property figures as predicate violate our understanding of what it is to assert something?

Be that as it may, an interesting part of his argument that we do not say of individuals that they exist consists in his insight that there must be a reason why nothing exists without being determined as thus and so. For him, the reason for the fact that there is no undetermined existence, no sheer or purified being, as it were, is that claims of existence mean that a propositional function has values to the effect that it is sometimes true.[7] It is sometimes true that 'x is a bottle of beer' because there are instantiations of 'x', such as that Negra Modelo bottle over there, which assign the truth-value *true* to the proposition 'That Negra Modelo bottle over there is a bottle of beer.' This view straightforwardly entails that there is nothing that does not have any properties whatsoever because existence is tied to propositional functions, and they always exhibit patterns of property-attribution. Of course, here a lot hinges on the question of why there would not be a propositional function 'x exists' that is true for that Negra Modelo bottle over there and false for Indiana Jones (assuming we are not speaking about the movies)? Also, is Russell not ultimately committed to claiming that the relation between a propositional function and the instantiations which turn it into a true proposition only comes to be if someone holds beliefs that are at least either determinately true or determinately false? But this would amount to a crazy form of idealism, or at least ontological anti-realism, in that this would mean that nothing had ever existed had no one ever had any truth-apt beliefs such that a certain propositional function is sometimes true. Thus, Russell would have to make a case for all-out Platonism about propositions according to which propositions sometimes also happen to be grasped, asserted, believed, denied, etc., but that they are 'out there', regardless of our further representation of them. But on this construal it would be difficult to see why propositions would not belong to the facts, given that we can have true or false beliefs about them so that they fulfil the function of truth-makers in any event.

Evidently, we must steer clear of the notion that nothing would have existed had no one had any beliefs about it, a proposition secretly driving modern ontology since Kant had suggested that to exist is to appear in the field of sense of possible experience, which will be discussed later. Any such theory of existence, that is to say ontology, will turn out to be incoherent as it will run into problems regarding the prior existence of objects and the obtaining of associated facts leading to something like creatures capable of truth-apt thought. We simply do not make it the case that generally or globally there is something rather than nothing because there is something about us (that we think or conceptually represent) that creates all the facts including those supposedly obtaining before or generally independent of our arrival.

According to the traditional model already to be found in Plato and Aristotle, the minimal requirement for there being facts is that some property is instantiated, which we can write down with the now traditional formula $F(x)$, where 'F' is a property and 'x' is a variable sign whose range is whatever objects (or object-names) can fit in the argument place according to some system of rules. That the cat is furry, the mug is round, the moon is shining, are all minimal facts in this sense. However, even though we can represent all facts in this form by just breaking them down to the fact that we can judge things to be thus and so (however complicated), this does not mean that facts always only have the logical form of some individual falling under some concept. Conditional facts such as: *Had I not eaten for three days, I would by now either be starving or already dead* can formally be represented as me falling under some concept (the conditional with variables), but this leads to an overly abstract form of representation and might mislead us into thinking that to exist is to fall under concepts. In the next chapter I will argue that to exist is not identical with falling under concepts. Falling under concepts is a local case of existence, but does not generalise to everything there is. Counterfactuals such as

(CC) Had Britney not eaten the cheese, she might have chosen the ham instead.

are also facts, as they hold good of something or other, in this case of Britney, the cheese and the ham. (CC) has an internal structure characterising how things would have been had certain conditions been met. As I will argue in the modalities chapter, there are no absolute modalities. Modalities are as restricted as ordinary exis-tential assertions, which means that we can legitimately regard (CC) as being about Britney, the cheese and the ham. (CC) describes a truth; it says what holds good of certain objects. To reduce facts to property instantiations or to any other logical equivalent of a grammatical structure we find in some natural language or other might be the right move at some point in a specific philosophical argument. But from an ontological point of view, identification of facts with property instantiation is *prima facie* unwarranted, as this rules out that there could be *sui generis* modal facts, among other things.[8] There might be reasons for a reductive account of facts according to which there are simple or atomic facts (property instantiation) that make up more complex facts. However, many of the reasons traditionally given for something like this hinge on foundationalist epistemology, that is, on the idea that we have to grasp the facts piecemeal and build a system of more complex beliefs on the basis of simple ideas, which to some extent is a dif-ferent topic.[9] Nevertheless, within the given context we can reject all versions of foundationalist epistemology that hinge on a con-ception of the external world as being the homogeneous totality of what is always already there, as this metaphysical world-picture can be rejected on the grounds developed here.

Given that we already know that even the most radically

anthropomorphic version of zoontology has to admit that there are interest-independent facts (at least the fact that all other facts, that is, almost all facts, are interest-relative), we have already succeeded in knowing something about things in themselves. We know that the domain of things as they are in themselves – those things that are utterly observation-, mind-, theory- and conscious-ness-independent – partly consists of interest-independent facts. This might not be a very substantive form of knowledge. It is not like knowing that some (many or even all) things in themselves are subatomic particles or free-floating Berkeleyan minds. Nevertheless, it is fully-fledged knowledge about things in themselves, as we know that they have at least the following structure: that they partly consist of interest-independent facts. The degree of cognitive or broadly epistemic satisfaction plays no essential role in telling the individuals in the interest-independent domain apart. They are just not distinguished by being distinguished by us.

Properties are introduced in order to explain the difference between individuals. Properties that serve this job without gener-ating paradox can be called 'proper properties'. A *proper property* accordingly is a property reference to which puts one into the position of distinguishing one object from another in a domain. In particular, individuals differ from each other by having differ-ent proper properties. We can now change our understanding of individuals and claim more generally that *individuals* are objects that have proper properties. A first and still rough understanding of the concept *object* would have it that it is anything that can become the content of a truth-apt thought. As I will lay out in more detail in Part II, these definitions actually have to be further qualified. However, at this point in the argument we can think of individuals as individuated by their proper properties, of facts as being truths about individuals, and of objects as the contents of truth-apt thoughts.[10]

Traditionally, individuals are understood as *completely* deter-mined objects, as *entia omnimodo determinata*, a criterion I will be rejecting. On the traditional model, what determines an indi-vidual as this rather than that other individual are its properties, and it is indeed hard to see how an individual could lack one of its properties: the cat has the property of being furry and is thereby distinguished from the Empire State Building (which as far as I know has never been successfully referred to as furry). The cat has its properties just as much as the Empire State Building or the number 273 have their properties. The fact that cats are often furry and that the number 273 is bigger than the number 2 do not obtain because we are interested in them, even though we only found out that they obtained because we were interested in them for some reason or other.

Individuals certainly are not literally different from their properties, for their properties define what they are. There is a sense in which some properties can justifiably be regarded as more essential, as long as this does not mislead us into thinking that there is a realm of essences delineated by some overall criterion of 'naturalness' or 'eliteness'.[11] There is no essence of essences, that is, nothing that generally makes it the case that all objects share some essence, such as only contingently having disjunctive properties or being a four-dimensional thing, say. Also, there is no independent reason for identifying individuals with some particular kind of individuals. Not all individuals are spatio-temporal, for example, and I believe that space-time is highly overrated in metaphysics as a principle of individuation – it is emphasised much more than in some self-descriptions of contemporary physics, which can itself do without space-time on some levels.[12] But there is no need to consult physics at this point given that we are not even engaged in metaphysics, but in ontology. We are on a journey to answering the question what 'existence' means, and not trying to uncover the fundamental nature of nature or the most fundamental layer of the universe. In his 1918 lectures on the *Philosophy of Logical Atomism* Russell already aptly remarked in a discussion of the existence of numbers, phantoms, and images (meaning: imagined objects):

> I know that this belief in the physical world has established a sort of reign of terror. You have got to treat with disrespect whatever does not fit into the physical world. But that is really very unfair to the things that do not fit in. They are just as much there as the things that do. The physical world is a sort of governing aristocracy, which has somehow managed to *cause everything* else to be treated with disrespect. That sort of attitude is unworthy of a philosopher. We should treat with exactly equal respect the things that do not fit in with the physical world, and images are among them.[13]

That the number 273 and the witches in *Faust* not only exist, but are also individuals should be obvious: they have all the properties they need in order to be what they are (even if the witches differ from, say, Tony Blair by not having all the properties a typical human being has, such as having a determinate number of hairs), and they are also clearly different from each other by virtue of their properties, even though there still is an interesting problem for semantics tied to the question of whether the fact that the witches in *Faust* have all their properties means that they are really individuals. It has often been argued in the philosophy of fiction – or rather in the philosophy of the semantics of fiction – that fictional characters are not completely determined, as we do not know, for instance, whether the witches in *Faust* have ever been to Paris or whether they are extremely hairy. There seems to be no fact of the matter deciding these questions.[14] Yet, I will maintain throughout this book that this does not conflict with the fact that these witches are individuals, as they are satisfactorily determined for them to be referred to. They might not be *completely* determined, but they are *satisfactorily* determined.[15] Complete determination is not necessary for individuals, even though individuals trivially do not lack any property they have, which is not to say that they are completely determined. The difference between witches in a work of fiction and actual people on planet earth might be that witches in fiction do different things, and that for some things it is unclear whether they do them or could have done them. Also, they might lack properties that typical actual people on planet earth have. Maybe witches in a fiction are not eligible for a certain hairstyle, which would not make them incomplete or more paradoxical for ontology.

Traditional ontology from Plato and Aristotle onwards has associated the relationship between individuals and their properties with the relationship between a concept and what falls under it, a relationship recognised in judgements. A concept is expressed in a predicate, and if the predicate is joined with a name in such a way that the result comes out true or false, we have a judgement expressing how some things are with some individual. 'Aristotle likes Alexander' is a true judgement because Aristotle has the property of liking Alexander. It does not matter that properties can be further distinguished from relations or that we might also say that properties and relations fall under the more encompassing concept of functions. All we need for the following argument is a highly formal notion of properties, one that does not distinguish between properties and relations as between two species of a higher genus.

It is crucial to add that the concept of individuals and their properties traditionally already brings in the concept of the world along with it, a fact Kant was the first to fully make explicit: if all individuals are determined by their properties, then it seems natural to bring in the concept of a domain of all individuals that is internally differentiated by containing clusters of properties. The individuals are these clusters. They are, however, not mere bundles of properties. By a 'mere bundle of properties', I understand a mere mereological sum: my left hand and the earth joined together as the individual having all the properties of my left hand and the earth (= 'my left hearth') is not exactly an individual, even though it formally satisfies the relevant criteria.

Plato and Aristotle are very keen to distinguish actual individuals from such mere mereological sums. They believe that some mereological sums are more natural than mere mereological sums, and I think that they are evidently right about this. However, as I will argue in later chapters, there is no over-arching rule governing all individuals *a priori* in such a way that knowledge of that rule would put the best knower in a position to tell in advance whether something is an actual individual or a mere mereological sum. Some odd combinations can result in amazing new individuals. This can be demonstrated with reference to the gastronomic realm: new unheard of combinations turn out to be surprisingly tasty and can even make history; every dish with a history once appeared on the scene as a potential mere mereological sum and turned out to be a fine individual. There just is no overall *a priori* way of telling a natural property from a mere mereological sum. A candidate often discussed is disjunctiveness, but that also does not work, as some objects or facts simply are disjunctive: my cell phone can be in my office or at home, which is where I always put it. This is why looking at those two places suffices to find it. Why would it be a more natural fact that my cell phone actually is in my office? Of course, only the latter fact is responsible for where I find my cell phone. Nevertheless, it holds objectively good of all objects involved in the disjunctive fact that they are related in the way I take them to be related. It is not the case that the non-satisfied disjunct is merely mereologically added to the satisfied disjunct (the fact).

Kant's reason for bringing the concept of the world into ontology can easily be illustrated: if you introduce some domain of individuals (and he thinks there is exactly one all-encompassing domain of individuals, the world), you can look at it as a differentiated and meaningfully structured distribution of objects. As an illustrative example, let us divide our overall experience into four-dimensional screenshots and pick the screenshot of my subjective visual field right now: Computer, the word 'computer' on the screen, coffee left of the screen in a mug, right of the screen two pencils, my Mandarin flashcards, parts of the window, my hands, and so on. This field is meaningfully structured; it does not contain nonsense, but presumably satisfactorily determined individuals with no obvious tendency to suddenly merge into unexpected mereological sums. Kant believes that he has arguments that generalise on the basis of screenshots of this kind to such an extent that he can define the world as the 'field of possible experience'[16] so that that very field is unified into *one* field by relevant epistemological factors: it essentially consists of knowables, of individuals we are equipped to refer to with truth-apt and articulated thoughts hanging together in a space of reasons. The field of possible experience for him is unified by a justified assumption of 'systematic unity',[17] an assumption justified by the alleged fact that we could not refer to determinate scenes containing individuals without assuming that all such scenes are related by being glimpses of the world as a whole.[18] We will scrutinise this in the next chapter.

We can add a further thought to the idea of a proper property, namely the thought that reference to proper properties puts us in a position to distinguish an individual *in a domain* from some other individual in the domain. For example, the computer significantly differs from my coffee: I can drink my coffee, but I cannot drink my computer. This holds of the computer and the coffee in the domain of my living room. The difference between my computer and my coffee is in no way due to any linguistic convention or the result of the meaning of words. It is a matter of fact that I cannot drink my computer, and this fact is not projected onto any raw meaningless material. At least, there is no reason at this point to introduce the concept of raw meaningless material underlying the distribution of individuals over the domain in question (and I do not believe that there is any such reason at all). It is thus also true that if something in the domain is drinkable, it is not my computer. This is the reason behind Hegel's claim that 'everything is an inference'.[19] All individuals in the domain are embedded in inferential facts that hold of them. These inferential facts are again not projections of semantic or linguistic meaning onto some raw material, but simply facts holding of the individuals in the domain. It is a fact of the most basic form of applied arithmetic that there are four cows on my lawn if there are two male and two female cows on my lawn. This holds regardless of whether this turned out to be the right thing to say in certain situations where this just means that everyone is prone to agree. The fact is the norm of thought and not the other way around. Under these circumstances, this is why it is objectively the right thing to say that there are four cows on my lawn.

It is a fact that the carpet in my current living room is white. It is true of the carpet that it is white. Now whatever holds good of something's being white is relevant for the carpet's identity: if something is white, it is not red; if in addition the white thing is a white carpet, one usually wants to avoid spilling red wine over it, and so on. If I reason that I should not go into the living room in a really inebriated state with a glass of red wine in my right hand, my thought processes move along the inferential joints of the domain in which I co-exist with my carpet, my living room, my glass of red wine, and so on. I do not project inferential facts onto an inferentially blank reality, but trace the inferential structure of a domain in order to adapt my interests to the facts, including the inferential facts. It does not matter for the individuation of the facts that I have to be equipped with the relevant neurobiology, be trained in the use of the relevant concepts, and be relevantly unimpaired when articulating the inferential facts. The analysis of our capacities to refer to how things are in themselves simply does not assume centre stage for ontology at this level of observation. The question of how we manage to refer to an independent reality is interwoven with the question of how this independent reality is in itself, but not in such a way that there would not have been such an independent reality had we not made it the case. In particular, the idea that the independent reality in question would not exhibit properties had we not individuated them by fabricating predicates is utterly misguided.

Let us call this false view 'property constructivism' and mean by this the claim that there would be no properties had we not constructed them, where 'constructing' means 'making it the case by being equipped with the relevant conceptual capacities'. Property constructivism is an incoherent view in ontology, whereas there might be some local coherent instantiation, such as gastronomic property constructivism according to which no mereological sum consisting of a chicken breast and rosemary would have been savoury had we (or some other animal) not been equipped with a relevant sensibility for chicken with rosemary.

Proper properties are discriminatory within a domain. They do not discriminate across the board, as we will see in Chapter 7. They discriminate between individuals in a domain (even where this domain is identified with the unrestricted domain Kant calls 'the world'.[20]) For instance, the property of being green is a proper property in domains in which some objects are green and other objects are not, whereas the property of being a circle might be a proper property in domains in which other objects have other shapes. There is no general fact of the matter regarding which properties are proper properties with the noticeable exception of ontological and some logical properties.[21] Existence is never a proper property.

Of course, some properties can be shared among individuals in the domain. My pencil is white and parts of my computer screen are white, too. Yet, my computer screen and the pencil will each have some property by which they differ. This is no surprise given that otherwise they would turn out to be identical. Identity of individuals in the traditional sense at stake here is just sameness of properties (one way of stating Leibniz' principle of the identity of indiscernibles). For two individuals in a domain to be identical is for them to be exactly the same cluster of properties. They might look different due to some mistake at our end or some misleading phenomenal feature of the domain, but if they have the same properties, they will be identical.

In contradistinction to a proper property, for now let a *metaphysical property* be a property that all individuals in a domain have in common, a property reference to which, therefore, does not put anyone in a position to distinguish between any two individuals in the domain. Even though this is ultimately misguided, it seems fairly straightforward to argue that existence is a metaphysical property in that sense, because all individuals in the domain exist.[22] In my subjective visual field there is no individual which is not there (even though some of the individuals in my subjective visual field might not exist in the objective visual field; they might be hallucinations).[23] In the domain no existing individual is missing. This underlies the idea that the fact that everything exists or that the domain of existence is complete is somehow analytic or *a priori*.[24] Of course, one could object in this particular case that something might exist in another domain, but not in this one (which is the basic idea of my own theory of negative existential assertions, to be defended later). Yet, the distinction between proper and metaphysical properties only becomes fully salient when we generalise the idea and claim that for something to exist is for it to be contained in the world, an idea accepted by many contemporary metaphysicians.[25]

As I said in the introduction, metaphysics primarily deals with the world. It is a theory of totality, of the world as world. The world itself is not an individual within the world, but the name for a unified domain of absolutely everything. And absolutely everything exists in the world, the domain to which every single thing belongs. If there is nothing in the world that does not exist, existence can, thus, not be a proper property.[26]

One way of dealing with this is to claim that it is a metaphysical property, a property of the world, namely the property that it contains absolutely everything. Given my belief that it is incoherent to think that all objects might be some way, even if that way is a contingent way, the only way to make sense of a metaphysical property then is as a property of the world. This avoids attribution of a single property to all individuals. If one accepts that only individuals have properties, this creates the conundrum that the world turns into an individual. Yet, Kant might have been the first to really point out that that conclusion is unwarranted; he identified an air of paradox surrounding the view that the world is an individual, even though it is not clear whether his articulation of the paradox is sufficiently laid out.[27] The air of paradox is due to acceptance of the following set of ontological principles. These principles are the cornerstone of what I would like to call *naïve ontology (NONT)* (in analogy to 'naïve set theory'):

(NONT1) To exist is to be in the world (to be contained by the world).
(NONT2) What is contained by the world has properties.
(NONT3) The world consists of different individuals, the difference being explainable with reference to their different properties.
(NONT4) To exist is to be an individual.
(NONT5) The world is not contained by the world (motivated by fear of set-theoretical worries or driven by a less articulated fear of paradox and antinomy).

If the concept of a proper property is introduced in order to explain the difference between individuals in the world, (and therefore has no motivated application for transcendent matters), the world itself cannot have proper properties. If it had, it would be an individual (by the definition of 'individual'). Therefore, so the argument goes, we can account for existence not being a proper property, which is not yet to say that it is no property. For now, we have said that it might still be a property of the world albeit one that must not turn the world into an individual (in the ordinary or default sense of something belonging to the world). The question whether existence is a property, and if so what kind of property, will be dealt with when we consider negative existentials, which is the locus of debate since Russell and G. E. Moore. The view that it is not a proper property is conceptually independent from the view that it is not a property, as one might defend that it is not a proper property, but a metaphysical or maybe a logical one.[28]

One way of arguing for the claim that existence is a logical property is the following.[29] Imagine a world in which everything is green. Let us call this the 'green world' and the following set of considerations 'the argument from the green world'. In the green world ... *is green* would be a metaphysical property. Reference to something as green would not distinguish an individual in this world from any other individual. Accordingly, we can introduce a red world or a flat world, and so on. In all these worlds, there is a metaphysical property. That the metaphysical property is this rather than that other property is contingent to the extent to which one can say that even if all things are green, they might have been red. It might be difficult for the inhabitants of the green world to realise something that is fundamental to their world view could be contingent, so they would likely inflate the greenness of all things to something logical or necessary. Now, how do we know that the fact that we are in a world in which everything exists is not exactly like the fact that everything is green in the green world? Maybe we inhabit the existence world where it is contingently true of all individuals that they exist? My answer to this puzzle would be to claim that existence is not a metaphysical property on a par with or completely symmetrical with greenness in the green world. First of all, in the green world all green things also exist. Therefore, the green world argument does not establish that existence might be a contingent total or overall predicate in our world. In order for the green world argument to get any critical grip on arguments against existence as an overall metaphysical property, it has to show that for some world there could be a total or overall predicate ranging over everything in it such that this predicate's applicability does not imply the existence of that to which the predicate is applied. Now, the green world theorist, of course, might object that from our perspective (that is, essentially tied up with the condition that we cannot even imagine objects that do not exist) we are simply in no position to pass any positive or negative verdict on the relation between greenness and existence in the green world. 'Who knows', the objection continues, 'whether in the green world all the green objects also exist in addition to being green'. Yet, it is not clear whether this vague suspicion of transcendent truth conditions for statements we can make in our world about other 'possible worlds' even resembles an actual counter argument. It rather looks as if the green world argument relies on a vague hint from beyond, as if it was saying that from some perspective or other that is somehow unavailable to us, the argument that existence is a metaphysical and, therefore, not a proper property, might not get to the core of existence.

However, I accept that the green world argument raises a legitimate challenge. Let me rephrase it in a language closer to the ontology defended in this book. Instead of speaking of 'worlds' or even 'possible worlds', let us speak about 'domains', a term I will later replace by the term 'fields of sense' for reasons that do not matter at this stage of the dialectics. The green world then becomes a domain in which all objects are green and so on for the red world, the hat world (where all objects are hats) and the existence world. We now have several domains that are individuated in opposition to each other by having different total or overall predicates contingently ranging over everything that appears within them. The total or overall predicate of each domain can easily be mistaken for metaphysical predicates by epistemic agents within the domain, which is not to say that the epistemic agents are necessarily mislead by the overall predicates in their domain. So, how do we know that we are not mislead by appearances in the same way in which the green person in the green domain might be mislead by her own and everything else's greenness?

Let us speak of 'the metaphysical fallacy': when someone is mislead by the fact that she inhabits a given domain with an overall predicate and overgeneralises by regarding this contingent overall predicate as a necessary overall one. For instance, the identification of existence with the property of being spatio-temporarily extended is a case in point. As animals living in the universe that appears to be a giant (maybe infinite) container in which we only observe things that are thus extended, we are easily prone to a fallacy of misplaced concreteness of this sort.

At this point it is relevant to recall that the claim that existence is not a proper property tends to be associated with the further claim that it is somehow second-order or second-level. What this could mean is that for every domain introduced there will be a property defining it as this rather than that domain. The green domain is the *green* domain and the red one is the *red* one: this is why they differ from each other. Yet, they have something more general in common, namely, that for each of them there is something that all objects appearing within them have in common. What the classical arguments to the effect that existence is not a proper property are driving at, accordingly, is to show that existence is precisely the more general or even universal property of all domains that there is some feature that defines what it is to belong to them, some total or overall (albeit only locally instantiated) property. So, even if there apparently might be a sense in which there could be a domain of contingently green objects that do not also exist in addition to being green, then in this domain greenness would just be the existence property. The overall existence property would thus consist in there being no domain that does not have its local version of existence. As Umrao Sethi pointed out in written conversation about a prior version of this chapter, this would amount to a defence of

> a fundamental asymmetry between existence and any other property like greenness: one might argue that in order to be green, one must also have the property of existence but in order to exist, one has to have at least *some* other property given that there are no bare existences, but no *particular* property. In order to exist one needs some other property, but in order to be green, one needs the particular existence property as well.

In this case, to be green would be for objects to exist in the green domain, whereas in our domain greenness is a proper property and therefore differs from the existence property. The privilege of our domain would consist in the easier epistemic accessibility of the thinner existence property that stands in an asymmetrical relation to all other properties that might look like it.

But how do we know that our domain is privileged in that way? Maybe there is a more or less straightforward sense in which it is not. Someone might say that we can imagine a domain in which all objects are green without imagining that they also exist. Yet, we have not ruled out the option that existence is really said in manifold ways. One might accordingly pin this point down and maintain that existence is *whatever* property all objects in an unrestricted domain have such that their having any other property entails that they have the property in question. So greenness could have been that property.[30]

My own argument will ultimately amount to a similar view with the essential caveat not to think of existence in terms of a more general or universal concept. The relation between 'bare existence' and its manifold shapes is one where 'bare existence' is never instantiated, which is to say that there simply is no domain for which it is the case that absolutely everything exists in it. There is no existence domain in the sense in which there could be a green domain. There really are the several domains, but they are not instances of a higher genus, the all-encompassing existence domain. For every domain there is something not appearing in it, something that does not exist (in it): in other words, we have to be located in a domain where for some objects it is true that they do not exist (in that domain). To put it a bit too speculatively: if there is anything whatsoever, there has to be some object that does not exist. We cannot be in any position to observe a domain where absolutely everything exists, a form of incompleteness not due to our finite understanding. I will argue later that this account of negative existential assertions does not mean that existence after all is a property of ordinary objects, but rather a property of a field to the effect that some determinate object does not appear within it. For instance, there are no pigs in my room right now, but there are pigs on a farm somewhere. Existence is a property of rooms and farms insofar as something or other appears within them.

There is one further problem stemming from the green world argument I need to address before we can move on. For the sake of simplicity, let us say that there are three domains: the green domain (where everything is green), the brown domain (where everything is brown) and the hat domain (where everything is a hat, all the way down and all the way up). My suggestion was that in each domain there is a specific predicate – greenness, brownness, and hatness – that fulfils the function of existence. However, the objection goes, is it not the case that the green objects in the green domain in addition to being green also exist? If this interpretation of the green world argument is correct, do we not have to say that it does not at all establish that our world could be an existence domain in the sense in which the green domain is a green domain. All domains would be existence domains with the difference that the green domain has an additional property, greenness, that is similar to existence in that it is not a proper property. Existence would after all have a universal structure, with the exception that the inhabitants of the green domain might confuse existence with greenness, just as in our domain many people typically confuse existence with spatio-temporal location or with being a spatio-temporarily located entity or agent, given that spatio-temporality at the very least abounds in our neck of the woods.

My reaction to this worry consists in claiming that there is no overall, be it metaphysical or logical, property of existence that is instantiated together with a further property that characterises a field as this rather than that field. For objects to appear (to exist) in the green domain is for them to be green. But then what about *our* domain? Do I not have to maintain that our domain is special in that for objects to appear *here* is for them simply to exist without further ado? But that is exactly what I am denying. There is no bare existence, but only existence as this or that. Existence is not the description-free pure being-there of individuals or objects below the threshold of further descriptive determinacy. In my view, 'our world' is not unified into the alleged existence domain. There simply is no existence domain, but there are only the several domains.[31]

In other words, greenness and existence coincide in the green domain, whereas in the hat domain hatness and existence (that-ness) equally coincide. For objects to exist is something different in each field. The manifold appearances are nevertheless held together by the thin property of existence, the ontological property par excellence. Existence is radically disjunctive without there being an overall disjunction such as for objects to exist is either X or Y or Z, and so on, as this simply adds to the stock of the meaning of 'existence'. To be on the list of the alleged overall disjunction would just be another instance of a coincidence of

existence with something else (in this case: with being on the list
of the disjunction). This is why existence is radically disjunctive,
that is, disjunctive without amounting to any even in principle
complete list of disjuncts.

NONT is an incoherent view, as I will extensively argue in
Chapter 7. Nevertheless, it underlies the common sense of first-
order materialist metaphysics. Let *first-order materialist metaphys-*
ics be the 'view' that deep down there are only elementary particles,
the material constituents out of which everything is made. There
might be other forms of first-order materialist metaphysics, but
currently the idea that we have to find a ground floor seems to be a
more prominent fantasy among philosophers.[32] In addition to the
fact that any such view merely appears to be a modern version of
Presocratic atomism backed up by 'science', I see no philosophical
motivation for first-order materialist metaphysics. I doubt that it
is motivated by actual science. It cannot be a view arrived at by
scientific fallible procedures. At best, it is a description of what has
to be the case metaphysically for some description or other of the
importance of 'science' to make sense to philosophers. First-order
materialism is an instance of bad metaphysics, the metaphysics
rightly attacked by the logical positivists, even though they ultimately succumbed to the temptation of grounding their project
with first-order materialist metaphysics themselves. Quine was
honest enough to flag his 'metaphysics' as 'mythology' and to give
it equal validity on his reading to Homer's Gods. He accepted
the requirements of first-order materialist metaphysics, ultimately
leading him to reject logical positivism's most cherished doctrines.[33]
At the same time, of course, he believed that any justification for
the posits of modern science would be superior to any justification
for the posits of ancient Greek mythology. Yet, he admits that there
is some circularity involved in this claim, as it defines what ought
to count as a better justification in light of its own posits. I take his
declaration of equal validity to be a *reductio ad absurdum* of his
premises, which I will not lay out here in detail.

More importantly let me emphasise that I do not believe that
physics is necessarily tied up with metaphysics. Metaphysics, rather,
is a temptation in the various descriptions or self-descriptions of
the activity of arriving at an insight within physics. For instance,
elementary particles are neither particles nor elementary. The language of elementary particles and the idea that everything is made
out of them in roughly the same way in which a Lego house is

made of Lego building blocks is infantile metaphysics. At least, no one can justifiably claim to know, for instance, how neurons could possibly be fabricated on the basis of elementary particles or how there are so many different larger scale stable objects if they are all made of the same 'stuff' (which, of course, is not really 'stuff' anyway). Here, problematic metaphors abound that should not be treated as water on the mills of our ancient Presocratic instincts of looking for the true world below the threshold of mesoscopic appearances.

First-order materialist metaphysics is associated with an inclination towards rampant nominalism. *Rampant nominalism* is the claim that there really are only individuals, and even their properties are nothing like universals, but individuals, too. I believe that rampant nominalism is really motivated by NONT; it is an attempt to state that to exist is to be part of the world and that to be part of the world is to be an individual.[34] Unfortunately, the rampant nominalist ultimately needs properties in order to have many individuals, because he wants to be able to pick out the individuals, to refer to them. Otherwise, what would it even mean for him to say that there are many individuals, if his (impoverished) language did not even credit itself with the means to refer to them. Rampant nominalists, therefore, try to deflate the concept of a property and invent substitutes that do not *look like* properties (because they wear exotic names on their sleeves, such as 'tropes'), but still *function* as properties. They are properties, which really are more individuals. The ultimate problem that I will later identify with this view is that it is metaphysical, that it presents a thesis that is supposed to be true of everything that exists. Now, one might wonder at this point how this view then is itself yet another individual and not anything universal. Yet, even if there were a good answer to this particular problem of self-application, the view would still be a world view and can therefore be rejected on the grounds laid out in Chapter 7.

NONT is a good example of the traditional relationship between ontology and metaphysics, a relationship Heidegger has correctly diagnosed as the ultimate driving force behind *ontotheology*, that is, behind the idea that ontology is essentially metaphysics, that our answer to the question of what 'existence' means is at the same time part of a theory of totality. NONT is a form of ontotheology. It is arrived at through the following reasoning. First, a certain ontology is adopted as a theory choice. This choice then becomes

accepted as obvious common sense (to be is to be contained by
the world). The choice is obfuscated by later statements within
the theory and changes its modality from a theory-decision to a
natural necessity. The resulting view in this day and age is called
'naturalism', where this term is notoriously unclear and tends to
name an ideology rather than the attempt at discovering some
truth.[35] In order to not confuse too many positions, I will stick to
the old name for the view: materialism. I believe that materialism
is false, but that there are various senses in which I am not thereby
a super-naturalist.

The metaphysics of first-order materialism combined with
rampant nominalism is a projection of some ontological theory-
decision onto some alleged fundamental layer of 'reality'. A
decision is confused with how things are deep down, which is,
of course, the very structure of a projection in the psychological
sense, in this case inflated into a whole world view.[36] It should
already be clear that the insight that existence is not a proper
property needs not amount to any particular form of metaphysics.
At this point we can choose between seeing existence as a metaphysical property or not seeing it as a property at all. All we know
is that reference to the fact that something exists does not explain
why it is this rather than that other thing. If all we know about an
individual is that it exists, we are not able to tell it apart from any
other individual in the domain.

In other words, the fact that all things in the domain exist is
not what turns them into different things. If to be is to be an
individual, then the reason for them being manifold cannot be the
fact that they all exist. This does not individuate them. If there
are many individuals, there are many of them because there are
different properties distinguishing the individuals from each other.
Individuals are not individuated by being individuals.

What then is existence, or rather what does 'existence' mean?
We have ruled out several options under the assumption that it is
not a proper property. It might, thus, be a metaphysical property.
In this case, ontology would intersect with metaphysics. Notice
that existence might still well be a property of individuals, but
not a proper property.[37] We have not ruled that out. In this case,
existence would be a property of each and every individual in the
domain, for example, the property that exactly it belongs to the
domain. All other individuals in the domain have that property
too, which is why it serves no discriminatory function.

What speaks against this option is that it strains the concept of a property by adding a different function to the theoretical role it has been playing. For we have introduced properties as explanations for the fact that there are many different individuals. Now we stumble over a property that does not explain the difference. Either not all properties serve the function of properties or, at least, there are some properties of individuals that are not properly so classified.

To summarise, these are the theoretical ontological options:

(OO1): Existence is a metaphysical property.
(OO2): Existence is a logical property.
(OO3): Existence is not a property at all.
(OO4): Existence is a non-discriminatory property of each and every individual.

We are not yet fully equipped to decide between these options here, even though my intention has been to rule (OO1) and (OO2) out. I will later argue for the position that existence is a property, but not a property of individuals, but rather of fields of sense, namely their property that something appears within them, a position not covered by the traditional spectrum of (OO1)–(OO4). To exist is to appear in a field of sense, which I take to be a property of the fields, but not of the elements appearing within them. It is first necessary to disentangle ontology from metaphysics, that is, we first need to give up the idea that we already have a grasp of a totality consisting of our preferred kind of individuals so that we can reassess the idea that existence might be a property of individuals, which at the same time serves the explanatory function of universals.

All options presented so far speak against the idea that existence is a proper property. If we have turned all the substantial stones, there should be no relevant option left for conceiving of existence in terms of proper properties. NONT, which is something like a default ontology, the lowest possible standard in ontology, is a threshold below which there might be entities (ὄντα), but no more theorising about them (no ἐπιστήμη ἢ θεωρεῖ τὸ ἦ ὄν).[38] Even according to NONT existence is not a proper property, but rather the fact that some individuals (namely all existing individuals) are contained by the world. NONT is a device for speaking about all things at the same time, as it defines a universal rule, namely the rule that for any one thing that exists, it is contained by the world. The associated world view accordingly sees the world as an all-encompassing container of individuals. This leads many people to identify the world with the universe, the physical spatio-temporal container of all physical individuals and events, even though more sophisticated NONTologists are aware that this identification is not necessary because the world might contain non-physical individuals, such as numbers.[39]

Notes

1. On this see also my 'Existenz, realistisch gedacht'.
2. Cf. Meillassoux, *After Finitude*; Boghossian, *Fear of Knowledge*. I give an account of the underlying reasoning under the heading of 'the argument from facticity' in Gabriel, *Die Erkenntnis der Welt*, pp. 335–6; Gabriel, 'Nachwort', pp. 135–56.
3. Boghossian himself in *Fear of Knowledge* (p. 22) restricts himself to defending a general 'objectivism about facts'. However, in this book he does not spell this position out, which is fully justified given that his aim is only to prove that there has to be a space for such an objectivism.
4. The locus classicus of this idea is Russell, 'Philosophy of Logical Atomism', pp. 182–4.
5. Interestingly, Russell himself sometimes talks of facts in the sense that I use as my starting point. For instance, in a context where he introduces his concept of proper names he writes: 'No further information as *to the facts that are true of that particular* would enable you to have a fuller understanding of the meaning of the name' (Russell, 'Philosophy of Logical Atomism', p. 202, my emphasis). Russell does not speak of facts that can *be truly asserted* about a particular, but of facts that *are true* of that particular. Being truly assertible of something and being true of something are not the same relation, as the first is epistemic and the second need not be. Many things would have been true of the moon, had no asserters ever evolved. In any event, Russell explicitly recognises that at least facts involving belief have the structure I would generally ascribe to facts. 'I said a while back that there was no distinction of true and false among facts, but as regards that special class of facts that we call "beliefs", there is, in that sense that a belief which occurs may be true or false, though it is equally a fact in either case' ('Philosophy of Logical Atomism', pp. 227f.).

6. Russell, 'Philosophy of Logical Atomism', p. 241: 'As regard the actual things there are in the world, there is nothing at all you can say about them that in any way corresponds to existence. ... There is no sort of point in a predicate which could not conceivably be false. I mean, it is perfectly clear that, if there were such a thing as the existence of individuals that we talk of, it would be absolutely impossible for it not to apply, and that is the characteristic of a mistake.'

7. Cf. Russell, 'Philosophy of Logical Atomism', pp. 228–40; Russell, *Introduction to Mathematical Philosophy*, pp. 164–5.

8. Sider makes use of a similar argument in order to motivate the idea that not only property instantiation, but also quantifiers are candidates for logical structures that characterise the structure of how things broadly are independent of how we carve them up. This corresponds to his notion of ontological realism. See in particular Sider, 'Ontological Realism'. See also Sider, *Writing the Book of the World*.

9. See on this my *An den Grenzen der Erkenntnistheorie* and *Die Erkenntnis der Welt*.

10. Notice that this formal theory of objects treats properties as further objects. There is no categorical or substantive distinction between objects and properties.

11. Cf. David Lewis, 'Putnam's Paradox'.

12. See in particular Krauss, *A Universe from Nothing*.

13. Russell, 'Philosophy of Logical Atomism', p. 257.

14. Cf. for example, Kripke, *Reference and Existence*, in particular Lecture III; Kripke, 'Naming and Necessity', in *Identity and Individuation*, in particular pp. 156–8.

15. Umrao Sethi raised the worry that I have to revise or even reject the law of the excluded middle given that it seems that I am saying that the number of hairs on a given witch's head (meaning: a witch in *Faust* or *MacBeth* and so on) is neither 2 nor not-2. My response to this is that the witches in *Faust* or *MacBeth* are not suitable candidates for having any determinate number of hairs on their head. The witches are just indeterminate in that respect. This is not a general point about 'fictional' witches or even witches in general. For instance, a witch in a given movie will have a determinate number of hairs as well as a witch in the Rhenish carnival. I take it to be a perfectly legitimate statement that there really are witches in the Rhenish carnival (as well as Cowboys, Indians, and Mexicans, to cite just a few of the politically incorrect categories of this event). Evidently, this does not entail that the witches in the Rhenish

carnival are witches in the sense of the Inquisition. Each witch in Carnival satisfied the law of excluded middle for her number of hairs.

16. Kant, *Critique of Pure Reason*, A 229/ B 282f.: 'For as far as concerns the void that one might think of outside of the field of possible experience (the world), this does not belong to the jurisdiction of the mere understanding, which only decides about questions concerning the use of given appearances for empirical cognition, and it is a problem for Ideal reason, which goes beyond the sphere of a possible experience and would judge about what surrounds and bounds this, and must therefore be considered in the transcendental dialectic.'

17. Kant, *Critique of Pure Reason*, A 648/ B 676: 'From this, however, one sees only that systematic unity or the unity of reason of the manifold of the understanding's cognition is a logical principle, in order, where the understanding alone does not attain to rules, to help it through ideas, simultaneously creating unanimity among its various rides under one principle (the systematic), and thereby interconnection, as far as this can be done. But whether the constitution of objects or the nature of the understanding that cognizes them as such are in themselves determined to systematic unity, and whether one could in a certain measure postulate this *a priori* without taking into account such an interest of reason, and therefore say that all possible cognitions of the understanding (including empirical ones) have the unity of reason, and stand under common principles from which they could be derived despite their variety: that would be a transcendental principle of reason, which would make systematic unity not merely something subjectively and logically necessary, as method, but objectively necessary.'

18. See John McDowell's clear way of stating this point in his 'Having the World in View', p. 435: '[T]he intentionality, the objective purport, of perceptual experience in general – whether potentially knowledge yielding or not – depends ... on having the world in view, in a sense that goes beyond glimpses of the here and now. It would not be intelligible that the relevant episodes present themselves as glimpses of the here and now apart from their being related to a wider world view.' This formulation, of course, is compatible with there being multiple wholes or scenes and need not lead to the assumption that there is a widest world view.

19. Hegel, *The Encyclopaedia Logic*, § 181.

20. For now I will ignore the fact that there is a sense in which the world in Kant is not the unrestricted domain as he grants that there might

be further domains, or even that there have to be in order to restrict human cognition to its domain, the world. For elaboration see pp. 72–90.

21. On this see Colin McGinn, *Logical Properties*.

22. One sense in which this is misguided is that it is easy to come up with an indeterminately large number of such metaphysical properties, such as the property of having properties or the property of being different from all other objects. The metaphysician would owe us an account of how we can ever guarantee that there is a finite or even coherent list of metaphysical properties. Thanks to Umrao Sethi for insisting on this point. I reject the idea of metaphysical properties along with the project of metaphysics itself.

23. On this distinction see John Searle's forthcoming book on perception with Oxford University Press. Thanks to John Searle for providing me with the manuscript for discussions during a recent stay at UC Berkeley.

24. Cf. Russell, *Basic Problems of Philosophy*, in particular chapters 9 ('The World of Universals') and 10 ('Our Knowledge of Universals'); Quine, 'On What There Is'.

25. A good example can be found in van Inwagen, *Metaphysics*, pp. 277f. Van Inwagen defines 'the world' as *'everything* – everything period, everything full stop, everything without qualification.' Given his later elaboration on the concept of existence he probably understands 'being contained by the world' as belonging to some kind of set.

26. One might try to understand 'existence' as a universal feature all individuals contingently have, or rather a property all individuals contingently instantiate. In this scenario, existence would still be a proper property, but one which all individuals happen to have. The reason why existential assertions are uninformative would then not be conceptually or logically deep, but only express the contingent fact that all objects happened, happen, and maybe even will happen to exist. How do we know that the fact that all objects exist differs from a scenario in which all objects happened, happen, and will happen either to be a geometrical point or bigger in geometrical size than a geometrical point, or one in which all objects happened, happen, and will happen to be green? My own solution to this will be laid out in detail in the chapters on modality (Chapters 10 and 11) that all rest on the no-world-view, that is, on the very rejection of the option that there might be some way all objects are albeit a contingent one.

27. Cf. Gabriel, *Der Mensch im Mythos*, Part II, § 5, pp. 104–15; Gabriel, *Transcendental Ontology*, pp. 104–6.

28. Cf., for instance, McGinn, *Logical Properties: Identity, Existence, Predication, Necessary Truth*, in particular chapter 3, pp. 15–51.

29. I owe this point to a discussion with Yitzhak Melamed who pushed me on a prior assumption I now have given up.

30. This paragraph is my attempt at a response to Umrao Sethi's comments on an earlier version of the chapter.

31. In a certain sense this turns my position into a kind of 'ontological superpluralism', as introduced by Ben Caplan. He draws a distinction between claiming that there is *a general fact* to the effect that there are many meanings or kinds of 'existence', which in his terminology is 'ontological pluralism', on the one hand, and claiming that there only are 'the several pluralisms' (see Caplan, 'Ontological Superpluralism', pp. 79–114) that do not hang together in an overall disjunction. However, I do not hold my view for any of the reasons he cites in favour of superpluralism from his considerations regarding the naturalness or elitist privilege of properties or positions.

32. Recall Harman's distinction between undermining and overmining as well as the overlapping distinction between micro-fundamentalism and metaphysical holism discussed above in note 8, p. 25.

33. Quine wrote, 'As an empiricist I continue to think of the conceptual scheme of science as a tool, ultimately, for predicting future experience in the light of past experience. Physical objects are conceptually imported into the situation as convenient intermediaries – not by definition in terms of experience, but simply as irreducible posits comparable, epistemologically, to the gods of Homer. Let me interject that for my part I do, qua lay physicist, believe in physical objects and not in Homer's gods; and I consider it a scientific error to believe otherwise. But in point of epistemological footing the physical objects and the gods differ only in degree and not in kind. Both sorts of entities enter our conception only as cultural posits. The myth of physical objects is epistemologically superior to most in that it has proved more efficacious than other myths as a device for working a manageable structure into the flux of experience' (Quine, 'Two Dogmas of Empiricism', p. 44). Cf. in addition Gabriel and Žižek, *Mythology, Madness and Laughter*, pp. 66ff., and Gabriel, *Der Mensch im Mythos*.

34. Cf. Armstrong, *Sketch for a Systematic Metaphysics*.

35. See Hilary Putnam's outspoken rejection of the term due to its lack of clarity in *Philosophy in an Age of Science*, pp. 109f.: 'Today the most common use of the term "naturalism" might be described as follows: philosophers – perhaps even a majority of all the philoso-

phers writing about issues in metaphysics, epistemology, philosophy of mind, and philosophy of language – announce in one or another conspicuous place in their essays and books that they are "naturalists" or that the view or account being defended is a "naturalist" one. This announcement, in its placing and emphasis, resembles the placing of the announcement in articles written in Stalin's Soviet Union that a view was in agreement with Comrade Stalin's; as in the case of the latter announcement, it is supposed to be clear that any view that is not "naturalist" (not in agreement with Comrade Stalin's view) is anathema and could not possibly be correct. A further very common feature is that, as a rule, "naturalism" is not *defined*.'

36. I discuss this under the Kantian heading of 'transcendental subreption' in my *An den Grenzen der Erkenntnistheorie*, pp. 100ff.

37. Cf. Miller, 'Exists and Existence', pp. 237–70 and again McGinn, *Logical Properties*, in particular chapter 3, pp. 15–51.

38. Aristotle, *Metaphysics*, 1003a20.

39. See, for instance, van Inwagen, *Metaphysics*, p. 277, where he rightly points out that even on a construal of the world as some collectively totalising name for absolutely everything 'the meaning of "the World" is not tied to any particular feature of things. If there are no spirits or other non-physical things, then a person who wrongly believes that there are spirits, and who expresses this belief – by saying, for example, "The World contains spirits" – will be saying something false, but will not be misusing the phrase "the World".'

3

What is Wrong with Kant and Frege?

In this chapter I discuss Kant and Frege's influential views on existence. The view that existence is not a proper property, maybe not even a property at all, is usually believed to hark back to Kant and Frege. As a matter of fact, both Kant and Frege indeed present different arguments for their belief that existence is not a proper property. Kant distinguishes between 'logical' and 'real' predicates and argues that existence 'is not a real predicate',[1] whereas Frege distinguishes between first-order predicates expressing 'properties (*Eigenschaften*)' of objects and second-order predicates expressing 'characteristics (*Merkmale*)' of concepts.[2] Frege's basic doctrine has it that objects satisfy functions in the formal sense of $F(x)$. An object is whatever produces a truth-value if replacing the x. If the concept is *X is a dog*, then Havannah (my dog) satisfies the function because *Havannah is a dog* turns out to be true. This is Frege's way of coming to the conclusion that Havannah is an individual. Sometimes Kant and Frege's views are simply identified.[3] However, the only essential feature they have in common is their rejection of the idea that existence is a proper property. In order to see this, I will first discuss the outlines of Kant's theory of existence and then move to Frege's enhancement of the view.

I think it is fair to say without going into complicated exegetical problems that Kant understands 'existence' to be the fact that the world contains individuals with properties. For him, existence is a property of the world and not of the individuals contained within it. Of course, in addition to this very thin notion of 'existence', which Kant in the famous quote calls 'being (*Sein*)', he has additional reasons to believe that nothing exists that is not actual (*wirklich*). For him, actuality is epistemically equivalent to existence, because understanding existence involves understanding that actual individuals are either straightforwardly spatio-temporal or at the very least related to the constitution of space-time. Roughly stated, his view is that individuals are either spatio-temporal objects or at the very least structures we can employ to describe spatio-temporal individuals. Ultimately, I believe his view of the necessary spatio-temporality of individuals is untenable, and I honestly have a hard time making sense of the idea that the individuals we can successfully refer to (which we can 'cognize (erkennen)') are necessarily (in some transcendental sense of 'necessarily') spatio-temporal. Further, his additional view that space-time is a set of forms of intuition and not itself a big individual is unintelligible and at best amounts to a very contentious revisionary understanding of the nature of space-time; a revision not up to our current scientific knowledge. It was discovered over the course of the nineteenth century that space-time is itself a big individual rather than a form of intuition. Transcendental idealism in its official version from the *Transcendental Aesthetics* has been tamed by mathematics first (non-Euclidian geometry) and then by physics (by the late nineteenth century and then the Einsteinian discovery that space-time really is itself something physical and not some abstract absolute 'spiritual' container of physical things and events).

However, Kant's theory of existence and actuality can be cleansed from the official doctrines of transcendental idealism. The minimal claim still defended by many contemporary ontologists amounts to nothing more than existence being the property of the world to contain something. To claim that there is something rather than nothing is 'merely the positing of a thing or of certain determinations in themselves',[4] that is, positing something within the world. Kant clearly distinguishes between positing something as something (the copula sense of 'is') and positing something absolutely (the existence sense of 'is').[5]

Kant conceives of the world as a field, the 'field of possible experience'.[6] For something to exist is for something to belong to this field. Actuality (*Wirklichkeit*), accordingly, is the additional property of the field that it only contains experienceable individuals, objects suitable for our understanding of them in terms of logical subjects, subjects we can have structured thoughts about.[7] The idea behind this is that we can know *a priori* that there are no objects of experience that we cannot think about as having some property or other. This insight cannot be derived from experience, because experience is a source of defeasible information, whereas the notion that all objects in the world are individuals we can think about with truth-apt thoughts precisely because they could not exist without being determined beyond their sheer existence is not itself derived from that source. To know that all objects can become contents of a truth-apt thought is not to know something that could be falsified by encountering an object that does not meet that condition. An object not meeting that condition cannot be met with in truth-apt thought. Yet, to experience something presupposes having a truth-apt thought about it. There is, therefore, an invariable minimal structure of intentionality built into the concept of truth-apt thought, an invariable structure not affected by the variable and contingent contents we encounter within the scope of our minimal intentionality.[8]

Now Kant believes himself to have reasons for concluding that only a certain kind of individual can be thought about as satisfying the constraints for there to be an invariable structure of intentionality. His arguments to this effect are complicated and most likely incoherent, but we do not have to take care of the business of deciding what Kant said about this particular issue here.[9] All we need is a good enough grasp of Kant's view that existence is a property, though not a proper property, but rather a property of the world and that the world is a domain or a field, as he himself writes. We do not need to accept his particular world view, which is notoriously broadly Newtonian, even though he also famously added further elements in the *Second* and *Third Critiques*.

Yet, it does not matter for ontology how we flesh out the concept of the world by attributing a nature to the world. By this I mean that it is possible to maintain that existence is the fact that the world (the domain where everything exists, and the place where everything takes place) is not empty, that it contains something rather than nothing, without claiming that the world is the (Newtonian or any other) universe. In this context, let the 'universe' refer to all of space-time (at least to the part of space-time of which we observers of space-time are a part if there are many universes). If the world is identical with the universe, then to exist is the fact that space-time contains something. And whatever space-time contains is what science, paradigmatically physics, tells us that it contains. This view is sometimes presented as the epitome of 'naturalism'. However, 'nature' is an even more vague term than 'the universe' and the idea that we need to protect nature from containing supernatural influences (such as souls, ghosts, or astral bodies) seems to me to be too trivial to be really worth mentioning. If someone believes in astral bodies or haunted houses, they are not in need of philosophical arguments. Philosophical rationality is not an effective therapy against these kinds of beliefs that are not usually rooted in mere 'fallacies of the understanding'.

But imagine George Berkeley, the Bishop of Cloyne, was right (of course, he wasn't): then the world would be the domain of all bodiless free-floating minds. It could not contain anything physical (as he argues that the very idea of something physical is incoherent). Berkeley in effect believed that the universe did not exist, but that there nevertheless was a world. He just claims that the world consists of nothing that even faintly resembles the objects needed to substantiate any claim to the existence of a material universe. Thus, for him, to exist is to belong to the domain of all bodiless free-floating minds (and everything associated with the constitution of that domain). However, he officially defined existence as the fact that something is perceivable by a mind and argued that minds themselves were not perceivable. In order to avoid the problem that this would amount to the claim that everything only exists because it is perceived by something that does not exist, he adds that to exist is to be perceived or to perceive, *esse est percipi aut percipere*. Any 'enhanced' version of his immaterialism would say that the world only contains minds and their contents, that is, only mental stuff. If there is only mental stuff, there still could be a world, namely the domain containing mental stuff, and we could accordingly define existence as the fact that the world is not empty, that, therefore, some (and ultimately all) stuff is mental. Berkeley could also easily be a rampant immaterialist nominalist and say that there are only individuals and that all individuals are either minds or mental contents. Thus, both the view that to exist is to be contained by the world and rampant nominalism are logically independent from materialism.

This is an important example of the fact that a single ontology can trigger different metaphysical systems. The answer to the question what 'existence' means need not amount to any particular 'ontological commitment' in Quine's sense, that is, to any particular view regarding which kinds of things populate the world as world and which kinds of things one will never be able to encounter in the universe. Ontology is not the attempt to answer the question what there is or the question what kinds of things there are. These questions, if even so much as meaningful, in this generality are not even philosophical. The answer to the question of what there is are the facts and objects that there are. They come into domains or rather fields of sense, an idea I will defend in later chapters, but this fact is incompatible with the idea that we could even write a list of all of the kinds of things in principle. Later, I will rule out the option that there could be a simplified way to list all the things that exist. There are all kinds of things, and no over-arching rule will ever be able to encompass them or to simplify them in the way that one could state any theory's real metaphysical commitments. The things in themselves are, if anything, meta-physically anarchical, because there is no all-encompassing rule one could hope to translate into an unrestricted universal quanti-fier to be used in sentences of the form: 'absolutely everything is such and such, or is of such and such nature, or belongs to either of the following very finite number of categories'.

But did Kant not reject the very possibility of ontology? There is no doubt that he writes, 'the proud name of ontology [...] must give way to the modest one of a mere analytic of the human under-standing' (CPR A247/B303). Yet, how is this claim compatible with the also obvious fact that Kant proposes a new concept of existence, that he himself sets out to define 'existence'?

I think one way of making sense of this tension is to see Kant as proposing a *revisionary ontology*. Let the *default ontology* be the view that to exist is to be there and that in order to be there, the things which are there have to have a certain property distinguishing them from the things that are not there. In other words, the default ontology implicitly postulates two domains: the domain of existing things and the domain of non-existing things. In this way, it comes to understand existence as a proper property after all, namely as the property of existing things that distin-guishes them from non-existing things. When Kant claims that this project is unfeasible, his main reason to reject it is the idea that we do not have access to a domain of non-existing things, reference to which would put us in a position to attribute the first-order property of existence to the things in the domain of existing things in contraposition to the other domain of non-existing things. For if we had, we would have to say that the actual hundred Euro bill (to update Kant's famous example) differs from all non-existing, but obviously possible hundred Euro bills (the ones not yet printed). If it did, we could never produce a not yet existing thing, that is, turn *it* into an existing thing. For the actual existing thing would always literally be different from the possible, not yet existing thing by at least the one property: existence.

Depending on how we flesh this property out, this could make all the difference in the world. Imagine that it turns out that the property of existing is co-extensive or even logically equivalent to the property of being extended in space and time. Then the non-existing hundred Euro bill would be a very weird kind of thing: it would maybe be extended in imaginary space and time, but would not thereby really be extended in space and time (even though Kant himself has a hard time distinguishing imaginary and real extension[10]). Once it comes into existence, it changes its very nature to such a degree that we could not really identify it as the same thing with the difference of now existing. This is why for Kant existence is not a real predicate; it does not single the existing things out in a domain encompassing both the non-existing and the existing things.

In reality, Kant therefore does not give up on ontology as such, but rather proposes a new or revisionary ontology that offers a reconstruction of all basic ontological terms from the tradition (existence, the modalities, entity and object, and so on) without any need to think of these as properties of the things in themselves. Instead, he restricts meaningful application of ontological vocabulary to the domain of things experienceable by us, or rather to the things systematically related to things experienceable by us. In this light, I would even venture to claim that Kant's distinction between things in themselves and appearances could in principle be defended as the distinction between things with first-order properties (things in themselves) and things with higher-order properties (existence, the modalities, entity and object, and so on). However, this rough outline for an interpretation offers no solace to Kantians, as it merely repeats the distinction between a domain of non-existing things and the existing things by claiming that only appearances exist, whereas things in themselves cannot even exist.

One line of defence against this highly unwelcome result is what I call 'Kantian modesty'. Kantian modesty consists in restricting existential claims to judgements concerning details within the field of possible experience (that Kant explicitly equates with the world). This just means that we have no way of deciding whether things in themselves exist or not. It is not a question to which there is a possible answer according to any standards of epistemic possibility available to us. It lies beyond 'the bounds of sense', to borrow P. F.

Strawson's famous metaphor.[11] Unfortunately, as in other cases, Kantian modesty will not work here. For Kant restricts actuality in such a way that nothing could possibly be actual without standing in a relation to our sensibility. To be actual just means to be experienceable according to Kant. But perhaps Kant's view of existence as 'absolute position' is completely independent of his problematic restriction of actuality to judgements. He could then say that we absolutely posit things in themselves without ever being in a position to verify whether there are such things. However, this creates the problem that for things to exist as objects of experience might mean something utterly different from what it is for things to exist as things in themselves. How can we guarantee that it makes any sense whatsoever to work with a unified account of existence, one which leaves room for the option that things in themselves exist in a sense in any way similar to our actual concept of existence?

Kant is at least committed to the following conditional, which lies at the heart of transcendental idealism, and which is the real formula of what Meillassoux wants to criticise as 'correlationism'. Let us from now on call it the transcendental conditional (TC):

(TC) Had no human understanding (and therefore no one of our species) ever been around, nothing would have been actual.

This conditional is a prime example of what I have elsewhere introduced as 'ontic nonsense'.[12] The idea that nothing was actual before human beings existed is straightforward nonsense, and it should tell us that something went wrong elsewhere. This is not a bullet anyone should ever be willing to bite. It makes it look as if once upon a time (actually, there was no time yet either ...) a vast nothingness reigned over itself. Nothing was actual, even though maybe some things in themselves existed (in a sense of 'existence' we do not have a cognitive grip on). Then, human understanding fell from heaven (which of course also was not actual at that time) and suddenly all sorts of things started existing: the actual earth, the actual moon, actual mountains, actual rivers and actual deer. Then the humans started hunting the newly created finally actual deer whose actuality (if not their formal content or essence) they created. This is how the world looks to a strange tribe of indigenous people from old Königsberg at the river Pregel, which they consider to be the cosmopolitan centre of the known world. At least, this is how Kant sees his own town.[13] I see no reason to accept this creation myth, even though it recommends itself to modern readers by being associated with modern physics: human beings, defined by their understanding, had no choice but to create the things according to the book of rules later discovered by the great human being Isaac Newton, who discovered the book of rules even though he was not from Königsberg.

Of course, there is a long-standing debate as to how to exactly interpret transcendental idealism and the associated claim that the transcendental ideality of space and time does not undermine empirical realism, however one defines these views exactly. There are various ways in which one could try to fix Kant by correcting the official statements of the view. The standard objection against transcendental idealism's central tenet, namely that there is some relevant distinction between phenomena and things in themselves, contends that Kant has to claim knowledge about things in themselves. For instance, he has to think of them as individuated in such a way that they can affect us, whatever exactly that means. There is no doubt that Kant held that things in themselves affect us, and debates about the exact meaning of that claim have been prominent since Kant's own days.[14]

In one way or other, Kant has to be in the position to claim that things in themselves are involved in facts that at least in part are open to our understanding of them. Something has to hold good of them, and we know something about what this means. I have the following train of thought in mind. We do need to claim that to know that things in themselves at the very least could not even in principle contravene the laws of what Kant calls 'general logic'.[15] Nothing in itself, whatever else holds good of it, could turn out to contradict the basic laws of logic, if indeed there are any. Also, things in themselves have to be further determined and sufficiently individuated so as to determine appearances as being thus and so even if the specific processes involved in this determination are not open to human cognition (*Erkenntnis*). It cannot be the case that the fact that right now a cup appears in front of me stands in no relation whatsoever with things in themselves. Rather, Kant has to admit that things in themselves contribute to the content of perceptual experience in some way even if he might be warranted in claiming that we can neither cognise (*erkennen*) nor know (*wissen*) *how exactly* this works. Nevertheless, we know *that* it does. In other words, we are justified in postulating some non-arbitrary or non-random relation between things in themselves and appearances so that we can legitimately claim that the latter are appearances of things in themselves.

I see two ways of dealing with this. Kant could argue (1) that we cannot cognise (*erkennen*) things in themselves, but that we can know (*wissen*) something about them.[16] Or he could draw on the distinction between thinking (*denken*) and cognising (*erkennen*) and argue that (2) we can think things in themselves, but not cognise them.

Unfortunately, Kant definitely did not choose the first option. First and foremost, he explicitly rules out that we can *know* anything about things in themselves in addition to not being able to *cognise* them.[17] However, might he not have claimed that we can know something about things in themselves without cognising them? In my view, here is how such a view could be fleshed out within a broadly Kantian framework. At this point it is important to remember Kant's distinction between 'having an opinion (*Meinen*)', 'believing (*Glauben*)', and 'knowing (*Wissen*)' from the methodology section of the *First Critique*. There, he writes:

> *Having an opinion* is taking something to be true with the consciousness that it is subjectively *as well as* objectively insufficient. If taking something to be true is only subjectively sufficient and is at the same time held to be objectively insufficient, then it is called *believing*. Finally, when taking something to be true is both subjectively and objectively sufficient it is called *knowing*. Subjective sufficiency is called *conviction* (for myself), objective sufficiency, *certainty* (for everyone).[18]

Now, Kant officially seems to claim that we can have beliefs (*Glaube*) about things in themselves that do not amount to knowledge.[19] But he explicitly denies in several passages that we can *know* anything about them, *cognise* (*erkennen*) them or even *be acquainted with them* (*bekannt sein*). That commits him according to his definition of belief to the view that taking something to be true of things in themselves is a form of belief that is objectively insufficient. On one reading, this means that even in the scenario where all humans agreed about certain restrictions regarding what we can believe about things in themselves, all of this would still only hold locally, within the realm of human belief-mongering, whereas knowledge extends beyond that and holds necessarily 'for everybody' in the widest sense of the term (including Gods and angels). Or it means that we simply cannot know anything about things in themselves, but nevertheless can have subjectively satisfying beliefs about them (say in terms of practically grounded postulates in a *Second Critique* sense). But just how could we not *know* that things in themselves are identical with themselves or know that if there are more than five of them, then there are also more than four of them? How is this not objectively sufficient? In order for Kant to actually justify his restriction of our knowledge to appearances, he has to add his premise that a form of taking-to-be-true only counts as *objectively* sufficient if it involves cognition. In that sense, it would be trivially true that we cannot know anything about things in themselves given that we cannot cognise them. However, Kant could stick to his favourite view that we cannot cognise them and give up the constraint on knowledge. This would fix a lot of the traditional problems associated with the things in themselves/appearances-distinction. For instance, he could argue that cognition is always and only possible under contingent physiological sensory conditions. Humans *see* colourful objects and events. They also smell and touch and hear and they do this under species-relative (be it transcendentally or neurologically more or less hardwired) conditions. We could then say that bats cognise differently, as they have access to different appearances, such as a nicely individuated sonar-bubble of appearances. Just as our senses do not address each other in the same languages (if I see an event of sauce-cooking I do not thereby have full access to the sounds it emits or to how it tastes), there might be a further translation problem involving other forms of cognition simply not accessible to us. This is what it means for cognition to be finite. Of course, Kant holds the much more contentious (if not to say crazy, and almost certainly completely false) view that space and time literally belong to our form of cognition in such a way that we have to grant that there might be forms of cognition for whom space and time are inaccessible in the same sense in which the sonar-world of bats is inaccessible to us (as of now, the status of future neurotechnology pending).

A purified or modified (at least a more modest) Kant would have said that we cannot *cognise* things in themselves, but that we can *know* something about them. This would put him in a position to give an account of non-random phenomenalisation, that is, of how things in themselves are likely to look once they appear under certain finite conditions, such as those defined by our sensory equipment. Yet, even on this construal it remains unclear why we should not be able to cognise things in themselves. Why not say that we cognise things in themselves under species-relative descriptions? Why not claim that it is a feature of things in themselves that *they* appear the way they *appear* to humans, whereas they again *appear* differently to bats, gods and angels? Kant seems to want to say that we cannot cognise things in themselves because we cannot cognise them completely. But that should never be evidence for the impossibility of accessing things in themselves, as it is not generally required that we know of something or successfully perceive it only if we know everything about it or perceive it in its entirety. Of course, cognition and knowledge are partial, which is part of the explanation of our fallibility, but this does not entail that we always only refer to appearances and never to things in themselves. It all hinges on how we think about phenomenalisation, a problem Kant wants to be intractable so as to continue speculating about things in themselves as if belonging to an immaterial 'kingdom of ends'.[20] After all, full-blown monadology for Kant is still possible in the mode of belief (*Glauben*). Yet, this only results if we accept the premise that appearances are closed under laws of nature in Kant's understanding of the Newtonian requirements for the nomological closure of nature. Given that all of this is much too controversial (or even misguided), it would be a bad idea to build our epistemology on such shaky soil, and as such we should simply dismiss the idea that the realm of appearances can only be made sense of in terms of Newtonian nomological closure.

To some degree, the model of phenomenalisation defended in this book would be in line with this attempt to fix Kant, that is, to the degree to which this turns out to be compatible with the no-world-view. My model is one on which we cannot only know things in themselves without cognising them, but we can also cognise things in themselves as they appear to us in species-relative ways. Things in themselves are revealed to true thought under species-relative conditions of appearing, such as those associated with human optics or tactility. The softness of a surface tells us something about the surface and not just about how the surface feels to us. Neither spatio-temporal relations nor other relations only accessible to true thought under specific sensory descriptions are in principle on the other side of some set of bounds of sense or other. Given that Kant officially rejects this option, my own view at most could count as a very deviant or heterodox form of Kantianism.

On the second model, Kant creates the following problem for himself. If we can *think* (*denken*) things in themselves without thereby *cognising* (*erkennen*) them or *knowing* (*wissen*) anything about them, this means that we have no reason to infer that they are actually individuated in any of the ways we could deem relevant for an understanding of how they even might be connected to appearances. Thinking by itself unaided by any form of cognition (be it divine archetypal cognition that creates objects by thinking about them) can never give anyone any clue as to the actual individuation of its objects. It certainly cannot tell us anything about the specific nature of the relationship between things in themselves and their appearances. In other words, for Kant we cannot construct a theory of phenomenalisation on the basis of thinking things in themselves, as mere thinking never is able to grasp appearances. Kantian modesty also implies withholding judgement in the area of any theory of phenomenalisation. This means that we cannot merely think the relationship between things in themselves and appearances, as we cannot merely think appearances. We have to cognise them. Regarding God's case (as invoked by Kant), he also does not merely think things in themselves; he cognises them by creating them in his reference to them, however that looks in detail. This means that no one can merely think things in themselves in such a way that something can be claimed about their relationship to appearances.

This is why I disagree with Sebastian Rödl's preferred solution of the problem as a reading of Kant. Rödl wants to think of Kantian thinking as having content: being itself.[21] If I understand him correctly, his reason for this interpretation consists in insisting on the logical generality of thinking. Thinking is not limited to any kind of 'phenomenal bubble';[22] it is general or universal. However, Kant does not say that we can apply thinking outside of appearances. It is not universal in the sense that we can know that it holds across the board, as we cannot know anything about the board as a whole (if there be such a board). Thinking for Kant, rather, is a mere form, albeit a form without exception. It is a form to which there cannot be any counterexamples, which also implies for Kant that there cannot really be any examples of it. Kant holds a correspondence theory of truth, which, among other things, also fulfils a justificatory function. It adds to his case that there has to be something like a transcendental logic if we ever want to be able to account for the fact that there are structured thoughts, even if they are so much as analytic truths. As soon as there are examples, some form of cognition is at work that relates to content (be it given or produced by the form of cognition at work) in a way that cannot be anticipated by inspecting the nature of thinking alone. This is why there will ultimately always be a gap between the logical modalities, most notably logical possibility, and the real modalities, as their reality is determined by the specific content processed or produced by some form of cognition or other. This is why the concept of thinking does not provide us with any grip on the individuation of things in themselves that would be sufficient even for the most general and unspecific solution of the problem of phenomenalisation. We certainly could not claim that things in themselves can bring about appearances in any way intelligible via insight derived from articulating the laws of general logic. In any event, this would always involve insight into the relation between appearances and things in themselves, which will cause the problem that we cannot have a purely formal-logical grip on appearances. This also explains why Kant introduces the concept of transcendental cognition. He famously writes:

> I call all cognition transcendental that is occupied not so much with objects but rather with our mode of cognition of objects insofar as this is to be possible *a priori*.[23]

The distinction between things and themselves and appearances can be drawn by us precisely because there is transcendental cognition. This means that thinking alone does not give us any insight into the problem of phenomenalisation, as this can only be posed as soon as we are confronted with a specific form of cognition, in our case, with human cognition. Thinking alone is without any content, which also applies to the case of divine thinking. The difference between the finite human thinker and God's *intellectus archetypus* is a difference in the form of cognition, not in the form of thinking. This means that God himself cannot think things in themselves, but has to cognise them. We cannot think them, as they are not even the content of the purest form of thinking, given that no actual form of thinking can have content without being associated with its specific form of cognition. In this sense, God (as imagined or stipulated by Kant) is as finite as we are, he just belongs to another species of thinkers, namely to the species of thinkers that produce their objects by cognising them in their specific way.

The best attempt at a charitable reading of the transcendental idealism/empirical realism distinction is in terms of theory-orders. Transcendental idealism would then be a higher-order claim about our epistemic relationship with spatio-temporal objects and not a first-order claim about those objects themselves.[24] However, there is hardly any doubt that Kant himself believed that transcendental idealism entailed, or even consisted in, the thesis that there would be no space and time if 'our subject' were not around to establish spatio-temporal relations. He explicitly writes:

> We have therefore wanted to say that all our intuition is nothing but the representation of appearance; that the things that we intuit are not **in** themselves what we intuit them to be, nor are their relations so constituted in themselves as they appear to us; and that if we remove our own subject or even only the subjective constitution of the senses in general, then all the constitution, all relations of objects in space and time, indeed space and time themselves would disappear, and as appearances they cannot exist in themselves, but only in us.[25]

Apart from all the manifold problems this passage raises (what does it possibly mean that space and time exist 'only in us'?), Meillassoux has recently reminded us of the good old problem that this means that there was no time before we made it true that there was time, which means that there is a paradoxical beginning of time somehow associated with the atemporal coming into existence of human beings and their specific sensorial equipment.[26] Evidently, this is in conflict with the fact that human beings originated *after* a very long time of evolution, which did not paradoxically or suddenly turn into the time of evolution at some point of time in the development of evolution. It is absurd to suppose that evolution first developed outside of time and then became temporal as a by-product of one of its products.

The real problem with the 'correlationalist circle'[27] is not so much that we can never have epistemic access to how things are independently of our access to them, but that there are no such things, or rather, that these things at least do not exist. I think that Kant's real answer to this challenge is that he invents a new concept, a concept we can call 'schmexistence'. Things in themselves do not exist, and they also should not be considered to be non-existing. Rather, they exist in some different way, in a way completely inaccessible to our cognition, even though we can have educated guesses about them and can even subjectively justifiably believe (*glauben*) that they are at least non-contradictory.[28] We only have the concept of their 'schmexistence' as referring to whatever it is that makes them more than non-existing. Schmexistence is as-if-existence, or noumenal being. Even though we cannot really know what it is for things in themselves to schmexist, we can have the hope that it is for them to be part of the 'kingdom of ends',[29] which means that the projection of moral categories onto schmexistence is at least not out of the question.

This amounts to an even deeper problem. Kant avoids default ontology by limiting existence to the domain of human understanding. For things to exist is for them to belong to the 'field of possible experience'. The real trick here is to understand existence as a field property, as the field's property to encompass something rather than nothing. Yet, this move ties existence to this specific field. But what if the field of things in themselves, which by definition differs from the field of appearances (which is true in any interpretation of the distinction[30]), contained something rather than nothing? This hypothesis is more likely than the hypothesis that there are no things in themselves at all, at least as a matter of Kant exegesis. Yet, it is, of course, not quite correct to surmise that there probably are some things in themselves. Rather, what we are thereby surmising is that there is (in some undefined sense of 'there is') a field of things in themselves, and that that field is not empty. Call this fact 'schmexistence'. There schmare things in themselves, or they schmexist, even though they cannot exist, as the full import of existence only enters the picture together with human understanding. But what about the field of things in themselves? Does it exist or schmexist? Kant certainly owes us an answer to that, but he would probably refuse to address that question due to its utter unintelligibility for human understanding.

Let us pin down the problem and define *revisionary ontological monism* as the view that there is only one domain encompassing everything such that we are justified in regarding everything within that domain as existing. It thereby seems as if we were qualifying the objects within the domain as existing, but existence is really the fact that the domain is not empty, that is, it is a relation between the all-encompassing domain and its denizens. It is revisionary precisely to the extent that it defines existence as the property of the domain to not be empty and does not ascribe the property of existence to the things within the domain. By this definition, if we assume that there is any possibility that there might be additional things outside of the domain, they cannot exist. But maybe something structurally similar applies outside the domain, something we cannot really access. It might be the case that there are further domains with different properties somehow similar to existence, for example, schmexistence, krexistence, and maybe also X-istence.[31] In other words, Kant's defence of revisionary ontological monism entails at the very least the possibility of *revisionary ontological pluralism*. I take him to be committed to revisionary ontological monism because he thinks that the domain of appearances contains within it everything that exists, and anything that is outside the domain cannot exist, but might perhaps schmexist. However, Kant's monism cannot make sense of this option, in particular, because it limits the concept of real possibility to the domain of existence.[32] Thus, the other domains – schmexistence, krexistence, X-istence, and so on – are not really possible, but are maybe schmpossible, krpossible, or X-possible. Actually, they are not even maybe schmpossible, but rather schmaybe schmpossible because the statement that they are *maybe* schmpossible is saying that they are possibly schmpossible, which already amounts to transcending the limits of human understanding.

In other words, Kant combines two ideas: the first (ontological monism) turns out to be untenable, whereas the second (field ontology) is the motivation behind the more general view that existence is a field-property and not a property of field-immanent objects. Given the premise that existence is not a real property, he first and foremost holds ontological monism. Note that *ontological* monism needs to be distinguished from *ontic* monism. Whereas ontological monism is the view that there is only one *domain* of objects settling which objects exist and which do not, ontic monism is the view that there is only one object, for instance, in the form of one *real* object encompassing other *apparent* objects by having them as parts.[33] However, all Kant motivates is that there is at least one domain of objects, namely the one whose denizens are defined by being cognisable by us.

Restrictions on cognisability include that the objects can be referred to by singular thoughts or judgements grounded in sensory experience (or contributing to making it possible), even though Kant argues that we have to think of all objects as belonging to an overall world. Although we cannot *cognise* (*erkennen*) their denizens, there is no good reason to deny that there could be further fields of inquiry, where Kant is believed to have at least good reasons for postulating one additional field unified by the fact that all its denizens are inaccessible to human cognition. Still, we can *think* (*denken*) that there could be further domains, in the minimal sense that it does not amount to contradiction.[34] According to Kant, we cannot assess other fields' *real* possibility (judged by their accessibility via sensory experience), but we can also not rule out their *overall* possibility given that they are *logically* possible, at least in the thinnest sense in which we can express any number of non-contradictory propositions about them without thereby being in a position to come to any warranted verdict about their actual truth value.

The problem with the distinction between *overall* and *real* possibility here is that it amounts to an acknowledgement that ontological monism could be false. Kant's formulation of ontological monism is at the very least a commitment to the overall contingent fact that for all we know there is only one domain of objects, the field of possible experience, and to exist accordingly is for this particular field not to be empty. But the meaning of 'existence' might have an overall sense we cannot grasp, where it would mean something like: to exist is to belong to any of the several domains of objects, such as, the field of possible experience or to any of the other fields not accessible to human understanding apart from human understanding's very thin quasi-reference to them under the description that they are all logically possible.

Now the real problem for Kant is not only that he allows for the possibility that his ontological monism could be shown to be false from without by someone who could at least never speak to us humans – if such a different form of actual intellect were to talk to us, we could not understand it.[35] Rather, his own position straightforwardly entails ontological pluralism. Here is why. If to exist is to belong to the field of possible experience, the field of possible experience must itself exist in some sense. Even if there are reasons that motivate the revisionary concept of existence, there must be some space for the notion that the domain within which everything exists itself *exists* in some sense. But what would that sense be? Certainly not the ordinary or default sense, as this was rejected so that we arrived at the revisionary concept. We cannot simply hold both.[36]

But if the field of possible experience did not exist in any sense, for all we could know, nothing would exist. At least, no ordinary objects would exist, let alone humans, because we exist both in that field (as human beings) and in a constitutive relation to the field (as particular instances of human understanding). But in order for the field to exist, it must either belong to the field itself or not. If it does not, we cannot tell whether it exists, because it would not be within our possible experience. This would amount to a very strange form of ontic-ontological scepticism: we could neither know whether the field of possible experience (the only domain of objects we thought we can know anything about) existed, nor could we know whether any particular object in the field existed (because no field entails no object existing in it). Thus, Kant's only two options are:

1. To acknowledge that there are at least several meanings of 'existence' available to us: existence in the field and the schmexistence of the field itself.
2. To claim that the field belongs to itself.

Let us briefly explore both options. Option (1.) amounts to a rejection of ontological monism. It introduces a twofold meaning of existence: *empirical* and *transcendental existence*. Both forms of existence are cognisable and not merely logically possible. To put it in Kant-o-nese: both standard first-order empirical objects and transcendental functions (categories, ideas, and so on) would have to be available to truth-apt thoughts (or judgements), the first as objects of cognition and the second as what? Probably not as more objects of cognition, as this would turn the categories, ideas, into appearances and transcendental knowledge into empirical knowledge of higher-order objects.

Option (2.) does not fare much better. It essentially claims that the field of possible experience is an object in that very field. If the field of possible experience were an object in the field, it would satisfy all conditions for being an individual among others. We can illustrate the resulting situation by a simple world-diagram:

The world (the field of possible experience) would encompass all objects belonging to it as well as itself. But if it encompasses itself in this way, then all objects immediately exist at least twice: in the world and in the world in the world. This, however, triggers an infinite regress and therefore an infinite proliferation

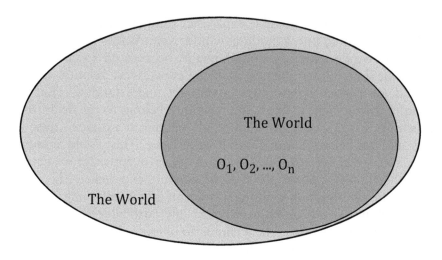

of the same objects all the way down and all the way up. The 'same' objects suddenly exist in infinitely many copies of themselves.

This option cannot even be made serviceable by thinking of it as an anticipation of the multiverse hypothesis because it really is nothing but an eternal and infinite recurrence of the 'same'. There are no different fields, but only the 'same' field copied into itself infinitely. If any infinite regress has ever been vicious, this one is. It could only be defended by giving up many cherished beliefs about the identity of world-immanent individuals.[37]

The upshot of this discussion of Kant's weaknesses is that Kant should not have pretended to be ontologically modest, for he is not. His view is ontologically significant and requires an array of aporetic presuppositions. Jacobi rightly emphasised that there is a threat that Kant's transcendental idealism generates nihilism, because it has to admit that the field of possible experience might not itself exist (in any sense), which entails that nothing could exist within it.[38] Even if the charge of his target officially differs from this point, they are evidently related, as 'nihilism' in Jacobi's sense results from transcendental idealism, a position I interpret as an ontological stance. This is the only concept of existence actually available to Kant's human-all-too-human understanding of existence.

This is where Gottlob Frege enters the picture. In my view, Frege sets out to repair the essential weakness of Kant's account by giving up ontological monism. Frege, in contrast to Kant, immediately allows for a plurality of domains of objects. According to Frege, to exist is to fall under a concept. In his analysis, to assert that something exists is to assert that some concept has an extension larger than the empty set. The idea behind this is quite simple. Like Kant, Frege accepts some version of the claim that existence is not a proper property. However, he explicitly rejects the notion that to exist is to be experienceable, for this is exactly what his interlocutor, the Neo-Kantian theologian Bernhard Pünjer, offers as his account of existence in Frege's *Dialogue with Pünjer about Existence*.[39]

Frege's trick is to only accept a thin notion of existence motivated by a general revision, namely, that it is some other-order property that does not hold of individual objects, but of something else. This thin notion can easily be divorced from any particular world view such as transcendental idealism or empiricism. For Frege the mathematician was evidently (and probably primarily) interested in vindicating claims such as *there is* only one prime number between 4 and 6 or *there is* no biggest natural number. He therefore came up with an account of mathematical existence that he deemed compatible with existence *tout court*, as his account can also explain what it means to claim that there are horses. It is, thus, sufficiently topic-neutral to be ontological in nature and not committed to any Kantian manoeuvres of compensating for an ill-formulated ontological monism.

Frege claims that the assertion of existence is 'in fact nothing but denial of the number nought (*die Verneinung der Nullzahl*)'.[40] Putting aside the number business for a moment (which causes him trouble, as we shall see in due course), the view is that to assert existence is to assert that some concept has an extension, that something falls under it. For instance, to assert that there are horses is to assert that the concept ... *is a horse* has an extension with a higher cardinality than the empty set or the null class. If Daisy is a horse, then she exists because she satisfies the concept function ... *is a horse*. The basic idea behind this account is very promising and it has (quite unfortunately) crystallised as a dogma of twentieth-century ontology in the form of the notion that all we need to say about existence is identical with what we need to say about the existential quantifier: ∃.[41]

The existential quantifier is not as harmless as it might appear at first glance or out of some habit of manipulating it symbolically. At best, it amounts to a reduced or inverted concept of existence, which is why I sometimes call ∃ the twisted E. As a matter of fact, the idea of existential quantification is rooted in Frege's ontology, in particular, in his idea that to exist is to be a member of some concept's extension. A concept, according to Frege, settles in advance what could be a member of its extension. On some readings, what Frege calls 'sense' is what one would more naturally call 'linguistic meaning', and they often see well-defined linguistic meaning as settling the possible extension of a concept.

Yet, notice that Frege's theory of concepts is not exactly part of a philosophy of language. On the contrary, it is part of a theory of concepts, and concepts are dealt with in his *Begriffsschrift*, a formal system defined in such a way that we can know *a priori* that all the referring expressions it contains actually refer to a determinate number of objects. In the formal system of a *Begriffsschrift*, for every object and every concept it is fixed once and for all (analytically) that there are exactly *these* objects that fall under it, and for every group of objects there is exactly *this* concept under which they fall. The very ontology of the *Begriffsschrift* is what Wolfram Hogrebe calls a 'discrete ontology'.[42] It quantifies over well-defined and analytically completely determined individuals, its objects.

Frege is explicit about the fact that the ontology of natural languages is not fully discrete, for there are vague expressions and also expressions with a sense, but without actual reference. It is, thus, a mistake to identify Frege's project as belonging to what later would be called the 'linguistic turn'. On the contrary, Frege is only interested in language marginally, to the extent that an analysis of language helps him to show the constraints his formal system has to meet in order not to be a language.

Of course, contemporary philosophy of language is well aware of the limitations of Frege's theory of reference for the philosophy of language in a broad sense, but since Frege the idea that there is nothing wrong with identifying the linguistic meaning of expressions such as 'there is', 'exists', and their cognates with their formal counterpart ∃ is rarely questioned. The reason behind this is a general prejudice in favour of discrete ontology, a phenomenon I have elsewhere attacked under the heading of the 'naïve ontology of individuals (*naive Einzeldingontologie*)' (which is not the same as 'naïve ontology' in the sense discussed above).[43] According to this ontology, there is an overall fundamental reality, the world. And this world consists primarily (if not only) of all the individuals. As some contemporary metaphysicians like to put it, there is a fundamental reality with a pegboard structure, and we hang predicates like rubber bands on the pegs already there.[44] Relations would be represented by rubber bands stretched between pegs, where the number of pegs varies according to the relation. What is really out there, as it were, in the mode of profound or grounding existence (the really real, τὰ ὄντως ὄντα) is the totality of individuals. The fundamentality of these individuals is supposed to be reflected in the fact that they are maximally modally robust: they would have been there anyway, had no one ever been around. This mythology often goes hand in hand with the idea that ultimately or fundamentally reality consists of elementary particles, which are the individuals postulated by metaphysics. What is not an elementary particle is supposed to be reducible to elementary particles, whatever that means.

This is flawed metaphysics and not ontology, but once more this form of rampant nominalism is a projection of bad ontology onto a world supposed to exist ancestrally, that is, in a maximally modally robust sense of absolute existence: it would have existed anyway – who cares that we are around these days trying to refer to individuals and throwing around our linguistic rubber bands from within the pegboard?

Be that as it may, Frege claims that for something to exist is for it to be the member of some extension. Almost naturally this idea could be associated with set theory (but it need not happen) if one were to identify a concept's extension with the set of all objects that are its members. Yet, with the help of Frege himself we can see why this move is not necessitated by the acceptance of his claim that to exist is to fall under a concept. The reason for this is that for something to fall under a concept is for it to fall under this concept (or these concepts) and not under another concept (or under those other concepts), which is one of the motivations behind his famous distinction between sense and reference. Here is what I mean. Imagine something falls under the concept ... *is the 38th Governor of California*. In this case, we could say that the 38th governor of California exists. It happens that the same object also falls under the concept ... *is the actor who played Hercules in 'Hercules in New York.'* It just so happens that the two concepts share the extension that has Arnold Schwarzenegger as its sole member. Only Arnold Schwarzenegger was the 38th governor of California and played Hercules in *Hercules in New York*. But things could have been otherwise. In this case, the member of the extension of the concept ... *is the 38th governor of California* could have been a different individual (say Sylvester Stallone). That Arnold Schwarzenegger exists turned out for him to fall under the two concepts we can call 'governor' and 'Hercules'. It is at least now essential for Arnold Schwarzenegger's existence that he falls under these concepts.

For something to exist is not for it to fall under any concept whatsoever, but to fall under suitable concepts. It is not enough to identify some bare individual essence of Arnold Schwarzenegger picked out by Kripkean baptism (that is, in the moment someone referred to the guy for the first time) and to say that 'Arnold Schwarzenegger' from now on refers to the same individual in all possible worlds in which this individual exists. This might be a way of rephrasing the modal claims involved in saying that Arnold Schwarzenegger could have lost the election (too bad, he won) or that he could have not been the actor who played the Terminator (fortunately, he was chosen). But no one wants to say that Arnold Schwarzenegger (the guy) could have been a Norwegian female sex worker (he could not!), even though there is some possible world in which the individual essence of Arnold Schwarzenegger (whatever that is!) could be a Norwegian female sex worker (maybe by having changed sex first depending on what the actual relation between his individual essence, his genetic code, and his gender is). If there is any essential relation between the fact that something falls under this concept and its existence, we cannot identify existence with extension. For such an identification means that for some particular thing to exist is for it to fall under any concept whatsoever, which is clearly not true. Objects fall under a suitable range of concepts, which is why there is the standing temptation to call this range 'essence'. It is indeed essential for Arnold Schwarzenegger if he is to be that guy that he is a human person and not just a wax figure or alien robot. Being a human person belongs to the suitable range of things to be said of Arnold Schwarzenegger, as much as it belongs to the suitable range of things to be said about water that pure water consists of H_2O, even though it is, of course, not precise to say that the stuff that flows in our oceans and rivers is H_2O, as all sorts of other things flow there too. We should not forget that when we account for our capacity to refer to the so-called 'surface qualities' of water. Just take the taste. The water we usually speak about has certain tastes that cannot be reduced to water being H_2O, which is why I doubt that the philosophical paradigmatic identity statement 'water is H_2O' is literally true.[45] It is also part of the meaning of water that it tastes somehow or that it is drinkable. But if these descriptions are involved in our capacity to refer to water, the actual chemical identity statements about water turn out to be highly disjunctive, as we now have to say that 'water is H_2O plus X or H_2O plus Y or H_2O plus Z, etc.'.

This might even motivate the claim that 'water' mostly refers to a more or less homogeneous set of surface qualities than to the chemical element H_2O, which is only a part of the story. And what happens if we add a third element to the classical thought experiment: triplet earth (trearth). On trearth, wherever we find a substance we identify it as water on the basis of our more or less homogenous set of surface qualities. However, this substance equally consists of H_2O as found on earth and of XYZ as found on twearth. Now, what does the word 'water' refer to in trearth-English? Should we say that the trearthians do not have a single concept of water, but refer to different things with just one word? And why does this not apply to ourselves given that H_2O strictly speaking is actually also not a chemical element but somewhat disjunctive.

I take it that for Frege existence is not only a matter of extension (or reference in his sense), but also of sense. For the concepts 'governor' and 'Hercules' differ in sense, even though they turned out to have the same extension. The distinction between sense and reference allows us to distinguish the scenario in which 'governor' and 'Hercules' have the same extension from the scenario in which there are both the governor and Hercules, but they are different individuals. Given the importance of number for Frege's view of existence, it surely is a different situation when there is one individual rather than two. Sense matters for existence. But if sense matters for existence, we cannot reduce sense to extension. In Frege's construal of the matter, $\exists$ and $\in$ (set membership) are different concepts; for something to exist is not for it to be a member of *any* concept, but at the most it should be a member of the extension of *this* concept.[46] To exist is not to be a member of any set, but rather a member of a set determined by a concept, and there is no such set without there being a sense individuating the concept as this rather than that other concept.

Frege accordingly admits that the things that exist as individuals exist as determined in specific ways. They exist under the description that holds good of them. In other words, existence is not bare existence and individuals are not bare particulars. He, thus, has no need to postulate a raw material of existence from which we could even in principle happen to be screened off because all our thoughts have sense and thus present the individuals under potentially distorting descriptions. Without modes of presentation, no thought could be about a specific object, and what exists according to Frege, is accordingly specific objects falling under specific concepts.

Although I just laid out some welcome features of Frege's view that tend to be ignored by later reconstructions of his work, his ontology still fails for some significant reasons. Let me begin by attacking the claim that existence is related to the existential quantifier in any relevant way. Even on the most superficial level of analysis it is rather obvious that the question, 'Are there any eggs?' is not identical with, 'How many eggs are there?' True, if there are three eggs then there are eggs, but the fact that there are eggs at all is not identical with the fact that there are three of them. It does not even matter that there is at least one, as there might only be half an egg left of all eggs. In a scenario in which there is only half an egg left and there will from then on always only be half an egg (someone might have frozen it for future generations), it does not mean that eggs ceased existing. Of course, we normally individuate eggs by referring to entire eggs, but this does not mean that in order for there to be eggs at all, there have to be whole eggs. Existence and quantity are just not the same concepts. What is more, the question, 'How many eggs are there?' only makes sense within a domain (a field of sense) in which one is looking for eggs. It might mean any number of things: 'How many eggs are there in the fridge?', 'How many eggs are there in these huge egg boxes in American supermarkets?', 'How many hidden eggs are there in the garden?', and so on. What all these instances have in common is that there is a domain (a field of sense) suitable for containing eggs: the fridge, the American supermarket, the garden. In this sense, existence, or rather the possibility of existence, is presupposed when someone asks a trivial number question whose answer is not more complicated than a natural positive number.

This leads me to my second objection to the identification of existence with the existential quantifier. Frege thought that he could ground numbers in concepts. That is the whole point behind his ontology. He is, after all, primarily a mathematician and his logicism serves the goal of determining what numbers are and how we can refer to them in a suitably precise formal language. From his point of view, the actual cash value of this ontology is that he can define numbers as properties of concepts and define concepts with a precise extension associated with the numbers. Famously, he argues that the number zero can be defined as 'the Number which belongs to the concept "not identical with itself"'.[47] Without any further argument, Frege assumes that there is nothing that is non-identical to itself. If this means that all individuals have all their properties, this might well be true, but it should not be assumed without argument. But let us grant this point. He then goes on and defines the number 1 as the extension of the concept defining the number 0: There is exactly one number 0, and one object falls under the concept defining 0, namely the number 0. Whatever one makes of this definition and the problems deriving from Russell's paradox and related aporias, the most straight-forward problem with this understanding of numbers is that it gives us, at the most, an understanding of positive natural integers including 0. However, what is the concept with the extension of π or of 0.3562? In other words, under what concept does 0.3562 of an object fall? Frege does not address this, as he is happy to have defined the positive natural integers including zero. However, this presupposes that the number term 0.3562 does not refer to what it seems to refer to, but rather refers to a combination of natural positive integers. There is no reality broken down into real numbers or more complicated mathematics if one sets out from the metaphysical assumption of discrete ontology.

In discrete ontology, it is assumed that reality consists of all the individuals, and that all the individuals are completely determined and certainly not vague. 'Our language might be vague, but the individuals must be determined!' I am not willing to accept this without arguments, and all the arguments or argument fragments for this view I have revisited are far from establishing this. On the contrary, discrete ontology is extremely counterintuitive and encounters many problems, such as Zeno's paradoxes. It has had a difficult time thinking about the infinite, continua, and so on. There might be ways of gerrymandering the concept of completely determined individuals within the range of concepts with an extension whose equinumerosity can be established with child-like counting in natural numbers, but these manoeuvres are not grounded in some mathematical necessity. Rather, they are introduced in ontology and have to be debated there. No reference to some preferred subdomain of mathematics can decide ontological questions, and reference to mathematics in ontology is usually a sign of an attempt to cheat oneself out of the real stakes of the debate. I will attack these manoeuvres under the heading of 'mathematicism' in the next chapters in more detail.

Be that as it may, the ultimate problem for Frege's ontology is that he is committed to a very explicit form of either conceptual realism or subjective idealism, depending on how one understands this commitment. He defines existence as the fact that something falls under a concept. To exist is to fall under a concept. This immediately entails the following conditional: had there been no concepts, nothing would have existed. Indeed, Frege is committed to saying that there would have been no mountains had there not been the concept of a mountain. This conditional has two very different meanings depending on how one thinks of the relation between concepts on the one hand and concept-use or concept-manifestation on the other hand. Frege seems to be a conceptual realist at least on a local scale as he explicitly insists that the concepts relevant for doing mathematics (including most notably logical concepts, if not only logical concepts) are independent of the further fact that we sometimes grasp them.[48] Large stretches of the logical space of logical concepts are already laid out in a maximally modally robust sense. We find the laws of being true and do not produce them. Yet, conceptual realism at the very least does not seem to hold across the board. For instance, what about defective concepts such as the famous concept of a boche, where 'boche' is a description of all Germans in terms of the additional idea that they are essentially cruel or just generally evil? There are all sorts of defective concepts not just in the ethical realm, which is why one can also think of logics as a regimentation of our actual concept formation in light of the *a priori* requirements of legitimate concept formation. At least, this critical aspect should be part of any meta-logical account given that we think of logics as a normative discipline of the rules of truth preservation that one ought to follow precisely because one is capable of not following them.

Frege would be much worse off if one could interpret the claim that nothing would ever have existed had there been no concepts as a claim about concept *use*. This would amount to the crazy view that we bring mountains and horses into existence by using the relevant mountain- and horse-creating concepts in judgements. Of course, there are reasons that might lead one to a commitment to anti-realism about mountains (reference to the arbitrary demarcation of these entities from the human standpoint might be part of this). But there is no general ontological reason to come to the conclusion that this holds for everything that exists as a matter of the analysis of the concept of existence.

Frege's preferred way out of this problem is a form of type theory, as he claims that concepts cannot really be talked about. If we refer to a concept by predicating something of it, it thereby turns into an object (by definition) and ceases to be a concept, as nothing is a concept that does not function like concepts function in logical forms.[49] But this means that concepts cannot fall under concepts by definition. If they did we could talk of them as if they were objects. Frege therefore says something to the effect that concepts do not exist, as they cannot fall under concepts while at the same time he is trying to say that concepts have features, such as the feature that something falls under them. Here, Frege resorts to fully-fledged stipulation: He stipulates himself out of the problem by distinguishing between 'properties of objects (*Eigenschaften*)', and 'features of concepts (*Merkmale*)'. Yet, this hides the problem that arises once one claims that nothing can exist if there is no concept for it. The basic problem is that if concepts indeed exist, then they have to fall under concepts (on Frege's conception of existence). But if concepts do not even exist, Frege should not be allowed to talk about the features of concepts either (as this amounts to subsuming a concept under a different concept).[50] For Frege himself, this is much less of a problem than for the ontologist, as he is not primarily interested in ontology, but rather in a non-psychologistic grounding of mathematical existence. He need not concern himself with the question of the existence of citizens or events experienced in the form of future-oriented time, as he believes his business to be with the problem of the existence of numbers.

Of course, Frege could respond that his concept of concepts is entirely formal and bears little relation to our overall concept of concepts, which is inextricably bound up with our capacity to use concepts in order to refer to how things are, which need not be the way we take them to be. Frege could simply give up the idea that concepts in any way essentially or conceptually relate to anyone's conscious grasp of them. However, there is no real textual evidence that this is the position he would like to espouse in general, and he probably should not go down this road, as it leads straightforwardly to Wittgensteinian objections against Fregean theories of meaning to the effect that they are (also) tied to use. At least Frege would have a hard time defending the idea that 'concept' does not mean anything even faintly resembling what we thought it meant before he stipulated a meaning for it we somehow can only grasp in the rare moments of our life where we have a logically induced intellectual intuition of sorts.[51]

However, Frege at least notoriously commits to there being some such objective concepts, namely the laws of being true.

> If being true is thus independent of being acknowledged by somebody or other, then the laws of truth are not psychological laws: they are boundary stones set in an eternal foundation, which our thought can overflow but never displace.[52]

Wittgenstein simply observed that meaning is not generally just found, but often, perhaps even mostly, historically produced by speakers. Whatever one makes of that famous rejoinder, it contains at least a grain of truth insofar as concepts have to be in some way related to language, for this is where we find them.

The ontology defended in this book follows the strategy of developing an ontological version of Frege's insights about the conditions of possibility of reference to objects and facts not being identical with being referred to. In order to get there, it is important to give up the undesirable aspects of Frege's programme, in particular the identification of existence with the existential quantifier and more particularly the view that generally to exist is to fall under a concept.

However, one might ask, what is left then? Why even bother with Kant and Frege if both turn out to be wrong about existence? The answer to this is twofold: First, because they were wrong in an interesting way that helps us to find the right answer, and second, because the Kant-cum-Frege-(cum-Quine) ontology is by far the most influential and widespread assumption in contemporary ontology, and is tied to a host of metaphysical assumptions I take to be problematic and not without alternative.

Let me systematically summarise the respective weaknesses and strengths of Kant and Frege.

Kant's ontology

1. Strengths

- Existence is not a *proper* property.
- Existence is the property of a domain, or rather of a field not to be empty.
- Despite himself, Kant is committed to ontological pluralism, that is, the view that there are many domains (in Kant: the field of possible experience = the world; the noumenal; the world under the description of as-if-teleology and as-if-causality-of-freedom, and so on).

2. Weaknesses

- Existence is a *metaphysical* property, a property of the one and only world.
- Kant wants to be an ontological monist, where ontological monism is the position that there is only one domain.
- This leads to incoherence, as the alleged singular world has to exist in a different sense (it has to schmexist or krexist or X-ist) than the intra-worldly individuals and facts.
- What is most problematic: the field of possible experience contains nothing that is not experienceable, which leads to ontic nonsense about spatio-temporal individuals, facts and events, such as: nothing would ever have occurred had no one ever been around to notice.

Frege's Ontology

1. Strengths

- Existence is not a *proper* property.
- Existence is not a *metaphysical* property.
- Existence is a property of domains (concepts). In addition, these domains are already seen as fields of sense given that the domains (extensions) only contain something if there are senses individuating them (the senses of the concepts having the extensions fall under them).
- Ontological pluralism: there are many concepts, and consequently many fields of sense, where the principle of individuation

of the fields is senses (even though these are in turn understood as features of concepts).

2. Weaknesses

- Identification of existence with the existential quantifier.
- Modelled along the lines of formal languages and therefore overly revisionary in nature: any actual use of 'exists' or 'there is' incompatible with the newly-created concept of existence has to be ignored in ontology.
- Mathematicism in the sense of the view that the ontology is explicitly developed for the sake of giving an account of mathematical existence.
- What is most problematic: his theory entails that nothing could exist unless there was a concept under which it falls. It remains unclear what this means (conceptual realism, subjective idealism or a very strange interpretation of the term 'concept').
- The only way out is a purely formal concept of concepts, according to which they are functions, open spots in reality, as it were, which are always satisfied even without the presence of an observer, unless Frege wants to say that there are ontological holes in reality prior to any concept-mongering creature's occurring thoughts about reality.

The identification of existence with the existential quantifier is largely a completely unquestioned dogma of contemporary ontology.[53] It dominates ontology far beyond the apparent distinction between analytic and continental philosophy. It ultimately originates in Greek philosophy. Both Plato and Aristotle defended discrete ontologies, and both took the number 1 to be the measure of all numbers, a μέτρον, the unity of which has to be fixed in order for us to account for anything's existence, which turned into the medieval dogma: *ens et unum convertuntur*.[54] The metaphysical idea behind this is that to exist is to be a unified object, an individual. Subsequent philosophers disagree about what it is that defines the unity of an individual: a Platonic form, the fact that it is a substance, the transcendental synthesis of apperception, the will to power, the laws of nature, the elementary particles and their clustering (chairs are elementary particles arranged chair-wise), and so on. All these philosophies are attempts to work out their preferred discrete ontology, and discrete ontology fits nicely with the identification of existence and existential quantification. In this context, Russell introduced his notion of a 'term', which he characterises in *The Principles of Mathematics* thus:

> Whatever may be an object of thought, or may occur in any true or false proposition, or can be counted as *one*, I call a *term*. This, then, is the widest word in the philosophical vocabulary. I shall use it as synonymous with it the words unit, individual and entity. The first two emphasize the fact that every term has being, i.e. *is* in some sense. A man, a moment, a number, a class, a relation, a chimaera, or anything else that can be mentioned, is sure to be a term; and to deny that such and such a thing is a term must always be false. It might perhaps be thought that a word of such extreme generality could not be of any great use. Such a view, however, owing to certain wide-spread philosophical doctrines, would be erroneous. A term is, in fact, possessed of all the properties commonly assigned to substances or substantives. Every term, to begin with, is a logical subject: it is, for example, the subject of the proposition that itself is one. Again every term is immutable and indestructible. What a term is, it is, and no change can be conceived in it which would not destroy its identity and make it another term. Another mark which belongs to terms is numerical identity with themselves and numerical diversity from all other terms. Numerical identity and diversity are the source of unity and plurality; and thus the admission of many terms destroys monism. And it seems undeniable that every constituent of every proposition can be counted as one, and that no proposition contains less than two constituents. *Term* is, therefore, a useful word, since it marks dissent from various philosophies, as well as because, in many statements, we wish to speak of *any* term or *some* term.[55]

A staunch defender of this dogma is Peter van Inwagen, who takes it to be the upshot of the Frege-Kant thesis: 'Being is a feature and it is this feature: it is what one says of a thing when one says that the number of things that *are* that thing is not zero.'[56] He even has the right hunch in suspecting that Heidegger is his real opponent, even though he misunderstands Heidegger's reasons for giving up on the idea that existence is quantity, as one can see from his criticisms of Heidegger based on a contentious selection and reading of the latter's texts.[57] Heidegger indeed questions the overriding assumption of Occidental metaphysics that to exist entails being one thing, to be an individual. Without getting into Heidegger exegesis, I think it is fair to say that Heidegger correctly saw that vagueness and indeterminacy abound, that fixed individuals are not the ontological rule or paradigm, because many objects and facts we can very successfully talk and think about are to some degree undetermined. He took this indeterminacy not to be a projection of human language onto an otherwise nicely and fully determined reality or universe, but an insight into how things are, an 'Einblick in das, was ist'.[58]

Interestingly, some theoretical physicists now seem to confirm the view that the universe does not even only or paradigmatically consist of individuals in the sense of completely determined objects. Independent of whether something like the uncertainty principle has any metaphysical and not only epistemological impact, structures and events such as quantum fluctuations, or the spontaneous emergence of space-time out of literally nothing have to be made sense of.[59] Of course, for theoretical physics this is ultimately a question regarding the interpretation of mathematical symbolism. However, no one should doubt that there is the phenomenon of indeterminacy, for example, in human action or in artwork. The anthropologist and neuroscientist Terrence Deacon recently even argued that at least with the appearance of life and then of consciousness in the universe, we need to give an account of absential causality, of absent and not-yet existing facts causing things to be a certain way.[60] But it is not necessary to ground claims to indeterminacy in the universe. Human action, for instance, comes with the concept of objectively existing indeterminacy. There is no need to ground this indeterminacy ontologically in the universe. Rather, it is perfectly intelligible and coherent to think of the universe as not containing human action, but only subject-less processes of some kind. Yet, this does not as such tell us anything about the grounding or, as it were, the ungrounding of the objectively existing indeterminacy of human action as long as we do not accept that there is exactly one world that is identical with the universe thus described. Apart from the fact that it is hard to see such a monistic view as an actual outcome of natural scientific research (how do you prove it experimentally, and what would it mean to be wrong about it?), it is ontologically untenable. Again, this ontological fact by itself does not prove anything about the grounding or ungrounding of the objectively existing indeterminacy of human action with regard to the universe. This is a further question that can be meaningfully raised in the discussion of the no-world-view that will be unfolded in subsequent chapters. Be that as may be, we will always be left with reference to human action as involving objectively existing indeterminacy, and even if we come to the empirically grounded conclusion that the concepts in question do not apply to anything physical (including the brain and its chemistry), we will still be left with the fact that there are these concepts we understand.

While presenting earlier outlines of the view argued for in this book, I was often asked about my take on quantum mechanics or physics more generally. Let me emphasise here that theoretical physics is an exciting field of enquiry, but that there is no particular reason to talk about physics in ontology. The meaning of 'existence' is not settled by the universe, as there are witches (for instance in *Faust*) that are not part of the universe. There are hobbits, numbers, dreams and the contents of hallucinations, governments, the past and plans I never carried out. These objects are not unified by the further fact that they are all part of the universe, let alone studied by physics. The metaphysical prejudice in favour of physics or science in general is not only largely unjustified by its own lights (it cannot be a result derived from physics, but at best can be seen as built into its heuristics); it is also irrelevant to ontology and arguably results from ontotheology, the identification of ontology with one's preferred metaphysics, the metaphysics of the day. Nothing in this book is supposed to be supported by, to support, or to be in conflict with any true proposition of physics or any other inquiry into the material/energetic conditions of there being spatio-temporal objects, things, or events of any kind whose nature is described by them as being instances of mathematical equations.

Let me conclude this chapter by stressing that my questioning of discrete ontology does not amount to an ontology, or rather metaphysics, of substance *per se*. What I am attacking is the idea that existence is significantly related to quantifiable individuation, whether the objects thus counted are substances, events, or absolute processes. I reject the idea that to be is to be one or a one, a unified object, be it unified in itself or unified by thought, language, discursive practices, the symbolic order, the neurochemistry of what we think of as intentionality or what have you.

Notes

1. Kant, *Critique of Pure Reason*, A 598/ B 626: 'Sein ist offenbar kein reales Prädikat, d.i. ein Begriff von irgend etwas, was zu dem Begriffe eines Dinges hinzukommen könne'.

2. Frege, *Foundations of Arithmetic*, § 51–§ 57, pp. 63–9. Ben Caplan ('Ontological Superpluralism', pp. 80–3) gives an interesting reconstruction of Frege's view in terms of an ontological pluralism. *Prima facie* it seems that Frege is an ontological dualist to the extent that he distinguishes between objects and functions (or objects and concepts). However, 'functions don't form an ontological category. Rather, functions form indefinitely many disjoint ontological categories' (Ibid., p. 81). On the basis of Frege's commitment to a genuine multiplicity of functions, Caplan infers: 'As a result, there is no concept *being a concept*: there is no concept that maps first-level concepts, second-level concepts, third-level concepts, and so on, to the truth-value True. For the same reason, there is no concept *being a function*. Nor is there a concept *being an object or a function*' (Ibid., p. 83). Even though I am very sympathetic to this view, I doubt that Frege holds it. In particular, his argument for his own version of a type-theory only works under the assumption that everything is either a concept or a function so that there has to be a concept *being an object or a function*. If there were no such concept, how could Frege rule out that there could be something that is both? It is important for an alleged Fregean ontological pluralism of the type envisaged by Caplan to get off the ground that we can draw a sharp and clear-cut distinction between objects and functions, which would be problematic if there were no sense in which all functions are at least functions. Caplan's reconstruction is an interesting attempt to circumvent the paradoxes that arise within the framework of Fregean dualism. The only problem is that Caplan's Frege is unmotivated, as the starting point of the envisaged type-theory is undermined by the result that there is no well-formed dualism of concepts and functions. Also, Caplan does not discuss Frege's explicit views about the meaning of existence and their relation to his alleged ontological pluralism, which might just be a lacuna in the presentation.

3. Cf. Stuhlmann-Laeisz, 'Freges Auseinandersetzung mit der Auffassung von "Existenz"', pp. 119–33.

4. Kant, *Critique of Pure Reason*, A 598/B 626. Kant writes here (brackets mine): 'Es ["Sein"] ist bloß die Position eines Dinges, oder gewisser Bestimmungen an sich selbst. Im logischen Gebrauche ist

es lediglich die Kopula eines Urteils' (A 598/B 626). The Guyer/ Woodruff translation reads: 'It is merely the positing of a thing or of certain determinations in themselves. In the logical use it *is* merely the copula of a judgment.'

5. Kant, *Critique of Pure Reason*, B 627; Heidegger, *Basic Problems of Phenomenology*, p. 40.

6. Cf. Kant, *Critique of Pure Reason*, A 227/B 280, A 248/B 304, A 610/B 638, A642/B 670, A 697/B 725, A 702/B 730.

7. Cf. the 'Postulates of Empirical Thought' in Kant, *The Critique of Pure Reason*, A 219/ B 265: 'The categories of modality possess this peculiarity, that they do not in the least determine the object, or enlarge the conception to which they are annexed as predicates, but only express its relation to the faculty of cognition. Though my conception of a thing is in itself complete, I am still entitled to ask whether the object of it is merely possible, or whether it is also real, or, if the latter, whether it is also necessary. But hereby the object itself is not more definitely determined in thought, but the question is only in what relation it, including all its determinations, stands to the understanding and its employment in experience, to the empirical faculty of judgement, and to the reason of its application to experience. For this very reason, too, the categories of modality are nothing more than explanations of the conceptions of possibility, reality, and necessity, as employed in experience, and at the same time, restrictions of all the categories to empirical use alone, not authorizing the transcendental employment of them. For if they are to have something more than a merely logical significance, and to be something more than a mere analytical expression of the form of thought, and to have a relation to things and their possibility, reality, or necessity, they must concern possible experience and its synthetical unity, in which alone objects of cognition can be given.'

8. This is the starting point of Fichte's project, which becomes most explicit in the *Wissenschaftslehre* 1804, where he refers to the invariable general structure of intentionality under the heading of 'absolute knowing'. See Fichte, *The Science of Knowing*, p. 149.

9. For an updated defence of the Kantian framework in its application to space-time see Koch, *Versuch über Wahrheit und Zeit*. See also his *Subjektivität in Raum und Zeit*.

10. G. E. Moore famously based his refutation of idealism on that insight into the shortcoming of Kant's theory of space. See Moore, 'Proof of an External World', pp. 127–50, and Gabriel, *An den Grenzen der Erkenntnistheorie*, § 3, pp. 66–75.

11. Cf. Strawson, *Bounds of Sense*.
12. Cf. Gabriel, *Transcendental Ontology*, pp. xx, xxi, 115.
13. Kant, 'Anthropology from a Practical Point of View' (AA 7:121).
14. Here is a selection of citations showing Kant's commitment to this from several works. Kant, *Critique of Pure Reason*, A 44/B 61: 'The representation of a *body* in intuition, on the contrary, contains nothing at all that could pertain to an object in itself, but merely the appearance of something and the way in which we are affected by it; and this receptivity of our cognitive capacity is called sensibility and remains worlds apart from the cognition of the object in itself even if one might see through to the very bottom of it (the appearance).' Ibid. A 190/B 235: 'For we have to do only with our representations; how things in themselves may be (without regard to representations through which they affect us) is entirely beyond our cognitive sphere.' Ibid. A 358f.: '[T]his Something is not extended, not impenetrable, not composite, because these predicates pertain only to sensibility and its intuition, insofar as we are affected by such objects (otherwise unknown to us). These expressions, however, do not give us cognition of what kind of object it is, but only that, since it is considered in itself without relation to outer sense, it is such that these predicates of outer appearances cannot be applied to it. ... If matter were a thing in itself, then as a composite being it would be completely distinguished from the soul as a simple being. But it is merely an outer appearance, whose substratum is not cognized through any specifiable predicates; hence I can well assume [that is, believe in Kant's technical sense of "glauben", M. G.] about this substratum that in itself it is simple, even though in the way it affects our outer senses it produces in us the intuition of something extended and hence composite.' Kant, *Prolegomena to Any Future Metaphysics*, § 13, Note II, 4:289: 'There are things given to us as objects of our senses existing outside us, yet we know nothing of them as they may be in themselves, but are acquainted only with their appearances, that is, with the representations that they produce in us because they affect our senses.' Ibid. § 32, 4:314f.: '[I]f we view the objects of the senses as mere appearances, as is fitting, then we thereby admit at the very same time that a thing in itself underlies them, although we are not acquainted with this thing as it may be constituted in itself, but only with its appearance, i.e., with the way in which our senses are affected by this unknown something.' Kant, *Groundwork of the Metaphysics of Morals*, 4:450f.: 'It is an observation for which no subtle thinking is required, but one that one may

assume the commonest understanding can make, though according to its own manner by an obscure distinction of the power of judgement, which it calls feeling: that all representations that come to us without our choosing (like those of the senses) enable us to cognize objects only as they affect us, while what they may be in themselves remains unknown to us; and hence that, as far as representations of this kind are concerned, even with the most strenuous attentiveness and distinctness that the understanding may ever add, we can achieve only cognition of *appearances*, never of *things in themselves*.'

15. Kant, *Critique of Pure Reason*, A 52/B 76: '[L]ogic ... can be undertaken with two different aims, either as the logic of the general or of the particular use of the understanding. The former contains the absolutely necessary rules of thinking, without which no use of the understanding takes place, and it therefore concerns these rules without regard to the difference of the objects to which it may be directed.'

16. This option is explored in Schafer, 'Kant's Conception of Cognition'. Schafer draws on the distinction between *Erkennen* and *Wissen* and believes that Kant himself appears 'to claim that we can know a good deal about what things-in-themselves are like' (p. 1). However, Kant explicitly rejects the latter possibility and opts instead for the unknowability of things in themselves. Of course, there is the option to claim that there is a legitimate non-Kantian concept of 'knowledge' that Kant maybe implicitly brings into play, according to which we can know things-in-themselves or what they are like. But this concept of knowledge is precisely not Kant's, and it is hard to show that he makes use of an implicit concept of knowledge officially unavailable to him.

17. Cf. Kant, *Critique of Pure Reason*, A 276/B 332f.: '[W]hat the things may be in themselves I do not know (*weiß*), and also do not need to know (*wissen*), since a thing can never come before me except in appearance.' Ibid. A 540/B 568: '[J]ust as in general we must ground appearances in thought through a transcendental object, even though we know (*wissen*) nothing about it as it is in itself.' Ibid. B 164: 'But appearances are only representations of things that exist without cognition (*unerkannt*) of what they might be in themselves'. Ibid. A 678/B 706: 'For by no means do I require, nor am I warranted in requiring, cognition (*erkennen*) of this object of my idea as to what it might be in itself.' Ibid. A 473/B 501: '[The common understanding] can still ratiocinate infinitely more about them, because it is wandering among mere ideas, about which one

can be at one's most eloquent just because one *knows* (*weiß*) *nothing about them.*' Ibid. A 565/B 593: '... as a transcendental object, but about which one knows (*weiß*) nothing'. Kant, *Groundwork of the Metaphysics of Morals*, IV 451: '... namely the things in themselves; even if – since they can never become known (*bekannt*) to us, but only ever how they affect us – we of ourselves rest content with being unable to get any closer to them or ever to know (*wissen*) what they are in themselves'. I take these passages to be decisive evidence against any reading according to which we can know anything about things in themselves, even modest things such as that they are identical with themselves or do not contradict the laws of general logic.

18. Kant, *Critique of Pure Reason*, A 822/B 850.
19. 'Thus I had to deny *knowledge* in order to make room for *faith*; and the dogmatism of metaphysics, i.e., the prejudice that without criticism reason can make progress in metaphysics, is the true source of all unbelief conflicting with morality, which unbelief is always very dogmatic.' Kant, *Critique of Pure Reason*, B XXX.
20. Kant, *Grundwork of the Metaphysics of Morals*, IV 433.
21. See his review essay on Smith and Sullivan, 'Transcendental Philosophy and Naturalism', forthcoming in the *European Journal of Philosophy*. Interestingly, Schelling reads Kant in exactly this vein based on his conception that the *omnitudo realitatis* as a necessary presupposition of the systematic unity of our knowledge and cognition is the successor concept of Platonic being or οὐσία. On this see my *Der Mensch im Mythos*, §§ 4–6.
22. On the scope and limits of this metaphor see Rödl's discussion of Adrian W. Moore's contribution in his review of Smith and Sullivan, 'Transcendental Philosophy and Naturalism'.
23. Kant, *Critique of Pure Reason*, B 25.
24. This seems to be the basic idea of Prauss, *Kant und das Problem der Dinge an sich*. For something like a defense of a similar view (but independent of the question of space and time) see my concept of 'idealism' in Gabriel, *An den Grenzen der Erkenntnistheorie* and Gabriel, *Skeptizismus und Idealismus in der Antike*.
25. Kant, *Critique of Pure Reason*, A 42/B 59.
26. Meillassoux, *After Finitude*, pp. 14–18.
27. Meillassoux, *After Finitude*, p. 5.
28. For further discussion of the prospects of knowing things in themselves in some way or other within a Kantian framework see also Langton, *Kantian Humility*, Langton, 'Elusive Knowledge of Things in Themselves', Jauernig, *How to Think about Things in Themselves*.

In 'Elusive Knowledge of Things in Themselves' Langton presents an argument (inspired by David Lewis) based on the assumption that we can imagine 'a true and complete 'final theory' of the world' (p. 131). She then proceeds to present Kantian humility with respect to things in themselves in light of the distinction between *intrinsic* and *relational* properties. Note, however, that Kant certainly does not base his account of the limits of knowledge (if that is the right way of putting it) on the conceivability of such a final theory, as this is exactly denied by his view according to which the world is and remains a regulative idea (even 'in the long run'). Let it be noted in passing that I also doubt that we can make sense of an *epistemic* distinction between things in themselves and appearances in light of a *metaphysical* distinction between intrinsic and relational properties. Kant also denies that we can know of things in themselves that they are substances, as this would amount to the epistemically successful application of categories to things in themselves, which is ruled out by Kant. For a defence of the applicability of a pure concept of substance to things in themselves see Langton, *Kantian Humility*, ch. 3.

29. Immanuel Kant, *Groundwork of the Metaphysics of Morals*, 4:439.
30. Even a two-aspect or description-dualism theory of things in themselves and appearances (where appearances *are* things in themselves, as they appear to us) treats them as different given that things in themselves and appearances still have to be described differently. They might be related, but they cannot be strictly identical.
31. Max Kötter pointed out in discussion that Kant at least has good reasons to unify all these other domains into the single domain he names 'the thing in itself'. His main reason might be that all other domains apart from the field of possible experience are unified by instantiating the property of not being cognisable by us due to the fact that cognisability by us is partly defined by our sensory equipment.
32. Cf., for instance, Kant, *The Critique of Pure Reason*, A 219/ B 265. See also Bxxvi: 'To cognize an object, it is required that I be able to prove its possibility (whether by the testimony of experience from its actuality or *a priori* through reason). But I can think whatever I like, as long as I do not contradict myself, i.e., as long as my concept is a possible thought, even if I cannot give any assurance whether or not there is a corresponding object somewhere within the sum total of all possibilities. But in order to ascribe objective validity to such a concept (real possibility, for the first sort of possibility was merely logical) something more is required. This "more", however, need

not be sought in theoretical sources of cognition; it may also lie in practical ones.'

33. For a contemporary take on this view, cf. Horgan and Potrc, 'Blobjectivism and Indirect Correspondence'.

34. Kant, *Critique of Pure Reason*, B 146: 'To think of an object and to cognize an object are thus not the same. For two components belong to cognition: first, the concept, through which an object is thought at all (the category), and second, the intuition, through which it is given; for if an intuition corresponding to the concept could not be given at all, then it would be a thought as far as its form is concerned, but without any object, and by its means no cognition of anything at all would be possible, since, as far as I would know, nothing would be given nor could be given to which my thought could be applied. Now all intuition that is possible for us is sensible (Aesthetic), thus for us thinking of an object in general through a pure concept of the understanding can become cognition only insofar as this concept is related to objects of the senses.'

35. For a discussion of this problem, see the illuminating reconstruction in Conant, 'The Search for Logically Alien Thought'.

36. Thanks to Umrao Sethi for pushing me on this point. This is my reply to her objection that my argument against Kant might rest on an equivocation between the ordinary concept of 'existence' and the revised, technical one.

37. Anton Friedrich Koch has argued that Kant really has resources to avoid this problem by tying transcendental idealism to a particular theory of the relation between indexicals and space-time, which leads Koch to reformulate an updated version of transcendental idealism. See his seminal *Versuch über Wahrheit und Zeit*. My objections against his approach hinge on a disagreement about what counts as an individual. For him, individuality is conceptually tied to the notion of indexical reference; for me this is not the case. An adequate discussion of his sophisticated work would require a whole book, so I leave it at that.

38. Jacobi, *Concerning the Doctrine of Spinoza*, p. 189: 'The whole thing comes down to this: from fatalism I immediately conclude against fatalism and everything connected with it. – If there are only efficient, but no final, causes, then the only function that the faculty of thought has in the whole of nature is that of observer; its proper business is to accompany the mechanism of the efficient causes. The conversation that we are now having together is only an affair of our bodies; and the whole content of the conversation, analyzed into its

elements, is extension, movement, degree of velocity, together with
their concepts, and the concepts of these concepts. The inventor of
the clock did not ultimately invent it; he only witnessed its coming
to be out of blindly self-developing forces. So too Raphael, when
he sketched the School of Athens, and Lessing, when he composed
his *Nathan*. The same goes for all philosophizing, arts, forms of
governance, sea and land wars – in brief, for everything possible.
For affects and passions would have no effect either, so far as they
are sensations and thoughts; or more precisely, so far as they *carry*
sensations and thoughts *with them*. We only *believe* that we have
acted out of anger, love, magnanimity, or out of rational decision.
Mere illusion! What fundamentally moves us in all these cases is
something that knows nothing of all that, and which is *to this extent*
absolutely devoid of sensations and thoughts. These, the sensations
and thoughts, are however only concepts of extension, movement,
degrees of velocity, etc. – Now, if someone can accept this, then I
cannot refute his opinion. But if one cannot, then one must be at the
antipodes from Spinoza.'

39. Frege, 'Dialogue with Pünjer about Existence', pp. 53–67.

40. Frege, *Foundations of Arithmetic*, § 53, p. 65.

41. Objections against this orthodoxy, for example, can be found in
Miller, 'In Defence of the Predicate "Exists"'; Miller, '"Exists" and
Existence'; Orenstein, 'Is Existence What Existential Quantification
Expresses?' and McGinn, *Logical Properties*, pp. 20ff.

42. Hogrebe, *Prädikation und Genesis*, pp. 46f.

43. Gabriel, *An den Grenzen der Erkenntnistheorie*, § 3, pp. 64–75.

44. Turner, 'Ontological Pluralism'.

45. Interestingly, Erwin Schrödinger points out that ὕδωρ in Thales *does
not* mean H_2O. He gives two reasons for this. First, Thales introduced ὕδωρ as a name shorthand for the description of whatever
it is that explains how everything is 'intrinsically the same stuff'
(Schrödinger, *Nature and the Greeks*, p. 59). Second, he points out
that 'we had better not associate this naively with our "H_2O", rather
with liquid or fluid (τὰ ὑγρά) in general' (Ibid.).

46. Philosophers of language after Frege, in particular Russell and even
more evidently Carnap and his followers, can be seen as agreeing
that the concept of sense is dispensable for existence. At the most,
they were looking for a way to force all senses into intensional
logic, which would be a way of dealing with them extensionally,
as with nicely separated linguistic entities. Honestly, I never quite
understood why people did not like Frege's elucidation of sense as

'modes of presentation' and rather wanted sense to be thoroughly linguistic. The reason behind this is probably the idea that language is our device to refer to 'the world', where the term represents the totality of individuals or their arrangements (the 'facts') in the sense of rampant nominalism. A very clear commitment to this is the following set of statements by Scott Soames: 'The central fact about language is its representational character. Exceptional cases aside, a meaningful declarative sentence S represents the world as being a certain way. To sincerely accept, or assertively utter, S is to believe, or assert, that the world is the way S represents it to be. Since the representational contents of sentences depend on their grammatical structure and the representational contents of their parts, linguistic meaning is an interconnected system.' Soames, *Philosophy of Language*, p. 1.

47. Frege, *Foundations of Arithmetic*, § 74, p. 87.

48. Frege, *Basic Laws of Arithmetic*, p. xxiv: 'If we want to emerge from the subjective at all, we must conceive (*auffassen*) of knowledge (*Erkennen*) as an activity that does not create what is known but grasps (*ergreifen*) what is already there (*das Vorhandene*)'. German additions mine.

49. Cf. Frege, 'On Concept and Object', pp. 169ff.

50. I owe this clarification to Umrao Sethi, which is not to say that she agrees with my overall point here.

51. Russell, 'Philosophy of Logical Atomism', p. 185: '[I]n very abstract studies such as philosophical logic ... the subject-matter that you are supposed to be thinking of is so exceedingly difficult and elusive that any person who has ever tried to think about it knows you do not think about it except perhaps once in six months for half a minute. The rest of the time you think about the symbols, because they are tangible, but the thing you are supposed to be thinking about is fearfully difficult and one does not often manage to think about it. The really good philosopher is the one who does once in six months think about it for a minute. Bad philosophers never do. That is why the theory of symbolism has a certain importance, because otherwise you are so certain to mistake the properties of the symbolism for the properties of the thing.'

52. Cf. Frege, *Basic Laws of Arithmetic*, p. XVI; Gabriel, *An den Grenzen der Erkenntnistheorie*, pp. 324ff.

53. Despite earlier criticisms of the idea in e.g. Miller, 'In Defence of the Predicate "Exists"', Miller, '"Exists" and Existence', and Orenstein, 'Is Existence What Existential Quantification Expresses?'

54. Cf. Aristotle, *Metaphysics*, 1087b33: 'τὸ δ᾽ ἓν ὅτι μέτρον σημαίνει' and *Metaphysics*, 1003b22–3: 'τὸ ὂν καὶ τὸ ἓν ταὐτὸν καὶ μία φύσις'.

55. Russell, *The Principles of Mathematics*, § 47, p. 43. Thanks to Marius Bartmann for reminding me of this passage. Against this see Badiou, *Theoretical Writings*, p. 40. Badiou there explicitly wishes to 'undo this bond between being and the one'. However, I disagree with his attempt of achieving this separation to the degree that it relies on a very revisionary and contentious ontological interpretation of set theory that I do not share.

56. van Inwagen, *Metaphysics*, p. 286.

57. Cf. van Inwagen, *Metaphysics*, p. 287.

58. Cf. Heidegger, 'Einblick in das was ist'.

59. Krauss, *A Universe from Nothing*.

60. Cf. Deacon, *Incomplete Nature*.

4

Limits of Set-Theoretical Ontology and Contemporary Nihilism

At this point, one could argue that there are versions of set-theoretical ontology that do without discrete ontology. In recent years, Badiou's ontology has been discussed as the prime example of a set-theoretical ontology, even though his basic ideas are broadly Platonic and very traditional. What he seems to add is that we can model a set-theoretical ontology along the lines of the *Cantorian-Russellian revolution.* This revolution consists in giving up the idea that there is an absolutely unrestricted totality, at least as long as one is forced to think of it in terms of a set of all sets. Without further ado, nothing corresponds to the concept of absolutely everything.

Badiou cites both Cantor's theorem and Russell's paradox as his main reasons for giving up on totality in the sense of an all-encompassing set, a set which has absolutely everything as its members.[1] To put it simply, if every member of the set of absolutely everything were assigned a real number, there would be some instance of the following list:

0.23457
0.34246
0.43235
0.12324
0.54321

We can now generate a new number by just adding 1 to each digit in a diagonal through the square.

0.2̲3457
0.34̲246
0.432̲35

0.123<u>2</u>4
0.5432<u>1</u>

This provides us with the number 0.35332, which was not included in the previous list. As is easy to see, even an infinite set of real numbers and actually every set of sets can be represented in such a way that we can devise a diagonal argument, amounting to a simplified version of Cantor's theorem.[2] There will always be one more set, a set missing in the alleged totality. Badiou sums up the result of Russellian and Cantorian arguments in the slogan that the One does not exist, where 'the One' is his name for an absolutely unrestricted totality. Even though, strictly speaking, I do not believe that set-theoretical arguments can ever establish that result, I accept the conclusion (albeit for different reasons to be laid out in detail in Chapter 7).[3]

My main objection against Badiou's approach is methodological: In ontology, set theory does not speak for itself. If utterly uninterpreted in the formalist mathematical fashion, not even a contradiction would ever give us a philosophical result. *Formalism* is the view that mathematical symbols have no semantics, but only syntax, that is, the view that they are meaningless signs, which is why they can be very successfully manipulated by computers, which need not have any grasp of meaning in a more demanding sense. A computer might show some behaviour we can interpret as paradoxical when confronted with a particular string of meaningless symbols. This happens when it halts in an infinite loop, a phenomenon known to every user of a computer. We can easily programme computers to halt when confronted with a string of meaningless symbols we call a contradiction. We can programme them to express any possible behaviour when deriving a contradiction, but this would never prove that the computer or even our formal system has contradicted itself. Almost trivially, neither a formal system nor a computer can contradict themselves, because they do not grasp any meaning whatsoever and in this sense do not speak. As printed out by a computer, the strings 'p and not-p' or even 'It is both the case that p and not the case that p (at the same time and in every respect)' do not disquote. There is no meaning within the parenthesis as long as we do not see it there, as little as in the strings 'XFGHSZZZ' or 'ÖÖ---ÄÄ###'. We can use a computer to derive a string (a theorem) from some systematic set of axioms or propositions, and *we* can use that information, but it never shows that the computer contradicted itself.

I wholeheartedly agree here with John Searle, who makes exactly this point with his Chinese Room Argument.[4] Imagine someone sits in a room equipped with a chart of instructions. There are two windows, one where someone hands in flashcards with Chinese characters, and one through which the person in the room hands them out to someone on the other side of the room in a particular order determined by the chart. One instruction, for instance, tells the person in the room that she has to hand out 我叫 马克思 when presented with the three flashcards 叫, 我, and 马 克思. Now imagine the chart recommends that the person at some point hand out: 我叫马克思，我不叫马克思. Did she contradict herself? Readers of these lines unable to read the characters would not know what to say. I had her hand out: 'My name is Marx and my name is not Marx.' Imagine a version of the thought experiment where everybody is informed about what is going on. The person handed the cards at the output end of the system might laugh out loud when handed the 'contradiction', as the person at the input end might have sent this message for fun. In the natural language case, we evidently do not conclude that Chinese is contradictory and should be given up, but only that we can state contradictions in this language, which is one of the many differences between an actual language and a formal system (which is, strictly speaking, not a language at all. Who speaks it? We should give up the idea that formal systems are languages. They are similar in some respects to languages, but they do not amount to the creation of new languages, much less even than Esperanto.)[5]

Uninterpreted symbols do not contradict themselves; they merely are or co-exist in some space or other. For contradiction or paradox to arise, there has to be meaning. I am not saying that every grasp of meaning is an act of interpretation, a claim I would certainly reject (on pains of a vicious infinite regress or paradoxes of radical translation). But where no interpretation has ever been imposed, where no one has understood anything against a background of prior lack of understanding, there is no meaning and consequently no contradiction.

Notice that this fact also affects the claim that Gödel's incompleteness theorems somehow refute formalism, as some interpreters have maintained.[6] On some presentations of the first incompleteness theorem, its conclusion can only be established by forcing any formal system that proves basic arithmetical truths to print out a Gödel sentence (G) of the form

(G) 'G is not provable in this theory T.'

On the reading I have in mind, the fact that it can be shown for any formal system that it has to print out a (G) is supposed to have established that formalism is incomplete in a problematic way. This is controversial for many reasons disputed among mathematicians and logicians. What interests me in the given setting is that the semantic fact that (G) *means* anything is not entailed by formalism itself. In formalism, we should resist the temptation to read (G) in this way by replacing it with a suitably uninterpreted equivalent, maybe

(G*) G wibnweob qewofb xqbfdɪcnff T.

The fact that some instance of (G) can be derived from any formal system is no more interesting than the fact that (G*) might be derived or that (G') can be derived:

(G') 'G provable in is theory not T.'

In a strictly formalist version of the first incompleteness 'theorem', it does not prove anything spectacular. At most it is like Magritte's *Ceci n'est pas une pipe*, which only causes problems if one takes the drawing of what looks like the French phrase to actually express: 'This is not a pipe.' However, the very reasons for believing that the mere drawing of a pipe is not a pipe should lead also to believing that the mere drawing of what looks like words is not a sentence. It is possible to interpret Magritte as claiming that there is also a difference between *drawing* objects in the form of words and *writing* words. One could frame this point with the help of Searle's distinction between *intrinsic* and *as-if-intentionality*: drawn objects in the form of words can be seen as if they had intrinsic meaning, which happens in the case where we draw objects in the form of words in order to write words.[7]

In this reconstruction, Gödel's first incompleteness theorem is not a refutation of formalism, but only speaks to those trying to *understand* mathematics. Its message is not even part of the formal system, as formal systems do not contain any message we do not interpret them as having. Running formal systems on a computer may *cause* the specific computer in question to exhibit self-destructive behaviour. Maybe it could even explode or run out of battery when confronted with an infinite loop for some specific reason or other. However, this is not at all like being committed to contradictory beliefs.

Of course, one might try to argue that if some person is in contradiction, this might cause self-destructive behaviour, but this is at least not the standard point behind acceptance of the principle of non-contradiction, which is not meant to be a scientific hypothesis about the self-destructive nature of systems running on contradictory programmes.

The first reason for rejecting the idea that any set-theoretical result by itself establishes that there is no absolutely unrestricted totality is, thus, that this only holds for certain *interpretations* of set-theoretical results. Badiou's identification of ontology with set theory and his conception of multiplicity are based on mixing formalism with his preferred interpretation of set theory. Yet, his interpretation is largely unjustified, as he bases it on an implicit combination of Plato's *Parmenides* and an implicit preference for some interpretation or other of the set-theoretical axiom system he employs. *Set theory unaided by philosophical reflection does not prove anything of any importance for philosophical reflection.* Set theory by itself is not a candidate for ontology, as it only contains information about the meaning of 'existence' under some sort of interpretation of its results.

A recent paper of Meillassoux' seems to happily embrace formalism as his philosophy of mathematics in general.[8] However, this understanding of the nature of mathematics leaves no room for any understanding of mathematical meaning or reference, and consequently eliminates the option that mathematics somehow brings us close to 'the absolute'. Here one might understand 'the absolute' in the minimal sense of a set of truths that hold independently of the contingent fact that at some point in the development of the universe some of its inhabitants were able to refer to facts. The 'glacial world',[9] the world in which there is no room for observers, cannot be substantiated by set theory or any other branch of mathematics understood in formalist terms. Therefore, the very idea of a subtractive, inconsistent multiplicity, the idea of sets without the One, untotalised and unrestricted proliferation, is utterly unmotivated; it is nothing but alienated meaning, the projection of the shadow of meaning onto the allegedly dark and empty space of meaningless nothingness.[10] Such gnostic existentialism might seem to be an attractive remedy against religious anthropocentrism and seems to be in tune with modern science. But, again, even this only holds under some interpretation of modern science that is far from what the major players of the scientific revolution themselves held as their world view. Newton, Galileo and Copernicus' universes are far from being 'disenchanted', and far from the acceptance of the meaninglessness of humanity for the universe.[11] This is not to say that humanity should be put centre stage again in a cosmic drama. However, commitment to 'glacial anti-humanism'[12] is as much an overgeneralised world view as the idea that all galaxies are merely there as the scene for human action on our planet. Anti-humanism is just humanism with a sad face, an expression of the disappointment that we are not as special as we think our ancestors believed we were. Yet, let it be noted in passing that the notion of our ancestors as religiously enchanted is also hopelessly anachronistic and probably a historicised form of exoticism.

Set theory generally is not a suitable candidate for ontology with a scientific outlook for several reasons. One reason to consider is quite simple, and was first pointed out by Georg Cantor himself, who was keen on distinguishing his results in set theory from a non-mathematical concept of what he explicitly calls 'the absolute'.[13] For Cantor, sets are grasped after a twofold act of abstraction: first, one needs to abstract from the specific qualities of some given objects, and, second, one needs to abstract from their 'order of presentation (*Ordnung des Gegebenseins*)', which I interpret as a predecessor of Frege's concept of a 'mode of presentation'.[14] Although Cantor's definition of the concept of a set is naïve in that it contains no defence against many of the paradoxes later discovered, the twofold abstraction is still part of axiomatic set theory. The fingers of my left hand and the fingers of my right hand belong to the set of all sets with five members; they thus belong to the same set. Even though all fingers involved are very different physical objects and belong to very different hands, insofar as they are fingers they can be counted, and as soon as they are counted, their specific qualities and their order of presentation is flattened out into the set F: $\{f_1, f_2, f_3, f_4, f_5\}$ underlying our grasp of the natural number 5. Set theory can only do ontology a service if we find a way of abstracting from specific qualities and orders of presentation as much as possible in order to arrive at a level of the sheer multiplicity of objects. It then becomes a universal theory of multiplicity, an *allgemeine Mannigfaltigkeitslehre*, as Cantor called it. On this hypothetical level it seems as if we have arrived at the inconsistent multiplicity Plato already talks of as 'the others (τἆλλα)',[15] and which subsequent Platonists called 'the infinite duality (ἀόριστος δυάς)'.[16] In Badiou's view this multiplicity is deemed inconsistent precisely because it is not governed by an axiomatic system that rules out the set-theoretical paradoxes. It seems as if set theory is able to quantify over an uninterpreted domain, the domain of sheer multiplicity, as long as no criteria are imposed on that very multiplicity that guarantees its consistency relative to some axiomatic base or other.

At least, this is Badiou's preferred interpretation, which is certainly not standard and stands in need of philosophical substantiation. On this basis, he claims that axiomatic set theory somehow tames inconsistent multiplicity and gives it a more determinate shape by never allowing for a single totalising operation and, thereby, preserving the indeterminacy of a transfinite proliferation of elements. Once again, let me emphasise that all of this rests on all sorts of contentious interpretations of set theory and is not just an undisputed evident mathematical fact, something like basic arithmetic.

Yet, existence cannot be a property only of this prolific and somehow unbound domain, as it only has very abstract objects, objects *tout court*, as its elements, an idea Jocelyn Benoist has rightly characterised as the myth of the white objects (*le mythe des objects blancs*).[17] The objects in Badiou's ontology are not even elementary particles; they are mere objects. But there are no mere objects at all, as we will see in due course. Note that if there were, there would be a set of all mere objects. But this very set is not so much as allowed by Badiou to exist. It would be a very bad solution for him to maintain that inconsistent multiplicity does not even exist, for this would turn his ontology into a complete farce: he would be claiming that what all objects have in common insofar as they are objects is that they do not exist, because they all belong to a single domain that does not exist. If there is only one domain of objects defined by the only predicate available for one's ontology (in this case the predicate or pseudo-predicate ... *is an object tout court*), this domain had better exist.

Ultimately, set-theoretical ontology is a remainder of Platonic mathematicism. Let *mathematicism* from here on be the view that everything that exists can be studied mathematically either directly or indirectly.[18] It is an instance of theory-reduction, that is, a claim to the effect that every vocabulary can be translated into that of mathematics such that this reduction grounds all derivative vocabulary and helps us understand it significantly better. Set-theoretical ontology is just one instance of mathematicism. Depending on one's preferred candidate for the most fundamental theory of quantifiable structure, one can wind up with a graph-theoretical mathematicism, a set-theoretical, category-theoretical, or some other (maybe hybrid) form of mathematicism. However, mathematicism is metaphysics, and metaphysics need not be associated with ontology. The no-world-view defended in this book argues that metaphysics is, strictly speaking, impossible. It is ontologically impossible; the object of metaphysics, the world, cannot exist, and therefore no particular claim regarding its nature (that it consists of sets, of elementary particles, of social facts, of solipsistic monads, or what have you) can ever be substantiated. Metaphysics is the error of Parmenides, as well as of some of his Asian contemporaries. It might have a longer prehistory and might be someone else's fault. It does not matter whom we blame, the temptation of metaphysics is universal anyhow, though it is not built into human nature, but is rather definitely the result of a long prehistory of human attempts to make sense of things. Nevertheless, it is always as overgeneralised as the view that everything is water, although its contemporary ramifications are much better disguised. Metaphysics cannot be a discovery, because it is a meaningless search for something that could never possibly exist. As set-theoretical ontology ultimately turns out to be a form of metaphysics, this is an additional and perhaps the best reason for rejecting it. It is not the case that everything is or ultimately is a set or the member of a set. This is both false and not entailed by set theory as such.

Badiou himself seems to have realised that set theory cannot be the correct answer to the question of what 'existence' means, as he changes his view from *Being and Event I* to *Being and Event II*. In his *Logics of the Worlds*, he starts thinking of existence as the degree of presence of something in a world, where a world in his sense comes very close to the concept of a field of sense laid out in this book.[19] However, it is far from clear how the two books can be made to cohere, and I believe that the better view is defended in

Volume II of the project. Nevertheless, Badiou's fascination with formalism and meaninglessness brings me to the concluding reflection of this chapter.

Contemporary global philosophy of all traditions in recent decades gives voice to the now more or less common sense view among academics that the position of mind or thought in the universe does not really matter for an understanding of the universe. The universe is just what is independent of any facts about our reference to it. Everyday poetry (often called folk psychology) matters less, and the reason for the decay of poetry is often associated with 'the disenchantment of nature',[20] a Weberian phrase almost always referred to without actual discussion of the meaning of the phrase in Weber's writings. Disenchantment is presented as a historical fact, the fact that we humans have discovered over the last five hundred years or so that there is no meaning in the universe, that it is just stuff spread out in space-time or spread out as space-time, maybe some really odd (but still meaningless) stuff oscillating in any number of dimensions surprisingly bigger than 4. Semantic stuff simply does not matter, or so they say.

Weber's dictum is usually read as a commitment to the view that modernity really begins with the scientific revolution, and this term in turn is understood as the progressive discovery of the meaninglessness of meaning-generating practices. Once religion is dispensed with in favour of the discovery that the universe is nothing but a vast container of matter resistant to any effort of reserving a special place for human interests and values within it, we might as well give up all the other illusions too: colours, ethics, semantic meaning, being someone, and more progressively in accordance with the advances of theoretical physics, maybe even bodies. Along this line of reasoning, it seems as if ultimately or fundamentally nothing has ever existed but some kind of arrangement of either individuals (elementary particles) or some more paradoxical-seeming gunk. This impression, this seeming itself, is evidently ruled out of existence by this line of thought (which, of course, again does not exist, at least not really). Our final achievement of a fusion with fundamental and meaningless reality seems to be haunted by the shadows of our semantically mediated grasp of that very reality, an illusion that has to be reduced or eliminated in one way or another.

Of course, all of this is going nowhere; it is and remains a hopeless effort to ornament Presocratic atomism with the terms of modern, sometimes twenty-first-century popular science. In order to have a theory, you need to account for the meanings invested in generating the theory. Thus, even if there were a large stratum of facts or objects one might be tempted to call fundamental (even though this is nothing but a metaphor suggesting a theory where there is none), one would still be *claiming* that there is such a stratum, an event supposedly not happening on the level of the stratum itself.

Apart from the more intricate forms of metaphysical overgeneralisation and ontological failure involved in the now somewhat fashionable forms of physicalistic nihilism (we will get to that), this whole picture is very ill advised to count Max Weber among its founding fathers. Weber is essentially making the opposite point, as he argues that the disenchantment of the world is not a historical fact, process, or event, following the grand mythical moment of Galileo's triumph over the dark forces behind cardinal Bellarmine. Rather, disenchantment for Weber is an ideologically distorted description of the social world. Here is what he actually writes when he talks about disenchantment:

> The increasing intellectualization and rationalization do not, therefore, indicate an increased and general knowledge of the conditions under which one lives. It means something else, namely, the knowledge or belief that if one but wished one *could* learn it at any time. Hence, it means that principally there are no mysterious incalculable forces that come into play, but rather that one can, in principle, master all things by calculation. This means that the world is disenchanted.[21]

What Weber is saying in this famous quote is that disenchantment is a certain way of looking at our 'Lebensbedingungen'. He explicitly rejects the assumption that rationalisation is a discovery or a form of knowledge. Rather, it is an illusory self-description, albeit one that characterises citizens of modern states. He certainly does not hold that modernity is a process of secularisation and of progressive discovery of the elementary forces behind the illusory surface of primitive beliefs, but on the contrary gives an account of the illusory potential of self-descriptions.

Disenchantment is fully-fledged zoontology: a human-all-too-human projection. Weber in another work rejects 'the enthusiastic spirit of naturalistic monism',[22] which he deems unacceptable in the social sciences. He is not saying that one should not be a materialist about the material universe. What he is saying is that naturalistic monism – by which he seems to understand the view that every object of scientific inquiry is material and can be studied by some ultimate science of matter – cannot be the right approach in the social sciences. However, I am not interested in defending Weber's conception of the social sciences. The point I am making is that the identification of modernity with the scientific revolution and the interpretation of that revolution as a unilinear process of reducing one meaningful item in 'the manifest image' after the other to some item in 'the scientific image' is modern mythology and not the discovery of some ultimate fact. The no-world-view straightforwardly entails that the very idea of an all-encompassing scientific image (or any other all-encompassing stance or entity for that matter) is strictly incoherent; it is a remnant of just the bad kind of metaphysics modernity is struggling to overcome.

Metaphysics is indeed unscientific, but it is implicitly drawn upon in many interpretations of the actual results of modern science. Humanity seems to be more interested in believing that everything deep down completely differs from the way it appears to us (including ourselves) than to find out how things appear to us. This is why phenomenology became prominent around the turn of the twentieth century, and this is why it is still so attractive: it helps us understand that there are appearances whatever we might believe about their grounding in some allegedly hidden realm. At the historical moment of its inception, phenomenology was introduced as a justified counter-reaction to the prevalent tendency associated with the scientific method of ignoring appearances and trying to get to their true nature.

Scientistic nihilism is a form of Presocratic cosmology typically combined with actual scientific results. There is no reasonable way to deny that we constantly find out more about the universe, and that we thereby come to know that there is no grand plan built into the universe that secures us safety in the jungle-planet we inhabit. I am not re-enchanting here, but I wholeheartedly reject the assumption that we should either be disenchanting or re-enchanting. If anything, this is a point we can accept from Nietzsche, who rejected nihilism for the simple reason that it does not make sense to ask for the value of the whole thing of which we are a part.[23] I am not sure if he would have accepted that there is no such whole thing. At least he would have accepted the sceptical equivalent of my view, namely, that we cannot ascribe any ultimate goal or structure to the whole thing (even if it existed). Nihilism is utterly meaningless, and that is the only ultimate meaninglessness it is confronted with.

The problem with any form of all-encompassing metaphysical fundamentalism in the name of science does not lie in science, but rather in that it is neither science nor really scientifically minded. Indeed, our concept of nature might not be sufficiently disenchanted in the sense that we tend to interpret many purely natural events in terms of some meaning related to human interests where no such relation should be projected. The problem with over-generalised metaphysical fundamentalism of any kind is the tacit monism according to which everything that even so much as exists is part of a single, all-encompassing domain. Naturalistic fundamentalism goes on to identify this domain with some actual fundamental stratum, fundamental natural reality, where something belongs to that stratum if it somehow grounds some phenomenon not strictly speaking belonging to the stratum. This whole project is hopeless, because it rests on the mistaken identification of ontology and metaphysics (that is, ontotheology), and the associated understanding of metaphysics in terms of the attempt to grasp the world as world, the all-encompassing domain. It does not matter whether our understanding of the domain is more liberal or more reductionist in outlook. The mistake is to get into the business of ontotheology in the first place.

Modern nihilism is continuous with the kind of religion it seeks to undermine. The standard objection against this observation points out that religion and science might indeed have a common ancestor, the human desire to know or understand the phenomena, 'the world'. Seen in this light, religion is a primitive attempt at explaining natural phenomena: Thunder is Zeus, love is Aphrodite, and so on. But this philosophy of religion does not meet the scientific standards of the philosophy or sociology of religion. It is a projection of the contemporary, mostly North American struggle between Christian fundamentalists and enlightenment-directed forms of atheism onto the overall shape of human consciousness and its historical development in pre-historic times. Human beings are seen as scientists from the outset: to be human is to try to explain natural phenomena, maybe for the sake of hunting or mating, or whatever goal one deems most primitive and evolutionarily hardwired. However, at the very least we do not know that the inventors of what later was called 'religion' were scientists without mathematics, let alone a decent laboratory. This view seems to be straightforwardly anachronistic and assumes what it wants to prove, namely that explaining phenomena presupposes that the phenomena be natural and accordingly material or physical (thunder, birth, death, and so on). Yet, scientistic naturalism is still involved in mythopoiesis in the production of an overall narrative designed to explain the world and its meaning or utter lack of meaning.

Generally, the fact that we have scientific knowledge and the authors of say *Genesis* or some creation myth or other did not should not be interpreted as evidence that we understand the world better than they did, for the simple reason that the world does not exist. However, I am far from denying that we understand many things better than they did: electrons, atoms, evolution, galaxies, set theory, toilet flushes, numbers, biological life, plants, animals, diseases, the brain, history and the list goes on. But who would deny that Solomon might have understood more about love than Richard Dawkins? Or that Goethe, Cézanne, and Beethoven understand more about art than Daniel Dennett? India during the creation of its major creation myths was full of people who understood more about enjoying themselves and overcoming the desire to constantly enjoy themselves than many of us. Who would deny that Queen Victoria understood much less about sex than the architects who built the temples in India that she would really have liked to destroy? Sophocles certainly understood more about Greek tragedies than any scientific interpreter or reductionist scientist, and the problems depicted and discussed are still with us, as is particularly well illustrated by the second season of the HBO show *The Wire*, which is a contemporary tragedy run by the Greeks (even though the criminal master mind in season two is only called 'The Greek' and turns out not even to be Greek, as he himself says in the season finale). Tony Soprano finally comes to the conclusion that Sun Zi (often misleadingly spelled as Sun-Tzu) is better than Macchiavelli:

> Been reading that — that book you told me about. You know, The Art of War by Sun-Tzu. I mean here's this guy, a Chinese general, wrote this thing 2400 years ago, and most of it still applies today! Block the enemy's power. Force him to reveal himself. You know most of the guys that I know, they read Prince Machiavelli, and I had Carmela go

and get the Cliff Notes once and — he's okay. But this book is much better about strategy.

My point is quite simple: You need not live after the alleged real-life historical event of the scientific revolution (it was a revolution only metaphorically) in order to be able to know many things better than someone maximally informed about the current state of knowledge in the natural sciences. There is no reason to believe that actual knowledge about the laws of nature changes our overall framework of knowledge in such a profound way that we somehow become more rational and less enchanted.

One epistemologically deeper reason for this is, as I will argue in Part II, Chapters 12 to 13, that neither the world nor knowledge can be unified into a single, univocal, and all-encompassing concept. 'Science' in the eminent singular does not exist either: it is the epistemological equivalent of the world, yet another totalising fantasy we inherited from tradition and simply need to give up in the name of modernity. To be modern is indeed to accept many of the obvious truths derived from various scientific breakthroughs we should have accepted by now: that there are at the very least a hundred billion galaxies, that the known universe in its observable shape has a determinable 'age' (current estimate: around 13.82 billion years), that we think with our brains (and not with our hearts, lungs, or toe nails), that homosexuality is not a disease or defect of any kind, that water is H_2O, and so on. But none of these truths commit us to the additional view that there is a totality of such truths, an overall final body of knowledge that tells us everything about the overall final state of things. Such a body of knowledge is more like the 'History of the World in Phone Numbers' from *Mulholland Drive*, that is to say, an awe and mystery-evoking fantasy, as it were, the core fantasy of the scientistic subject (to be thoroughly distinguished from the scientist).

What is true about the insistence that modernity somehow is driven by demystification is that we are now in a position to overcome ontotheology. Overcoming ontotheology for good is indeed an aim of this book, because I believe that it is still the most widespread overall assumption in professional and common sense philosophy. Most people believe that there is an overall totality, the world, and that this totality is identical with some substantial structure or even entity. Contemporary nihilists therefore do not attack the right enemy when they are trying to undermine 'enchanted' religion by pointing out the meaninglessness of the universe.

Badiou's set-theoretical ontology is also utterly ontotheological because it is driven by the fantasy of a language more expressive than any other and yet without any meaning. For him, transfinitely many truths can be typed by set theory, and they are supposed to be both completely devoid of meaning and radically universal, truths about essentially everything. His insistence that no such thing as everything can exist due to set-theoretical paradoxes only holds for certain interpretations of the paradoxes, not for sets in themselves, for the subtractive or whatever it is that he is trying to commit to. Badiou's opening move, the insight that the One/ the Whole does not exist, is not coherently carried out as long as the subtractive prime matter of inconsistent multiplicity is even implicitly treated as more fundamental or as regimenting any ontological discourse.

Set theory is not ontology and nihilism is metaphysics. It is indeed bad metaphysics, but this is because all metaphysics is ultimately bad metaphysics to the degree that it rests on the assumption that there is an all-encompassing domain or most universal (most fundamental) stratum or layer of reality, sometimes simply called 'reality'. It is unclear whether Badiou really gives up reality in that sense. It seems to me that the two tomes of *Being and Event* rather map a profound dualism, the dualism between the ultimately unified domain of sheer multiplicity (unified by the axioms and rules of inference holding it together) and the manifold worlds of *Logics of the Worlds*. How do these two levels of observation relate to each other? Is set theory a world among worlds (in my language: just one field of sense among others)? In this case, why would Badiou want to claim that mathematics and ontology coincide? Or is set theory somehow ontologically privileged (which is the official view)? This threatens to open up a gap between sheer inconsistent multiplicity and the manifold worlds. For Badiou, mathematics in the sense of a regimented consistent discourse occupies a 'transitory', that is to say special, intermediary status between the inconsistent multiplicity and the manifold worlds, so that his ontology is actually split into three parts whose connection is not further clarified.[24]

To some extent, the ontology of fields of sense opts for a middle ground between *Being and Event I* and *Logics of the Worlds* in that it puts the concept of sense at the heart of the investigation into the meaning of 'existence'. Sense is responsible for the individuation of fields and this means that sense-less extension is not as sense-less as it appears. There is no uninterpreted sheer multiplicity, no bare existence below the threshold of descriptions. Sets and their extensions also exist *as* something or other (as the set with four members, say), which is why there are truths about sets. There are no sets on this side of the facts (and no facts on this side of their differentiation into manifold fields).

Notes

1. Badiou, *Logics of Worlds*, in particular Book 2, Section 3.1, and Badiou, *Being and Event*, part I, chapter 3.
2. On the philosophical significance of this and some more details see Moore: *The Infinite* and Berto, *There's Something About Gödel*.
3. Patrick Grim has presented arguments similar to those found in Badiou in his *The Incomplete Universe*. For an elaboration and generalisation of Grim's position see Kreis, *Negative Dialektik des Unendlichen*. Whereas Kreis is trying to generalise the set-theoretical arguments in such a way that they become relevant for the theory of facts and thereby for rational cosmology, Badiou explicitly rejects the application of his procedure of detolisation beyond set-theoretical ontology in his sense of the term: 'First of all, it is being as such that we are here declaring cannot constitute a whole, not the world, or nature, or the physical universe' (Badiou, *Theoretical Writings*, p. 190).
4. Cf. Searle, 'Minds, Brains and Programs'.
5. Interestingly, the actual Chinese word for contradiction 矛盾 (máodùn) consists of two characters. The first means 'spear' and the second shield. The explanation of this goes back to the book *Han Feizi*, a book from the second century BC. In this book the following anecdote can be found: 'There was a man in Chu who sold shields and spears. Praising the shields he said: "My shields are so strong that nothing can pierce them". And praising the spears he said: "My spears are so strong that there is nothing that they cannot pierce". A person asked: "What if someone pierces your shields with your spears?" He could not respond.' Thanks to Li Min for pointing this out to me.
6. See, for example, the reconstruction in Berto, *There's Something About Gödel*.

7. See Searle, *The Rediscovery of the Mind*, pp. 78–82. Searle makes a different, even if similar use of this distinction given that he uses it in order to show that no program computes anything intrinsically, but only operates in the mode of as-if-intentionality due to the fact that some creatures are endowed with intrinsic intentionality.

8. Quentin Meillassoux in his Berlin lecture, *Iteration, Reiteration, Repetition*.

9. Meillassoux, *After Finitude*, p. 117: 'The world of Cartesian extension is a world that acquires the independence of substance, a world that we can henceforth conceive of as indifferent to everything in it that corresponds to the concrete, organic connection that we forge with it – it is this *glacial* world that is revealed to the moderns, a world in which there is no longer any up or down, centre or periphery, nor anything else that might make of it a world designed for humans. For the first time, the world manifests itself as capable of subsisting without any of those aspects that constitute its concreteness for us.'

10. Cf. Benoist, 'Alien Meaning and Alienated Meaning'.

11. For further elaboration of this point see my *Warum es die Welt nicht gibt*, chapters IV–V.

12. Badiou, *Theoretical Writings*, p. 11.

13. See Cantor, 'Mitteilungen zur Lehre vom Transfiniten', p. 378: 'Es wurde das A.-U. [Aktual-Unendliche] nach *drei* Beziehungen unterschieden: *erstens* sofern es in der höchsten Vollkommenheit, im völlig unabhängigen, außerweltlichen Sein, *in Deo* realisiert ist, wo ich es *Absolut-unendliches* oder kurzweg *Absolutes* nenne; *zweitens* sofern es in der abhängigen, natürlichen Welt vertreten ist; *drittens* sofern es als mathematische Größe, Zahl oder Ordnungstypus vom Denken *in abstracto* aufgefaßt werden kann. In den *beiden* letzten Beziehungen, wo es offenbar als beschränktes, noch weiterer Vermehrung fähiges und *insofern dem Endlichen verwandtes* A.U. sich darstellt, nenne ich es *Transfinitum* und setze es dem *Absoluten* strengstens entgegen.' See also Cantor, *Briefe*, p. 139: 'Der Ausdruck "absolut" wird, wie ich sehe, von Ihnen in demselben Sinne gebraucht, wie von mir der Ausdruck "eigentlich". Dagegen gebrauche *ich* das Wort "absolut" nur für das, was *nicht mehr vergrößert*, resp. *vervolkommnet* werden kann, in Analogie des "Absoluten" in der Metaphysik. Meine eigentlich unendlichen oder, wenn Sie lieber wollen, transfiniten Zahlen w, w+1, ... sind nicht "absolut", weil sie, obgleich nicht endlich, dennoch der Vergrößerung fähig sind. Das Absolute ist jedoch keiner Vergrößerung fähig und daher auch für uns inaccessible.'

14. Cantor, *Contributions to the Founding of the Theory of Transfinite Numbers*, p. 86.
15. Plato, *Parmenides*, 159b–60b.
16. Aristotle, *Metaphysics*, 1007b27. He discusses here the nature of indeterminacy, using the term τὸ ἀόριστον. He doesn't use the term ἀόριστος δυάς until 1081a13, where there is a lengthy subsequent discussion of indeterminate numbers: 'ἐκ τίνων γὰρ ἔσονται ἀρχῶν αἱ ἰδέαι; ὁ γὰρ ἀριθμός ἐστιν ἐκ τοῦ ἑνὸς καὶ τῆς δυάδος τῆς ἀορίστου, καὶ αἱ ἀρχαὶ καὶ τὰ στοιχεῖα λέγονται τοῦ ἀριθμοῦ.'
17. Benoist, *Éléments de Philosophie Realiste*, p. 59.
18. Badiou seems to be committed to the idea that the appearances in his sense can be studied mathematically, because their being (that is their multiplicity) is governed by mathematical laws. See, for instance, Badiou, *Theoretical Writings*, p. 15: 'mathematics is the science of being qua being. Logic pertains to the coherence of appearance. And if the study of appearance also mobilizes certain areas of mathematics, this is simply because, following an insight formalized by Hegel but which actually goes back to Plato, it is of the essence of being to appear. This is what maintains the form of all appearing within a mathematizable transcendental order.' See also Ibid., p. 172: 'the science of appearance must itself be a component of the science of being, and therefore of mathematics'.
19. Badiou, *Logics of Worlds*, p. 208: '*Given a world and a function of appearing whose values lie in the transcendental of this world, we will call "existence" of a being x which appears in this world the transcendental degree assigned to the self-identity of x.* Thus defined, existence is not a category of being (of mathematics), it is a category of appearing (of logic). In particular, "to exist" has no meaning in itself. In agreement with one of Sartre's insights, who borrows it from Heidegger, but also from Kierkegaard or even Pascal, "to exist" can only be said relatively to a world. In effect, existence is nothing but a transcendental degree.'
20. Cf. McDowell, *Mind and World*, p. 70, and Brassier, *Nihil Unbound*, p. xi.
21. Weber, 'The Disenchantment of Modern Life', pp. 129–56.
22. Weber, 'The "Objectivity" of Knowledge in Social Science and Social Policy', p. 122.
23. Cf. Nietzsche, *Beyond Good and Evil*, p. 16: 'The eagerness and subtlety – I might even say, shrewdness – with which the problem of "the real and the apparent world" is today attacked all over Europe makes one think and wonder; and anyone who hears nothing in the

background except a "will to truth", certainly does not have the best of ears. In rare and isolated instances it may really be the case that such a will to truth, some extravagant and adventurous courage, a metaphysician's ambition to hold a hopeless position, may participate and ultimately prefer even a handful of "certainty" to a whole carload of beautiful possibilities; there may actually be puritanical fanatics of conscience who prefer even a certain nothing to an uncertain something to lie down on – and die. But this is nihilism and the sign of a despairing, mortally weary soul – however courageous the gestures of such a virtue may look.'

24. See Badiou, *Briefings on Existence: A Short Treatise on Transitory Ontology*.

5

Domains of Objects and Fields of Sense

Let us first draw a broad distinction between *adverbial* and *domain ontology*. According to *adverbial ontology* 'to exist' is a verb that describes an activity of objects and can correspondingly be qualified by an adverb. Adverbial ontology claims that objects exist differently, that there are different modes of existence: numbers exist abstractly, planets exist materially, and so on. Heidegger and Aristotle are sometimes credited with such a view, and one could take Heidegger's view that the world does not exist, but that it 'worlds', or that inanimate objects do not exist (that is Dasein's privilege), but merely are present, as evidence for some underlying adverbial ontology. Aristotle's distinction between *dynamis* and *energeia* seems to lend support for an adverbial reading of his ontology, as he sometimes seems to be saying, that *dynamei on* (δυνάμει ὄν, existing potential-ly) is different from *energeiai on* (ἐνεργείᾳ ὄν, existing actual-ly). Peter van Inwagen has objected to Heidegger and Sartre for having defended an adverbial ontology, as he rightly deems it absurd to think of existence as something's activity.[1] Yet, it is far from clear that either Heidegger or Sartre generally hold the view that to exist is to perform a certain activity (that of existing). What they claim is that our existence (*Existenz*) is a reality (*réalité humaine*) that sustains itself via a conception of itself, that it only exists as this or that kind of human existence as long as every single one of us acts upon an overall idea of the purposefulness of our individual lives.

Even though I disagree with the upshot of van Inwagen's reasoning, I agree that existence is not an activity of objects. Even if it were an activity, it would not be a proper activity, and therefore, nothing objects do in any ordinary sense of doing. As Austin famously remarked about the even loftier meaning of being in general: 'The word is a verb, but it does not describe something that things do all the time, like breathing, only quieter – ticking over, as it were, in a metaphysical sort of way.'[2]

On closer inspection, neither Aristotle nor Heidegger (let alone Sartre) defend an adverbial ontology. Aristotle is probably rather the first domain ontologist, and Heidegger has followed him in this regard throughout his whole career, as he persistently thinks about domains (*Bereiche*) in his ontology. Actually, Aristotle introduces domain ontology in the very same passage where he gives the historically first definition of the theory that was much later called ontology:

> There is a science which investigates being as being and the attributes which belong to this in virtue of its own nature. Now this is not the same as any of the so-called special sciences; for none of these others treats universally of being as being. They cut off a part of being and investigate the attribute of this part; this is what the mathematical sciences for instance do.[3]

Here Aristotle clearly suggests that we should think of being qua being more as a (maybe all-encompassing) domain than the regional or local domains investigated by the special sciences. The metaphor of cutting off a part of being wrongly suggests spatial metaphors. What really does the job of distinguishing between the various sciences in light of their relation to ontology as the most general theory is that they give an account of being as something other than just being. Famously, Aristotle claims that mathematics is about being *as* ($\tilde{\mathring{\eta}}$) countable or physics about being *as* ($\tilde{\mathring{\eta}}$) moved.[4] The word he uses for 'as', namely $\tilde{\mathring{\eta}}$, can also be translated as 'insofar'; it corresponds to the Latin 'quatenus', which plays an important role throughout the history of modern metaphysics. Most prominently it serves in Aristotle to unify all sciences in light of the fact that they study being under different overall descriptions, which is responsible for them not being in contradiction. It is not contradictory to think of being under different far-reaching descriptions or in different far-reaching theories, because these different descriptions approach being from a particular angle compatible with the objective validity of other angles. What further individuates special sciences are their various methods, which literally translated means their ways of going with their objects by tracing their essential ways of being under the description in question.

This picture is still with us today, albeit with some special science or other as occupying the position of ontology or rather metaphysics: physicalism, for instance, can be stated as the view that physics deals with the first causes, and therefore with the all-encompassing domain, whereas all the other sciences cut off a part from the big thing and investigate that region. Aristotle himself explicitly says that knowledge of the first causes, or the set of principles structuring everything, amounts to a formal way of 'knowing everything'.[5] More generally, the idea is that there is an overall domain of investigation and local, regional domains investigated by the special sciences: French Studies takes France as a socio-cultural entity, political science studies political systems, sociology studies social systems, physics studies physical systems, and so on. The special sciences deal with objects in particular domains, which leaves room for an over-arching, non-special or universal science that asserts propositions about all other sciences in light of the fact that they all share the feature of studying what there is in general under a local form of description.

Given that philosophy at the very least since Kant was eager to give up its methodological supremacy, its status as the queen of all sciences, the position has been vacant. Kant thought that no one should try to occupy the position on the ground that, given that no survey of the world in its totality would ever be possible from the standpoint of human knowledge, it is ultimately illusory anyway. However, circumstances have changed, and Kant's modesty has been overruled by the vast successes of nineteenth and twentieth-century science in penetrating the things in themselves and in giving up most of the constraints on human knowledge Kant deemed essential. Some contemporary physicists explicitly reject the principle of sufficient reason and even endorse the claim that out of literally nothing (physical) comes the basic stuff making up the universe.[6] No one literally believes that there are twelve categories (and associated content-determining structures such as the Kantian kind of schematism or a finite clear-cut number of axioms of intuition), some permissible combination of which defines the limits of human cognition and consequently of human knowledge.

Note that Aristotle introduces the science of being qua being in such a way that he goes from ontology immediately to metaphysics.

Now since we are seeking the first principles and the highest causes, clearly there must be some thing to which these belong in virtue of its own nature. If then those who sought the elements of existing things were seeking these same principles, it is necessary that the elements must be elements of being not by accident but just because it is being. Therefore it is of being as being that we also must grasp the first causes.[7]

Aristotle thus introduces the notion of a domain ontology and at the same time argues that there has to be a universal or all-encompassing domain, from where it is only a short step for him to conclude that the all-encompassing domain is itself a thing with a nature, a nature determined by its properties, the first causes. Aristotle accordingly runs ontology and metaphysics together. To some extent, in line with Heidegger's understanding of the matter at hand, I call the identification of ontology and metaphysics 'ontotheology', and I take Aristotle to be the creator of ontotheology in a demanding sense of the term. It is not an accident that it is very hard to tell metaphysics and theology apart in Aristotle, as 'God' for him first and foremost is the placeholder for the ultimate first cause or the ultimate first causes.

It would get us into a long exegetical detour to determine what the thing underlying the ultimate domain is. Elsewhere I have argued that it is indeed 'God', and that God for Aristotle is pure activity beyond thought.[8] Aristotle's God does not think, he just exists, which is why Aristotle ultimately defends both a domain and an adverbial ontology, as he believes that for things to be in a domain is for them to do something that things in other domains do not do: humans live in political communities and think, God merely is, fire goes up, the earth rests, the stars move in regular spheres, and so on. Aristotle therefore not only falls prey to ontotheology (which he invented alongside Plato) but on the highest level of investigation mixes elements from adverbial and from domain ontology. As Heidegger rightly pointed out time and again, Aristotle here left us with a rotten heritage that we somehow need to sort out by ourselves.

Aristotle's heritage still largely determines the structure of the academic system in the contemporary world in that we think of scientific knowledge in terms of being about the all-encompassing domain, but in the form of a division of labour. What divides the labour is not merely constructed by us, but corresponds to knowledge's capacity to 'carve nature at its joints', a reference to Plato that has returned in a different disguise in contemporary philosophy.[9] The division of labour corresponds to different domains of objects – an expression commonly used in order to mark off the difference between, say, the social sciences and chemistry – they are about different kinds of objects, or rather facts. However, domain ontology in the traditional sense has a built-in drive to a totalising closure, it projects an absolute or all-encompassing domain and seeks to identify a corresponding discipline, a discipline uncovering the ultimate ground.

The search for the ultimate ground essentially takes two shapes. It either looks for the biggest thing (the universe) or for the most fundamental (the smallest) units out of which a potentially or maybe even actually infinite superthing (the multiverses, or if you take all of them together the 'hyperverse', as it were) could be constructed. Kant was right in pointing out that the problem of the world I am addressing here typically runs into paradoxes of the infinitely big or paradoxes of the infinitely small, paradoxes he deals with in the *Transcendental Dialectics* of the *Critique of Pure Reason*. However, he was wrong to identify this as a 'natural illusion'[10] of human reason, for the search for the 'unconditioned', as Kant called it, is not natural and, thus, inevitable for animals able to think about anything in scientific terms. The unconditioned is rather the projection of fully-fledged fallacies. There is no such *thing* as the unconditioned, either in the shape of the biggest thing (an all-encompassing universe), or in the shape of the most fundamental (a finite number of elementary particles, a finite number of laws of nature, and absolutely everything else consisting of the elementary particles arranged by the laws of nature). There simply is no such *thing* as absolutely everything, not even in the sense of a regulative idea. Such an idea could never guide any investigation, for it is as incoherent as the search for the biggest natural number. If anything, this is an illusion, but one that can easily be dispelled and is not somehow grounded in rationality as such, as Kant thought.

Now, the simplest arguments for this can be drawn from domain ontology without yet specifying the rules of individuation that turn a domain into a domain and distinguish it from other domains (I will call these rules senses). For the sake of the following argument, let us recall that there are domains of objects, and that domains of objects are accessible by different disciplines (maybe defined by their methods of investigation). In order for domain ontology to even get going, it has to assume a revisionary ontology, that is, the view that existence is not a proper property. One way to achieve this is to maintain that to exist is to belong to a domain, and accordingly for domains to exist is to exist in some other domain. Existence is a relation between a domain and its objects (its denizens). As a result, objects could not exist alone; they are not absolutes, but only exist as *relata*. Objects only exist relative to their domain, as existence is the property of their domain to contain exactly them.

Now this straightforwardly entails that there cannot be a domain of all domains, or an all-encompassing domain, as this domain would have to belong to a domain in order to exist. The all-encompassing domain cannot belong to any of the domains it encompasses. It cannot belong to itself, as belonging to it is defined in such a way that whatever belongs to it appears alongside other domains. Imagine there were only three domains: Chemistry, sociology and Indian studies. If the domain encompassing these three domains belonged to one of its sub-domains, it would either be a chemical object, a sociological object, or an object relating to India (a language or linguistic item, an artwork, a religion, part of India's democratic government, a state, or local cuisine). In order to keep the argument manageable, let us take chemistry as an example and let us imagine that the domain of all domains belonged to chemistry. In this scenario, it would be a chemical object, say H_2O. But this would straightforwardly amount to the good old view that everything is water. For everything would exist within the domain of H_2O, as we picked it as the domain of all domains, the domain within which all domains and everything they encompass exist. Of course, no other object will do: the domain of all domains is neither Uttar Pradesh, nor the social structure of Northern England, nor the electoral behaviour of Indiana, nor some chemical reaction or other. The domain of all domains cannot exist as one of the objects it encompasses.

For almost the same reason you cannot identify the domain of all domains as whatever is within the scope of some particular investigation. The last decades have seen an unfortunate elevation of physics to metaphysics. Along those lines, one might claim that the all-encompassing domain is the universe and define the universe as the domain investigated by physics. However, the universe as a domain is nothing within the domain; it is not some object of investigation or other. It cannot belong to itself (where in the universe is the universe?). The universe as a domain encompassing any other domain cannot be identical with any object within one of its sub-domains and still be within the domain investigating the general aspects of it, such as galaxies or even space-time considered in terms of its maximal extension (whatever that might happen to be).

Nothing is wrong with physics as such. But it is set on the wrong track if we praise it as the new metaphysics, for that identification rests on bad ontology. If the universe were an all-encompassing domain, it would have to exist in a more-encompassing domain that could not in turn be investigated by physics.

In a recent discussion with a Google manager, a Buddhist from Nepal and a software engineer, I found myself confronted with the ancient idea that one should not identify the all-encompassing domain (the universe) with the biggest, as this indeed amounts to paradox, but with the smallest. After some discussion, I found out that they were defending the idea that the universe is all-encompassing precisely because an investigation into the universe is an investigation into the fundamental constituents of all objects. I take it that this idea underlies much of contemporary metaphysics, even though it is yet another contemporary resurgence of Presocratic metaphysics in the disguise of modern science. Here the idea is that we can think of the all-encompassing domain as a fundamental level to which we can reduce all higher-order phenomena in the following manner: tables are elementary particles arranged table-wise, galaxies are elementary particles arranged galaxy-wise, and so on. Yet, current physics has not identified any fundamental elementary particle or set of particles, and no one should claim that it is the Higgs Boson, as it is simply not true that *all* elementary particles somehow consist of it. This is a popular myth. At this point, we simply do not know whether there is such a thing as a most elementary particle, an atom in the ancient sense. But nothing hinges on this point, as I am willing to grant that it could turn out that all elementary subatomic particles consist of some kind of particle or other, call it the super-elementary particle. Even if there were either a single super-elementary particle, or a finite array of kinds of super-elementary particles (say three different kinds), the following argument would still hold. It would also hold if there were only strings oscillating in some surprisingly high number of dimensions and generating the objects we are confronted with in doing physics.

Imagine the all-encompassing domain were the most fundamental domain, the domain of the super-elementary particles. If there is more than one domain, the relation between the most fundamental domain and the others would have to be *reduction*. The higher-order domains could be *reduced* to the most fundamental one, but they would still have to exist, of course – even if only in the form of an illusion, they would be grounded in some way or other.[11] Reduction is not elimination; it needs to keep the objects reduced in one way or another somehow in existence as it reduces them.

This also means that the most fundamental domain cannot be all-encompassing. If it were, we could legitimately raise the question whether it exists in itself or in some other domain (as we are still accepting that to exist is to belong to some domain or other). If it existed in itself, it would have to be identical with some of the objects existing within it, some super-elementary particles (maybe even all of them, if their number is finite), because this is all you can ever hope to find within it. But in this case, nothing could even so much as exist in the form of an illusion that could be investigated by another method. The most fundamental domain would be entirely occupied by the super-elementary particles with no place for the domain of illusions. There could be no observation of tables, because tables would not even exist as super-elementary particles arranged *table*-wise. There literally would only be super-elementary particles without any chance that they even could look different (like tables or galaxies).

But this is not reduction anymore but *elimination*. Reductionism is the claim that the explanations needed in order to account for some objects under some description ought to be replaced by explanations needed in order to account for the same objects under some other description. *Prima facie* reduction, as it were, leaves the illusion intact, but offers a revisionary explanation of it in terms of something grounding the illusion. Elimination, however, gets rid of the illusion in one stroke by denying its very existence such that no need for reduction can even possibly arise. In elimination we would be left with just one single domain of super-elementary particles (where the domain is nothing in addition to this fundamental layer). This would be the view that there literally only are super-elementary particles with no chance whatsoever that illusions could possibly ever exist on top of that. For if they existed, they would be the object of investigation of some observation and as such form a domain in addition to the material remainder we are left with after elimination (although we are saying that we need not even perform such an elimination, as this performance would have to be eliminated together with all other illusions).

This 'position' of *eliminativist microphysicalism* is ultimately ineffable. It cannot state itself as even so much as a view, as it is trying to say that there are no views, just the super-elementary particles. It does not say that we should think of views as of super-elementary particles arranged view-wise (and, by the way, good luck defending that), it rather says that there really are no views. I surmise that this underlies the nowadays-popular Pseudo-Buddhist idea that we are our brains and that no self is around to be even so much as the illusion generated by our brains.[12] This popular or rather popularised version of an identity-theory of mind and brain forgets that if two things are indeed identical (in whichever form one prefers here) there is no point in saying that either of them is an illusion or does not really exist. This is as fallacious as claiming that we are identical with our brains and that, therefore, our brains generate our consciousness or our minds, as this would mean that we are certainly not identical with our brains, but at the most with some parts of them. But even then we could not go on to claim that the parts of our brains with which we are identical generate our consciousness or our minds, as these parts are supposed to be identical with our consciousness or our minds. An identity-theory of mind and brain should not claim without further qualification that there is any sense in which the brain generates the mind. This is precisely why the actual traditional position of the identity-theory avoids the claim that the brain generates the mind. The combination of identity-theory and the claim that the brain generates the mind rather seems to be underlying some popular journalistic distortions of the actual views discussed in the philosophy of mind.

The real problem for both reduction and elimination generally is that they owe us an account of the structure of illusion; they owe as an account of phenomenalisation. Reduction fares slightly better in that it at least accepts that constraint, whereas elimination simply ignores this rejoinder by shrugging its shoulders. According to elimination, illusion does not even so much as exist; it is somehow nothing, at least nothing worth analysing, it is what the hoi polloi believe. Why even bother to eliminate the view that the sun turns around the earth once you know that it is false full stop; why bother explaining away the impression that there are mesoscopic ordinary objects if you know that they do not really exist?

On top of all the metaphysical exaggerations and overgeneralisations built into the ineffable view from (really) nowhere hinted at in the last paragraph, we must not forget that we are looking for a stance that allows us to think of the domain of all domains as existing within some sub-domain of itself. However, in the process of attempting to identify a viable position amounting to a relevant insight, we lost everything we were looking to account for. We are left with nothing to account for, as we eliminated all domains in one stroke. We are left with a form of the absolute One, which is an absolute manifold: all the super-elementary particles, but no concept around which to unite them, no domain of objects suitable for forming some discourse or other. Whatever else one might think of microphysicalism for independent reasons, it cannot be the result of accounting for the domain of all domains, as it cannot even account for a single domain. It gets rid of all domains and tries to state that there are only microphysical states, objects, processes, or events, without these being unified by the further fact that they form a domain. Eliminativist microphysicalism is not an option, as it results in claiming that nothing exists, for existence – so much was agreed upon – is not a property of objects, but of domains, and now we are left with no domains and accordingly with nothing that could be a candidate for existence.

So far we have seen how domain ontology must avoid two traps: The trap of the all-encompassing domain on the one hand and the trap of the most fundamental domain on the other hand, although both traps are ultimately the same. In a sense, these traps are the utmost vanishing points of two tendencies nicely identified by Graham Harman: overmining and undermining.[13] The domain overminer postulates an all-encompassing domain in order to account for the existence of all other domains and finds himself in paradox. The domain underminer wants to ground all domains in a most fundamental domain and finds himself in still further paradoxes. Both are unable to keep everything they wanted to explain in the first place in existence. The overminer is looking for an ultimate science and its ultimate domain of objects, but is unable to reach his goal. The underminer loses everything in the act of attempting to ground it.

Both are wrong because they assume either that there has to be something all-encompassing or something most fundamental. Of course, there are possible combinations of the two tendencies, but they all ultimately run into the conundrum created by Aristotle and anticipated by Plato in his discussion of the One in the *Parmenides* that inspired Plotinus and subsequent Neoplatonists from antiquity to the Renaissance.[14] They all believe in the One, the really big thing or the really big domain of which other domains are a part. Parmenides himself might be the culprit for this, as his idea of being as a sphere with no outside might well be the first expression of the view that there is a One in the form of a domain. Even though Parmenides also seems to argue that the One itself does not have parts, one might attempt to read this, rather than as the claim that it is not a thing suitable for having parts, as a domain simply unsuitable for having parts. This would make him an ontological rather than an ontic monist, a description more likely to account for the fact that he also held views about the make up of nature in terms of the then standard idea of elements.[15] As I said earlier, 'ontological monism' is the view that there is only one domain whereas 'ontic monism' is the view that there is only one object or one kind of object.

In this reading, Parmenides really invented the concept of the world, the idea of an all-encompassing immanence. Whatever exactly he was after, the ensuing history of Occidental metaphysics can legitimately be called world history in that it is based on developing the concept of the world, of the domain of all domains in various shapes.

Here Heidegger was certainly right when he spoke of 'The Age of World-Picture'.[16] This age is the veritable creation of the world out of nothing, as the world (the domain of all domains) is a mere figment of human imagination to which nothing could possibly correspond. It is an illusion with no content whatsoever, a nebula spread out over the human mind as we know it. My own view is metametaphysical nihilism, a version of elimination that leaves all other domains and their objects fully intact. I only claim that the existence of the world is an illusion, not that there are no other domains, let alone many objects.

What I have said about domains of objects so far in addition to the problems I just sketched hinges on the still vague notions of a domain and of objects. These notions are commonly used in many disciplines in addition to philosophy, and most of the time they slip into a theory almost unnoticed. Interestingly, in *The Logical Structure of the World*, Rudolf Carnap speaks about 'spheres of objects (*Gegenstandssphären*)' and also uses the metaphor of a region (*Gebiet*) to express the same idea.[17] He himself explicitly claims that there is ultimately only one such region, but grants that there are different ways of specifying it, though all of them follow his method of structural reduction.[18] Nelson Goodman, one of the most original readers of Carnap, inherited this notion and transformed it into a plurality of worlds and 'ways of world-making'.[19] Around the same time as Carnap, the idea of regions or domains of objects seems to be a standard presumption in German philosophy, and it can be found in Nicolai Hartmann, Husserl and Heidegger, who also suggested a domain ontology in his earliest books.

Be that as it may, the assumption is almost unarticulated and is apparently based on the old Aristotelian idea that domains of objects correspond to different disciplines. Yet, Carnap explicitly wants philosophy to be the grounding discipline insofar as he introduces a formal theory of objects, with whose basic idea I agree. Carnap understands objects as 'anything about which a statement can be made'.[20] From now on, let us restate this in the following form as the first version of a *formal theory of objects*. This theory has it that an object is anything that can become the content of a truth-apt thought. This is not at all to say that there are no objects if no one refers to them, but rather that had anyone capable of referring (and it need not be a human organism, just any system capable of referring) been around in any situation whatsoever, they could have referred to either something in the situation or to the situation itself.

The point I am making is not that being (object) and thought somehow are structurally correlated, but only that we can refer to objects. We can refer to every single object. Yet, as we will see in Chapter 7, we cannot refer to all objects at once, as this would amount to a world view, and world views are impossible in any sense of impossible. No one really holds a world view, as there is nothing to be viewed that could fall under the concept of 'the world'.

However, the concept of a domain is more problematic than the concept of an object. Traditionally it remains utterly unclear what individuates a domain. The most prominent attempt is still the Aristotelian idea that a domain is individuated in terms of disciplines: the domain of physical objects is the domain investigated by physics, the domain of social objects is the domain investigated by the social sciences, the domain of art is the domain investigated by art history, or its contemporary successors, and so on.

Yet, this threatens to implode into constructivism in the following sense. *Constructivism* evidently is the view that something is constructed, which usually means that it would not have existed had no discursive practice brought it into existence. Trivially, discursive practices themselves are constructed. They depend for their existence on themselves and are, therefore, the real candidates for a *causa sui*-structure. Now, all scientific disciplines are discursive practices and consequently they are all constructed. If all of this is true, then the domains are not maximally modally robust: they would not have been individuated had the discursive practices not individuated them.

But this is an extreme form of correlationism, for constructivism says that there would have been no domains had there been no discursive practices. Yet, if existence is tantamount to a domain not being empty, and if there were no domains before the advent of discursive practices, then nothing would even have existed had there been no discursive practices. This consequence is a necessary unpleasant consequence constructivists like Rorty or Niklas Luhmann regularly and sometimes reluctantly accepted, for they believed that they could be sceptics about the world in itself, which Luhmann explicitly equates with the unobservable One. Yet, this should not be considered a positive feature of constructivism, as it is not really a sceptical view, but rather a correlationist one. It claims that there really is a plurality of domains and therefore a whole array of objects existing in them, but that this array unfolds from nothingness as soon as discursive practices create themselves (by very spontaneous *autopoiesis* I suppose). If the plurality of domains is discourse-dependent, and if discourses are constructed, at best we wind up with an ineffable One as the origin of the multitude of domains. It does not matter if we take ourselves to have additional reasons to identify the ineffable One with super-elementary particles or with some historically lost origin from 'ancient European heritage', as Luhmann ironically calls it.

In post-Kantian philosophy, domain ontology is tied to a transcendental division of labour between objects and our reference to them. Even though this strand again has predecessors in ancient philosophy and resurfaces at various moments in later history, Kant certainly laid out the idea that referring to objects is not itself an object most explicitly. I call this idea 'transcendental asymmetry'. According to transcendental asymmetry, there is something essentially elusive about reference in that it can never itself become the object of reference.[21] On looking more closely, Kant and contemporary Kantians actually defend a variety of versions of transcendental asymmetry. It can be spelled out as an epistemological claim, as a semantic claim, or as a claim about mind and world. However, the lowest common denominator of all these readings is the idea that objects can only appear to truth-apt thought under conditions defined by truth-apt thought. Truth-apt thought settles its own truth-conditions from within, as it were, independently of what it is actually about. Thoughts determine their truth-conditions, but do not thereby determine their actual truth. What makes a thought true is the object or fact it happens to be about, and it cannot be anticipated *a priori* what that object or fact really is, which is why Kant generally rejects the idea of a material criterion of truth while clinging to a correspondence theory of truth.[22]

According to Kant the concepts we employ in truth-apt acts of thinking (in judgements) are horizons determining a range of things to be observed from their points of view. He spells this out in a remarkable passage that is widely ignored with the notable exception of the German philosopher Josef Simon, one of the most original contemporary Kantians.[23] In the passage I have in mind, Kant writes that one can

> regard every concept as a point, which, as the standpoint of an observer, has its horizon, i.e., a multiplicity of things that can be represented and surveyed, as it were, from it. Within this horizon a multiplicity of points must be able to be given to infinity, each of which in turn has its narrower field of view; i.e., every species contains subspecies in accordance with the principle of specification, and the logical horizon consists only of smaller horizons (subspecies), but not of points that have no domain (individuals).[24]

Now for Kant this structure of logical horizons is *a priori* in that it is not determined by the objects that happen to be observed when directing the apparatus at an independent reality, that is, a reality mostly consisting of non-intentional objects or rather spatio-temporal things, which for him are essentially incapable of thinking.

The essence of transcendental asymmetry is a very general form of internalism according to which domains of objects (logical horizons) are *constructed*, whereas the objects appearing within the domains usually are *encountered*. This is just what it means to be both a transcendental idealist and an empirical realist: if no one had been around, there would neither have been any horizons nor any appearances in the form of objects one can refer to with truth-apt thoughts, but there would still have been non-intentional objects (whose nature – according to Kant – we cannot sufficiently assess in order to *know* anything about them). Famously, Kant himself is ultimately not able to keep this distinction fixed, as the non-intentional objects collapse into the horizons. They are only effectively individuated by concepts whose logical form derives from the horizons, which is why the manifold of appearances in Kant's formulation often collapses into the lump of an essentially undifferentiated thing in itself. Hegel points this out pithily in the following passage, which is full of his typical enjoyment of perverse metaphors:

> Objectivity and stability derive solely from the categories; the realm of things in themselves is without categories; yet it is something for itself and for reflection. The only idea we can form of this realm is like that of the iron king in the fairy tale whom a human self-consciousness permeates with the veins of objectivity so that he can stand erect. But then formal transcendental idealism sucks these veins out of the king so that the upright shape collapses and becomes something in between form and lump, repulsive to look at. For the cognition of nature, without the veins injected into nature by self-consciousness, there remains nothing but sensation. In this way, then, the objectivity of the categories in experience and the necessity of these relations become once more something contingent and subjective.[25]

Contemporary versions of transcendental asymmetry of course are mostly trying to do without the distinction between appearances and things in themselves in that they stick to a formal distinction between the analytic and synthetic, between form and content, or between the normative and the natural. What all these views have in common is the idea that the distinction between truth-conditions and actual truths can be divided into two camps. These camps define their own truth-conditions in order to then have 'the world', as they say, confirm or disprove thinking in a process of trial and error.

If we grant the obvious, namely that there was a time when no

one referred to anything (Meillassoux'ancestrality), the very idea
of domain constructivism becomes incoherent, as we generally
need to make sense of objects being grouped in themselves: up
quarks would have been up quarks, the moon would have been the
moon, and the sun would have been the sun had we not grouped
them as we group them scientifically. Trivially, some of our
groupings are indeed constructed in the sense of merely optional
groupings: that the sun and the moon have a cultural significance,
the moon being related in many cultures to melancholia and in
others to ultimate beauty, or in general, the idea of a human or
even personal significance of celestial bodies is not a grouping we
ought to expect to be objective, that is to say, maximally modally
robust. But for very many contemporary facts it is just not hard
to tell whether they are maximally modally robust and therefore
anchored in ancestrality.

Every contemporary maximally modally robust fact, such as
the number of planets in our solar system, affords us a glimpse
into ancestrality, which also shows that the point drawn from
ancestrality ought not to be chronological.[26] There is no need for
a mathematical detour through set theory to vindicate our capacity to have truth-apt thoughts about facts that are not themselves
truth-apt thoughts, but relations between non-intentional objects.
We need not refer to the speculative power of our preferred mathematics to account for this, as the point is much more down to
earth: I know that the earth was not identical to the sun before
someone ever was around to notice that, unless it happens to
be the case that there was no point in the history of the universe
without referrers in it. This is very unlikely given what we know
about the universe, as it was impossible for anyone capable of
truth-apt thought to be around at the time of the Big Bang with
the irrelevant exception of God, because whatever one means
by 'God', she, he, or it was certainly not around and engaged in
thinking at the 'time' of the Big Bang. This is mere superstition and
not worth refuting. It is just a form of madness to believe this. It
needs therapy and not refutation, as it is a form of sceptical coun-
terfactual scenario with no support from actual insight, a relic of
the human past unfortunately still with us.

I reject transcendental asymmetry and the associated constructivism. The scientific division of labour is not as such arbitrary
and cannot be sustained if it is not directed at truth. Referring
to how things are in their domain is not generally constructing a

domain first and then locating things in the constructed domain. If it were, things would only begin existing with the advent of referrers, unless there was just one domain of objects in the first place that could then be investigated under different aspects. This makes it possible to claim (1) that there must be one domain, say the one only containing the super-elementary particles, and (2) that all other domains are constructed by us when we investigate the different aspects of these particles (or any other kind serving the function of unconstructed particulars).[27]

For this reason, we need to give up the general idea that there is an antecedent active (be it conscious or somehow unconscious) constitution of a domain of objects (utterly independent of the objects) to which the actual objects are then added after the fact of constitution, that is to say, empirically. Even if there were transcendental frames of reference, potentially distorting glasses or forms of intuition, they would themselves still be the objects of another constitution in order for them to exist. A pure constitution out of nothing is inconceivable, which is to say that there is no chance that there is a pure constitution. It is not even possible to claim that there might be pure constitution beyond our human imagination or human capacity of conceiving possibilities, as a pure constitution has to amount to a relation between some act of constitution and a domain thereby constituted. The act of constitution only exists as a relatum of this relation and, thus, exists in a domain encompassing both the constituted and the constitution. But where does this domain come from, as it cannot be in turn constituted by the act of constitution appearing within the domain?

This problem has been pointed out by Schelling and Hegel's objections to Kant in general and to Fichte in particular. Interestingly, later Fichte consequently gave up the idea of constitution and replaced it with the idea of a domain he called 'being', which gives rise to the relation between an act of constitution and a constituted domain of objects. However, this ultimately boils down to the introduction of an *ad hoc* regress blocker. In order to avoid the problem that every alleged act of constitution turns out to be constituted by some other act of constitution (so as to exist in a domain), Fichte blocked the regress by postulating the domain he calls 'being', which is just the traditional name for what I call 'the world'. But why introduce a non-constructible domain at the third-order level? Why so late? If we are forced to acknowledge a reality whose existence is completely independent of any construction of concepts, there is no reason to defer it to such a high level of reflection. If something is the case anyway, why would it consist in the construction of concepts or any other condition of our epistemic access to how things are? Even though this fact must be accounted for in some way or other, we need very good reasons to grant it such an extraordinary explanatory privilege.

The later Carnap notoriously introduced a distinction between internal and external questions that can be helpful here.[28] Internal questions are questions arising within some overall accepted framework needed in order to have scientific objectivity. Internal questions include: how many tables are there in my living room, what is DNA, how many moons does Jupiter have, and so on. Whether or not there are spatiotemporal things and not only our representations of them, on the contrary, is external. It cannot meaningfully be asked. One of the problems with this distinction is that it inherits transcendental asymmetry even though it changes its value. Why should any question be external? The trouble with the problem of the external world is not that it results from external questions, but that it is utterly ill-posed and simply rests on false assumptions. Carnap presents the problem as if it could be derived from some kind of *a priori* reasoning gone wild, but it cannot be derived, as it is just a confused impression of a problem. How can it be a problem to refer to a table with the thought that there is a table in front of me?

There are various strands of arguments that make it seem more difficult than it appears at first glance, but no argument ever reaches the generality required by the problem of the external world, namely a position from which we can withhold judgement about all possible references to how things are independently of how we take them to be. The main reason for the failure of the 'problem' of the external world is its assumption of an overall external world as the total object of knowledge divided into bits and pieces by different acts of knowing. That total object is then called 'the external world'. This object indeed does not exist outside of epistemological imagination. It is a product of fantasy, which is not to say that there are no spatiotemporal ancestral things. On the contrary, they belong to different fields that are not constituted by our reference to either the objects or the fields within which they appear. The things not necessarily referred to and the maximally modally robust facts in which they are embedded are not unified into a single domain we can call the external world. The point is that the fields cannot be unified into one big field to which we could then try to refer with a big singular thought about all of external reality. The notion of the external world is metaphysical poppycock, not because there are only representations, but because not all spatiotemporal ancestral things belong to the same domain, the world as it existed before we came onto the scene. The world has never existed, nor does it exist, nor will it ever exist. The world's existence is out of the question. It is not even an external question.

Notes

1. Cf. van Inwagen, *Metaphysics*, pp. 287–9; van Inwagen, 'Being, Existence and Ontological Commitment', in particular pp. 476–9.
2. Austin, *Sense and Sensibilia*, p. 68, footnote 1.
3. Aristotle, *Metaphysics*, 1003a21–b16.
4. Cf. Aristotle, *Physics*, Book II, chapter 2 (193b22–4b15): 'Now the mathematician, though he too treats of these things, nevertheless does not treat of them as the limits of a natural body; nor does he consider the attributes indicated as the attributes of such bodies. That is why he separates them; for in thought they are separable from motion, and it makes no difference, nor does any falsity result, if they are separated. The holders of the theory of Forms do the same, though they are not aware of it; for they separate the objects of natural science, which are less separable than those of mathematics. This becomes plain if one tries to state in each of the two cases the definitions of the things and of their attributes. Odd and even, straight and curved, and likewise number, line, and figure, do not involve motion; not so flesh and bone and man–*these* are defined like snub nose, not like curved.'
5. Aristotle, *Metaphysics*, 982a20–b10.
6. Cf. Kraus, *A Universe From Nothing*. Considerable public controversy on the issue was provoked when philosopher (and physicist) David Albert wrote a scathing review of the book in the *New York Times* article 'On the Origin of Everything: A Universe From Nothing by Lawrence M. Krauss' (23 March 2012). Lawrence Krauss responded in a similar vein in an interview on 23 April 2012 in the Atlantic where he expressed doubts about the relevance of philosophy in general and in particular the philosophy of science as a field. In a further article in the *New York Times* on 10 June 2012

entitled 'Physicists, Stop the Churlishness', philosopher Jim Holt defended the relevance of philosophy and the fruitful relations that can be had between philosophy and physics.

7. Aristotle, *Metaphysics*, 1003a24–33.

8. Cf. Gabriel, 'God's Transcendent Activity'.

9. Cf. Lewis, *Papers in Metaphysics and Epistemology*, p. 13: 'Properties carve reality at the joints–and everywhere else as well. If it's distinctions we want, too much structure is no better than none.' See also Sider, 'Ontological Realism'. The origin of the metaphor is Plato, *Phedrus*, 265c1–3, where Plato talks about κατ'εἴδη δύνασθαι διατέμνειν κατ'ἄρθρα ᾗ πέφυκεν. As a matter of fact, he does not talk about nature here at all. The idea in Plato is not to cut nature at its joints, but to cut the forms along their natural joints. Plato would certainly object against the identification of what there is with nature in the sense of what is always already there anyway regardless of any thinking activity. On this see Gabriel, *Skeptizismus und Idealismus in der Antike*, § 3.

10. Cf. Kant, *Critique of Pure Reason*, A 396, A 582/B 610, A 615/B 643.

11. A different concept currently under discussion is that of 'grounding'. For an overview see the papers in Schnieder and Correia, *Metaphysical Grounding*.

12. Cf., for instance, Metzinger, *Being No One*. Metzinger, on the one hand, wants to argue that no one ever had or was a self, but his argument is really that a self is always a phenomenal self, and that such a self is a process intransparent to itself (in his language, this is called transparency). In any event, at the most, Metzinger makes a case to the effect that a self differs from what some people might have thought a self was. Despite frequent references to Buddhism (what he refers to as 'system consciousness' in Metzinger, *Being No One*, p. 566), Metzinger does not even come close to the Buddhist view that we are really no one, as this view means that there is not even the illusion of a self. There is only the false belief that we are selves, but this does not amount to a stable illusion of a phenomenal self or an 'ego-tunnel' to use Metzinger's other metaphor. For more on this see Metzinger, *Ego-Tunnel*. Certainly, classical Buddhism does not rely on any claims about how the brain creates the illusion of a stable self or any such thing, as such metaphysics is precisely beside the very point that we ought to give the idea of identifying ourselves with anything (including the brain, which is an ordinary physical thing like a liver or a mountain).

13. Harman, 'On the Undermining of Objects', pp. 21–40.
14. Cf. Gabriel, *Skeptizismus und Idealismus in der Antike*, § 3.
15. For an interesting reading along those lines see Thanassas, *Parmenides, Cosmos, and Being*, p. 109.
16. Heidegger, 'The Age of World Picture', pp. 115–54.
17. See Carnap, *Logical Structure of the World*, § 42, p. 70: 'Following an occasionally used terminology, one could speak of the different "modes of being" of the objects of different object spheres.' See also § 162, p. 260: '[W]e must not overlook the fact that the objects on the different levels belong to different object spheres (§§ 41, 29) and thus belong to logically totally separate and independent domains.' See also § 23, pp. 39f.; § 29, pp. 51f.; § 41, pp. 69f.
18. For an updated version of this kind of structuralism see, of course, Chalmers, *Constructing the World*.
19. Cf. Goodman, *The Structure of Appearance* and Goodman, *Ways of Worldmaking*.
20. Carnap, *Logical Structure of the World*, p. 5: 'The word object is here always used in its widest sense, namely, for anything about which a statement can be made.'
21. This is an idea prominently defended by contemporary Kantians like John McDowell, who makes use of an updated version of this point when he says that there is no 'sideways-on point of view' on the relation between a particular act of referring (a thinking) and the object of reference. See, for instance, McDowell, 'Intentionality as a Relation'.
22. Cf. Kant, *Critique of Pure Reason*, A58–9/B 83: '[A] general criterion of truth would be that which was valid of all cognitions without any distinction among their objects. But it is clear that since with such a criterion one abstracts from all content of cognition (relation to its object), yet truth concerns precisely this content, it would be completely impossible and absurd to ask for a mark of the truth of this content of cognition, and thus it is clear that a sufficient and yet at the same time general sign of truth cannot possibly be provided. Since above we have called the content of a cognition its matter, one must therefore say that no general sign of the truth of the matter of cognition can be demanded, because it is self-contradictory.' And in addition A58/B82: 'The nominal definition of truth, namely that it is the agreement of cognition with its object, is here granted and presupposed; but one demands to know what is the general and certain criterion of the truth of any cognition.'
23. See Simon, *Kant*. See also Simon, *Wahrheit als Freiheit*.

24. Kant, *Critique of Pure Reason*, A 658/B 686: '... jeden Begriff als einen Punkt ansehen, der, als der Standpunkt eines Zuschauers, seinen Horizont hat, d.i. eine Menge von Dingen, die aus demselben können vorgestellet und gleichsam überschauet werden. Innerhalb diesem Horizonte muß eine Menge von Punkten ins Unendliche angegeben werden können, deren jeder wiederum seinen engeren Gesichtskreis hat; d. i. jede Art enthält Unterarten, nach dem Prinzip der Spezifikation, und der logische Horizont besteht nur aus kleineren Horizonten (Unterarten), nicht aber aus Punkten, die keinen Umfang haben (Individuen).'
25. Hegel, *Faith and Knowledge*, p. 77. For an interpretation of this see Gabriel, *Transcendental* Ontology, pp. 34–48.
26. This is Heidegger's objection against the idea that objectivity is grounded in the fact that the earth is not necessarily inhabited by referees, which follows from the fact that for a long time it was not inhabited. See Heidegger, *Das Argument gegen den Brauch*.
27. Umrao Sethi made me aware of this relation between ontological monism and constructivism. It seems that ontological monism serves the function of grounding the otherwise incoherent idea of an overall constructivism by helping itself to one relevant exemption to the rule that motivates constructivism in the first place.
28. Carnap, 'Empiricism, Semantics and Ontology'.

6

Fields and the Meaning of Existence

So far I have discussed two ways of making sense of the idea that existence is a domain-property: set-theoretical ontology and traditional domain ontology. However, it transpired that both are problematic. Sets are not phenomenologically fine-grained enough: if I know that I am holding a glass of wine in my right hand, I only accidentally gain access to the set of the fingers of my left hand. What exists, the glass of wine in my left hand, is not identical with its set-theoretical representation. The latter actually distorts the glass of wine in my left hand; it misrepresents it. In some contexts, mathematical abstraction is needed, but there is no good reason to generalise this local fact.

Traditional domain ontology fails because it is premised on transcendental asymmetry, which is an untenable idea. Set-theoretical and traditional domain ontology both tend to over-generalise (to the extent to which they accept the existence of an all-encompassing domain) and to accept constructivism for the transcendental constitution. Yet, the very plurality of domains cannot be constructed. There really are many domains of objects corresponding to the right division of scientific labour whether we have already reached it or not. The individuation of domains cannot hinge on the existence of our disciplines.

My use of the concept of a field is designed to replace the concept of a domain in ontology. Fields are generally unconstructed, and their force is felt by the objects entering them. An electric field, for instance, can be detected by some bodies entering it, and we can detect it by using things manifesting certain properties when inter-acting with the field. The field provides objective structures and interacts with the objects appearing within it. It is already there, and objects can pass through it and change its properties. Fields are not horizons or perspectives; they are not epistemological entities or objects introduced to explain how we can know how things are. They are an essential part of how things are in that without fields, nothing could exist.

To put some more cards on the table, I understand existence to be the fact that some object or objects appear in a field of sense. For something to exist is for it to appear in a field. I could have said 'belong to' instead of 'appear'. My worry with this is that belonging is associated with set-theoretical ontology. To belong to a set is only one way of appearing in a field of sense. The notion of 'appearance' is just the stand in for whatever it is in each case for something to be in a field of sense. For physical objects to appear in the field of sense of the universe is for them to be physical, where this might be defined in terms of what can ideally be observed or claimed to exist by some idealised future physicist. For unicorns to appear in the colouring book *Unicorns are Jerks* is for them to be associated with our standard fantasy of unicorns. If there happen to be unicorns on some far away planet, then for them to appear in a field of sense would be for them to appear in the field of sense studied by zoology, which makes them subject to laws very different from the ones characteristic of fairy tales and dreams. For democratic elections to appear in a field of sense is for them to take place in the context of constitutions and institutions. Neither of those is studied by physics or by the science of dreams, the history of fairy tales or zoology. 'Appearance in a field of sense' is just a technical version of 'being in a context'.

Given that generally a lot of fields are already laid out, for something to exist is generally for it to be part of how things are in a maximally modally robust sense. However, this is not to say that all objects are involved in maximally modally robust facts. Some objects are constructed, at the very least in the undemanding sense that they are involved in facts produced by human beings, such as trivially a lot of truths about human beings. Just as mental states are trivially mind-dependent in the sense that no one would have had them had there been no mind (whatever 'mind' ultimately refers to), some facts are produced by us. It is, thus, neither true that all objects are constructed nor that no object is constructed. There are constructed and non-constructed objects. For all we know right now, generally facts are unconstructed. However, there might be all sorts of reasons for revising this picture. It all depends on how we individuate the relevant facts and how we count them. If it turned out that life is an incredibly widespread phenomenon not even coming very late in the development of our universe, we might have reasons to think of facts as generally constructed. Or imagine the multiverse-hypothesis is true. In addition, imagine there has never been an overall multiverse situation (call it a hyperverse) without any fact-producing intelligent beings in it. In this case, there would be even less reason to ontologically privilege utterly inanimate facts, or rather things, over occurring thoughts and fact constructing activities.

I am not saying that this is the case, as I see no reason to privilege any particular kind of fact or object over others from the standpoint of ontology. Given that the no-world-view entails that there is no particular way everything generally or universally is (as that way would be the world), it is also not exactly true that everything generally is constructed or unconstructed. In other words, some fields are indeed domains of objects and some other fields are indeed sets. Yet, the concept of a field of sense is more neutral with respect to the manifold natures of what exists than the concepts of domains and sets. It allows for domain-like structures (in the plural) to be laid out in advance to any theory-decision or ontological commitment. It prioritises truths (and therefore facts) over what we believe (and therefore commit to) about them. What matters are the facts, and our constructions of them only matter to the degree to which they are in turn embedded in facts.

This even holds of illusions and false thoughts. If I wrongly believe that it is raining in Los Angeles while I am typing this sentence, it is a fact about me that I believe this. It is thus true that my belief is false. My belief is objectively false; we can investigate the origin of my error and in one way or other detect it. Even if for some contingent reason we will never find out what led me to my false belief, we know that my false belief has a structure and this structure consists in its being embedded in some set of facts or other.

Now, as I will argue in more detail in the next chapter, if there is anything whatsoever, there are at least indefinitely many fields. The basic argument goes roughly like this: if something exists, it has to appear in a field, which entails that there is a field. For this field to exist, there has to be another field within which it appears, and so on infinitely. If there only were one kind of field, there would be an all-encompassing field, namely the universal kind. But this universal kind cannot exist (as it would be identical with the world, which cannot exist). Therefore, there has to be a plurality of kinds of fields. To put it paradoxically: if overall or total reality existed, it would consist of indefinitely many regions that differ in kind and not just in location. If it existed, overall reality would be a mesh of meshes indefinitely spreading out in every possible direction in logical space: everything conceivable would be the case in some field or other. But that picture suggests an overall unification where there really is none.

I said that the concept of a field is more neutral than the concepts of domains and sets. I do not intend to claim that it is more general than the other two concepts, because I am not committed to the idea that the relation between different fields generally is one of one field falling under another field. This is a decisive difference between the ontology of fields of sense and a possible Fregean alternative that could be devised by radically objectifying Fregean concepts. Objects fall under concepts (they satisfy functions). But not all fields that appear in other fields are objects falling under a concept. For example, the coffee in my mug is itself a field (the coffee) appearing in another field (my mug), which is not to say that every object is its own field. I am just saying that the coffee is an object insofar as it appears in the mug and a field insofar as many objects (of a chemically describable nature, say) appear within the coffee. They appear in the coffee independent of the fact that the coffee appears in the mug. The mug itself appears in some field or other, for instance in my room, or in San Francisco. Objects appear in indefinitely many fields of sense at the same time. Given this, the coffee does not thereby fall under the concept ... *is a mug*. Appearing-in (existence) is not generally identical with falling-under-a-concept. Another perhaps more perspicuous example that will continue to play a role in my account is that of the manifold hands. My left hand is both a hand and an arrangement of atoms. It is also an arrangement of cells, an object with a certain significance, and could become an artwork if some famous artist, say, decided to tattoo it with one of his designs. As an arrangement of cells and as an artwork, my left hand is in different fields.

Another way of looking at this is through reversible figures, such as Wittgenstein's famous duck-rabbit. What I am effectively saying is that there really is both a duck and a rabbit. Yet, the duck and rabbit are different fields. In the duck-field there is a beak, whereas in the rabbit-field there are rabbit ears. On the contrary, there are neither rabbit ears in the duck-field nor is there a beak in the rabbit-field. We can also look at the black ink on white paper in order to explain how our brain reacts to certain drawings by going back and forth between a duck- and a rabbit-field. Yet, this only adds a third figure, the black-ink-on-white-paper-field. All these fields equally exist and there consequently is no ontological reason to privilege any of the fields over any other. As I will argue in the next chapter, it is a consequence of the no-world-view that there is no overall way of individuating fields. There is no categorical, most general notion of fields with an associated notion of overall, categorical or most general appearance. It is not the case that all fields have something in common beyond the function they serve insofar as something appears within them.

The contrast I have in mind here is that of *ontology* and *metaphysics*. From a metaphysical point of view there should be some particular feature that all fields have in common that makes it the case that something appears within them and that differentiates fields from all other objects. From an ontological point of view, the concept of fields is introduced in order to serve the traditional function of sets and domains with the difference that fields do not inherit the metaphysical background assumptions of either set-theoretical or domain ontology. To this extent fields are already conceptually individuated by the theoretical role they play in ontology. They are further individuated by being fields of *sense*, where the idea is that each field is delineated by objective modes of presentation. We can make it explicit by looking for norms or laws that have to be met by objects in order for them to stand in the relation of appearing in the field. This only gives us a very restricted number of *a priori* restrictions on fieldhood, such as that there can be no all-encompassing field, which rules out many prevalent metaphysical assumptions. If we want to substantiate the often vague assumption of naturalism (that everything is natural and that nothing is super-natural) by claiming that there is just one world (the universe, the cosmos, material reality as a whole) we will need clearly to distinguish this from the view that there is only one field of sense.

Of course, there might be all sorts of different reasons to privilege some of the fields for some explanations. When explaining the neurobiology behind our capacity to react to reversible figures by representing them as reversible figures we will privilege the black ink on white paper over the rabbit because we do not want to say that there is a rabbit that can both be seen as black ink on white paper and as a duck, and that our brain turns the rabbit into black ink on white paper under certain conditions. Evidently, there is some sense we can attach to the aforementioned explanation, but it certainly is not the sense in which there is a rabbit our brain interprets as black ink on white paper. The rabbit in the neurobiological explanation is always the rabbit as projected onto black ink on white paper.

But if the rabbit is drawn in such a way that it is part of some story (*Alice in Wonderland* or *Inland Empire*), there are truths about the rabbit that do not pertain to neurobiology or to black ink on white paper. In this case we would have good reasons to privilege the rabbit over the duck and the black ink on white paper and tell the relevant stories about the rabbit. Ontologically, the rabbit, the duck and the black ink on white paper are all equal; they all equally exist.

The point is that fields, domains and sets sometimes relate to each other more like rabbit, duck and black ink on white paper than like a concept and an object falling under it. Fields are just not generally concepts: even though a lot of concepts are fields, not all fields are concepts.

The relation of falling under a concept is ontologically overrated and the reason for this derives from the tradition of thinking of being or existence as disclosed to some sort of most basic categorical judgement, thought, or proposition (*logos*). That tradition is as old as Plato and has prominently been renewed by Kant. The idea is that our access to what exists is fundamentally constructed by way of adding singular demonstrative thoughts, such as 'This is an F', 'This other thing is a G', and so on, to our belief system. This is not only epistemologically misleading, but causes problems often discussed under the heading of foundationalism. What is more problematic about it is that it is used as a stepping-stone to ontology. Here I agree with Kant, who distinguished between epistemology and ontology: whatever holds good of our access to how things really are is not necessarily the most general frame for all things regardless of our access. If we (human beings) somehow needed to grasp things piecemeal in terms of building up a belief system from singular demonstrative thoughts, this would not necessarily tell us something about the things we thereby grasp beyond the fact that we can so grasp them. This is the rationale behind the Kantian distinction between appearances and things in themselves.

Fields do a better job in ontology than domains. They explain what domains are supposed to explain, namely how anything can exist given that existence is not a proper property, without inclining in advance in the direction of constructivism or anti-realism. Constructivism and anti-realism are more generally motivated by analyses of truth-conditions for some paradigmatically simple forms of propositional thought about what there is. But if we give up the idea that our projected truth-conditions generally matter for how things are, we might grant some terrain to anti-realism, but never give up a realist conception of fields and accordingly of facts.

Let us call the relation between an object and a field 'appearing'. Objects appear in fields of sense. This relation differs from the relation of falling under a concept in that it is again more neutral. Some objects fall under concepts, no doubt. However, there are many objects that will never fall under concepts, objects for which we will never have a concept. The concept

(C#) ... is an object that will never fall under any concept

is defective for the simple reason that it can never serve the actual function of concepts, namely to make an object available to truth-apt thought. If anything satisfies the formal concept function (C#), it paradoxically follows that it does not satisfy it. Yet, from a logical point of view, (C#) is just another concept with interesting features. For instance, it is not defective when used to express that there are some objects that will never fall under any concept as long as we do not individuate those objects by having them fall under some other concept. Imagine O to be an object that will never fall under any concept. If all we can know about O is that it satisfies (C#), O is not individuated. It remains a generic object, an anything, any thing that will never fall under any concept. O is some object, but we do not know which one. It therefore slips away from our attempts to grasp it with recourse to (C#), as does any other object satisfying (C#). All objects that will never fall under any concept together make up some kind of semantic lump, an undifferentiated mass we cannot differentiate into parts. Arguably, this corresponds to the traditional concept of the unknowable, transcendent One: it is not a determinate object of thought, and it certainly is not God or any other object worthy of praise, awe and wonder, but rather the undifferentiated lump of objects never referred to and only accessible through paradoxes such as those incorporated by (C#).

But what about the concept __ *is an object*? Does O not fall under that concept by satisfying (C#)? Here I make use of an argument one can find in Husserl's *Formal and Transcendental Logic*, an argument probably also to be found in Kant's distinction between these two disciplines. Husserl there argues that our notion of an object as such, a *Gegenstand überhaupt*, is the result of an abstraction from specific objects belonging to different domains. He there even speaks of 'fields', 'regions of objects (*Gegenstandsgebiete*)', 'field of objects (*Gegenstandsfeld*)' and 'field of sense (*Sinnesfeld*)'.[1] In this context, he even considers the possibility that set theory might be a formal ontology in the sense of an a priori theory of objects (*apriorische Gegenstandslehre*).[2] However, his major argument is that in order for the very concept of objects as such or in general to satisfy the restrictions necessary for it to be a concept we can articulate coherently, criteria of 'Sinn', that is, of meaningful articulation have to be met. But our grasp of those conditions or criteria is tied to our practices of judging things to be so and so, where these practices are not formal but related to actually given objects and things. He points out that we have no specific idea how we could extend our actual given criteria of meaningfulness to all objects as such on the basis of a purely logical extension of our criteria. According to Husserl, all our regimented logical vocabulary is only meaningful to us at all because it is usually related to our actual practices of judgement from which many distinctions are borrowed, such as the distinction between a predicate and what the predicate applies to.[3]

Let me give you an example of what I take Husserl to be hinting at. In S5 in modal logic, the following inference from necessity to possibility is valid:

(NP) $\Diamond\Box p \rightarrow \Box p$.

The intuitive reasoning behind this can be summarised as follows. If it is possible that p is necessarily true, there is at least one world in which it is actually true that p is necessarily true. Yet, if there is any world in which it is true that p is true in all possible worlds, then it is true in *all* possible worlds. Now, on one interpretation, however, (NP) is an instance of the evidently inacceptable modal statement

$(NP^\#)\ \Diamond p \to p.$

If p is possibly true, there is a world in which it is true, but this does not entail that it is true in the world of the asserter of $(NP^\#)$. In any event, there are interpretations of $(NP^\#)$ that turn it into the absurdity that for anything that is possibly true it is true that it is actually true. Before we can fully settle the coherence of any modal logical system (or any other formal system for that matter), we need an independent grip on the meaningfulness of the symbols. We cannot first define our actual concepts of 'necessity' and 'possibility' and then regiment them in a formal system in order to then interpret our regimented conclusions by bringing in elements of the original unregimented concepts that we eliminated in the course of regimentation. This would amount to a form of equivocation. Any actual use of a formal system within philosophical argumentation requires an independent grasp of conditions of meaningfulness in order to avoid equivocations and mere nonsense. Independent of an articulated relationship between, say, '□' and 'it is necessary that __' we can have no idea what '□' might mean. This is why Husserl comes to the conclusion that it is an illusion that our formal logical vocabulary in any of its forms provides us with a metaphysical insight into the range of the concept __ *is an object (as such)*. As he puts it: '[t]he theory of sets and the theory of cardinal numbers relate to the empty universe, *any object whatever* or *anything whatever*'.[4] This is why – without further ado – we cannot base our grasp of

$(C^\#)$ __ is an object that will never fall under any concept.

on our grasp of

(C) __ is an object.

We have no general or generally accepted concept (C) independent of our grasp of specific (kinds of) objects. My conclusion is that 'objecthood' is a functional concept, that is, the concept of whatever appears in a field of sense, where this relation is defined by the senses by which a field is constituted. Again, here I replace 'domain' with 'field' in order to flag the differences between traditional domain ontology and the corrected view of it I am presenting here.

We can now use the following as our definition existence: *Existence is appearing in a field of sense.* To exist is to objectively appear in a field of sense, where the relation of appearing is in no way generally restricted by any local human-all-too-human conditions of grasping it. Appearing is fairly inhuman. What appears comes forth; it stands apart from a certain background. This is what both the etymology of 'appearance' and 'existence' suggest. I am not arguing that we cannot escape the roots of our words or that they somehow determine the essence of things, but only that appearance and existence in many languages refer to the coming forth or standing out of objects against a certain background. The Latin 'existere' quite literally means 'to stand forth' and it also just means 'to appear', 'to enter the scene'.

Jonathan Barnes has rightly pointed out that many expressions for 'existence' are locative in nature.[5] Let me just list a few examples from languages I am familiar with: Dasein, existence (Existenz, existência, and so on), il y'a, c'è and last but not least (to avoid Eurocentricism): 存在 (cúnzài), where 'cún' by itself means 'to contain' and 'zài' means 'it, at, on'. 'cúnzài' is also used in the Chinese translation of 'existentialism'. However, the word comes later in the history of the Chinese language, yet its age old counterpart 有 (you) also is familiar in that it means 'to have' as in the French *il y'a*. As Heidegger in particular pointed out, the Greek word φύσις is close to the concept of existence. Originally it just means the coming forth independently of our grasp or manipulation of that which thus comes forth.[6]

The defining claim of the ontology of fields of sense is that to exist is to appear in a field of sense.[7] A field here is the background of what exists, what stands out from the field. This idea also underlies domain ontologies in general. Yet, as I emphasised in the last two chapters, traditionally, from Aristotle at least to Carnap, domains of objects are regions of discourse delineated by different methods associated with disciplines and, therefore, need not correspond to maximally modally robust joints in nature. Nature itself is undivided into regions; the regions only come into play with our discursive distinctions. However, as will become particularly salient from the next chapter onwards, if nature were undivided it could not even exist. The idea of some all-encompassing undivided flat primordial domain of non-intentional, inanimate and maximally modally robust elements, objects, or rather things, is ontologically misguided. Reality or the world, had they existed in anything even so much as approaching a *singulare tantum*, would still have been divided into fields and not just into objects always already falling under the concepts necessary to individuate them as elements, objects, or rather things.

If anything exists whatsoever, if there is something rather than nothing, there is a plurality of fields of sense. If there is even one single object, in order for the object to exist it has to appear in a field of sense, stand forth from some background or other, and that means that there has to be a background, the field. Yet, for the field to exist in its own right it has to appear in another field. Fields cannot be the type of thing that can contain objects without being contained themselves, as they have to exist in order to contain anything. But if 'existence' means 'being contained' (in the sense of 'appearing in a field of sense'), there has to be some field or other for any given field in which it appears.

We can now introduce another important manoeuvre, namely the *functional concept of objecthood*. According to this concept, objects fulfil the function of appearing in a field of sense. To be an object is not to have a specific nature such as the specific nature to be a thing, where a 'thing' is a spatiotemporal material physical object like a car or a star. What defines an object is not the fact that it appears in a specific field, such as the universe, but rather that it appears in some field or other. The beer I did not have yesterday but fantasised about is as much an object as the beer I had the other day, even though the former is not a thing, whereas the latter was. For something to exist is for it to be an object in a field. 'To exist', 'to be an object', and 'to appear in a field of sense' are ontological synonyms; they all refer to the same fact. Every field, therefore, is also an object insofar as it exists. Field is a functional concept too: it serves the function of designating the background from which an object stands forth. Fields ground objects, and they are themselves grounded in other fields, where the 'grounding' metaphor traditionally serves the function of what I call 'appearance'.

Insofar as fields are grounded, they are objects, and insofar as they ground, they are fields. Without intending to spell this out exegetically here, it might be illuminating to point out that this idea derives from Schelling's *Freedom Essay*.[8] The book actually bears the title *On the Essence of Human Freedom and Objects Related to it*. As the title says, the book is not primarily about human freedom, but about its essence. At a famous juncture of the text, Schelling introduces a distinction between 'essence, insofar as it exists' and 'essence, insofar as it is the ground of existence', where the German word for essence, 'Wesen', very unfortunately is often translated into English as 'being', obscuring the relation between this distinction and the project laid out in the book.[9] Essence, insofar as it is ground, is what I call 'fields of sense' and 'essence, insofar as it exists' is what I call 'objects'. Schelling himself believes that he can in turn ground the distinction in the neutral and empty essence he calls 'the unground (Ungrund)', which I give up in favour of the indefinite and ungrounded proliferation of fields individuated by their sense. Yet, it might be possible to read Schelling in a similar vein, that is, if it is possible to read his concept of the 'unground' as a commitment to ultimately ungrounded appearances. For in my view, it is indeed appearances all the way down, even though this again is a misleading way of putting it, as it suggests that there is one way, the way down, and that this way can be completed, that there is some way to go *all* the way down.

Notice that I am not working with the contrast between appearance and reality, and that I am consequently not claiming that there are only appearances and no reality. Appearances are as real as it gets. Right now my computer appears in the field of sense of my living room, and it thus exists. It would have appeared in my living room had I today not appeared in it. Anybody can come and see it. Right now all sorts of events appear in all sorts of regions in the universe that no one will ever observe or even be in a position to observe, which does not mean that these events are less real than my computer. On the contrary, they can be quite real, such as a large-scale, forever-unobserved supernova hidden from our view by some factor or other.

The classical general distinction between appearance and reality and the associated general distinction between fiction and reality result from metaphysical overgeneralisation. They pertain to metaphysics and not to ontology. Ontology need not and should not be committed to the idea that to exist is to really exist, where the adverb 'really' is designed to emphasise that something is not fictional or not a mere appearance. It is tempting to say that the content of an illusion, such as a Fata Morgana, does not really exist: it only looks like water on the road, but there really is no water on the road. Yet, at the same time, it is legitimate to say that there is water in the Fata Morgana. For instance, someone who has never experienced a Fata Morgana might wonder whether there are Fata Morganas when it looks like there is blood on the road rather than water. In this case, we could reassure that person that there is no blood in Fata Morganas, but only water.

The reality/appearance distinction is orthogonal to the existence/non-existence distinction. First of all, appearances in the usual sense exist (by appearing in the usual sense and, thus, by 'appearing in the field of sense of the appearances'). And second, they have content by which they are individuated. Appearances usually are to the effect that p. It appears that there is water on the road. The content exists as an individuating part of the appearance. The water on the road exists in the Fata Morgana, but it does not exist on the road. In this sense, there is no water on the road, even though there is water in the Fata Morgana. The ontological relation of being-in (of bein') is not always transitive, which is no surprise given that there cannot be an overall sense of being-in, no most general form of bein'. From an ontological point of view, there is no reason to privilege facts about the road over facts about the Fata Morgana. That the Fata Morgana involves water and the road does not is a fact, indeed. But this fact does not entail that nothing generally exists in Fata Morganas. This would deprive appearances of their content and thereby of their individuation. All appearances would merge into an undifferentiated illusion-lump if nothing existed within them.

Similar truths hold about fiction. It is enough to point out that the reality/fiction distinction is orthogonal to the existence/non-existence distinction, as there is embedded fiction. Instead of giving yet another account of the dagger in *Macbeth*, let us consider *Faust* for once. In the first part of the tragedy, there is a scene called *Witches' Kitchen*. In this scene, the witch hands Faust a magic potion that makes him fall in love with women in general. From now on, he will project an archetypical ideal type onto all women he meets and will fall in love with the first woman he encounters. As Mephisto says,

> With that elixir coursing through him,
> Soon any woman will be Helen to him.[10]

Faust, in other words, suffers from a mild form of hallucination in that he will project a mirage of the ideal woman, of the One, onto the first female he meets (Gretchen). The object of this encounter does not matter. Later in the tragedy, in *Walpurgis Night*, a lot of the events Faust is confronted with are hallucinations, and it is not quite clear what is fiction and what is reality within the fictional world; what is hallucinated and what is the real causal trigger of the hallucination in each instance. The situation, of course, gets more complicated with *Faust II*, where Faust travels through the ages, from antiquity through the Middle Ages to some utopian future in the end of the tragedy. The point is that we can draw a distinction between reality and fiction and apply it to the fictional world. Part of what we disagree about in the interpretation of a narrative work of art is which events that are supposed to take place within the so-called fictional world are fictional and which are real.

Evidently, embedded fiction plays an important role in many works of art. It is one of the central manoeuvres in Proust's *In Search of Lost Time*. For the purposes of ontological illustration, a simple example suffices to make the point. Within the world of the novel, there is an artist by the name of Elstir who never existed as a painter in nineteenth-century Paris, but who plays an important role in the book. Some of his paintings are described in detail by the narrator, so that we are in the situation of reading a description of a painting that never existed outside of that description in our world. Contrary to Elstir, Monet, whose paintings also play a role in the book, exists in our world in addition to the world of the book. Within the fictional world, there are paintings we deem real and others we deem fictional. However, within the fictional world, they are as real as Monet is in our world.

Another prominent example of dealing with embedded fiction is Thomas Mann's *Death in Venice*. Evidently, the Venice in the title refers to Venice, the city in Italy. Neither Venice nor Munich (another important place in the book) is a fictional city. Rather, some of the essential properties of both cities are nicely brought out by the work of art, and being acquainted with *Death in Venice* is an integral part of knowing Venice and Munich. The novel is part of the history of the places now, just as Picasso's famous painting of Gertrude Stein became an essential aspect of Gertrude Stein. Legend has it that Stein told Picasso that the painting did not look like her, to which he responded: 'It will.'

Within *Death in Venice*, Gustav von Aschenbach regularly hallucinates, but he does not hallucinate that he is in the English Gardens when he hallucinates. At the beginning of the novel

Gustav von Aschenbach really is in the English Gardens. This sense of reality is underlined by the detailed description of the landscape and architecture in the garden with which the novel begins. Suddenly Gustav von Aschenbach is said to notice a

> ... figure in the portico above the two apocalyptic beasts guarding the staircase, and something slightly out of the ordinary in the figure's appearance gave his thoughts an entirely new turn. Whether the man had emerged from the chapel's inner sanctum through the bronze gate or mounted the steps unobtrusively from outside was uncertain. Without giving the matter much thought, Aschenbach inclined towards the first hypothesis. The man – of medium height, thin, beardless, and strikingly snub-nosed – was the red-haired type and had its milky, freckled pigmentation. He was clearly not of Bavarian stock and, if nothing else, the broad, straight-brimmed bast hat covering his head lent him a distinctly foreign, exotic air.[11]

The contrast here is between the English Gardens and the suddenly appearing man who is the harbinger of von Aschenbach's later confusion and madness. Reality and fiction are opposed within the realm of fiction. There are indefinitely many other examples of embedded fiction from literature and also from film (just think of the TV-genre of mockumentaries, paradigmatically exemplified by the British *Office*). The upshot is that the reality/fiction distinction is functional and not substantial in the sense that *prima facie* there is no need to draw an overall metaphysical distinction between reality in a substantial sense and fiction as a separate form of discourse-generated mock reality. Heavy revisionary metaphysical argumentation is needed to make sense of the idea that there is a single, all-encompassing reality underlying all appearances and generating fictional discourse as one unified block opposed to another unified block called reality. It is not the case that there is no distinction between fiction and reality or between appearance and reality more broadly, but that distinction equally well applies to embedded fiction or to the content of many kinds of illusions. Thus, appearance and reality do not make up two worlds or two overall domains; they are functional concepts that apply within different kinds of worlds, or rather fields, to use my own terminology.

From an ontological point of view, no arguments via the appearance/reality distinction are necessary, as the answer to the question of what existence means does not at all hinge on the distinction between real existence and some other form of existence. The question of whether something *really* exists might turn out to be meaningful in various contexts, but there is no meaningful overall question regarding the status of reality in its opposition to appearance, and most certainly not in the form of profound physical reality and its sensory distortion.

Forms or modes of existence are equally ruled out as ontological options. It is not the case that fictional entities exist in a different mode from the mug on my table or that social entities such as institutions have a different form of existence than molecules. There are no modes of existence, but only different fields of sense and objects appearing in them. Having said that, I grant that there are different forms of appearing in the sense that it is different for a mug to appear on my coffee table than for a mug to appear in a poem. The mug I think about when I go into the kitchen to fetch it first and foremost exists in my plan to fetch it, and it happens to also exist in my kitchen, which is why the two fields of sense of my plan to fetch the mug and of the kitchen merge as soon as I successfully grab the mug.

The inherited ontologies of modes of existence are not sufficiently clear about what the expression 'modes of existence' really denotes. In our days modes of existence talk is prominently used by Bruno Latour and John Searle in order to make sense of the idea that facts and accordingly objects can be generated in different ways: institutions differ from mountains by their modes of existence. Given that Latour's general and Searle's more specific mode of existence ontologies are prominent alternative attempts to allow for multiple forms of existence, it is important to distinguish the outlines of their views from the position defended here.

Latour and Searle make very different use of the basic idea of modes of existence. Yet, they do not dedicate much attention to the concept of a 'mode of existence' itself, and I believe that the concept is ultimately not very useful, as modes are traditionally thought of as adverbial qualifiers. Having said that, the phenomenon of a construction of social reality they set out to explain can be reframed in the language of a domain-ontology.

Against talk of modes of existence we need to object first of all that existence is not an activity. To repeat Austin again: 'The word is a verb, but it does not describe something that things do all the time, like breathing, only quieter – ticking over, as it were, in a metaphysical sort of way.'[12] Objects do not exist in different modes, if that means in different ways. My table does not exist material-ly or physical-ly, whereas the restaurant in my dinner plans for tonight exists (in this respect) imaginari-ly, and all institutions in one way or other exist imaginari-ly. Adverbial ontologies rest on too many unclear assumptions. Therefore, one could try to articulate the idea of modes of existence in a domain ontology, but this will lead to the accounts discussed so far and does not add anything to ontology. 'Modes', then, are either sets, domains, fields, or whatever else could do a better job according to the constraints discovered and defended up to this point in this book.

Let us take a brief look at Searle's way of making use of the concept of 'modes of existence'. What particularly interests me is his way of individuating the modes. Searle individuates modes of existence by associating them with a logical form. His most explicit account of modes of existence is found in his social ontology. There, his famous idea is that social objects, such as institutions, are 'created and maintained' by activities that have the same logical form as declarative speech acts.[13] In other words, social objects are produced by activities bringing about and accepting their existence. Social objects are dependent on accept-ance in the weak sense of an attitude of awareness first creating them and then keeping them in existence. The institution of the city of London is created and maintained by people's accepting awareness of London's existence. As I objected elsewhere, Searle's notion of 'acceptance and recognition' nevertheless is problematic in that it models the actual mode of existence of social facts along the lines of explicit declarative speech acts, a feature of his view not entailed by the basic claim that social objects and facts share the defining logical form of declarative speech acts.[14] There are unconscious social facts, not produced by any form of accepting or recognising awareness, something perhaps recognised by British Common law. Acceptance and recognition come after the fact of the institution, they are explicit attitudes built on people going along with facts they might not even be able to refer to with any explicit description.

Yet, the important point here lies not in the details of Searle's account of social facts, but in his idea that modes of existence are individuated by logical forms. By that I mean that for a social fact to obtain and for a social object to exist is for them to be related to the logical form of declarative speech acts, that is: existing by being accepted as existing. Accordingly, for a mountain to exist is for it to exist as a thing referred to in the logical form of an assertive speech act. It is not produced by our reference to it, but we assert that it is so under the assumption that its existence always already antecedes the speech act. There is no sense in which the speech act of asserting creates the mountain as a geological object. Even though Searle is not explicit about this point in his writing, the only viable option I see for his account is to divide modes of existence according to the most basic types of logical forms deriving from the most basic types of speech acts.[15]

This does not amount to linguistic idealism – that is, to the view that language creates all of reality by being the only means of individuating objects – as assertions do not *produce* the objects and facts they are about, but *state* that they are such and so. Searle presupposes that there is (as he puts it) 'at most' one single all-encompassing reality he calls 'the world', and that this reality is the universe. The introduction of modes of existence mainly serves to single out social facts, and not to differentiate between physics and biology, say. Searle's deflationary pluralism of modes of existence rests on a traditional materialist monism.[16]

We now have the conceptual tools to flesh out the no-world-view, which is the essential result of this part of this book. On closer inspection, the no-world-view itself is pluralist in that it generates different patterns of its own appearance. The fact that the world does not exist is itself not monolithic, as it is not a truth about the world. The world's necessary non-existence is not a truth about an object, the world. The world is not even an object, and it absolutely does not exist.

Before we can fully appreciate this view, it is helpful to give you my account of non-existence. What is it to negate existence? In my view, if we assert that something does not exist, we are generally not claiming that it absolutely does not exist, but only that it does not exist in a certain field of sense. For instance, it would not be wise to absolutely deny the existence of unicorns. There is at least one unicorn, namely the one in the movie *The Last Unicorn*. Any interpretation of the movie according to which there really is no unicorn at all in the movie absolutely misses the point of the movie. The unicorn is not a disguised pony only pretending to be a unicorn. There really is a unicorn in *The Last Unicorn*, namely the last unicorn. I am not saying that the last unicorn therefore exists in our imagination. Imagine that all human imagination has died out in some near or (hopefully) distant future. There still is at least one unicorn in the movie *The Last Unicorn*. If human imagination has died out, this does not imply that all the products of it have gone out of existence, too. If future Martians find their way to earth, they can still watch *The Last Unicorn*. Maybe they are downloading it right now for future research programmes just in case the earth and its documents are destroyed.

That there is such a unicorn is a mind-independent fact about the movie and the unicorn, even though it is a fact produced by a work of art, and works of art exist in fields produced by us. But that there is a unicorn in *The Last Unicorn* is a fact that is not identical with how it was produced, just as the existence of the earth's moon is not identical with its production by some meteor impact, say, that certainly did not involve minds. That minds are part of the history of *The Last Unicorn* is a noticeable fact about the movie; there is a trivial sense in which it is constitutive of the first appearance of the movie itself (for instance in the field of sense of Hollywood productions). Had our imaginations ever existed, the movie would not have existed either. Even though this is (unsurprisingly) true, it does not follow that the unicorn in the movie only exists relative to any given set of human imaginations. Imagination might still be a condition of our access to the world of a movie, but this does not mean that it is true of the last unicorn that we thereby gain access to the fact that it only exists relative to our imagination.

The existence of a unicorn in *The Last Unicorn* is as objective, real and mind-independent as the existence of the earth moon. Minds might be involved in the former's and not in the latter's first appearance, but that does not turn the unicorn into a construction, into something that only exists as long as a certain number of people sign up for recognising its existence. If we all now decided to interpret the movie as not containing a real unicorn, if someone wrote a really influential book on the movie in which she makes a seemingly strong case that the unicorn in the movie is really a cunningly camouflaged pony, this would simply not change the fact that there is a unicorn in the movie. Every interpretation in conflict with this fact is just completely wrong about the movie. How things come into existence is not immediately relevant for whether they exist. That there is a unicorn in *The Last Unicorn* does not mean that there only is such a unicorn for as long as our imagination keeps it in place. We are not asserting anything about our imagination when we assert the existence of the unicorn in *The Last Unicorn*. The fact that *The Last Unicorn* exists is not maximally modally robust, whereas the fact that the last unicorn exists and is not imagined by someone in the world of the movie is more modally robust than the existence of the movie. Even if no one in the field of sense populated by the actual last unicorn (which is not the field of sense of the movie theatre or the living room in which we watch the movie) including the unicorn itself had ever discovered or imagined that it is a unicorn, it would still have been a unicorn.

However, there is, evidently, a sense in which there are no unicorns. For instance, there are no unicorns in Milwaukee or in Coventry. There also are no unicorns in any other state or country of this planet. For all we know, there are no unicorns in our solar system, and what exactly are the odds that there are unicorns anywhere in the universe? We really do not know, but somehow I am inclined to believe that the odds for unicorns in the universe are really low. It seems to me that it is more likely that there are pigs in space than unicorns in the universe, but that might just be idiosyncratic.

At this point it is important to counter a possible objection from Kripke. In his *Reference and Existence* he argues that we could not even look for a unicorn, as unicorns have been invented by us as fictional objects such that it is indeterminate what we would have to look for when searching for unicorns. Do they even have a specific DNA, which seems to be a prerequisite for finding them among all the other animals?[17] The imagined unicorns are not completely determined, and they might not even be sufficiently determined in order to compare them to some animal we happen to encounter under the suspicion that it is a unicorn.

This argument sounds like Kripke presupposes his externalist causal account of reference. Against this background we could not find unicorns, as 'unicorn' in our language could not refer to unicorns. It would lack the relevant feature. At most, it could refer to unicorns in novels, but these unicorns are excluded from the kind of existence to be expected of animals. Now, apart from the fact that Kripke's claim in *Reference and Existence* that we could not even find unicorns, that we could only ever find something with certain surface qualities we attribute to unicorns (that is, animals that look like ponies but have a horn), seems counterintuitive, there is a deeper problem.[18] The argument with the counterintuitive conclusion that we can never find unicorns generalises to an argument with the untenable conclusion that we can never find anything we have not already encountered. What if someone imagines a life form not based on earthly chemistry, but on XYZ? Is it impossible to ever find it on *a priori* grounds, namely on the ground that we introduced XYZ in a context where we are currently cut off from any causal contact with XYZ? Note that this problem can be locally circumvented for some parts of earthly physical discovery. We could find the Higgs Boson because we were already in causal contact with it, even if we did not always have the slightest hint of a description of it available. But what about a subatomic particle we can imagine, but with which we have not hitherto been in causal contact? Could we imagine it based on some earthly data? Also, is it impossible to find out that there really lived a man by the name of Peter Smith who meets all the descriptions Arthur Conan Doyle gives of Sherlock Holmes such that we would cry out in surprise: 'Sherlock Holmes existed all the time!'?

Negation of existence (for one field) is often assertion of existence (for some other field). This is a consequence of the fact that our existential statements are restricted to some field or other. Negative existentials, such as 'there are no unicorns', are not straightforwardly about unicorns, but about some field or other. The meaning of unicorn is usually settled when we assert that there are no unicorns. In this sense, we do not learn anything about the meaning of unicorn when we learn that they exist or do not exist. The information conveyed by assertions of existence and negative existentials is information about some field or other, namely that the X in question appears or respectively does not appear in some field F or other. If insights into existence could be achieved by reference to the modes of operation of quantification, I could make my point by saying that there are only restricted quantifiers. There is no unrestricted universal quantification, or rather most cases of assertion and negation of existence can be made intelligible as restricted in the following sense. To assert that there are unicorns is to speak about the fields in which they exist, and not about all fields. There are unicorns in some fairy tales, in *The Last Unicorn*, and in contemporary art museums.

Yet, one might object, we tell our children that there are no unicorns when they tell their friends that they are scared of unicorns.

We even insist on telling them that unicorns do not really exist, when confronted with a suspicious case such as the unicorn in the art exhibition. But this is loose talk. What we really tell our children when we inform them that unicorns do not really exist is that the kinds of unicorns the children refer to only exist in specific fields, but not in the one where they could be frightening. There is some sense in which unicorns cannot hurt us, unless we mean that the unicorn in the art exhibition falls on my foot during an earthquake and thus hurts me. This is also why children do not stop watching *The Last Unicorn* after we tell them that unicorns do not exist. They do not acquire the false information that there is no unicorn in *The Last Unicorn*. They are able to distinguish the claim that unicorns do not really exist from the all-out universal claim that there are no unicorns – period. The all-out universal claim is clearly false.

From an ontological point of view, it does not matter how we gloss over the fact that unicorns do exist in some conversations or disciplines of thinking about unicorns. The question is what assertions of existence mean and how we can account for negative existentials. And here my view is that to assert existence is to claim that some object or objects appear in a field of sense, and to negate existence is to claim that some object or objects do not appear in some field of sense or other. As I will argue in the next chapter, absolute non-existence is impossible. Everything exists, but in different fields of sense. It does not co-exist.[19] There is no all-encompassing field in which surprisingly there somehow are unicorns and there are no unicorns. There are unicorns (for instance, in *The Last Unicorn*), and there are no unicorns (for instance, in Milwaukee). There are witches (for instance, in *Faust*), and there are no witches (for instance, in Portugal or Norway).

I take it that this account *mutatis mutandis* corresponds to Plato's notion that non-existence is difference (that μὴ ὄν is θἄτερον).[20] Without going into exegesis here, his main intention in ontology was to overcome Eleatic monism by showing that we can both account for the univocity of being or existence on one level and be ontological pluralists on another level. His proposal is to see negative existentials as claims that some objects differ from some objects. However, his account is mostly designed to account for negation in general. He wanted to explain how we can assert that 'Socrates is not flying' is true, and he wanted to do this by an analysis of assertions into their elements. This makes it a condition of Socrates not flying that Socrates and flying are not identical. This can mean many things, but one reasonable thing to mean by this expression is to say that Socrates has many other properties (not that of flying), and that there are flying things that are not identical with Socrates. In other words, for Plato the assertion 'Socrates is not flying' consists of the elements 'Socrates' (a name, ὄνομα) and a verb or predicate 'is flying' (ῥῆμα). If we negate this predicate about Socrates, we are not thereby claiming that nothing flies. Rather, we are saying that something else might be flying. To claim that Socrates is not flying is not to claim that nothing flies, it is to claim that Socrates is not flying, but that something else might well be flying. If asked, someone who claims that Socrates does not fly ought to be aware that many other things are likely to fly, or even that many things actually fly, just that Socrates is not among them. At least, one must be aware of what it would mean for something to fly so that one must be able to entertain the possibility of something flying.

Even though Plato's theory of non-existence as difference thus serves the job of an overall theory of negative statements, it comes at least close to the idea that non-existence is not absolute, but concerns field-difference. Yet, I guess that Plato would stick to Eleatic monism in that he would want to defend the idea that there is an all-encompassing field, being itself, which is somehow divided into parts or regions by negation in general, an idea I explicitly reject. This form of monism is not necessary for the account of negative existentials as assertions of existence in some other field.

But how is this different from all-out Meinongianism? Let *Meinongianism* be the name of the views that result when we claim that everything exists, and more specifically that we cannot deny existence of anything without thereby committing to its existence (at this point it does not matter that Meinong himself distinguishes between existence and subsistence). More specifically, the view usually associated with Meinongianism is that to assert that unicorns do not exist is to claim something about unicorns that consequently have to exist, at least, as the objects we are talking about. This looks like 'Plato's beard', to recall Quine, namely the apparent paradox that we cannot talk about anything without presupposing its existence.[21] We cannot talk about nothingness without presupposing that it exists; we cannot say that there are no unicorns without committing to their existence. Of course, actual Meinongianism distinguishes between existence and subsistence, and it would only say that although unicorns might not exist, they have to subsist when we deny their existence.[22] This view is often construed as the outcome of a mistaken conception of intentionality according to which objects can either be merely intentional objects (objects of intentions) or in addition also real objects. When I look at the table, it is both an intentional object (I am looking at it) and a real object (I am really looking at it and not simply dreaming it). As we will see in the epistemological chapters of Part II, there is no reason to hold the mistaken conception that we reduplicate a reality by looking at it. We do not multiply things by having reality in view, even though we change it by adding the property of having been seen to it, and by finding out that it already had the property of looking this way from this angle. Sensory objects are echoes in the sense of the first of T. S. Eliot's *Four Quartets*:

> Other echoes
> Inhabit the garden. Shall we follow?
> Quick, said the bird, find them, find them,
> Round the corner. Through the first gate,
> Into our first world, shall we follow
> The deception of the thrush? Into our first world.
> There they were, dignified, invisible,
> Moving without pressure, over the dead leaves,
> In the autumn heat, through the vibrant air,
> And the bird called, in response to
> The unheard music hidden in the shrubbery,
> And the unseen eyebeam crossed, for the roses
> Had the look of flowers that are looked at.[23]

At this point, we should distinguish between two different claims. Let *formal Meinongianism* be the view that we cannot claim that something does not exist without thereby committing to its existence. In contrast to this formal version, let *substantial Meinongianism* be the view that we cannot claim that something does not exist without thereby committing to its subsistence, where this is a form of intentional inexistence, that is, a being in our realm of thoughts.[24] My view commits to a specific version of formal Meinongianism in the sense that to claim that something does not exist is to claim that it exists in some field of sense other than the one originally under consideration. If I claim that there is no more beer, this might be restricted to many fields of sense. Let us say it is restricted to my apartment. Then the claim that there is no more beer implies that there is beer somewhere else. The same holds for witches. To claim that there are no witches is not to claim that witches only exist in our imagination, as there are witches in carnival (people dressed up as witches), and there are witches in a variety of cultures where 'witch' does not mean any such thing as a red-haired evil woman flying around on a broom, but, say, a quasi-medical doctor or whatever exactly the anthropological study of magical practices tells us the beliefs are. If existence claims are restricted in the way envisaged here, there is no straightforward road to substantial Meinongianism, only a commitment to its formal counterpart.

The motivation behind my theory of negative existentials is not semantic. I am not claiming that we, or rather our statements, cannot refer to anything without assuming its existence and that this also holds for negative statements of any kind such that we generate the Eleatic riddle of non-existence (if it is their riddle). Semantics comes second in the order of explanation in ontology, for we should not develop a theory of existential statements, but of the meaning of 'existence', or rather a theory of existence. Language does not get in our way here, as we are not studying what we do when ascribing or denying existence. For instance, imagine someone says that there are no tigers in Germany. By this, they would usually convey the information that there are no wild tigers in German forests or elsewhere within the borders. Yet, there are tigers in German zoos (I suppose). In this scenario, we are not claiming that tigers are intentional objects in the sense that they are not real objects. We are claiming that tigers exist in German zoos, but that they do not exist in German wildlife, walking around like everybody else and hunting animals in the Black Forest. The contrast between intentional tigers and real tigers is thus orthogonal to the contrast between assertions of tiger-existence and their negation. When denying the existence of tigers in Germany, we are not in any sense committing to imaginary tigers or mentally represented tigers, but committing to there being tigers in flesh and blood, just not in the Black Forest (maybe in a show or on display in the Black Forest). That there are no tigers in Germany does not necessarily mean that there are tigers in our imagination, but rather means that there are tigers elsewhere on the planet, but just not in Germany.

Umrao Sethi pointed out that there is a general worry here about whether in making a negative existential claim, I am necessarily committed to a particular positive existential claim as well. With many negative existential claims, even if they are restricted and I recognise them to be so restricted, I have no idea which positive existential claims are true. My view is that the range of positive claims one might explicitly or implicitly be committed to in denying (in a suitably restricted way) that some (kind of) object exists is not itself unrestricted. This is how I distinguish my formal position from substantial Meinongianism as the latter says that I always know that the object whose existence I am denying at least exists in my mind in virtue of conceiving it as not existing. This is only one case of many, for instance, if I deny that the green patch over there exists on the ground that I become aware that it is an afterimage. In that case, denial of existence might be commitment to existence in my mind, but this model does not generally apply, as substantial Meinongianism suggests.[25]

Some and really only some cases of existential claims about so-called fiction also seem to be of this kind. For instance, when I claim that Gustav von Aschenbach does not really exist, I am indeed committing to his imaginary existence. I might be saying that he only exists in our imagination, in the imagination of Thomas Mann, and subsequently in the imagination of Fellini, Mann readers and Fellini viewers. This account of the meaning of existence in or for fictional discourse is, however, utterly limited and only covers the least interesting and troublesome cases. For instance, what about the last season of the American *The Office*? In this season, the protagonists become aware that there is a documentary about them. They see the trailer online. But we know that the documentary in the show is not the show we are watching, as this show is not a documentary, but a mockumentary. Now what about the characters' existence in the documentary in the mockumentary? This is a special case of embedded fiction. It is actually reality embedded in fiction. The protagonists really only exist in the documentary. They have no life outside of the footage presented as the show *The Office* to us, but within the show that footage turns out to be fragments from a documentary we cannot watch, as it is a documentary never made in the field in which we are watching *The Office*. But what if the trailer of the documentary were online in Denmark right now? The crew is really making another *The Office*, this time the documentary version. Or are we watching the documentary? Is the mockumentary we are watching identical, or at least partly identical, with the documentary watched by the protagonists in the show? Throughout the history of art there are a host of intricate examples of different levels of uncertain reality that cannot be accounted for simply by drawing a distinction between real objects and intentional objects.

The point is that I am not claiming that generally negative existentials presuppose the existence of the object whose existence is then denied, and that they do this by adding the object to the domain of imaginary, imagined, or some way or other intentional objects. I reject this substantial view according to which there are modes of existence or of being: real being and intentional being (world and mind), say. The argument just given shows that there is no reason to think of the account of non-existence as field-difference in terms of literal Meinongianism. If I deny the existence of tigers in Germany, there is no straightforward sense in which I thereby claim that they have intentional being rather than real existence. Tigers are as real as it gets, but they just do not exist in German wildlife.

Notes

1. Husserl, *Formal and Transcendental Logic*, pp. 199, 38, 131.
2. Husserl, *Formal and Transcendental Logic*, p. 78.
3. See in particular, Husserl, *Formal and Transcendental Logic*, §§ 89–90, pp. 215–21.
4. Husserl, *Formal and Transcendental Logic*, p. 77.
5. Barnes, *The Ontological Argument*, pp. 63–5.
6. Cf. Heidegger, *Introduction to Metaphysics*, p. 15: 'Now what does the word *phusis* say? It says what emerges from itself (for example, the emergence, the blossoming, of a rose), the unfolding that opens itself up, the coming-into-appearance in such unfolding, and holding itself and persisting in appearance–in short, the emerging-abiding sway.' This is supported by usage, as seen in the Lidell-Scott-Jones lexicon entry on φύσις: 'II. the natural form or constitution of a person or thing as the result of growth (οἷον ἕκαστόν ἐστι τῆς γενέσεως τελεσθείσης, ταύτην φαμὲν τὴν φ. εἶναι ἑκάστου Arist.Pol.1252b33).' Also, see Frisk, *Griechisches etymologisches Wörterbuch*, pp. 1052–4. Frisk writes that φύσις, which he defines as 'growth [Wuchs], kind [Beschaffenheit], origin [Abstammung], nature [Nature], essence [Wesen], etc.' is derived from the verb

φύομαι, which in the intransitive middle voice means 'to grow [*wachsen*], to emerge or develop [*entstehen*], to become [*werden*]' and in the perfect and aorist 'to be created by nature [*von Natur geschaffen*] or to be created [*beschaffen sein*], to be there [*da sein*]' and in the transitive (factive) active 'to be allowed to grow [*wachsen lassen*], to be brought forth [*erzeugen*], to be produced [*hervorbringen*]'. He also notes that although the nouns derived from φύομαι have many similarities, because of the many divergent meanings, in many cases it is better to see these meanings as parallels of one another rather than as representative of some common faithfulness to the meaning of their Indo-European root: 'Die Nomina steuern mehrere Gleichungen bei, die aber wegen der abweichenden Bedeutungen in mehreren Fällen eher as Parallelbildungen denn als Vertreter indogermanischer Grundwörter zu betrachten sind'. Heidegger himself observes this when he writes further, 'This emerging and standing-out-in-itself-from-itself may not be taken as just one process among others that we observe in beings. *Phusis* is Being itself, by virtue of which beings first become and remain observable' (Ibid.).

7. My use of the term 'appearance' here is similar to Badiou's when he writes: 'Clearly, it is intrinsic to the being of entities to appear, in so far as being as a whole does not exist. All being is being-there: this is the essence of appearance' (*Theoretical Writings*, p. 170). Yet, I disagree with the continuation of this passage, where Badiou comes to the conclusion that 'being qua being is, for its part, absolutely unbound. [...] This excludes that there may be, strictly speaking, a being of relation. Being, thought as such, in a purely generic manner, is subtracted from any bond' (Ibid., p. 171). But this raises the worry that Badiou thinks of being as multiplicity on this side of any relation, which puts him, among other things, in the problematic position of having to explain away the fact that he related to being in his thought of being as such. Badiou also characterises 'appearance' as some entities belonging to a situation and presents this as a 'the consequence of the fact that there is no Whole' (p. 180f.) Here I wholeheartedly agree with him, even though I do not believe that his arguments are able to establish this result due to his set-theoretical commitments in ontology.

8. Cf. Gabriel, 'Schelling's Ontology in the *Freedom Essay*'.

9. Cf. Schelling, *Philosophischen Untersuchungen über das Wesen der menschlichen Freiheit*, SW VII, p. 357: 'The natural philosophy of our time has first advanced in science the distinction between being

in so far as it exists and being in so far as it is merely the ground of existence.' (All translations of the *Freiheitsschrift* are, unless otherwise noted, from Schelling, *Philosophical Investigations into the Essence of Human Freedom*.)

10. Goethe, *Faust: Part One*, v. 2603–4.
11. Mann, *Death in Venice*, pp. 3f.
12. Austin, *Sense and Sensibilia*, p. 68, footnote 1.
13. Gabriel, 'Facts, Social Facts, and Sociology'.
14. Gabriel, 'Facts, Social Facts, and Sociology'.
15. In conversation, he clarified his view to me by saying that the question of modes of existence is the question of what kind of facts make something true. Thus, he draws a distinction along the lines of different kinds of facts. The question still remains what individuates kinds of facts. One part of his answer to this question could be that they are individuated by exhibiting a particular logical form, which at least seems to be his answer regarding the individuation of social facts.
16. See, for instance, John Searle, *The Rediscovery of the Mind*, pp. 25f.: 'If we think of the make-up of the world, then of course everything in the world is made of particles, and particles are among our paradigms of the physical. And if we are going to call anything that is made up of physical particles physical; then, trivially, everything in the world is physical. But to say that is not deny that the world contains points scored in football games, interest rates, governments, and pains. All of these have their own way of existing—athletic, economic, political, mental, etc.'
17. Kripke, *Reference and Existence*, pp. 44ff.
18. Marius Bartmann has made me aware of this problem in discussion. He left it open whether this problem really affects Kripke's account. However, I believe the problem is certainly worth presenting here.
19. Umrao Sethi remarked that this might be read as a commitment to the view that conceivability not only implies possibility, but also actuality. It does, indeed. But given my restrictions on modal vocabulary, this is not outright crazy. That there actually is a unicorn, because we can imagine one, does not mean that we therefore have reasons to look for a unicorn in our or any other galaxy. 'To be actual' does not entail 'to be physical' and 'to be possible' does not entail 'to be possibly physical'.
20. Plato, *Sophist*, 257b.
21. Cf. Quine, 'On What There Is', pp. 1ff.
22. 'How little truth there is in such a view [that the non-real is a mere

nothing] is most easily shown by ideal Objects which do indeed subsist (*bestehen*), but which do not by any means exist (*existieren*), and consequently cannot in any sense be real (*wirklich*). Similarity and difference are examples of objects of this type: perhaps, under certain circumstances, they subsist between realities; but they are not a part of reality themselves. That ideas, as well as assumptions and judgments, are nevertheless concerned with such Objects (and often have reason to be very intimately concerned with them) is, of course, beyond question.' Meinong, 'The Theory of Objects', p. 79.

23. Eliot, *Burnt Norton*, v. 19–31.
24. This distinction is a response to Umrao Sethi's objections against an earlier version of this chapter, where it was unclear to which form of Meinongianism I am committed.
25. Abby Rutherford pointed out to me that my view at most amounts to a kind of Meinongianism with a much less simplistic notion of existence. Whereas he draws a distinction between what exists 'out there' and what exists (or rather subsists) in our reference, I reject any such principled distinction. The point of similarity boils down to my acceptance that things we make negative existential claims about exist in some field of sense or other.

7

The No-World-View

This chapter is the heart of the matter, as I will argue in some detail that the world does not exist.[1] By 'the world' I mean any kind of unrestricted or overall totality, be it the totality of existence, the totality of what there is, the totality of objects, the whole of beings, or the totality of facts or states of affairs. The world is usually meant to designate the ultimate, all-encompassing unity or entity. It is supposed to be the place where everything takes place. Let me repeat that I understand metaphysics to be the investigation into the world as world. Metaphysics is primarily about the world in that it specifies what it is for something to belong to the world, to be part of the furniture of reality, or whatever (mis-) conception one prefers.

I am myself a meta-metaphysical nihilist. *Meta-metaphysical nihilism* is the view that metaphysics has no object. In that respect metaphysics is like witchology, the discipline of witches, which assumes that there are witches in some European country or other (say, in Spain). At best, it is like *Seinfeld*, which famously is 'a show about nothing' in various senses. More directly, it is a show about a show that has never been shot, as Jerry and George's proposal of a show about their lives is not realised. At the same time, it is realised insofar as we are watching it. On this scale it is also a show about nothing, as there is no object or theme it could be about. The show just is what it is; it does not refer to a hidden dimension.

The reasons for accepting meta-metaphysical nihilism presented here all stem from ontology, from the investigation into the meaning of existence. So far, we know that for something to exist is for it to appear in a field of sense. This entails that for the world to exist would be for it to appear in a field of sense. The issue of the existence of the world is accordingly the issue of whether an unrestricted all-encompassing field of sense (the world) can appear in any field of sense. If it can, the world exists, if it cannot, it does not (cannot exist). Let us state what we know about ontology so far:

1. To exist is to appear in a field of sense.
2. If there is any object whatsoever, it appears in a field of sense.
3. There are fields of sense.
4. There are fields within which fields of sense appear.

Let me emphasise here that I do not rule out that some field can appear within itself. The problem is not that generally there is no self-reference or self-containment for fields of sense, but that there is a problem in the combination of totality and self-containment, a problem loosely connected to issues from set theory, albeit different in that not all fields are sets.

The natural conception of the world in this framework would be to define it as the field where *all* fields of sense appear. The world could thus mean the *totality* of fields of sense. There are at least two ways one could think of such a totality. The first thinks of this totality according to an additive model. Let us call this *additive totality*. The second emphasises the unification of the totality and says that the world somehow has to be a field on top of or in the background of all other fields. Let us call this *unified totality*.

If the world were an additive totality, it could be something like the mere co-existence of all the particular fields. It would not be a field in addition to the several fields. But this immediately raises the question of what would motivate the closure associated with the term 'totality'? In what sense would there be a totality of *all* fields of sense? This requires some rule or other that allows us to achieve an overview so that we can guarantee that the singular term 'the world' refers to *all* fields of sense at once without somehow unifying them into a field that is different from each and every one of the several fields. Given that fields change, that fields are added, whereas other fields disappear, this picture runs into problems with time and change. Even if the world were identical with the physical universe, it would be unified by being structured according to the laws of nature, which unify the several physical entities and processes. We would not say that the world is identical with the universe and that the universe is just the arbitrary combination or unprincipled co-existence of whatever it is that happens to be physical.[2] And even if there would be a sense one could attach to this view, what would justify speaking of the universe in its entirety or totality?

This is why the traditional view is rather to think of the world in terms of a *unified totality*. But then this unified totality differs from each and every single thing that is unified by it and accordingly becomes an additional field of sense, the field of all fields. If to exist is to appear in a field of sense, this raises the question in which field the world itself appears. There seem to be only two options: The world either appears in itself or in another field.

Now imagine the world appears in any other field. If it appears in any other field, it appears alongside other fields, as there has to be a field within which the field appears within which the world appears. Evidently, this field would encompass more than the world, as it encompasses the world. The only way to avoid this problem is by claiming that the world is both the field of all fields, and that it appears within itself. The field where the world exists is the world itself.

Now that cannot mean that the world appears within the world alongside other fields, as this would repeat the problem of the world being a field among others (now within itself). The problem was that the world appeared alongside other fields, and we cannot overcome the difficulties with this by adding that the world appears alongside other fields within itself. If the world itself (and not something like its Doppelgänger shadow) really appears within itself, it cannot do so alongside other fields. But then how does the world manage to appear within itself?

One objection against this basic argument for the no-world-view first raised by the Brazilian philosopher Eduardo Luft says that my conception of existence is local and has to turn out to be somehow finite. In effect, he says, I claim that existence is being-in or being-encompassed. Against this he proposes to add a concept of existence in terms of networks. To be precise, his intention was not to argue that for some objects existence is being-in, whereas for other objects it is some network-property. Rather, he claims that I have no means for ruling out that existence ultimately is something other than appearance in a field of sense, as I cannot claim that by necessity existence always and in each instance is being-in. I could only claim this, he believes, if unrestricted universal quantification were available to my position. In other words, he believes that I maintain that there is no object for which to exist is not to be in a field. If this is not a universal proposition stating an essential truth about everything and therefore a metaphysical assertion *par excellence*, then what is? Thus, he believes it is warranted to oppose my stance with his preferred version of network theory plus some sufficiently fundamental discipline of mathematics, which he considers to be graph theory.[3] It looks indeed promising at first glance to give up set theory as a model for ontology (which I do myself) in order to then replace it by a different mode of presentation that captures the motivation behind the idea that set theory is ontology without inheriting the difficulties of set theory (I reject this second move). Graphs can represent quite a lot of the properties of networks in a way abstract enough to aspire to universality. Or so it seems.

At this point, it might be interesting to note that even Latour has a hard time introducing a second theoretical mode of existence in addition to networks, to 'réseaux', symbolised as [NET]. For him, networks or actor-networks are still privileged in the plurality of modes, even though he now grants different modes. Yet, networks continue to be the most universal tool in his toolbox, and part of the motivation behind this might be that he is not willing to give up the world on pain of the fear of relativism. If we give up the idea of any privileged mode of existence, how can we avoid relativism? This is a tricky question to be dealt with in the epistemological chapters of Part II. Suffice it to say that the fact that there are at least infinitely many fields of sense without any all-encompassing background in front of which they all stand out together (in the form of networks, graphs, sets, atoms in the void, or whatever candidate concrete notion of the world there might be) as such does not contribute anything to relativism. The fear of relativism only enters the picture when we ask which fields of sense we want to inhabit or privilege in a given explanatory setting.

The issue of relativism appears when we are in a fallible position and need to adjudicate between competing claims. The relativist argues in one way or other that disagreement cannot be rationally solved because there is a plurality of incompatible positions that are held relative to some frame of reference, and we cannot adjudicate between the frames themselves so that we are necessarily stuck with frame-immanent claims. Yet, this is not at all the position in ontology. Here, the question is what the meaning of 'existence' is (if any). By ruling out alternative and widespread answers to the question, we were left with the position that existence is appearance in a field of sense. We can now formulate a precise argument for the non-existence of an all-encompassing totality (the world). There is no relativism involved in this procedure, as it explicitly rules out other frameworks and positions derivable within them as false full-stop, not as false for me but not for someone else. It is absolutely false that to exist is to always fall under a concept as much as it is false that it is a proper property or the world's property not to be empty. Different ontologies exist and compete for truth, but this does not make them equally true, or make it impossible to adjudicate between them. Ontological pluralism is very different from either epistemological relativism or even metaphysical relativism, which would be the view that we cannot adjudicate between competing claims because they all exist within their respective domains or fields. I am a pluralist in ontology (that is, a pluralist about existence), but this does not commit to pluralism about truth. It is true that there is beer in my fridge. This truth (and its assertibility) is not somehow relativised in such a way that truth should not be thought of as monadic. The fact that there are many descriptions that equally well capture what there is does not mean that there is one situation that we can describe using different standards, criteria or forms of truth.

My argument does not hinge on the metaphor of being-encompassed or being-in if this is understood as a spatial container. The point is not that the world is spatially bigger than anything that is a part of it. I am not myself committed to the idea that the world is a whole where this means that it has parts relative to which it is bigger. Otherwise, network theorists could simply say that the world is just the fact that all objects are related in different ways by being nodes of networks. Yet, they also need to address what it is for something to exist in this view. And the only answer they have is that for something to exist is for it to be local, to be a node or a local network. Latour, for instance, draws a local/global-distinction. Of course, he wants to carefully replace any domain ontology with his picture of overlapping networks. But this contradistinction implies that domains are limited in such a way that nothing can travel between them, which is not even a necessary ingredient in traditional domain ontology. From an ontological point of view, it does not matter much whether objects can appear in many fields of sense and how they manage to move between the fields. It also does not matter whether there are any more or less general phenomena such as the phenomenon that many fields are permeable. To claim that existence is appearance in a field of sense is not to claim that fields are closed domains, that they are spatially segregated, or that they are vague and nebulous. On the contrary, the ontology of fields of sense entails the no-world-view, and the no-world-view rejects the notion that there even could be anything substantial that all fields of sense or all objects have in common.

This leads me to a second prominent objection I have been confronted with. This objection invokes my definition of 'existence' and argues that it is inherently universal. Everything that exists thereby appears in a field of sense. Thus, the objection continues, the world has to exist; it is the field defined by the concept of existence that in turn exists, as the concept of existence falls under itself: it exists. My reply is that the concept of existence, or rather existence, is manifold (not that it is *said* in manifold ways, it *is* manifold). Existence is just not generally a concept. The notion of existence as *appearance* in a field of sense is essentially malleable: for elements in set theory to exist is to be bound by an axiom system and rules of inference, for Spanish citizens to exist is to be subjected to a number of laws, for Picasso's *Les Demoiselles d'Avignon* to exist is (among other things) to be part of the history of art, and so on. There is no such thing as an answer to the question of what it is for an object just insofar as it is an object to appear in a field of sense just insofar as it is a field of sense. There simply is no *a priori* property of appearance in a field of sense that is instantiated in just the same way by everything falling under it. Existence is not the highest genus.

But does this not mean that I am giving up any right to make a substantial explanatory claim based on the insight that to exist is to appear within a particular field?[4] Well, it depends on what would count as a substantial explanatory claim here. The explanatory power the view has consists at least in being able to criticise positions in ontology that lead to metaphysical (hyper-substantial) claims in specific regions of philosophy or scientific discourse. Identification of existence with a specific metaphysical property often leads to the explanatory programme of ruling out certain entities or fields from existence in light of a tacitly metaphysical norm. This phenomenon is so widespread that a motivated rejection of its premises is sufficiently substantial. At the very least, ontological pluralism is designed to make us rethink many of our methodological assumptions in specific fields of enquiry, such as the philosophy of mind or ethics. For instance, we cannot motivate any version of reduction or elimination of certain apparent phenomena on the basis of a world view that is itself based on a biased and arguably wrong ontology. In that regard meta-metaphysical nihilism is a fairly substantial claim.

That existence is not the highest genus is also the upshot of Aristotle's claim that existence or rather being is not the most universal concept. He famously illustrates this with the concept of analogy. However, the concept of analogy is traditionally interpreted as part of semantics. From this perspective, being has analogical meaning; it means all sorts of things, but in a systematically related way. Analogical meaning always falls short of fully-fledged equivocation, as that is part of its definition.[5] However, we need not interpret Aristotle as being committed to the idea that being has analogical *meaning*. Rather, he seems to be saying that objects relate differently to their analogical focus. His most widely discussed example is that of the relation of a doctor, food, a knife and a patient to health.[6] A doctor, food, a knife and a patient are healthy (the example does not quite work in English) in that they are health-related. Yet, they do not all equally fall under the concept of health, where the relation of falling under a concept is determined as the relation between a universal and rules of specification. A doctor is conducive to health, so is some food. A knife can also help in establishing health in an operation. If people and other animals are healthy, they are neither conducive to health (unless served as food), nor do we usually mean that they are used in an operation (of course, some people are used in operations in some sense). Aristotle's point is that the relation between health and the different objects relating to health is not generally that of falling under a determinate concept such as ... *is healthy*. Rather, he maintains that we consider a doctor, a patient and food under the condition that they relate to health, even though they might relate to all sorts of other things, goals, or objects, in general. The point, then, is that we come to think of the patient, the doctor and food in a particular way when we consider them as healthy or health-related. We might come to think of them in a variety of other ways: as related to political economy, as consisting of molecules, and so on.

These ways of coming to think of objects reveal properties of the objects. There is no general obstacle to thinking about them as real. When I find out that red wine is healthy in a similar way in which chemotherapy is healthy, namely as preventing the further growth of cancer cells, I find something out about red wine and chemotherapy, and not about our use of language or about the analogical meaning of 'healthy'. Here the concept of a focus might serve as a helpful illustration. Health brings certain objects into focus. This focus brings out properties of the objects, or at least, it need not generally obscure real properties of the objects brought into focus.

For instance, if I take the BART from San Francisco to Berkeley (if I 'bart' there, as the locals say), someone might enter my car with a bike in one hand and a hot dog in the other hand (which happened to me once). Now, it is actually against the rules to eat on the BART, and the way the guy was eating his hot dog was quite annoying to me, as I was attempting to finish reading Kripke's *Reference and Existence*, which had been released recently. Some other people were annoyed too, whereas many people simply did not care. The focus of the situation or scene just described is that of a BART-ride. All objects in the scene relate to the BART-ride. Yet, they do not fall under the concept of the BART-ride; they are not BART-rides, although they relate to this focus. Appearing in the field of a BART-ride is not identical with falling under the concept of a BART-ride.

In my interpretation, Aristotle is trying to make this point with his discussion of analogy. This is clear from his overall project of overcoming Plato's mathematicism, that is, the view that everything is structured mathematically. According to Aristotle, this paradigmatically does not hold for human action. Human action is only intelligible in light of contingent time management and risky decision-making. The objects appearing in the field of human action thereby differ modally and in the degree of determinacy from natural numbers and the laws they obey. What we ought to do next is not generally computable or subject to an algorithm. In this sense, 'being is said in manifold ways': for something to *be* a human action is different than for something to *be* the largest prime number between 3 and 77. The reason is that the objects in question appear in a different field of sense; they are brought into a different focus.

To maintain that the world does not exist is to maintain that there is no overall focus. Another way of putting this is to assert that there is no such thing as *the* meaning of it all and that this is the reason why there is no such as *it all*. Things in themselves mean

all sorts of things; objects necessarily appear in a plurality of fields
of sense. A phenomenological description (in a non-terminological
sense of the term) might be adequate to capture the idea I mean to
convey. Imagine you sit in a restaurant with friends. You met for
a nice Friday-evening dinner in one of your favourite spots. This
determines the focus as that of a Friday-evening dinner. Within
that focus or in that sense, the objects reveal a certain number of
properties: the waiter is nice as usual; it is a good surprise that
they after all changed their dessert selection; it is a good idea to
find an adequate wine; the tablecloth is appropriate, but remains
discreetly *zuhanden* in that no one feels the need to comment on
it; and so on. The scene is revealed in light of the focus 'Friday-
evening dinner', and all objects involved in that scene, everything
appearing in that field of sense, has real properties contributing
to the scene. Yet, the objects do not fall under the concept of that
scene. The scene is not a more general concept than the tablecloth,
such that we can assert that the tablecloth is a Friday-evening
dinner (which is straightforward non-sense, at least, outside of
the field of sense of figurative language use). At this point we can
ask whether 'Friday-evening dinner' therefore is the meaning of
it all, or at least, of everything involved in the scene described.
Is it the ultimate meaning of the event to be a Friday-evening
dinner? Evidently not as we can bring the objects into focus
just as well by considering their appearance in the field of sense
of mesoscopic objects. This changes the scene quite radically,
as the tablecloth immediately becomes as salient as my friends,
and quite a lot of other objects we did not want to consider in
the Friday-evening scenario assume a new role: the well-hidden
spiders in the corner of the restaurant, the huge number of hairs
in the room, fingernails, lungs and livers, and so on. Now why
would the Friday-evening scene be either more or less real than
the mesoscopic object scene? From an ontological point of view,
I see no reason to privilege one of the scenes over any other. This
is why my account is only faintly phenomenological, as the goal
of phenomenology is usually to 'save the appearances', or even to
privilege the *zuhanden* and absorbed being-in-the-world over the
mere being-there of spiders and hair. Yet, in my view, there is no
monolithic domain of appearances to be saved, but manifold fields
with their related appearances.

There are no ontologically privileged scenes: scenes that exist in
an out-and-out sense are not more significant than scenes that are

constructed, which are often considered to be less important, or merely painted by the human imagination. There is no meaning of it all, as 'it all' does not refer to anything. There just is no reason to look for the meaning of it all, as this is not an object we could possibly look for. In my ontology, 'the meaning of it all', insofar as it is one way of describing the world, is one of the very few absolutely empty names in that the expression cannot pick out and refer to what it claims exists.

'The world', 'the meaning of it all', 'the domain of all domains', 'the One', 'absolutely everything', 'unrestricted totality', 'reality', 'Being', 'Beying', 'Being and Time', and so on, are all short-hand (overgeneralised) terms for failed attempts at cashing out Parmenides' misguided impression that we are somehow part of an all-encompassing sphere, the big thing, the universe, *una substantia*, *Deus sive natura*. The world does not even exist on such a small scale as that of an isolated Friday-evening dinner. Not even that everyday (or once a week) affair encompasses all the objects appearing within it and itself in such a way that there is no further focus. We cannot bring everything into focus at once, because there is no focus into which we could thus bring it. Finitude, therefore, is not at all a special property of human or any other form of cognition. If it existed, reality itself would be incomplete. Of course, it is imprecise to say of reality that it is incomplete, as it does not even exist. What there is is an indefinite proliferation of fields of sense, not of objects unified on some homogeneous plain, Deleuze's plane of immanence, or Badiou's inconsistent multiplicity.

This is not itself a world view. I am not revising our world picture or adding to the stock of already existing and competing world-pictures. Instead, I argue that we need to give up the very idea of a world-picture or world view in general. The 'era of the world-picture' has come to an end, as we are by now in a position to know that there is nothing to picture in the first place. Heidegger thus was almost right. However, he still thought that *Dasein* was a function of projecting world views, such that without *Dasein* there might well be ineffable objects, but no-world-view. Heidegger still has room for a positive conception of the world as an overall focus (the meaning of being) that shifts from epoch to epoch. For Heidegger, the world is, as it were, a question of style: the world of the Aztecs and the world of French monarchy differ in style; they are different worlds in that they are different overall ways of making sense of how things are. Independently of these overall ways, either nothing exists or at least we have no means of determining what there is independently of our ways of constructing world-pictures.

In *Being and Time* Heidegger clearly argues 'that reality is grounded in the being of Dasein'[7]. In this context he introduces reality as a term for 'modes of being of innerworldly beings'[8]. He maintains that *Zuhandenheit* and *Vorhandenheit* are 'modes of reality'[9], and adds that nature is neither *zuhanden* nor *vorhanden*. To be precise, he does not speak of nature, but of 'nature', where the quotes seem to indicate that there ought to be a different concept of nature available, one possibly not conceived of as a mode of reality. At least, nature in the usual sense, as that 'which "surrounds" us'[10] according to Heidegger 'is indeed an innerworldly being'.[11]

Right after this discussion, Heidegger begins to oscillate, an ambivalence already exhibited by the fact that he seems to be considering a different concept of nature (where nature is possibly not a mode of reality). He first writes:

> The fact that reality is ontologically grounded in the being of Dasein cannot mean that something real can only be what it is in itself when and as long as Dasein exists.[12]

He distinguishes between reality and the real, where reality corresponds to what is intelligible under the condition that someone (Dasein) is around to understand what the real is. Reality is interpreted; it is explicitly claimed to be such and so, which is compatible with things (the real) being thus and so regardless of the further fact that we now understand them to be thus and so. This is also the upshot of the passage immediately following the discussion of the distinction between reality and the real, where Heidegger reframes this as a point about being and beings:

> However, only as long as Dasein *is*, that is, as long as there is the ontic possibility of an understanding of being, 'is there' [*gibt es*] being [Sein]. If Dasein does not exist, then there 'is' no 'independence' either, nor 'is' there an 'in itself.' Such matters are then neither comprehensible nor incomprehensible. If Dasein does not exist then innerworldly beings, too, can neither be discovered, nor can they lie in concealment, *Then* it can neither be said that beings are, nor that they are not. It can

now indeed be said that as long as there is an understanding of being and thus an understanding of objective presence, that *then* beings will still continue to be.[13]

Heidegger here clearly commits to ontological anti-realism or constructivism. Had there been no Dasein, there would not have been being, where being is tied to understanding and understanding is understood as a condition of possibility of truth in the sense of the appearance of objects in light of the option that they are thus and so or something else. At the same time, he also clearly rejects ontic anti-realism, the view according to which there would not have been any real objects or things had no one understood or individuated them.

Nevertheless, there is a tension between the two tenets in the way Heidegger holds them, as he attributes independence and dependence only to being and not to beings. Beings are independent of being only to the extent to which 'there is' being. Had there been no one to understand being, beings would not have been independent of being. Of course, they would also not have been dependent on being, given that 'there would not have been' any being. That means that the ontological difference between domains and what appears within them (existence in my sense of the term) is constructed such that we would also have to come to the conclusion that nothing would have existed (in my sense of the term) had no one ever understood being. Only as long as understanding of being takes place is it the case that something appears or even possibly appears.

Heidegger's preferred way out of this dialectics, his way of avoiding full-blown commitment to the tension I diagnosed, is to maintain that the ontological realist is liable to commit *the fallacy of misplaced ontological concreteness*. This fallacy consists in identifying specific conditions of our capacity of abstraction with a concrete condition of how things are. In particular, it can be found in contexts where one might be tempted to count our conditions of access to concrete (material or physical objects) among those very objects. Husserl, for instance, identified this fallacy behind naturalist metaphysics, behind the idea that to be an object *überhaupt*, to be anything whatsoever, is to be part of nature. This fallacy misses the point that the generality of the concept of an 'object *überhaupt*' is not a discovery of there generally being such objects (in particular, say, those of nature), but a construction of a category out of our understanding of what it is to understand how things are. In order to fend off this fallacy, Heidegger commits to ontological anti-realism. Yet, this is an overreaction, as long as we take care to not project our conditions of understanding onto what there is. As I argued, the ontological difference between fields (domains) and objects cannot generally be a construction or projection; it cannot depend on us being around, as this fully undermines the relevant independent existence of objects. If we completely subtract being from beings, we are not left with beings, but with free-floating meaningless object-shadows, to which we cannot legitimately attribute existence, as there are no domains left with the property of having something appear within them.

This is also the upshot of Heidegger's recently published text *The Argument against Use/Custom (For the Being-in-itself of Beings) (Das Argument gegen den* Brauch *(für das Ansichsein des Seienden))*.[14] However, Heidegger there considers ontological realism to be an option in the following sense. By 'Brauch', he means the idea that Being needs (*braucht*) humans (*den Menschen*). At the same time, Brauch, of course, also means 'custom' or 'habit', a way of dealing with objects and others. His idea now is that it is a modally robust property of being that even had there never been any human being, being would still have needed them. It would just have happened that the correlation of humans and being was never actualised by the relevant cosmic accidents, as it were.

Given Meillassoux's (ultimately misplaced) charge against Husserl and Heidegger according to which they get into problems with the idea of ancestrality, that is, with the very idea of a temporarily prior universe without human inhabitants, the context of this Heidegger text is quite interesting. Heidegger is commenting on an exchange of letters between a Zürich-based geologist and the psychoanalyst Medard Boss with whom Heidegger taught the Zollikon seminars in the 1960s. The geologist ironically writes:

> For us geologists there can be no doubt regarding the reality of a very long pre-human history of the earth. It might be the case that ultimately this reality only exists thanks to the retrospective activity of the human mind – but in this case one becomes somewhat afraid of one's own similarity to God.[15]

On a funny side note, the geologist tells us that at the time (1955) the estimate is that the earth is 3–4.5 billion years old, and that this probably also determines the age of the 'universe (*Weltall*)' to be the same, which means that the idea was that the earth came into existence together with the universe or shortly thereafter (whatever that means ...). Heidegger's comment on this is that 'this argument *for* the fact that human beings are not necessary when it comes to beings in themselves is correct'.[16] He clarifies his position in his text by making it explicit that he only maintains that there is no being in itself without humans, which is not to say that there are no beings (entities) in themselves without humans. The latter view is incorrect, a trivial fact Heidegger does not dispute. Nevertheless, he qualifies his earlier views from *Being and Time* in that he now thinks of the correlation between being and humans as modally robust, that is, as not depending on the actual existence of humans on earth. Translated into a different vocabulary, Heidegger now argues that things in themselves must have the property of possibly becoming intelligible, of becoming objects of truth-apt thought regardless of whatever else individuates them. This allows Heidegger to hold both that the earth would have been the earth anyway, but that the fact that we are now in a position to know this tells us something about the being of beings, namely that they are not on the other side of a dualistically construable gap. The claim that being and humans are correlated is a commitment to epistemological realism beyond the idea that to be available to human thought is to belong to a specific category of objects that might as well be located on the other side of a dividing line. In other words, Heidegger's argument for the correlation between being and humans is thoroughly antisceptical, and he suspects that the idea that the earth existed before we were around to notice might give rise to micro-fundamentalism, even though this is a typical fallacy of his (and our time), the time of the atomic age.

In this highly qualified sense, Heidegger oscillates between *weak* and *strong correlationism*, that is, between the weaker view that we cannot know how things are independently of a historically shifting meaning of being and the stronger view that there is no way things are independently of a historically shifting meaning of being. The latter view differs from the no-world-view, among other things, in that it still reserves a meaning for the term 'world' and 'world view'. For Heidegger, aspirations to totality are not absolutely null and empty, as they are according to my no-world-view. For me, saying anything about the world is plain nonsense, like saying the following: 'XCEANNRs12*' or the following: ''.

As Frank Ramsey said in a similar context about Wittgensteinian nonsense: 'But what we can't say, we can't say, and we cannot whistle it either.'[17] Of course, Wittgensteinian nonsense is a more general problem, as it is not restricted to the notion of the world. At least, most interpreters do not put the problem of the world centre stage for the discussion of nonsense in and according to the *Tractatus*, which, however, might be a mistake given that the work begins with a definition of the world (the moment of creation) and then goes through seven propositions (the seven days of creation) to the last day when the transcendental subject creating the text has to rest and remain silent. But therein hangs a tale and I do not wish to engage in Wittgenstein exegesis at this point. It suffices to emphasise that Wittgenstein was certainly aware of some problem with the problem of the existence of the world and that he unfortunately thought that the existence of the world itself would remain a mystery, something mystical, not to be stated in language, but maybe experienced. But that is just to say that we can whistle it, where we cannot.

Heidegger runs into very similar difficulties, but instead of whistling it *sotto voce* or behind our backs, he invents new poetical expressions, such as the verb 'to world'. The world does not exist, but it worlds. But this is just another form of pretending to not be whistling it, where one really is whistling it. And again, we cannot whistle it, as there is nothing to whistle or whistle about.

On several occasions, it has been objected to the no-world-view that if the assertion that the world does not exist were true about the world, it would thereby exist (by my definition of 'existence').[18] A similar objection has it that the world at least exists in the proposition expressed by any claim about it (for example, that the world is certainly more encompassing than a tiger's stomach). Am I not committed to claiming that some (a lot) of things are true about the world, and that it, consequently, is an object embedded in facts and therefore exists insofar as it appears in the field of all these facts?

The principle statement of the no-world-view, that the world does not exist, does not say of a particular object, the world that it does not exist. The reason for this is that 'the world', had it existed, would have been a very peculiar object. Had it existed, it would have been all-encompassing. Thus, it would certainly never only exist in a proposition, as the proposition itself would rather exist in the world. The world, with which the proposition deals as its object, cannot be identical with the world in which the proposition exists. Let us just examine two paradigmatic instances of alleged counter-examples:

(1) The world encompasses more than a tiger's stomach (or a bottle, or any old galaxy, or any other object within the world).

The objection says that the world appears in (1), that (1) is a field of sense, and that consequently the world exists after all. But what exactly appears in this assertion or the proposition expressed by it? Imagine the world existed in (1) and similar statements (maybe in infinitely many statements, although naturally not in all statements). Now the world is supposed to designate unrestricted totality. If the world exists in (1), unrestricted totality exists in (1). This can, therefore, not be the opponent's intended understanding of (1). That the world exists in (1) cannot mean that the entire world exists in (1). But then, what exactly exists in (1)? The only solution I see is to say that some representation of the world exists in (1), some way of identifying the world with relevant conceptual means, some way of pointing to it, of referring to it captured by the singular term 'the world' used in (1). Now, interestingly this works in ordinary cases. For instance,

(1*) Any old galaxy encompasses more than a tiger's stomach.

Here, we have independent means of identifying any old galaxy. We see one in the evening sky, we use our telescope, we check for coloured images of Hubble photographs online, some informant tells us about it, and so on. We can refer to any old galaxy independently of the technical device of introducing it as a singular term in a statement true of anything we consider a galaxy. According to our overall acquaintance with galaxies, we know that any old galaxy, any galaxy one could possibly refer to, encompasses more than a tiger's stomach. Of course, there are all sorts of scenarios which would make this come out false, but they currently seem very far-fetched: there might be wrapped up galaxies in currently unobservable dimensions on a very small scale relative to our measurements; there might be gigantic tigers in other regions of the hyperverse that could easily swallow any old galaxy we have ever managed to refer to, and so on. But all these imaginary variations of truth-conditions for (1*) are premised upon a successful instance of reference to some galaxy or other. And this is just what is missing in the (1). We have no independent means of referring to the world so that we can then claim that IT also appears in our statements about IT.

But, so the objection continues, we are not considering what the semantic conditions are for (1) being true or false. The question was not how exactly we could settle the meaning of (1), but whether (1) could be thought of as the expression of a fact. Something has to be true of the world, at the very least, that the world is the world, or that the world, had it existed, would have been the world, and so on. In order to claim

(2) The world does not exist (and it does not world either. In fact, it does not do anything).

one also has to be able to claim

(3) The world is the world.

or

(4) It is true of the world, that it is no other object, that it is not my left hand, no tiger's stomach, and so on.

The no-world-view does not say that (2), (3) and (4) are false, but that they have no truth-conditions. In this respect (1) is similar to

(5) The round square is bigger than some square that is not round.

No one would immediately object against (5) that it presupposes that the round square is identical with itself, that is, as long as one identifies a problem in attributing self-identity to contradictory objects.

In order for statements about the world to have truth-conditions, reference to the world would have to be possible, be it with the help of a singular term ('the world') or with some definite description ('the unique object that is the totality of everything'). We tacitly assume that (3) has already managed to pick something out before we can fix its truth-conditions as that of a tautology. But the point is that 'the world' has no meaning; that the term cannot refer to anything if it means what it traditionally means

204 Fields of Sense

(the all-encompassing). To claim that it is true that the world is the world assumes that there could be an object – the world – that then evidently would at least be self-identical. There is therefore a significant difference between the following tautologies:

(T1) The world is the world.

(T2) Markus Gabriel's (me) penthouse in Manhattan is Gabriel's (me again) penthouse in Manhattan.

I do not own a penthouse in Manhattan, but if I owned one it would be mine and it would be my penthouse in Manhattan. Other people own penthouses in Manhattan. But (T1) does not contain any expression that refers to any actual or possible object. It is at best metalinguistic in that it says something like

(T1*) 'the world' is 'the world'.

where this means nothing different from

(T1**) 'xvdas' is 'xvdas'.

Now let us take a look at objections derived from (4). To the best of my recollection, this objection was first clearly raised by Eduardo Luft during a set of lectures I gave on this topic in Porto Alegre. Luft objected that I pretend to know of any object he could point out to me that it is not identical with the world. Therefore, the objection goes, it is true of the world that no object ever encountered is identical to it.

Here we have the interesting case that all we can know of some alleged object, aka the world, is that no other object is identical with it.[19] Now this either changes the meaning of the world, as it does not think of it as the totality of anything anymore, or it is supposed to amount to a technical device of identifying the world as the unique object that no other object is identical with. But the property of being the unique object that no other object is identical with is not a proper property. It is a particular way of expressing the property of self-identity, a property the tradition has often equated with being. Now any object satisfies the predicate ... *the unique object that no other object is identical with*. The question is whether the world can have any property in addition to this one. If we can have no reason for this, if all other ways of referring to the world have been eliminated, and we are left with the desperate attempt of claiming nothing more than its self-identity or non-contradictoriness, we are not able to pick it out. If the world only had the property to be no other object than itself, every single object would be a candidate for the world, and we could never tell when confronted with a suspicious case whether or not it is the world: when seeing a hamster, we would have to seriously wonder whether it is the world. Yet, we already know that the world cannot appear within itself as one object among others, and that it consequently cannot have any proper property. However, an object with no proper property cannot be referred to. We can only refer to hamsters by saying that they are hamsters or that they are unique objects that no other object is identical with because we have independent means of referring to them. These means are not available in the world case, which is why the statement that the world does not exist is not a statement about an object at all.

Of course, this is part of the reason why many philosophers following Kant, from the post-Kantian idealists via classical phenomenology to Habermas, all argue that the world is not an object, but something else, whether a regulative idea, a horizon, or a source of infinite eidetic variations. However, this manoeuvre does not help to bring the world back into existence. Let us say that the world as the field of all fields is not an object, but rather only a field within which all other fields appear. If in addition it is not an object, we have to come to the conclusion that it does not appear in a field of sense. Yet, this still implies that it cannot exist. In Heideggerese: the world at best can be being, but not *a* being. Yet, Heidegger's point is that this ontological difference is not substantial, as this would imply that being after all is *a* being, insofar as it is a relatum in a relation. Heidegger does not claim to have discovered the ontological difference. Rather, the ontological difference is precisely the destiny of metaphysics; it is the metaphysical idea that being is not *a* being, where this means that there is a relation between being and beings. Yet, this turns being into *a* being, which is the basic move behind ontotheology. Replacing the concept of the world as object with the concept of the world as a horizon that does not appear within itself does not amount to a defence of the existence of the world, but introduces a paradoxical object that is not really an object, something we can only indirectly talk about, and so on. It results in whistling.

Of course, there is the Husserlian version of Kant's understanding of the world as a regulative idea. It might already be Kant's intention to go there, but given that he believes that he can only solve the problem of the antinomy of the world by introducing transcendental idealism, there is more exegetical work to be done for a rehabilitation of Kant on this point than of Husserl. In Husserl's version in *Formal and Transcendental Logic*, the incoherence of the notion of the world arises only from thinking that 'the world' actually refers to an entity. What it really refers to is to a norm of theory-building, a norm according to which we have to think of all of our knowledge as potentially integrated and uniform. If we mistake this norm of unification of knowledge into a systematic whole with the object of all research, we confuse the first-order level of enquiry with some second-order requirements of the universality or unity of reason.[20]

The no-world-view is like a declaration, the declaration of the end of world views, the declaration of a new era after the illusory epoch or the illusory epochs of world-pictures. In other words, I maintain that one of the characterising features of the axial age pointed out by Karl Jaspers, the alleged striving for an insight into the whole or totality was a mistake, or rather something even less than that: a full-blown illusion, as there never was such an object as 'the world' about which one could even have truth-apt thoughts. We mistake the objects as shadows of the all-encompassing, which is why I speak of an illusion rather than of a hallucination.

When Parmenides was believed to have stated an insight into totality or into its uniqueness, he was in fact suffering from an illusion, an illusion that is as meaningless as it gets. Hegel's famous claim that 'Pure being and Pure nothing are therefore the same',[21] should accordingly be interpreted as stating that there literally is nothing we can say about being (totality; the most universal 'concept'), for it cannot be referred to at all. His radical departure from any mystical insight or any form of 'Anschauung' of the absolute, as he puts it, is a rejection of metaphysics in the sense of the discipline that studies totality.[22] When we look for the world, there is nothing to be seen, nothing to be referred to, nothing to be described. There is no way the world could possibly have existed.

The no-world-view entails a lot of immediate consequences, in particular and most obviously, that no one should hold any world view whatsoever. World views are illusions, and if we hold them we are prone to delusion. This applies to religious as well as scientific (or any other) world views. We cannot save the world by regarding it as a regulative idea, as Habermas in line with his Kantianism suggests at various stages of his career.[23] The world cannot exist, not even at the limit of inquiry or in the form of a discursive presupposition. We cannot even presuppose it as an all-encompassing, albeit somehow inaccessible or unsurveyable domain. There really is nothing to be seen, heard, felt, or thought about when it comes to the world.

Apart from these evidently destructive consequences of the no-world-view, consequences I subsume under the heading of 'negative ontology', it proves to be a useful tool in actual positive ontology. The fact that we need to avoid postulating the world in any of its traditional or avant-garde disguises is more than just a caveat for theory-building in ontology. We now already know that ontology can be done independently of metaphysics, and that it actually has to be thus conceived in order to be a meaningful enterprise. In the following part of this treatise that deals with positive ontology, it will be important to revise our theory of modality in light of the impossibility of metaphysics. In particular, we need to find a way to avoid even the idea of overall modality, such as the modality of 'the actual world' or of 'possible worlds', as these concepts are inextricably bound up with the idea of complete worlds. In addition, I will draw positive consequences from the absolute impossibility of any theory of everything of any nature whatsoever, as this will lead me to a proof of the necessary existence of indefinitely many fields of sense with an in principle open texture. It is impossible that all fields of sense have the same overall structure or logical form in virtue of being fields of sense, for this presupposes the availability of an all-encompassing algorithm or transcendental matrix, a blueprint of what it is for fields of sense to exist in general or *überhaupt*, as the natives say in my country. *That* there are indefinitely many fields of sense is therefore accessible *a priori*, *what* they are is only accessible *a posteriori*, which is itself a fact accessible *a priori*. What there is by necessity constantly surprises us. The problem is therefore not how there can be innovation, creation, or the new, as immanentist philosophers like Deleuze traditionally put it, but rather how it is not the case that we are constantly surprised, as this would also overthrow any rational form of expectation.

Notes

1. On this see also my *Why the World does not Exist.*
2. On this see Schaffer, 'The Action of the Whole'; 'The Internal Relatedness of All Things'; 'Monism: The Priority of the Whole'; 'Spacetime the One Substance'. I disagree with Schaffer's equation of world and universe and not with his equation of the universe with space-time as the one (physical) substance. Again, I disagree with his equation of his concept of the one substance with Spinoza's concept of the one substance, as 'nature' in Spinoza's mouth simply does not mean what it means in our mouth. It certainly is not identical with the material universe.
3. Luft, *Deflationary Ontology as Network Ontology* (forthcoming). This paper is based on a series of lectures given at the University of Bonn in June 2012.
4. This worry was regularly expressed during my presentation of the view in various lectures and earlier texts. Thanks to Marius Bartmann, Jens Rometsch, and Umrao Sethi for pushing me to clarify my position in this regard. I do not know if my response is satisfactory, but at least there is a response.
5. On the theory of analogical meaning see Ross, *Portraying Analogy.*
6. Aristotle, *Metaphysics*, 1003a33–b4: 'There are many senses in which a thing may be said to "be", but they are related to one central point, one definite kind of thing, and are not homonymous. Everything which is healthy is related to health, one thing in the sense that it preserves health, another in the sense that it produces it, another in the sense that it is a symptom of health, another because it is capable of it. And that which is medical is relative to the medical art, one thing in the sense that it possesses it, another in the sense that it is naturally adapted to it, another in the sense that it is a function of the medical art. And we shall find other words used similarly to these.'
7. Cf. Heidegger, *Being and Time*, p. 203.
8. Ibid.
9. Ibid.
10. Ibid.
11. Ibid.
12. Ibid.
13. Cf. Heidegger, *Being and Time*, p. 203f.
14. See Heidegger, *Das Argument gegen den Brauch.*
15. My translation of *Das Argument gegen den Brauch*, p. 6: 'Für

uns Geologen kann es keinen Zweifel an der Realität einer sehr langen vor-menschlichen Erdgeschichte geben. Diese Realität mag letzten Endes nur dank der rückblickenden Tätigkeit des menschlichen Geistes existieren – aber da wird einem doch vor seiner Gottähnlichkeit etwas bange.'

16. *Das Argument gegen den Brauch*, p. 69: 'Dieses Argument *für* die Unnötigkeit des Menschen hinsichtlich des Ansichseienden ist richtig'.

17. Ramsey, 'General Propositions and Causality', p. 238.

18. As far as I can recall, this objection was first raised by Marius Bartmann in conversations at the time I was starting to develop the details of the view, that is, around 2008–9.

19. Arguably, this is the case Hegel discusses under the heading of 'Being' at the very beginning of the *Science of Logic*, but I will not spell this out here in order not to create too much distraction. Suffice it to note in passing that I take Hegel to claim that being and nothing are one and the same insofar as both expressions do not refer to anything in particular. They are not even empty names that happen to not refer to anything these days (or ever), but radically or absolutely empty gestures. They are nothing.

20. In Gabriel, *Der Mensch im Mythos*, §§ 4–5, I tried to argue that this is already Kant's take on this issue. However, this assumes that Kant's preferred solution, namely transcendental idealism, is not as central to the argument as Kant himself officially believes and declares. This is why I want to leave it open whether Kant really made exactly this point, even though it is often attributed to him.

21. Hegel, *The Science of Logic*, p. 69.

22. To spell this out will require a book on Hegel that I intend to write in the future. In particular, it will be important to show that Hegel's constant use of 'the world' as in 'world history' is precisely not committed to the idea of totality. 'The true is the whole' does not mean that there is a whole, but it means that the true is the principled list of errors leading to the illusion that there is a whole. On a similar reading along those lines see, of course, Žižek, *Less than nothing* and already his Žižek, *For They Know Not What They Do*.

23. See Habermas, *Truth and Justification*, p. 16, pp. 30–1, and p. 57.

Part II

Positive Ontology

8

Indefinitely Many Fields of Sense

The results of the preceding chapter were negative in that they culminated in the no-world-view. However, there are many positive results that will be unfolded in this chapter: at this point, we can justifiably claim to know that metaphysics and ontology need to be clearly distinguished, and that existence is appearance in a field of sense.[1] In particular, we also know that there is nothing all-encompassing, that the world does not exist. Now, the world can take many shapes in a variety of kinds of thought in addition to philosophically trained thinking. The idea of an all-encompassing entity or domain has become ingrained in humanity's conception of itself and its position in the widest or broadest possible context. In that particular sense, there is a history of the world that consists in the unification of humanity under the illusory heading of the world. Humans have become world-beings (*Weltwesen*), that is, beings that are struck by the illusion that the world exists, an illusion we need to disabuse ourselves of.

As already noted several times, the world currently primarily manifests itself in the shape of the domain of a physical theory of everything, where the world is identified with the universe. However, the world need not be identified with any *object* of investigation. The world-illusion is operative in many forms, not just in the form of the idea of an extant unity. The no-world-view undermines all claims to the all-encompassing, including claims to the existence of an all-encompassing theory, algorithm, rule, principle, or concept. Nothing encompasses everything, no thing, no thought, no abstract operation or computation, no god.

Not even a god could have created the world. Trivially, he would have to have created himself together with the world (as he himself would have to have existed). This trivial fact traditionally generated paradoxes for theology that were usually solved, or rather accepted, in the form of celebratory nonsense such as that God created himself (*causa sui*), even if not quite out of nothing. Ontotheology is of no help when it comes to ontology, as we cannot make it the case that the world exists by *fiat* or by claiming that it indeed cannot exist, but that God somehow manages to make the paradox go away or that the world's existence is not paradoxical from God's point of view that happens to be inaccessible to human reason. The all-encompassing cannot exist behind our backs, as it were. It cannot exist in an incomprehensible or transcendent manner. It is impossible for it to exist, full stop. No further qualification can make it the case that the world exists.

In this second part of the treatise, I shall argue in detail that the world is the only thing (or object, or event, or domain, or field) that necessarily does not exist. Here, 'necessity' means that there is no field in which there is a relation between an all-encompassing field (the world) and anything it would have to encompass so as to be *all*-encompassing. In general, I shall argue that necessity is a field-immanent modality characterising a relation between objects in a given field, namely a relation that could not be otherwise. There is no field in which such a relation can appear between the world and anything it is supposed to encompass, as I have already claimed in Chapter 7. Even though my account is incompatible with standard contemporary modal metaphysics quantifying over possible worlds, at this stage of the argument one could also illustrate my point by saying that the world itself is not itself part of any possible world. Given that it does not exist in any possible world, its non-existence is necessary on the standard contemporary account of necessity.

We can now raise the question concerning how many fields of sense there are. Evidently, the answer cannot be just one, as this would amount to metaphysical monism. *Metaphysical monism* claims that there is only one field of sense (the world). *Metaphysical dualism* according to which there are two fields of sense is utterly arbitrary and consequently certainly does not fare any better than metaphysical monism. Why should there only be two fields of sense of all things, say, *res extensa* and *res cogitans*? Traditionally, at least from Plato to Descartes, arguments for metaphysical dualism hinge on a distinction between thinking and what can be thought about. It is designed to account for the fact that thought can generally be both about non-intentional, non-thinking objects and about itself, which is, for all we know, a feature or capacity limited to thought. Thus, one can distinguish between thought and the moon, or generally, between thought and all the objects it can be about that are not themselves thoughts. In short, there is a distinction between intentional and non-intentional objects, where the intentional objects are traditionally called 'subjects'. By 'intentional object' here I do not refer to objects of intentions, to that which is represented by an intentional state or system, but rather as that which represents or is intentional. Accordingly, the relevant distinction is between intentional objects (such as photographs and subjects) and non-intentional objects (such as stones and earthquakes).

With more precision one would of course have to draw an additional distinction between intentional subjects (intentional objects aware of themselves as intentional objects in special ways) and other intentional objects, such as photographs or footprints on the moon. Intentional subjects are intentional objects insofar as they themselves appear in fields of sense. Otherwise, they could not exist. Yet, the class of intentional objects not only comprises intentional subjects, that is, the kinds of objects we traditionally call 'subjects'. Footprints on the moon, or any other trace recording of an event on the moon, are also intentional in that they are *about* some event. For something to be about something it is not necessary that someone with certain capacities be aware of this fact. Cosmic background radiation is evidence for the events that caused it (for all we know right now: the Big Bang). In that sense it is about the events that caused it. This relation between cosmic background radiation and the events that caused it such that the events can be recovered from an understanding of the radiation does not hold because someone makes it so. It is as real or 'out there' as anything and certainly need not be constructed or individuated by some theory or other in order to obtain. Here, the idea is that intentionality is not generally reference-dependent on awareness.[2]

Brandom has proposed a distinction between *sense-dependence* and *reference-dependence*, according to which concepts are reference-dependent if and only if something only falls under one of the concepts in virtue of falling under the other concept and sense-dependent if one can only grasp one concept in virtue of grasping the other one.[3] Many traditional accounts of subjectivity (most prominently Fichte's) presuppose that subjects have a reference-dependent form of self-awareness, that is, a form of awareness that could not have existed had no one been aware in this way. Here, the object, awareness, might be construed as reference-dependent on the awareness within which it appears. Self-awareness and awareness are reference-dependent in the sense that nothing falls under the concept of being self-aware without falling under the concept of being aware and *vice versa*. Yet, as Hegel points out in his *Phenomenology of Spirit*, this reference-dependence does not cover the entire range of forms of awareness, as the awareness in lower animals (where 'lower' just means not endowed with this special self-awareness) is not reference-dependent on self-awareness. The reference-dependence often discussed under the heading of 'self-consciousness' traditionally goes by the name of 'subjectivity', which was intended to be the special status we assign to ourselves in creating a new form of awareness that is reference-dependent on our awareness of it. This concept significantly differs from the contemporary concept of subjectivity, where this is often understood as the domain of phenomenal content. Yet, when Kant and his successors speak of subjectivity, the subject, or the I, they do not refer to the subjective in the contemporary sense, but rather to a particular relation between awareness and self-awareness, one which can be characterised as reference-dependence.

Yet, even if we grant that the structure envisaged by Kant and Fichte applies to us such that we are subjects in this somewhat special sense, it does not even hold across the board in our own case. If I am aware of the small sculptural representation of the owl of Minerva on the right-hand side of my desk, this awareness of the sculptural representation is not there by virtue of my awareness of it. The awareness is as independent from the higher-order awareness as the sculpture is independent from the first-order awareness within which I introduced it as long as there is such a sculpture on my desk and I have not made it up, for instance, in the context of the illustration of the concepts I am hereby individuating. Nevertheless, the idea of the subject in the peculiar way it has shaped philosophical accounts of the self in Kant's wake has introduced the concept of a form of self-awareness, in which the awareness one is aware of only exists in the higher-order awareness we have of it.[4] In particular, Fichte has insisted on the fact that our awareness of our awareness in general is reference-dependent on the higher-order awareness necessary for understanding the proposition I express with this sentence. His 'original insight', as Dieter Henrich has notably labelled it, has it that the discovery of a topic-neutral structure of awareness, according to which we can become aware of essentially everything – at least, of a lot of things from sculptures to quarks – is the creation of an object, namely the creation of an object that can be about essentially everything.[5] In addition, this object is created by the awareness realised in each instance by whoever currently reads and understands the paragraph at hand. We are not constantly aware of the topic-neutral structure of our awareness, and such a higher-order awareness is not needed for the function of standard survival-driven object-level awareness. Other animals are aware of all sorts of things without being aware of this very fact. Fichte pointed out that the status of a subject in general is the status of someone capable of creating the structure of topic-neutral awareness by becoming aware of it.

However, he underestimated the modal requirements that inform the articulation of his account. For, even if no one had ever been around to notice, their awareness would still have been topic-neutral. Against this background, he later, most clearly in his 1804 lectures on the *Wissenschaftslehre*, revoked the idealistic idea of reference-dependent topic-neutral object-awareness in favour of a concept he then calls 'being', by which he refers to the topic-neutral general structure of awareness of which we can become aware by articulating it. 'Philosophy should reveal and discover *being in and of itself.* – Correct, and exactly our purpose.'[6] Yet, he then believes that the structure would have existed or truths about it would have obtained had we not noticed it, as he realised that he should not say that we ultimately only become fully self-aware through philosophical self-awareness. He gives up on the idea that this articulation is a creation from nothing, a kind of ultimate bootstrapping, for the ultimate reason that the structure of subjectivity, that is to say, of self-awareness of topic-neutral awareness, either is all-out maximally modally robust or at least has some relevant modally robust properties. This accounts for the fact that we find ourselves in the position of subjects adjusting their beliefs in light of their capacity to become self-aware in the general sense, which is an important ability we actualise in the form of autonomous autobiographies: we manage our beliefs and desires in light of the fact that we might have different beliefs and desires at every point, which is why we are able to distance ourselves from commitments of any kind in order to assess their range and value.

A better motivation for metaphysical dualism, dispensing with the mythology of souls, minds, or subjects, for that matter, could invoke the distinction between objects and facts. At this point we can say that an object is something about which something is true. Objects are embedded in facts, this is their functional role. In the human realm this manifests itself as the property of objects that something can truly be said or thought of them. It is true of the moon that it is not the earth and as soon as someone is around to assert this it can also be truly said of the moon that it is not the earth. That the moon is not the earth is a fact. It is neither identical with the moon nor with the earth. On this construal, it might seem as though there is an enhanced metaphysical dualism, a dualism of facts and objects, which at least goes beyond the subject-object-dichotomy.

'Fact' and 'object' accordingly seem to denote *categories*, that is, the most general distinctions right below the most universal concept of being or existence. Yet, we know that being or existence cannot be the most universal concept, insofar as this is supposed to mean that there is a concept under which everything falls. This would amount to metaphysical monism. Therefore, one might be tempted to assert that fact and object are not categories, specifications of a more universal concept, but rather independent meanings of being, substance, or existence. Notoriously, Descartes himself oscillates between metaphysical monism and metaphysical dualism, or rather trialism. Sometimes he says that there are two kinds of substances (forms of existence), thinking and extended substance, and sometimes he defines substance in such a way that there ultimately can only be one, namely God.[7] This tension could be 'reconciled' by maintaining that there are three substances: thinking, extended and divine substance, which, of course, triggers the question of why all three of them are called substance, and whether there is a substance-substance, as it were, the substance of all substances. Descartes did not really answer these questions, but they nevertheless became salient in his wake. It is not a coincidence that the major post-Cartesian metaphysicians, Spinoza and Leibniz in particular, were eager to unify the Cartesian account of substance.

Generally, let us call *metaphysical finitism* any view according to which there are a finite number of distinctions to be drawn in order to summarise everything. Metaphysical finitism is either immediately identical with metaphysical monism (in this case the number of distinctions is very finite, namely one) or it specifies some other number. Yet, all traditional forms of metaphysical finitism where the number of distinctions is bigger than just one happen to be ultimately themselves committed to some form of monism. For instance, Leibniz was willing to increase the number of substances to the infinite, even though he did not really commit himself to the idea that there are infinitely many kinds of substances. There is a residual conception of the One or even God, which interestingly is utterly unmotivated by Leibniz' own epistemological standards.[8] However, note that the view that there are infinitely many kinds of substances, categories, or modes of existence is a possible instance of metaphysical finitism as long as there is a principled way of generating the kinds of substance. Even if there are infinitely many categories such that insight into some principle triggers insight into that very infinity, we are still stuck with monism. If being were a principle governing the unfolding of a unified reality consisting of infinitely categorical joints one level down from being, being would fulfil the function of the world: it would be the world.

Paradoxically, metaphysical nihilism, the view that there are no distinctions to be drawn, that there is a big nothingness or oneness, that there is no substance, but only emptiness, Śūnyatā Śūnyatā, or what have you, is also just another instance of metaphysical finitism.[9] Metaphysical nihilism is the most parsimonious and most obviously false instance of metaphysics, as its answer to the question of how many kinds of objects there are is zero. It leaves us with an empty domain, or rather with emptiness, which is why it has to resort to metaphor (at best) and meditation in order to cover up the obvious fact that it has literally nothing to say. Metaphysical nihilism denies that there are any domains. It thereby unifies reality into something like radically unhinged appearances, into becomings without anything becoming, into fragments not even intelligible as such. Everything turns into an illusion as soon as we give up the idea of there being any domain whatsoever. Metaphysical nihilism is, therefore, not a no-world-view. Rather it is a world view denying the articulation of its own assumptions.

Metaphysics always remains embroiled in monism in one way or other, as it is an answer to the question of what the 'fundamental nature of reality' is. Answers to this question have been manifold, and they typically disagree about the number of categories, usually ranging between two and twelve. The problem, however, is not how many categories there are, as we already know that there are no categories at all. Categories are the most general distinctions specifying the concept of being or existence. Plato in *The Sophist* introduced them under the name of 'the highest genera (μέγιστα τῶν γενῶν)'[10], where he particularly mentions 'being itself, movement, and rest (τό τε ὂν αὐτὸ καὶ στάσις καὶ κίνησις)'[11] and informs us at the same time that this list is only a sample (ἄττα[12]) of a broader categorical structure that is an articulation (λόγος) of the 'idea of being (τοῦ ὄντος [...] ἰδέα)',[13] which is the object of philosophical investigation in opposition to Sophistic engagement with not-being.

> Visitor: But the philosopher always uses reasoning to stay near the form, being. He isn't at all easy to see because that area is so bright and the eyes of most people's souls can't bear to look at what's divine.[14]

Aristotle took over the idea and transformed the highest genera into categories in his attempt to circumvent the problem of a most universal concept of being under which the categories fall. Kant was under the right impression that Aristotle's categories are a 'meaningless rhapsody'[15] insofar as Aristotle ultimately postulates only an analogical unification of the categories as they relate to the all-encompassing principle that 'everything is coordinated with respect to one (πρὸς ἓν γὰρ ἅπαντα συντέτακται)'.[16] The one with respect to which everything is coordinated is the distinction between *dynamis* and *energeia*: everything there is is a realisation of its potential and can, accordingly, be measured by specifying its potential and its degree of realisation.[17] Despite his discovery that being cannot be the most universal concept, Aristotle failed to implement this discovery when he postulated a unifying hierarchical structure with unhampered paradigmatic *energeia* as the *causa exemplaris* of all becoming.

Even metaphysical infinitism is supported by metaphysical monism. The claim that there either are infinitely many substances or infinitely many kinds of substances assumes that there either is a rule triggering the infinite progression of substances or that this progression at least takes place within an all-encompassing domain. Aristotle famously claimed that the alternative to this would be a 'bad tragedy',[18] or in more contemporary terms, a movie without any plot whatsoever. Of course, he could not anticipate that we moderns are long used to plotless and pointless narratives and would not consider it as an objection against a narrative that it progresses through random twists and turns. *Last Year in Marienbad* has become a metaphysical option. However, insofar as even *Last Year in Marienbad* is unified by the sheer fact that it is one movie – this-movie-rather-than-another – one could still claim that its reality is encompassed by a formal unifying principle. Spinoza comes closest to the second kind of metaphysical infinitism even though he only concedes that there are infinitely many attributes (categories) of the one all-encompassing substance. Both Leibniz and Spinoza ultimately postulate an underlying all-encompassing principle they call God and believe that their respective versions of metaphysical infinitism are still grounded in a somewhat deviant version of the One.

However, the no-world-view straightforwardly entails that there is no all-encompassing or underlying principle of any sort whatsoever. The number of fields of sense is accordingly indefinite, albeit in a sense that naturally differs from the set-theoretical concept of the transfinite. In contemporary philosophy, Badiou approaches this point with his insistence on the transfinite. According to Badiou there is a transfinite proliferation of sets generated by Cantor's theorem.[19] The theorem states that the set of all subsets of any given set S (be it finite or infinite), its so-called power set, has a greater cardinality than the original set, that is, roughly speaking that it has more members than the original set. The idea behind this is quite intuitive for finite sets. Let S be the set with two elements a, b: S = {a,b}. This set has the subsets: {a}, {b}, {a,b}, {∅}. The set of these subsets, the power set P(S), accordingly, is the set: {{a}, {b}, {a,b}, {∅}}. Whereas S has two members, P(S) has 2^2, that is, four members. Cantor's theorem holds both for finite and infinite sets and its proof establishes that there are different orders of the infinite studied by transfinite set theory.[20]

There are different devices one can use in order to actually demonstrate that there are such orders of the infinite.[21] However, as argued in Chapter 4, none of them suffice as an ontological argument for the simple reason that not all objects are discrete in the sense needed by the discrete ontology projected by any mathematical method. Despite Badiou's welcome attempt to do ontology without the One, without an all-encompassing principle, his attempt fails for a simple reason: his idea of an all-encompassing operation (Cantor's theorem) generating the transfinite, here the order of different infinities, is itself another version of the One or the world. Badiou's intention was praiseworthy insofar as he was looking for a way of doing ontology without metaphysics, of inquiring into the plurality of domains without postulating a unifying principle. Yet, his methodological identification of ontology with set theory surreptitiously reintroduces unification and has the disadvantage of pretending that uninterpreted set theory would be an immediate conceptual representation of inconsistent multiplicity, that is, of a proliferation without the One. The disadvantage is that Badiou contradicts himself by presenting the reader with a (highly contentious) interpretation of set theory and not with an itself uninterpreted formalism. The very concept of a set is introduced intuitively as some collection or other even when it is refined, that is to say, technically defined by the axiom systems devised in order to overcome the paradoxes brought to light in the immediate wake of Cantor's introduction of transfinite set theory. However, what it is to be multiple is not defined by set theory for every multiple entity or group, but remains only partially articulated on such discrete ground. The idea of set theory as ontology, or rather the idea of a replacement of philosophical ontology by some idealised form of intellectual activity or other, is insufficiently motivated in Badiou's writings. My insistence that no formalism interprets itself, for instance, is not subject to Badiou's criticism of the linguistic turn approach within the philosophy of mathematics. My aim is not to reduce the objectivity of mathematics, but rather to put ontology in the right place with respect to our capacity to develop formal systems in order to regiment our mathematical discourse. Yet, our capacity of said regimentation should not mislead us into identifying the objects we thereby come to study with the regimented discourse we have invented in order to study them.

As already discussed, *mathematicism* is the position that everything is subject to mathematical structures and, therefore, can be thought of with recourse to some subfield of mathematics or other. Aristotle already pointed out against Plato's mathematicism that there are many objects and events we cannot think of mathematically, as they involve contingency and vagueness in forms that are not accessible to any discrete description. Actions have ever since been invoked in order to counterbalance the fantasy that everything there is is subject to mathematical laws ranging from set theory to probability theory aided by statistics. Badiou himself paradoxically constantly invokes a good example for the shortcomings of mathematicism, namely love, or rather falling in love. If two people fall in love, this event transcends their computation and rational choices even where some probabilities are involved. One cannot fall in love with someone while one is informed about the statistics that are supposed to explain why one falls in love, which is one of the many reasons why online dating or the intervention of dating agencies in general does not really work. It only works by accident via the fantasy of those involved regarding the functioning of the procedure. No combination of insight into personal interests or the social and biological factors of attraction and repulsion is able to make people fall in love. Even if a huge range of factors – including brute ones such as economical, neurochemical and sociobiological factors – play a role, being aware of these factors rather undermines the prospects of falling in love.

Outside of limited circles of philosophers, it usually does not need a lot of convincing for people to understand that mathematics cannot be an all-encompassing form of insight. Mathematicism is one shape the world takes among many others, including *sociologism* and *politicism*, by which I mean to refer to the idea that social structures or political structures underpin everything, in particular our own theoretical preferences. The view that everything can be made to be political, that there is no neutral truth or insight, is hopelessly overgeneralised and famously does not withstand self-application. It also misses the most trivial facts, such as my insight that the road in front of my building is longer than even my longest hair. I do not hold this latter belief because I belong to a certain group of people with certain overall interests (whatever that group may be). No politics is responsible for my belief that there are more moons in our solar system than one or, to play it safer, for my belief that there are stones.

The no-world-view entails a different version of the very idea behind invoking the transfinite in philosophy. In order to see this, it is sufficient to spell out another simple example inspired by Hilary Putnam's argument for his internal realism, whose penchant for anti-realism I evidently do not share. I call my version of the argument *the allegory of the cubes*, and I will draw conclusions from the arguments that differ significantly from Putnam's anti-realist intentions at the time.[22] Imagine there are three cubes on a table: a red cube, a blue cube and a white cube. Someone approaches the table and is asked how many objects there are on the table. A natural response to the question would, of course, be three. In this case, the passer-by might have counted the cubes.

Her rule of count accordingly was the maxim: 'count the cubes!'
Yet, there are evidently different ways of grouping the objects on
the table according to different rules of count. If we count the sides
of the cubes, the answer will be eighteen; if we count the colours,
the answer will again be three; if we count the abstract representations of the French flag, the answer will be one. In addition,
we might count the atoms, which is much harder to achieve and
would certainly provide us with a number of objects much larger
than three or eighteen. In a similar context, Frege once pointed out
the obvious when he said that the same object can be described as
three trees and as one group of trees.[23]

Let us call the respective rules of count used when specifying
an answer to the question of how many objects there are in the
allegory of the cubes, the *senses of the situation*. A 'sense of a situation' is a response to the question 'What is on the table?' rather
than to the question 'How many objects are there on the table?'[24]
The senses individuate a field of sense about which a limited
number of things can truly be said. It is true that in the field of
sense of atoms, there are n atoms on the table, just as much as it is
true that there are three objects in the field of sense of cubes. The
rules of count used by the passer-by are objective rules and not
mental constructions or linguistic representations, which is why
we can count them too. There is a field of sense of the fields of
sense listed. In this field, there are x senses, where x is indefinite, as
we have not individuated a clear-cut rule limiting the proliferation
of senses.

We can now draw a distinction between the objects in the
respective fields and the sense insofar as they are objects in the
field of sense of the fields of sense listed above. In this context, it
is crucial to introduce the *principle of functional flexibility*. This
principle states that to be an object is to be embedded in a field of
sense. Objects are denizens of fields of sense. The sense individuates the objects and accounts for the specific truths about them. It
is objectively true about the cubes that there are three of them on
the table. There is nothing mind-dependent, imaginary, or constructed in this truth. At the same time it is objectively true about
the atoms on the table – or rather in some yet to be defined region
of space-time related to the table situation – that there are n of
them in the situation. The rules of count are not linguistic projections onto some raw material, the objects, as the very concept of
an object is functional. It describes something insofar as it appears

in a field of sense. Objects are individuals insofar as they exist, that is, insofar as they appear in a field of sense by being in part individuated by the senses determining them as these rather than those kinds of objects. Now, for every field of sense, we know that it exists insofar as it appears in some field of sense or other. All above-mentioned fields of sense appear in the field of sense of the allegory of the cubes and, therefore, are objects within that field. Insofar as fields of sense themselves exist, they are embedded in fields of sense as objects or individuals.

By an *individual* I understand anything that is at least in part individuated by some sense or other as that about which something is true. Correspondingly, any old truth-apt description characterises an individual, as it is true of something or other. I will use 'individual' and 'object' more or less interchangeably, where the only substantial difference between the two consists in the emphasis on individuation carried along with the term 'individual', whereas 'object' might emphasise the fact that something is true about it, that it can become the objective (and by no means always mind- or reference-dependent) correlate of a true thought.

A field of sense in contradistinction to its individuals is not necessarily or not generally individuated by the sense or senses characterising its denizens. The concept of cubes is not itself a cube, the concept of an atom is not itself an atom, and so on. However, the concept of a cube and the concept of an atom are themselves concepts, which is why they both exist in the field of sense of concepts. One of the differences between cubes and concepts is that concepts fall under the concept of concept such that the field of sense of concepts can appear within itself. Some fields are self-referential. Cubes and concepts (such as the concept cube) fall under concepts. Yet, insofar as we refer to the concept 'concept', it is an individual alongside other individuals, such as the concept 'horse' and the concept 'cube'. The difference between the concept 'concept' as an individual and as a field of sense is functional and not substantial. It functions differently when regarded as an individual and as a field of sense. In this way, I disagree with the idea behind type-theory or Frege's dualism of object and concept. Of course, a concept can become an object of thought, but nothing can both function as object and concept in the same respect or in the same sense. If I think that it is raining, the event of raining at least appears in my thought about it. My thought serves the field function. Yet, someone else might think about my thought that it is raining, believing that I am wrong, say. In this case, my thought appears as an object in another field. At the same time, it is both a field and an object, but in different respects. There might be local restrictions on functional flexibility, as one might suspect that too much functional flexibility might generate the paradoxes tamed by type-theory or any other version of the claim that function and argument simply differ. It might be necessary for some formal systems to so much as get off the ground that functional flexibility is limited within their scope, but this does not undermine the point I am putting forward.

The functional division of labour entails that no field of sense can account both for all of its objects and for itself. When accounting for all its objects and for itself, it has to count itself among its objects and thereby changes the arrangement of the individuals by appearing among them. The difference between the concept 'concept' as an object and as a field of sense is that *qua* object it does not differ from the concept 'horse', whereas *qua* field of sense it differs from the concept 'horse' precisely by not being among the objects falling under it, but by having them fall under it. The concept 'horse' does not have the concept 'moon' fall under it; it falls under the concept 'concept' alongside the concept 'moon'. In that respect it differs from the concept 'concept' insofar as it functions as the concept 'concept' and is not referred to in our thoughts about concepts. The concept 'horse' falls under the concept 'concept'. In this light, the concept 'concept' encompasses more than the concept 'horse', and it appears on a different level. Yet, given that the concept 'concept' is as much a concept as any other concept, it also appears alongside all other concepts.

The concept 'concept' is both the most universal concept and a particular concept; it appears on both levels, which is why Hegel notoriously believed that he could solve the problem of the appearance of the whole within itself with recourse to the theory of conceptual content. He calls 'the Concept' the structure of the concept 'concept' according to which it both falls under itself and thereby appears alongside other objects, such as the concept 'horse', and is such that all concepts fall under it. In the latter perspective, it is the concept encompassing all concepts, which it is not in the former. Hegel celebrates this with his early Jena formula of 'the identity of identity and non-identity',[25] which just means that the concept 'concept' is both the universal concept and a particular object within the realm of concepts.

Hegel was well aware of the problems addressed by the no-world-view, and he detected the argument behind it from his reading of the antinomies in Kant's *First Critique*, where Kant puts the problem of the world centre stage.[26] Although I disagree with Hegel's solution of the problem of the no-world-view, his attempt to reformulate the problem of totality in terms of meta-theory of theories of totality still is one of the most ambitious and detailed attempts to hold on the world despite the antinomies and paradoxes it generates. This is why it is helpful to recall the outlines of Hegel's strategy.

In Hegel's language the problem of the world is the problem of the absolute. According to him, we need to find a way to think of the absolute as related to our thoughts about it in order to avoid a dualism of being (in-itself) and appearance (for-us). We need to conceive of how things are (in themselves) as graspable by us if we want to avoid overgeneralised forms of scepticism. In the *Science of Logic*, most centrally in the *Subjective Logic*, Hegel argues that there is at least one thing in itself we can grasp, namely the truth itself. Truth is the object of investigation of the last part of the book.[27] Hegel's assumption is that truth is intimately related to the relation of falling under a concept. Given that the concept 'concept' falls under itself, Hegel's account of concepts, his theory of conceptual content, operates under self-referential conditions in order to achieve insight into our overall capacity to grasp conceptual content. The trick is that we can know that if anything falls under concepts, the concept 'concept' does. If the concept 'concept' is not a concept, nothing is, because one would have to admit that all concepts falling under the concept 'concept' fall under something that is not a concept. But then what if the concept 'concept' is not a concept in the sense that it is not suitable for having objects fall under it (which is what a concept is)? Therefore, for there to be any concepts whatsoever, the concept 'concept' better fall under itself.

Yet, we need to distinguish between three different levels on which the concept 'concept' appears within its overall domain. First, the concept 'concept' is the most universal concept under which all concepts fall. Hegel calls this 'the universal (das Allgemeine)'. This is Hegel's concept of the world.[28] Second, insofar as the concept 'concept' appears alongside other concepts it is 'the particular (das Besondere)'. The concept 'horse' is a particular concept; it is less universal than the concept 'concept', but more encompassing than the concept associated with the indefinite description 'the horses who live on that lawn'. Third, the concept 'concept' is 'the individual (das Einzelne)' insofar as there is exactly one concept 'concept', the one fully individuated by Hegel's overall descriptions of it (granted that he gets it right). The concept 'concept' appears on these three levels and Hegel believes that this corresponds to our overall world-picture: the world/absolute is the most universal all-encompassing structure, which is repeated as a unifying principle at every local level. This guarantees for Hegel that there is exactly one world or one absolute in all its manifold manifestations.

Concepts make fields of sense explicit where they successfully individuate senses, which is not to say that all senses are concepts or conceptual – unless one wants to call all structures 'conceptual', which would be a question-begging way of proving the 'boundlessness of the conceptual'.[29] Against this background my objection against Hegel's attempt to guarantee that the concept 'concept' falls within its own reach claims that it only amounts to a coherent theory of totality (a world view) if it can be shown that the conceptual is actually boundless. Yet, Hegel does not show this, and it is hard to say what it would mean to claim that that flower there already fell under a concept before there were concept-mongering creatures. What about objects we cannot ever actually conceptualise even though there are no *a priori* limits of knowledge, but say, physical restrictions on the knowability of certain objects (which is almost certainly the case)? In a similar vein, Timothy Williamson objected against McDowell's version of the boundlessness of the conceptual that it rules out the existence of 'elusive objects' on an *a priori* basis, that is, of objects, reference to which in terms of any specific concept fails because they withdraw whenever someone tries to refer to them with any concept more specific than that of 'potentially existing elusive objects'.[30]

The relevant self-referentiality of concepts does not spread out over totality by itself. It would, if we had reasons to think of totality as encompassed by a given actual thought no thinker we are acquainted with holds. But if such a form of idealism is the only way of solving the puzzles of the no-world-view, the no-world-view has the advantage of not being committed to the idea that totality is always already encompassed by some actual thought or concept. As Guido Kreis shows in his *Negative Dialektik* on the basis of Hegel's treatment of Kant's antinomies of the world in the first part of the *Science of Logics*, Hegel owes us an answer to the question how he can guarantee *a priori* that everything falls under some concept or other? Even if Hegel might have established that every concept falls under the concept 'concept', which might be his somewhat more modest project in the *Science of Logics*, he does not thereby prove that all objects fall under concepts. However, on one reading, Hegel did not even intend to show this, which is why he dubs his *Logics* 'a realm of shadows'.[31] This is why any adequate account of Hegel's concept of totality would have to go through the *Encyclopedia*, which is a long story. Without going into details here, let me just state that Hegel ultimately seems to think of the proof that everything is conceptual as an open-ended activity, which would lead him back to Kant. The difference between him and Kant would only lie in Hegel's insistence that the open-ended activity of proving that objects fall under specifiable concepts (an activity Hegel calls 'science') is not restricted to phenomena. Hegel might be read as Kant without any assumption associated with limits of thought based on *a priori* epistemological or semantic considerations.

In my own view, the very fact that there is a plurality of concepts is due to the fact that there is a plurality of senses. Senses come first and we partially unify them into concepts. Here, I agree with Frege to the extent that what distinguishes a concept from other concepts and turns it into this rather than that concept is its sense and not what satisfies it. The concept horse is satisfied by Larry (say). If Larry dies, it still refers to some horse or other, and if all horses are extinguished, it could still refer to horses, but happens not to refer to them anymore. Thus, concepts are not governed by an axiom of extensionality according to which they would be identical with their extension. In set theory predicates (concepts) are used as a contingent way of accessing a set, and they are chosen in such a way as to rule out temporality and contingency. This is why Frege defines pure concepts for his *Begriffsschrift*, whose individuation guarantees that they always refer to the same number of objects. His logicism is not a general theory of concepts or thought, but only a limited theory of idealised mathematical thought.

Frege introduces the concept of a sense so that he can account for the individuation of concepts independently from considerations involving contingently existing individuals. Linguistic meaning has to exhibit an autonomous feature that does not necessarily vary with the objects individuated by it. This point can be illustrated by considerations from the theory of descriptive content. Here we might come back to the notorious case of water. Imagine you drink a sip of water right now. As it drips down your throat, the sensation is of some liquid, and you say to yourself: 'This is liquid.' That this is liquid is an essential part of the descriptive content of what is going on when you drink a sip of water. The experience of drinking water corresponds to H2FLOW, as they put it in an episode of the TV show *Parks and Recreation*. Now, Kripke and subsequent developments in the theory of reference have famously taught us that what the description is of need not be essentially picked out by the description. Trivially, that this is liquid holds for other substances (in the non-technical sense of 'substance') too. Also, a description can be superficial in some cases, or even be bad, and nevertheless serve to pick out an object among others. Just consider the case where someone says about someone in the corner of a party that 'Francey's husband is the most drunk person in the room', intending to refer to the very drunk person in the corner under the right description. Even if it was not Francey's husband, but someone else, the referrer nevertheless can successfully refer to the person with the help of some description or other. But the question is not to what degree false or bad descriptions might still be useful for referring to an individual by pointing it out. Imagine the person in the corner is neither Francey's husband, nor even drunk at all, but the speaker pointed him out with her finger. In this scenario the bad descriptions are not at all used to individuate the person, but rather the finger individuates the object by pointing at it. The point I want to convey is not that we can use bad and good descriptions alike for the purpose of manufacturing useful reference conditions, but rather that objects themselves have to be individuated by senses, which are the objective correlates of good descriptive content. That some bad descriptions refer despite the fact that their descriptive content is somewhat off the mark is important evidence to be respected in the theory of reference, but does not prove that objects are different from all descriptions that could be used to truly characterise and partially individuate them.

Objects are bundles of senses or objective modes of presentation, that is to say, objects are identical with the totality of what is true about them, where this totality is more often than not infinite in quantity, which is the ontological reason behind the claim that our access to what there is is finite. Let us call this view *ontological bundle descriptivism*. Our grasp of what there is is not explicitly infinite, because we are constitutively limited by a number of definite categories governing the structure or horizon of our cognition, as our structure or horizon of cognition is itself just another at least potentially infinite object. The finitude of cognition and knowledge boils down to the fact that we cognise and know objects under some of their descriptions, which is not an obstacle, but rather an enabling condition for successful epistemic states. An epistemic state (such as belief, cognition, knowledge, reference) is successful to the extent to which it involves things as they objectively are in themselves, even if these things are sometimes objects only appearing when we make them appear. This is to say that even descriptions of objects or facts we justifiably deem constructed or created by the beliefs we have about them appear under descriptions that actually describe them.

A typical problem for bundle theories is that they need to explain how they avoid essences altogether. Even if objects are bundles of descriptions, is it not the case that the bundles are unified in that some senses or others are privileged? My answer to this is that there is governing sense, as it were, that holds the various senses of an object together, and it depends on the object in question what kind of governing sense might play this role. For some material objects, such as H_2O molecules, what Kripke says about natural kinds might be the right way to go, while for other objects, such as Sherlock Holmes, what holds the descriptions true of Sherlock Holmes together is the governing sense of the various novels and films in which he is involved. There is no reason to assimilate the bundle conditions of Sherlock Holmes to those of H_2O, as Kripke does. Why would H_2O or any other natural kind be ontologically paradigmatic? If one wants to call governing senses 'essences', I am perfectly happy to accept this weak form of essentialism, as long as one does not postulate nature as a totality of essences, as no such totality can exist.[32] There is at least an open texture of governing senses such that it is useless to try to reduce the number of governing senses to oversimplified categories like fiction and reality, or mind and nature. There are no categories of governing sense; the essences are not unified into the domain of the essential or nature. Kripke models all governing sense according to his seminal insights into the governing sense of some natural kinds. And indeed he rightly discovered that Sherlock Holmes is not a natural kind, which is not at all evidence against ontological bundle descriptivism, as long as we keep in mind that this view is directed against the idea of a possible table of categories of governing senses in the first place. Governing senses are as functionally flexible as objects and fields of sense.

It is not the case that in general the governing sense accounting for the fact that a relevant number of (truly ascribable) senses orbit around an object is that the object is of a particular kind. Kripke still privileges material objects as candidates for natural kinds. Yet, Hamlet is not a natural kind in the way I am, and he nevertheless is the focus of all true descriptions of him.[33] What holds these descriptions together is not Hamlet, some spatio-temporarily located person we can point to independently of our use of descriptions. You can point to me with the help of all sorts of false descriptions and still be a more or less successful referrer. However, to be more precise, pointing at someone with your finger involves visual descriptions, such as the description: whatever it is I am pointing to over there. What is visually presented to anyone is already described in the objective sense of a mode of presentation. There is an objective sense of 'description', where a description is not an overt linguistic activity. The fact that the drunk person attending the party looks to me like Francey's husband only obtains because something seems to be the case. If there is a visual illusion involved, there is an object in space-time on the other end of my attempted reference, and the true descriptions associated with that object individuate it even though I might add wrong descriptions (Francey's husband) to the true ones (the person in the corner over there). The relationship between true descriptions (senses as ways things are in themselves) and wrong descriptions (in particular, illusions and hallucinations) will be discussed in the epistemological Chapters 12 and 13. From an ontological point of view, we are not asking how we can distinguish true from false beliefs, but rather whether objects can be individuated independently of all facts in which they are embedded. My view is that a fact can only be expressed with the help of descriptions, and that these descriptions, therefore, are objectively true of the object they actually describe. Indeed, true articulated thought does not stop short of the facts, to borrow McDowell's phrase.[34] The reason for this does not lie in indeterminate reference, but in articulated sense. A true description is a fact, such as the fact that Arnold Schwarzenegger is the actor who played Hercules in *Hercules in New York*. Actually true thought therefore covers parts of what there is, namely all the parts someone has had a true thought about, which is not at all to say that all facts are true thoughts. Rather, all true thoughts are facts – they are true of something – which is the definition of a fact with which I am working here.

At this point, three major objections have to be met before we can proceed. All three objections deal with problems from the theory of negative existential assertions.

The first objection calls attention to impossible objects such as round squares. Is it true of round squares that they are impossible and, therefore, do not exist? If it is indeed true *of them*, they are objects in my functional sense of the term and, consequently, exist, for instance, in the field of sense of the impossible. To assert without further ado that there are impossible objects, where an impossible object is precisely an object whose non-existence is necessary, surely amounts to a straightforward contradiction. The assertion says of the same object that it both exists (that it is there) and does not exist. This point, focusing on impossible objects, differs from my claim that negative existentials such as 'there are no cats' usually mean that there are no cats in such-and-such a field of sense. On my account, standard negative existentials are restricted in a way similar to standard existential assertions. But the non-existence of impossible objects does not seem to be thus restricted. Their non-existence is unconditional. Or so the objection goes. If successful, the objection might be developed into the claim that the world exists in the same sense in which round squares exist, namely in the field of the (absolutely) impossible.

The objection can only fully be met after I have dealt with the modalities in later chapters in more detail. However, the idea will be that for a round square to be impossible is for it to be incompatible with the senses associated with a specific governing sense. For instance, in a space defined by Euclidian geometry, nothing is both round and square. But if I draw a square on a spherical surface there is a sense in which there now is an object one could legitimately call a round or rather curved square. Settling the meanings of 'round' and 'square' and making it impossible for there to be a round square is defining a field of sense in which there are no round squares. They cannot appear there. Now, the sense in which there are no round squares does not apply everywhere, but depends on a prior (not necessarily *a priori*) settling of meanings. To say that round squares are impossible is thus not to say that they are impossible *tout court*, but that they are impossible in some field or other. But, the objection might continue, once we have specified the meanings of 'round' and 'square', both terms rigidly refer across fields. They are incompatible everywhere. However, this incompatibility is subject to further specifications, such as the specification that nothing is wholly round and square at the same time and in the same respect, to put it in Aristotle's formulation of the law of non-contradiction. Further conditions have to be met in order to make 'round' and 'square' incompatible across the board. Round and square do not relate to each other as p and $not\text{-}p$. We need more meaning in order to make round and square incompatible. At least, we need definitions of round and square, say geometrical definitions. But then, the terms of which the definitions will consist are subject to further qualification and limitation. The conditions introducing the impossibility for something to be a round square simply do not hold across the board, and it is far from clear and generally accepted that no thing is a round square in exactly the way in which it is not the case that both something and its contradictory negation are true.

In short, my counter-argument against the objection from impossible objects is that there is no single unified field of sense of impossible objects in which they all exist, as there are very different conditions of possibility and impossibility associated with different fields of sense. More specifically, there is no *unified* field of impossible objects in which they all exist. The field in which we could try to unite them will have to present them as appearing in different fields, as their respective forms of impossibility are governed by different concrete forms of modality. What is impossible in one field might be possible in another. Nothing is absolutely impossible in the sense required by the objection. As I will argue later, this is not trivially self-undermining, as the assertion does not amount to the claim that it is absolutely impossible for something to be absolutely impossible.

My response to the first objection can be summed up as the claim that there are no unrestricted modalities. To say that there are impossible objects is to say that some descriptions are not jointly true of the same object in some field or other, and not to say that there is no field in which they can be jointly true of some object. There is no overall logical generality or universality governing all fields of sense, such as the most universal law of non-contradiction quantifying over all truth-apt structures (all instances of p), an insight which is yet another instance of the no-world-view.

The *second objection* is associated with what Kripke has

recently officially labelled 'the final problem of negative existentials'.[35] The problem is how to 'analyze a singular negative existential statement'[36] such as 'Sherlock Holmes does not exist.' Kripke's solution to the problem is in conflict with the account here presented, and as such it is possible to construct an objection out of Kripke's alternative. According to the first step of the objection, there are empty names such as 'Sherlock Holmes', 'unicorn' and 'bandersnatch' that are empty insofar as they are not even determined. To say that Sherlock Holmes does not exist according to Kripke cannot mean to say that Sherlock Holmes is merely a fictional character. And here I agree with him for exactly the reason that he himself gives, that is to say, because there is embedded fiction, so that we can say of a fictional character that he really exists (in the story), whereas some other character in the story is merely fictional (in the story), what Kripke calls a 'fictional fictional character'.[37] Accordingly, Kripke argues, negative existential statements do not generally say of some object that it is merely fictional rather than situated 'on the level of reality'.[38] His example is the possible discovery that Napoleon never existed. He claims that such a discovery would not amount to the insight that Napoleon was merely a fictional character rather than a conqueror of Europe. As a matter of fact, we do not always claim that some object that does not exist therefore only exists in a story.

Now, Kripke distinguishes the case of fictional discourse about Sherlock Holmes from the negative existential discovery that Napoleon never existed and the associated case of the true modal statement that Napoleon might never have existed. His solution of the first case is that Sherlock Holmes is not sufficiently determined. There are some descriptions of Sherlock Holmes, but they do not single out anyone in particular. In a similar context, the German philosopher Uwe Meixner draws a distinction between an 'Individuum' and an 'Individual'.[39] For him, an 'Individuum' is roughly a completely determined object, whereas an 'Individual' is a fragment of an 'Individuum', that is, something about which some truths can be formulated, but which nevertheless remains incompletely determined. For instance, it is undetermined how long Sherlock Holmes' fingernails are, or even whether he has fingernails. How do we know that he did not lose some of his fingernails if we do not know whether he ever had any?

For Kripke, something analogous holds for predicates such as that of being a unicorn. For him, there is no such thing as the possible animal 'unicorn', as unicorns are only fragments of individuals. Reference to unicorns or completely undetermined objects, such as Lewis Carroll's 'bandersnatch' from his nonsense-poem *Jabberwocky*, is governed by a different 'ontology' than reference to historical figures such as Napoleon or your down-stairs neighbour. Kripke therefore distinguishes at least between historical figures, fictional characters such as 'Hamlet', fictional predicates such as 'is a unicorn', and nonsense-poetical predicates such as 'is a frumious bandersnatch'. His original contribution to ontology consists in the additional move of interpreting this distinction not as an overall dichotomy between fiction and reality that would then be paired with the non-existence-existence distinction. Rather, he concludes that the different treatment of existential statements in the cases he distinguishes is evidence for existence being a predicate that helps to individuate objects.

Unfortunately, it is not fully clear what concept of existence Kripke exactly intends to analyse. Having said that, he tentatively commits to the view that for something to exist is for it to be a sub-stance in the traditional sense of 'a thing for properties to be attrib-uted to'.[40] For Kripke it is important that there is an individuated thing, Napoleon, whose non-existence we might modally consider when claiming, for instance, that 'Napoleon might not have existed.' In his view, this 'is as much a statement about Napoleon as any other that predicates a genuine property of him'.[41] Thus, at least possible non-existence and consequently contingent exist-ence seems to be a property of some objects, whereas unicorns do not behave in modal contexts like Napoleon does, as they never were sufficiently determined in order to be eligible for membership in the realm of substances in the first place. So, at least, Kripke makes an interesting case to the effect that contingent existence is a property (albeit maybe not a genuine one, as he seems to be saying in the above quoted passage). And if contingent existence is a property (again, albeit a deviant one), why not reconsider the question of existence being a property?

The focus of the second objection is Kripke's general insistence that objects cannot be identical with the totality of descriptions holding of them. Otherwise, they could not have contingent properties, and even their existence would turn out necessary. Everything that exists would both necessarily exist, and necessar-ily have all the properties it has, and necessarily be involved in all facts that hold of it, which would be an extreme form of ontological determinism. Yet, this is not only implausible, but could not account for the ontology of fictional characters or for nonsense predication in nonsense poems, which is why such an account is both generally implausible and implausibly incomplete on top of that.

Kripke's account of the substance-property distinction presupposes that we have an independent means of referring to an object such that we can then start describing it both with good and with bad descriptions. His account is thus a bottom-up picture: we first are acquainted with an object in one way or other, by pointing it out, by referring to it with a name, a description, or whatever is needed to turn a merely causal encounter with an object into rigid designation based on baptism. He, therefore, rejects the idea that in general sense and sense alone determines reference. This might still be a valuable insight for the philosophy of language. I do not doubt that. What I doubt is that it amounts to the right ontology, for there will always be a description holding of an object, even where we are partially wrong about the object. *The fact that we can use bad (that is to say: false) descriptions in order to make contact with an object just does not amount to evidence for the object existing below the surface of descriptions, as a pure object of reference.* The second objection simply does not show that, beneath the articulated plurality of descriptions holding of them, objects are substances (objects corresponding to logical proper names) after all.

My account is top-down in that the identity of an object across the plurality of descriptions holding of it does not consist in the fact that the object is a substance to which we then ascribe properties, but rather in the fact that there is a governing sense unifying the various senses in which the object is presented. This is a particular version of a bundle theory of objects compatible with a weak top-down essentialism.[42] I claim that objects are bundles of facts, that is, bundles of everything that is true about them. The idea of an underlying substance of reference that is always only partially presented under its various modes of presentation is itself another mode of presentation. I again have to defer further discussion of this to the modalities chapters, where I will argue in addition that this does not entail ontological determinism. My modal pluralism, that is to say, the view that there are no unconditional or unrestricted modalities, will serve the job of fending off ontological determinism.

Here, let me spell out my point with the help of a famous example. Evening Star and Morning Star are modes of presentation of the planet Venus. The description 'the evening star' presents Venus as a star seen at a particular location in the evening, whereas the description 'the morning star' presents Venus as a star seen at a particular location in the morning. Frege notoriously uses this case to argue that the meaning of the identity statement that the evening star is the morning star is that there is some star that is both the evening star and the morning star, that they are different descriptions of the same thing. In my view, 'Venus', in this theoretical construal of the case, is just the relevant governing sense. 'Venus' has as much a sense as 'evening star', which can be seen by inspecting the truth-conditions of the identity statement that Venus is identical with the evening star. In other words, the following two identity statements have to be treated equally:

(IS1) The evening star is the morning star.
(IS2) Venus is the evening star.

In (IS2) 'Venus' has a mode of presentation. For instance, we might use 'Venus' in order to denote the referent of the two modes of presentation in (IS1). However, to present something as something presented differently by different modes of presentation is to present it under a mode of presentation. The idea of a bare reference, of an independent means of referring beneath the threshold of the manifold modes of presentation, is just another mode of presentation. There simply is no bare reference without sense, a conclusion Frege himself explicitly draws from his discussion of the curious case of informative and non-contradictory identity statements.

> The sense of a proper name is grasped by everybody who is sufficiently familiar with the language or totality of designations to which it belongs; but this serves to illuminate only a single aspect of the *Bedeutung*, supposing it to have one. Comprehensive knowledge of the *Bedeutung* would require us to be able to say immediately whether any given sense attaches to it. To such knowledge we never attain.[43]

Proper names have a sense as much as any other referring expression for the simple reason that we can use them to pick out a finite number of senses belonging to the governing sense they envisage.

Frege gives an account of informative identity statements according to which A = B means that there is an X that is both A and B, a form of predication Schelling has called 'emphatic', in that they let the X 'shine through' in the form of something said about A and B, which is his understanding of the etymology of 'emphatic'.[44]

The point of the top-down-account of the relationship between sense and reference, or fact and object for that matter, is that we can say of A and B that there is an X that is both of them and of A, B and X that is there some Y that is all of them, depending on the field of sense and the governing sense determining the field as this rather than that field. We can equally well attribute properties to properties, refer to facts about facts, and think about some object having some property. My functional account of object and fact, reference and sense, has the advantage of being topic-neutral from the outset, whereas Kripke sets out from an ontology of natural kinds for which he develops a semantic theory of how we manage to refer to them. He operates with the idea of the actual world as being the universe and only adds that this need not amount to untenable reductionist or rather eliminative manoeuvres. But the basic metaphysical decision underlying his theory of reference is that the material substances, the natural kinds, serve as reference magnets, as it were, that they anchor our descriptions in a realm that is in itself completely determined regardless of our more or less successful attempts to describe it.[45] This might be the right presupposition for a theory of our reference to natural kinds, but it is not the right presupposition in ontology, as there is no essential relation between the fact that there are substances in the form of natural kinds and the fact that something exists.

The *third objection* invokes worries associated with the claim that there is a *plurality* of fields of sense, which seems to commit me at least to some quantified statements about the fields. The objection states that this amounts to a local version of Russell's antinomy in the form of the claim that there is a restricted field of all fields not appearing within themselves (call it 'the field of all normal fields') and restricted field of all fields appearing within themselves (call it 'the field of all abnormal fields').[46] It looks like we can single out an antinomical Russell field. But can there really be such a field, can it exist? Can there be any object about which contradictory statements are true such that p is true of it iff *not-p* is true of it?

In order to address this worry, it is important to raise the question under which conditions an antinomy is a problem. Pointing out that a view amounts to antinomy means to claim that the view is either explicitly or implicitly committed to a contradiction in that it asserts both *p* and *not-p*. In our context, the antinomy would consist in a relevant commitment to the field of all abnormal fields either being normal or abnormal. But the field of all abnormal fields would only be subject to such a complete disjunction if it had to appear in either kind of field. Yet, this presupposes that *all* fields are either normal or abnormal. However, this is ruled out by the no-world-view: such a complete disjunction would have to quantify over all fields; it would be a truth about all fields, namely the truth that they exclusively either appear in one kind of field or the other. But the field of all abnormal fields needs not itself either be normal or abnormal. The fields of normal and abnormal fields are separated by a space of alternatives not defined by there being normal and abnormal fields alone. The objection, therefore, needs to establish the premise that all fields are either normal or abnormal (and nothing else), which would then accordingly apply to the field of abnormal fields too.

The space of alternatives separating normal and abnormal fields such that they do not form a *complete* disjunction encompassing all fields of sense as such can never be an all-encompassing field. It is simply not the case that all fields are either normal or abnormal, and accordingly that the field of abnormal fields might exist in an indefinite number of fields. But might it exist in all fields? The answer is obviously no, as the field of all abnormal fields does not appear, for instance, in my coffee mug or in the dream of some Peruvian farmer. But again, one might insist that the fact that the field of all abnormal fields does not exist in the Peruvian farmer's dream is different from the fact that it does not exist in itself or in the field of all normal fields. It might have existed in the Peruvian farmer's dream, but it could neither have existed in itself nor in the field of all normal fields. Yet, at this point it can already be repeated that there are no out-and-out modalities. Accordingly, the question becomes in which field and under which respective modal conditions is it the case that by necessity the field of all abnormal fields is neither normal nor abnormal?

For instance, consider a coffee mug with a photo of itself printed on it. Now, there is a sense in which the coffee mug appears within itself, but that sense is utterly different from the sense in which the concept 'concept' appears within itself (it falls under itself).

Appearing is not univocal; it is said in manifold ways. The field of all abnormal fields is not sufficiently unified so as to add up to a field with the overall characteristic of either being itself normal or abnormal.

In a recent discussion of similar problems Gerhard Ernst objected against the no-world-view that it underestimates the fact that according to its own premises embedded appearing often is not transitive, that is to say, that if O appears in P and P appears in Q, this does not always entail that O appears in Q, at least not in the same sense.[47] His example is a bucket with a hole in it standing in a closet. The hole is in a bucket, which is in a closet, but this does not mean that there is a hole in the closet in the same sense in which there is a hole in the bucket. My own prior example was that there are trolls in Norwegian mythology, which in some sense is located in Norway (in the history of Norway), which does not make it the case that there are thereby also trolls in Norway.[48] Ernst suggested that the world might exist in our discussions of it (including my no-world-view), which then need not entail that it exists within the world in the same sense in which Norway or chemistry would exist in the world. To this my reply is that the world problem arises because the world is all-encompassing. Wherever it appears, it brings everything else with it, so that there are further restrictions on the world's world-immanent appearance. The no-world-view does not hinge on the isolated principle that no domain can appear within itself, as there might be harmless forms of self-reference that deserve to be described, as some domains appear within themselves.

One horn of the world problem arises due to the highly specific condition that the world is supposed to be both all-encompassing and appearing within itself. The other horn consists in the fact that the world cannot appear in anything beyond the world, as this would only introduce another more encompassing world now consisting of the initial world and what is beyond it. One way out of the problem for the world-theorist (the metaphysician) could be to maintain that the world neither appears within itself nor in another on the very grounds given above meant to establish that there is no complete disjunction when it comes to normal versus abnormal fields. Why not say that the world's existence is neither its appearance within itself nor its appearance in another? The problem with this attempt to save the world is that it relies on the non-existence of a totalising operation in order to hint at the vague possibility that there might be a sense in which the world exists, but just not as a totality. In that case, I see no more reason at all to stick to the concept of the world, which precisely fulfils the function of grounding a universal ontology, a fiction deeply attached to the concept of the world, as Husserl quite rightly points out in *Formal and Transcendental Logic*.[49]

Back to the point under discussion, we now have a grip on the idea that there is no unified field of abnormal fields, as the relation of appearance in a field of sense is not univocal. There are indefinitely many senses of appearing that are not unified by an overall concept under which they all fall. This does not indicate that we cannot understand each of them or discover local patterns that allow for local unification (as performed by the various sciences). All this means here is that no ontological version of Russell's antinomy threatens the view.

Russell's antinomy arises in a limited and fairly well defined context, namely in the context of set theory. This context is not ontological, as not all fields are sets. In order to cash out the worry that the ontology of fields of sense is subject to the same paradoxes or antinomies as naïve set theory, one would have to show that the exact same considerations triggering an unpleasant antinomy for naïve set theory would also trigger an unpleasant antinomy for ontology. But the very incompleteness of fields of sense, the constitutive openness of the proliferation of fields, makes it impossible to unify them into a single system that can then be separated into local structures by procedures such as the ones leading to complete disjunctions. Some fields of sense are ontologically vague, open and subject to change that cannot be accounted for *a priori* by stating their transcendental boundary conditions. A business meeting, for example, even though subject to legal norms and determinable economic interests, contains elements of surprise by the sheer fact that it is interlocked with other fields, such as the field of the psychology of the people engaged in the meeting, cultural differences, sudden weather changes, and so on.

In this respect, I agree with Latour when he insists that there is a sense in which the actual structure of fields (of 'modes of existence' in his language) is not at all like the structure of *being-qua-being*, but more like *being-qua-other* (*être-en-tant-qu'-autre*).[50] Many fields are hybrids, and what is mixed in them cannot be anticipated *a priori*. There is change and creativity. There are also different forms of temporality, change and alteration, which is not to say that we should replace being by becoming. Unrestricted process ontology is just one more case of metaphysical overgeneralisation, which misleads Latour into postulating an absolute 'mini-transcendence' of alteration that is indeed operative even in the reproduction and maintenance of a field of sense over time or its partial change. As he writes, alteration 'is the default position, that it is thus *without a contrary*'.[51] This is why he subsequently sets out to explain the immanence and stability of a field (a mode in his terminology) as a side effect of alteration. Stability and continuity (what he calls 'habit') for him are only the result of bridging one *hiatus* after another, a picture universally privileging alteration over continuity.[52] Latour, therefore, does not really depart from the model of ontology as a metaphysical investigation of being-qua-being, that is, from ontotheology, but only adds that beings that are subject to change and production are subject to conditions of continuity that involve maintenance of structure over change.

The plurality of fields is not generally numerical. They are certainly not recursively enumerable, as there is no possible rule singling out all fields of sense. In other words, fields of sense are really individuated without recourse to an overall principle of individuation or an overall set of rules of individuation, however complex or abstract.

At this point of the argumentation, people regularly ask me how fields can be individuated if there are no overall rules of individuation? The motivation behind this question is often epistemological, and gives voice to the concern that we might lose our grip on individuation if there was no *a priori* overall way of knowing what it is for objects to be individuated. My response to this is the *gorilla argument*. In a remarkable episode of Louis C. K.'s brilliant show *Louie*, one of Louie's daughters wants to tell a joke at breakfast. Louie, the protagonist of the show (who resembles Louis C. K. and is played by him), immediately wants to put her off for the simple reason that he is convinced that she cannot tell a joke capable of surprising him. As Louis reports the scenario that inspired the event on the *Louie* show on the *Late Night Show*, he comments on the situation by saying: 'You know, you know jokes after a while. Someone starts a joke, you know what's going happen, but not hers.' In other words, her joke is real; it is a surprise transcending even the specialist's expectation. In the *Louie* show, Louie recalls the joke in his stand up set in the following way:

She said, 'Who didn't let the gorilla into the ballet?' I love this joke. I have not heard this joke. This is a new joke for me. Who didn't let the gorilla into the ballet? And she said, 'Just the people who were in charge of that decision. Just the folks who made the assessment.'

The gorilla argument points out that we cannot generally know what individuates a field of sense in advance by knowing anything that holds of all fields of sense by their very 'nature'. Some fields intersect, some fields don't, some fields ground other fields, others don't. The fact that the gorilla is not in the ballet is nothing more than the fact that someone did not let him in, that the gorilla simply cannot appear in the ballet (as either actor or audience). What happens to be the case is not generally engulfed by transcendental, necessary, and universal, boundaries. This is why facts surprise us and why they often exceed our expectations. We need methods to find out what is the case precisely insofar as what is the case is not identical with our methods of finding out what is the case. Our methods are only a small region of what there is, even though they belong to what there is with the same right as moons, fingernails and nucleons.

On my preferred reading there is an interesting argument in Husserl to a similar effect that drives his account of formal ontology in *Formal and Transcendental Logic*.[53] The argument begins by claiming that the formal theory of objects relies on a concept of 'Somethings whatever'.[54] However, he tells us, that there is no such region or domain as that of all objects as such, or *überhaupt*; this region is nothing but 'the empty region, object as such (*Leerregion Gegenstand überhaupt*)',[55] as he explicitly concedes. There are no objects that correspond to the flattest most universal concept of objecthood. However, that fact does not undermine our capacity to think of the domain of objects *überhaupt* as structured insofar as we can say what would have to hold of them, if they existed. Flattening our ontology to this degree of nullness of appearance (an operation I constantly rely on in this treatise) is not a meaningless enterprise, but gives us insight into the actual constraints on something counting as something rather than nothing. Husserl in this light is fully justified in claiming that the concept of objects as such, the formal theory of objects, is derived from a theory of judgements without succumbing to the temptation of postulating a realm of flat objects or even natural kinds that make it the case that our judgements are anchored in a realm of such objects.

This is a confusion of levels of theorising clearly diagnosed by Husserl.[56]

> Formal logic determines objects with pure universality by that form. It is also true that nowhere but in the judgement does the empty concept Something make its appearance, the concept in which all objects are thought by logic.[57]

Transcendental insight is, therefore, limited and finite, albeit not exactly in the way traditionally envisaged by Kant and his followers. It only deals with abstractions, which does not turn it into a meaningless enterprise, as it puts us into a position to critically diagnose reifications of what we can see through as abstractions. Here I still agree with Husserl's point that transcendental philosophy thus is a critique of misguided interpretations of our evident capacity for abstraction.[58] It is not limited by somehow being our human-all-too-human kind of insight (a misconception Husserl calls humanism),[59] but because facts and knowledge of facts conceptually diverge given that there is a *contrast of objectivity* potentially separating what is true from what is taken to be true. It is a realist platitude that some facts obtain not because we believe that they do, but rather we believe that they obtain because they do.[60] This fact, the contrast of objectivity, is orthogonal to the mind-dependence/mind-independence distinction. For instance, the claim that Britney believes that it is raining in London is as objective as the claim that it is raining in London, and the realist platitude is operative in both. That a belief is about a belief does not make it less objective. Yet, whatever our beliefs are, our actual beliefs will never be entirely identical with what they are about, even if we have meta-beliefs. We can be wrong about what we believe, for instance, by not fully being aware of the meaning of the concepts involved in our belief formation.

The no-world-view involves a commitment to a radical form of non-transcendental empiricism. It entails that there is no overall way to individuate facts, not even by the insight that all facts are facts or that all objects are embedded in facts. 'Fact', 'object', 'existence' and other concepts defined in terms of the ontology of fields of sense have a constitutive *functional plasticity*: they acquire their actual meaning by referring to facts, objects and fields of sense that define what it is for some facts, objects and fields of sense to exist. In other words, what there is co-determines the meaning of existence, and for some fields of sense this can only occur through ordinary empirical enquiry. If I find something out about some objects insofar as they belong to a particular field of sense, I find something out about the actual meaning of existence, namely in this particular field of sense. From the point of view of the ontology of fields of sense, there is no *a priori* verdict on which facts and objects exist apart from the one verdict that derives from the demonstration that the world does not exist. What exists and what does not exist is generally an empirical matter with the exception of the world, whose non-existence is *a priori*. But then, the non-existence of the world is not a fact about the world, namely the fact that *it* does not exist. The no-world-view really claims that the world is not qualified for any existential claims. The negative existential statement that the world does not exist is shorthand for the ontology of fields of sense; it limits the operations that can legitimately be carried out by ruling some operations out as overgeneralised. In other words, I am, of course, not talking about the world when I say that it does not exist. It is not an object of any kind of reference; it simply is not there to be thought about or referred to, not even as a fictional object. In this deflationary sense I can even agree with Slavoj Žižek's recent notion of 'less than nothing'.[61] The world is less than nothing; it does not even fall within the scope of the impossible. There really is nothing to be said about the world, but this very fact matters, as it has been neglected by ontology for most of its (ontotheological) history. Ontotheology has tried to create the world, and it misconceived its own activity with the activity of God to create the world. However, we need to overcome this 'wisdom of the world (σοφία τοῦ κόσμου)',[62] as St Paul has critically called the philosophy of his time.

Notes

1. If you are not convinced by my arguments that this covers the entire range of meaning of 'existence' and its cognates in natural languages (maybe including parts of the meaning of 'being'), you can read me as giving an account of 'existence' insofar as it means 'appearance in a field of sense', which, at the very least, arguably is an important sense of 'existence'. Of course, there are many other ways of regimenting the manifold meaning of 'existence' in natural languages, some of which substantially compete with my account. However, a

criterion of success of the analysis offered in this book is the extent to which it can make sense of existence without the idea of absolute existence, aka existence – full stop, aka absolutely unrestricted quantification. I believe that these concepts derive from a defective and ultimately metaphysical interpretation of the meaning of 'existence'. Of course, this interpretation forms the basis of the entire history of Occidental metaphysics, but that is another topic.

2. I, therefore, disagree with Searle's view that all non-conscious intentionality is derivative, which is not to say that there is no intentionality, which is borrowed from conscious intentionality. Just imagine that no conscious being existed, but that there nevertheless were living beings leaving traces (which used to be true at some time in the past of this universe). We can now understand these traces, that is, grasp their intentional content without thereby treating something without any intentional content *as if* it had intentional content. There is no as if involved here. The intentionality of photographs is derivative of our conscious intentionality in some sense, namely at least in the sense that we have consciously created photographs. Yet, this also does not mean that we read intentional contents into the photographs. We are able to recognise intentionality in the photograph, as we have produced it consciously, which is not to say that we treat photographs as if they had intentional content.

3. Brandom, *Tales of the Mighty Dead*, p. 50: 'Concept P is *sense dependent* on concept Q just in case one cannot count as having grasped P unless one counts as having grasped Q. Concept P is *reference dependent* on concept Q just in case P cannot apply to something unless Q applies to something.' On this distinction see Gabriel, *An den Grenzen der Erkenntnistheorie*, pp. 387–401.

4. Sebastian Rödl has recently argued that we need to make sense of the idea that self-consciousness is sufficiently like higher-order intentionality in order to fulfill the functions traditionally assigned to it, but that it, nevertheless, always only arises in one stroke with consciousness such that there is a sense in which they are always the same or the same act. See Rödl, *Self-Consciousness*, in particular chapter 4, pp. 105–32. However, as in all traditional accounts sharing this feature from ancient Neo-Platonism (most prominently Plotinus) to Dieter Henrich's discussion of this option and beyond, the problem is that this threatens to undermine the fallibility of self-consciousness. What would it mean to be wrong about consciousness in self-consciousness if not that the second-order intentionality directed at the first-order intentionality potentially misconstrues its

object as much as its object (the first-order intentionality) always potentially misconstrues its (more ordinary) object? For further recent discussions of this see also the theory of subjectivity in Cf. Koch, *Versuch über Wahrheit und Zeit*, pp. 206–57, as well as Hindrichs, *Das Absolute und das Subjekt*.

5. Cf. Henrich, *Fichtes ursprüngliche Einsicht*, pp. 13ff. Henrich originally borrowed this point from Hermann Schmitz. Cf. Henrich, *Fichtes ursprüngliche Einsicht*, p. 13, footnote 5 and Schmitz, *System der Philosophie I*, pp. 249f.

6. Fichte, *The Science of Knowing 1804*, p. 139. Fichte construes being in line with the tradition of zoontology, which follows from his claim 'that both being and living, and living and being completely interpenetrate, dissolve into one another, and are the same, and this self-same inwardness is the one completely unified being' (Ibid., p. 116).

7. Descartes, *Principles of Philosophy*. In § 51 of the *Principles*, Descartes speaks of God as the one true substance insofar as it is the only thing that depends on nothing else, and all other substances are dependent on it. However, in § 52 he speaks of corporeal and thinking substances as the only things that depend on nothing but God. Because nothingness has no attributes, he argues, we can infer from our interaction with any attribute that we are in fact interacting with something that exists, a substance that has that attribute.

8. Cf. Gabriel, 'Ist der Gottesbegriff des ontologischen Beweises konsistent?'

9. Śūnyatā might, however, also be interpreted as a version of the no-world-view. Buddhist nothingness would then not be a claim about the world, but rather articulate a perspective from which there is no residual need to even postulate the slightest possibility of anything all-encompassing. All we are left with are the manifold appearances.

10. Plato, *Sophist*, 254d4.

11. Ibid., 254d4f.

12. Ibid., 254c4.

13. Ibid., 254a8f.

14. Ibid., 254a8–b1.

15. Kant, *Critique of Pure Reason*, A 81/B 107.

16. Aristotle, *Metaphysics*, 1075a18–19. On this see Gabriel, 'God's Transcendent Activity: Ontotheology in Metaphysics Λ'.

17. Heidegger interestingly argues that this corresponds to a different sense in which being is said in manifold ways, namely on the one hand as the ten categories and on the other hand as *dynamis*

and *energeia*. See his Heidegger, *Aristotle's Metaphysics* Θ 1–3, pp. 1–7.

18. Aristotle, *Metaphysics*, 1090b19–20: 'But the phenomena show that nature is not a series of episodes, like a bad tragedy.'

19. Badiou, *Being and Event*, pp. 62–6.

20. Russell himself sometimes derives the necessity of a type of theory explicitly from Cantor's theorem. See, for instance, Russell, *Logic and Knowledge*, pp. 260f. Guido Kreis recently argued that Cantor's theorem can be applied to the concept of the world in the sense of any kind of unrestricted totality regardless of whether facts can be modelled in terms of sets. See his *Negative Dialektik des Unendlichen*. His argument proceeds by defining facts that both belong and do not belong to some local domain within any alleged totality of facts. In his view, we can only avoid these facts by giving up on cherished assumptions about concept-formation, which is why his conclusion is that there is an antinomy in our thought about totality (and not that totality does not exist). However, he does not address the version of the non-existence of the world presented here, even though he mentions an earlier version of my claim and discusses Patrick Grim's incompleteness view.

21. On this see the philosophically illuminating presentation in A. W. Moore, *The Infinite*.

22. Cf. Putnam, 'Truth and Convention'; Putnam, *Ethics without Ontology*, pp. 33–51; Gabriel, *Die Erkenntnis der Welt*, pp. 330ff.

23. Frege, *Foundations of Arithmetic*, § 46, p. 59.

24. Thanks to Umrao Sethi for suggesting this distinction to me.

25. Hegel, *The Difference Between Fichte and Schelling's System of Philosophy*, p. 83.

26. Hegel, *The Science of Logic*, pp. 157–65. On this see the detailed reconstruction in Kreis, *Negative Dialektik des Unendlichen*.

27. Consequently, Hegel's highest logical category, the 'absolute idea', is defined as 'self-knowing truth' ('*sich wissende Wahrheit*'). Cf. Hegel, *The Science of Logic*, p. 735 (GW 12.236).

28. Even though I agree with Kreis' upshot that Hegel gets himself into trouble by not addressing certain problems with the concept of 'absolutely everything', I disagree with the details of his presentation, as he does not work out the structure of the Hegelian concept, but only focuses on the paradoxes of quantity in the first part of the *Science of Logics*. This is not sufficient to undermine the concept of the concept.

29. McDowell, *Mind and World*, pp. 24–45.

30. See Williamson, *The Philosophy of Philosophy*, pp. 16–17; 'Past the Linguistic Turn'.

31. Hegel, *Science of Logic*, p. 58.

32. Thanks to Patrick Zoll for making me aware of the innocence of weak essentialism after my talk at the Hochschule für Philosophie in Munich on 9 December 2013.

33. The concept of a governing sense is a successor of what I called 'focus imaginarius' in earlier works with reference to Kant's introduction of this concept. On this see my *An den Grenzen der Erkenntnistheorie*, p. 237f. and *Transcendental Ontology*, p. 11.

34. McDowell, *Mind and World*, p. 33.

35. Kripke, *Reference and Existence*, p. 144.

36. Kripke, *Reference and Existence*, p. 144.

37. Kripke, *Reference and Existence*, p. 60, footnote 3, and pp. 73, 78, 81.

38. Kripke, *Reference and Existence*, p. 74.

39. Meixner, *Einführung in die Ontologie*, pp. 51–60.

40. Kripke, *Reference and Existence*, p. 146.

41. Kripke, *Reference and Existence*, p. 146.

42. Thanks to David Papineau for insisting on this point after a talk I gave on this topic at King's College.

43. Frege, 'On Sinn and Bedeutung', p. 154. See also Frege, 'The Thought', p. 298: 'Accordingly, with a proper name, it depends on how whatever it refers to is presented. This can happen in different ways and every such way corresponds with a particular sense of a sentence containing a proper name.'

44. On this with the Schelling references see Hogrebe 'Sein und Emphase', and Frank, *Auswege aus dem Deuteschen Idealismus*, pp. 312–74.

45. On the concept of reference magnetism see Sider, 'Ontological Realism'.

46. The objection is due to Jens Rometsch.

47. Thanks to Gerhard Ernst for his objections during a presentation of my basic ideas in ontology at the Literaturhaus München on 17 October 2013.

48. See my *Warum es die Welt nicht gibt*, p. 114.

49. See his distinction between formal ontology, which need not be a theory of absolutely everything, and the world as the object of a material ontology, in particular in the following passage: 'Is not every existent – thought of concretely as materially determined and determinable – essentially an existent in a *universe of being*, a

"*world*"? Is not every *possible* existent (as this word "essentially" indicates) something that belongs to its *possible* universe of being; accordingly, is not every material Apriori something that belongs to a universal Apriori, namely the Apriori that predelineates the apriori material form [*die apriorische sachhaltige Form*] for a possible universe of the existent? It seems therefore that we must now steer toward a material ontology, an ontology proper, which would supplement the merely analytic-formal ontology' (Husserl, *Formal and Transcendental Logic*, p. 150). However, this passage is not clearly committed to there being only one world or only one totality, as there might as well be different universes of being corresponding to the different regions Husserl distinguishes on the level of formal ontology.

50. Latour, *An Inquiry into the Modes of Existence*, p. 151.
51. Latour, *An Inquiry into the Modes of Existence*, p. 266.
52. Cf. Ibid.: 'If it is true that mini-transcendence is the default position, that it is thus *without a contrary*, immanence is not going to be introduced in this study as what is opposed to transcendence but only as *one of its effects*, as one of its ways – a particularly elegant one, to be sure – of adjusting the junction points *without splices* and without any *visible* break in continuity. Habit has the peculiar feature of *smoothing over*, through what must be called an *effect of immanence*, all the little transcendences that *being-as-other* explores.'
53. Special thanks to David Espinet and Paul Livingston for insisting that I take a second closer look at Husserl's contribution to a no-world-view account of formal logics.
54. Husserl, *Formal and Transcendental Logic*, p. 148.
55. Ibid.
56. I rely on similar arguments in my objections against the naive ontology of individuals in my *An den Grenzen der Erkenntnistheorie*.
57. Husserl, *Formal and Transcendental Logic*, p. 110.
58. Cf. Ibid. § 105 and § 106.
59. Ibid. p. 166. Here the German word 'Humanismus' as used in the original is translated as 'Humeianism', which *might* capture what Husserl had in mind but which is by no means a literal translation as the literal translation of the German 'Humanismus' is 'Humanism'.
60. On the concept of a contrast of objectivity see my *An den Grenzen der Erkenntnistheorie*, p. 45. For similar considerations see Koch, *Versuch über Wahrheit und Zeit*, § 5, pp. 51–7.
61. Žižek, *Less than Nothing*.
62. 1 Kor 1, 20.

9

How Flat Can Ontology Be?

In his *Intensive Science and Virtual Philosophy* Manuel DeLanda has given the term of a 'flat ontology' an influential meaning by opposing it to 'hierarchical ontology'. His statement of the position of flat ontology presents it in terms of a metaphysical picture:

> [While] an ontology based on relations between general types and particular instances is hierarchical, each level representing a different ontological category (organism, species, genera), an approach in terms of interacting parts and emergent wholes leads to a flat ontology, one made exclusively of unique, singular individuals, differing in spatio-temporal scale but not in ontological status.[1]

What DeLanda describes is rather a flat metaphysics than a flat ontology. Let me, thus, reformulate the idea of flatness and say that an ontology is *flat* as opposed to *hierarchical* if it unifies all objects insofar as they exist. A flat ontology claims that all objects are equal insofar as they are objects or that all fields of sense are equal insofar as they are fields of sense. In other words, flat ontology resists the idea of a governing principle that unifies all objects.[2] It replaces the idea of a substantial unification of objects or entities by the idea of their mere coexistence such that the actual structures of the objects determine their nature and not the fact that they relate to some more substantial concept. Flat ontology results from leaching out actual objects and from breaking them down to their bare bones, whatever they actually are supposed to be. It is a case of undermining some of them by reducing them to a fundamental deflationary structure, a structure deflated in the sense that reference to it does not amount to substantial insight.[3]

DeLanda's concept is often invoked in the context of debates about the pre- and post-human (or generally trans-human) world.

It is supposed to be an ingredient of the cure against anthropo-centric ontology or zoontology in the sense of Chapter 1 (see above, pp. 33–42). The idea is that objects are only individuated with reference to conceptual hierarchies by concept-mongering creatures, and that we should not project our conceptual necessi-ties or needs onto the pre-conceptual realm. However, it would, of course, be a mere fallacy to argue that our concepts cannot refer to trans-human objects or events. That we refer to something does not make the object of reference reference-dependent in the sense of an object that could not have existed had we not referred to it. Imagining a flat world without spectators is as impossible as imagining a hierarchy of world plus spectators due to the no-world-view. However, the concept of a flat ontology poses a challenge that needs to be addressed, as I am certainly opposed to a hierarchical ontology according to which there is an all-encompassing bottom-up or top-down structure determining what it is for objects in general to exist, for facts in general to obtain, or for fields of sense in general to appear and to have appearances occur within them.

However, the constitutive functional plasticity of the onto-logical concepts introduced so far also blocks the possibility of a completely flat ontology. Some fields are flat and some fields are curved. Nevertheless, the comparison between the ontology of fields of sense and the very idea of a flat ontology brings out an important positive feature of my new realist ontology, namely the point that it is impossible that everything is determinately an object or a fact at any given time.

Let me illustrate this with a simple allegory, *the allegory of the bulb-board*. Imagine there is a wooden board with small light bulbs attached to it. There are two colours in which the lights can be switched on: blue or red. Let a blue light be switched on if something is a field of sense, and a red light if something is an object, and remember that both concepts are functional. An object appears in a field of sense and fields of sense have objects appear within them. Now the question is whether all lights on the board could be switched on in the same light, say red. In this case, everything would be an object and we would have reached the level of a flat ontology. If all lights were red, there would be no more lights, as the lights only exist by appearing in a field of sense. Therefore, there is once again at the very least one field of sense. At least, one light has to be blue. On the opposite extreme, if all lights were switched on blue, there would only be fields of sense and no objects. But then the fields of sense could not appear in any field of sense, as this would turn them into objects. Thus, in order for there to be mostly blue lights, there has to be at least one red light, an object that exists in a field of sense that then in turn might exist in a field of sense and so on, and *vice versa*. The point is that from the standpoint of ontology, all we know is that some light has to be blue and some other has to be red. All other distributions of colours over the board and their change over time cannot be subject to ontological necessities or *a priori* principles.

In any event, the difference between the blue and red lights remains a *functional ontological difference*, where this contrasts with a *substantial metaphysical difference*. Substantial metaphysical differences consist in there being categorical distinctions. These might then be cashed out in terms of hierarchies such that, for instance, concepts determine objects top-down. The most general traditional substantial metaphysical difference is a hierarchy with the most general concept on top of the order of things (the One) and the manifold distinctions falling under the most general concept. This is probably the highest common factor of all onto-theological systems. There is then a disagreement in this tradition about the precise relationship between the most general concept or principle and everything else.

In opposition to this tradition, flat ontology rightly insists that there need not be a hierarchical structure in order to account for the difference among actual objects. They need not be individu-ated by reference to different levels of reality. Let us call the idea behind ontotheology *hierarchical individuation*. Hierarchical indi-viduation immediately poses the problem that the individuating principles themselves have to be individuated, a problem already pointed out by Aristotle against Plato. The most general concept has to have some relevant features that account for the facts of individuation coming forth from it. There has to be room in the most general concept for there to be manifold instances falling under it. Yet, what distinguishes the instances from each other cannot be contained in the most universal concept. Rather, there has to be a plurality of concepts interacting so as to individuate objects that actually fall under the alleged most general concept. The most general concept will always be too empty to have an actual grip on individuated objects, which is the core idea behind Hegel's insight that being and nothing are one and the same.[4]

Against flat ontology we need to have in view that it is impossible for there to only be a unified level (a plane of immanence, as it were, to misuse Deleuze's metaphor) of equal objects that happen to differ from each other in one way or other (most likely by their properties). Without the functional difference between fields of sense and objects neither objects nor fields could exist. The difference is functional in that something is both an object in some field and a field in which some object appears depending on the functional specification. For instance, the play *Faust* is a field in which there are witches, mountains, a bar in Leipzig (*Auerbachs Keller*), and many other objects (including events, which are just more objects in the sense of the functional theory of objects). Yet, *Faust* is also an object, for instance, in the field of literary studies or in a library owning several copies of *Faust*. Insofar as *Faust* is contained in a library, it is a copy of the play. If I remember having read *Faust* and think of the play as an object of my recollection, it is not a copy of the play, but it is still an object in the field of sense of my recollection. If I think about the development of Faust, the protagonist, over the different acts, Faust is an object and *Faust* a field of sense.

In order to fend off general subjectivism about functional ontological difference, a different example might be helpful. The moon is an object in the field of sense of the gravitational range of the earth (which from a physical point of view is limitless, but that does not matter for the argument). There is nothing subjective about the fact that the moon is such an object or that there is a field of sense in which the moon appears under the conditions defined by the gravitational range of the earth. At the same time, if there are footprints on the moon, these footprints appear on the surface of the moon, which can be the relevant field of sense for the footprints. Of course, the footprints also appear in the field of sense of the gravitational range of the earth, but not *as* footprints, but as some arrangement of sand that looks like footprints in a different field of sense. Yet, that they are footprints is as objective as the arrangement of sand. The moon also appears in many other fields of sense, such as poetry, and many other objects apart from footprints (if there are any left) appear on the moon insofar as it is itself a field of sense.

The different functional foci are not generally foci of attention. Rather, our foci of attention only serve as an individuating vehicle because they trace senses. Our attention stretches out to objects in fields and it itself is a field within which other fields appear as objects. It is just not the case that generally fields of sense are reference-dependent, which is why so many trivial counter-examples to the idea of overall subjectivism or constructivism are ready at hand. The notion that there are only distinctions if we draw them is so incoherent that one should wonder why we still need to remind ourselves of this fact.

But then what about hybrid cases such as the following? I focus my attention on the moon as a field of sense in which objects appear. In this scenario the moon is both a field of sense and an object. This is true, but the point is that the field of sense of my attention is not an object in this scenario. There will always be some field or other that is not an object in a given determinate situation. In the first-order attention case, it is the field of my attention that is not an object; in other scenarios it might be a number of fields interacting with each other that function as a meta-sense in which some arrangement of fields and objects appear.

But in general, conditions of appearing do not appear alongside the objects within their range, and even if they did, the appearing conditions would not be identical with the conditions of appearing precisely because of their functional ontological difference. If the conditions of appearing are reflected among the appearances, this either changes the field or creates an interesting possibility for error where the appearing conditions can be confused with the conditions of appearing. These two options deserve to be illustrated by respective examples.

The first case is the case of field-change by reflection that can happen in a social situation such as a dinner. Let us take a real-life example. If you meet friends or acquaintances for dinner in a restaurant in San Francisco, say, it is expected that the dinner does not take longer than ninety minutes, two hours at most. It is expected that you do not get utterly drunk, which is already symbolically flagged by the high prices for alcohol in the restaurants and the fact that the service focuses on the food and does not really allow you to stay at your table for drinks after the food is consumed. The bill comes with the dessert. In Germany, at least in my neck of the woods, it is expected that you stay much longer, drink at least twice the very modest Californian amount of wine, and are not pushed out of the restaurant in order to make room for the next set of consumers. After dinner you might go out to some other place or invite your friends to your home. Probably just due to the beautiful sun and daylight, in San Francisco almost everybody goes to bed at ten o'clock even after social dinners, whereas in Germany the cut off time is much later, as it does not really matter whether it is night or day given the usual grey sky. Famously, Spain and Portugal again differ for different reasons, as people only go to dinner after the cut off time in most other places on our planet.

An interesting thing happens as you put these facts on the table in the different situations. There is a principle of social inertia according to which every different group will take their dinner rules to be absolute or justified by some consideration or other, and the very fact that you discuss other options while inhabiting one of the above mentioned dinner fields changes at least some of the fields. It is simply inappropriate in some fields to let their conditions of appearing appear alongside their objects. If you nevertheless do so, the field will change and one will experience objective incompatibilities and real consequences. This is not at all to say that one should accept some given standards of propriety, or that one should not strive for a more global dinner culture. Some of the dinner proprieties actually reflect conditions of appearing of the wider fields in which they themselves appear (larger social structures with political impact), and some proprieties of the wider field might even be ethically obnoxious (here a lot depends on considerations regarding the production and consumption of the food and drinks presented including wages of cooks, waiters, the ecological conditions of the consumed plants and animals, and so on). But the point is that dinners are a particularly salient case in which many of the conditions of appearing for their objects have to remain implicit and must not themselves become objects. Social dinners are possible because we can expect that implicit rules are accepted without being constantly made explicit – a fact under heavy scrutiny in contemporary comedy, most prominently in *Curb your Enthusiasm*.

The second case is one where conditions of appearing are reflected among objects. An illustrative example is language acquisition. At the beginning of the process of acquiring an initially foreign language, grammatical rules appear alongside meaningful sentences and building blocks. The objects of the language, what the language speaks about in the way it does, appear together with the grammatical rules. However, the actual use of the rules differs from having them appear as objects in the language. Imagine that you have been learning Spanish for a while and your teacher talks to you in Spanish about some new rule you have not learned yet. While he explains the rule to you he might use it at the same time. The use of the rule differs from the rule as it appears in the field of the language, even though it is the same rule. Following a rule in language is different from mentioning it, even where one correctly individuates the rule. A grammatical rule is a condition of appearing that might itself appear alongside its objects and could be confusedly identified with one of its objects. However, notoriously, no one really speaks a language as long as they are thinking *about* rather than *in* the rules.

Conditions of appearing are only operative when they are functionally implicit, which is not to say that they cannot be made explicit. But their explication differs from their functional role as conditions of appearing. Conditions of appearing are thus similar to what Schelling in the *Freedom Essay* calls the 'ground of existence'.[5] Here, his concept of 'Grund' should not be translated as 'reason' or 'cause'. The ground of existence is rather a ground in the sense in which a hunting ground is a ground, that is, a certain structured region in which certain objects can stand out and, therefore, exist. Let it be noted in passing that this is exactly what Heidegger intends with his use of 'Grund'. His famous text *Der Satz vom Grund* does not deal with the principle of reason, as it has quite unfortunately been translated, but is rather about the relation between objects that appear and their conditions of appearing. Here it is important to emphasise that 'Satz' in German does not only mean 'sentence', 'principle', 'statement', or 'proposition', but also a 'leap'. 'Einen Satz machen' means 'to pounce', 'to lunge', 'to make a leap'. 'Der Satz vom Grund' can thus literally be translated as 'a leap off the ground', a leap that generates a distance between the ground and that which takes off from the ground. And this is exactly what Heidegger is interested in: the functional ontological difference between conditions of appearing (being) and what appears (beings). His point is that this difference is not ontotheological, that is, a substantial metaphysical difference, but functional.

What serves as a field of sense and what serves as an object is not fixed by any transcendental standards, but negotiated on a case by case basis. This is precisely what Heidegger was trying to make explicit with his concept of 'the event'. Heidegger's event is not a special event, but his name for the fact that what appears and how it appears can only be made out in case studies.[6] What there is is not determined by some overall considerations regarding what can be the case. What is the case, therefore, happens to be the case, which is not to say that there only is chance and contingency, but that there is no metaphysical overall structure determining what could possibly be the case in general.

Both Schelling and Heidegger draw on Kant's particular version of the insight that the world does not exist. Kant's own stance towards the no-world-view remains ambivalent. On the one hand, he gives arguments to the effect that the world cannot exist as an object of knowledge, or even of reference, that resembles the arguments laid out here.[7] Yet, he sticks to the view that the world still fulfils an irreplaceable function in the overall epistemic economy of beings whose cognitive life extends to 'the All of reality', to the *omnitudo realitatis*, as he also puts it. For Kant, reality as a whole is a necessary fiction, that is to say, a fiction necessary for the maintenance of a 'systematic unity'[8] of knowledge. We unify the pieces of information we receive from the senses by presupposing that there is a unified source of information, the world, even though we cannot know anything about that source independent of the fact that we thus presuppose it. The world is introduced on the second-order level of theorising: it is not an object of first-order knowledge, but a presupposition of our understanding of the overall unification of first-order knowledge into a world picture.[9]

This is exactly the paradigm of Heidegger's claim that we live in the era of the world picture.[10] The world has become a picture; it moved from a first-order object of inquiry, from the given totality of what there is, to a second-order concept introduced in an account of the unification of first-order inquiry. We can call this peculiar kind of second-order fictionalism about the world *meta-metaphysical fictionalism*. The central concept of metaphysics, the unified whole, develops from an object of inquiry into an indispensable fiction. However, we already know that the narrow Kantian view is untenable, as it still assumes that the world could have been an object of inquiry, that it just so happens that we are unable to refer to the unified whole as an object of inquiry due to our contingent sensory equipment (our epistemic finitude). Kant was on the right track when he discovered that some fundamental features of human knowledge have to be accounted for in light of the question of totality. In particular, he discovered that the world is involved in creating illusions. Yet, he believed that these

260 Fields of Sense

illusions were 'natural',[11] where this just means that they were indispensable or necessary side-products of any account of human knowledge as a whole. He was not yet able to appreciate the possibility of either ontological or epistemological pluralism. Be that as it may, we owe Kant the insight that the concept of unrestricted or overall totality is tied up with paradoxes and surrounded by illusions, even though he himself ultimately wound up adding to the stock of paradoxes by creating the second-order illusion of the world as a necessary illusion.

Notes

1. DeLanda, *Intensive Science and Virtual Philosophy*, p. 58. Tristan Garcia has recently spelled out a far-reaching flat ontology in his *Form and Object: A Treatise on Things*.

2. '[F]lat ontology signifies that *the* world or *the* universe does not exist. ... The claim that the world doesn't exist is the claim that there is no super-object that gathers all other objects together in a single, harmonious unity.' Bryant, *The Democracy of Objects*, p. 246. For Bryant's argument for the connection between flat ontology and his (in many respects different) version of the world's non-existence see chapter 6.2 in the same volume. One of the main differences is that the no world view defended here does not rely on the idea of the world as an all-encompassing entity, but generalises the idea of the non-existence of anything all-encompassing by neutralising the arguments. It, therefore, does not matter whether one conceives of the world as an all-encompassing super-object, a regulative idea, a totally universal principle of thinkability, or a set of laws that governs everything.

3. Harman, 'On the Undermining of Objects'.

4. Hegel, *The Science of Logic*, p. 66 (GW II.27).

5. Cf. Schelling, *Philosophical Investigations into the Essence of Human Freedom*, p. 27 (SW VII 356): 'The natural philosophy of our time has first advanced in science the distinction between being in so far as it exists and being in so far as it is merely the ground of existence.' Crucially, Schelling does actually not speak of being in so far as it exists, but of essence (Wesen) in so far as it exists, which is an important distinction that carries a lot of weight given that it cashes out the concept of 'essence' from the book title. On this see Gabriel, 'The Unground as the Irretrievable Other of Reflection'.

6. Heidegger, 'The Question Concerning Technology', p. 7: 'Causa,

casus, belongs to the verb cadere, "to fall", and means that which brings it about that something falls out as a result in such and such a way.' See also: Gabriel, 'Ist die Kehre ein realistischer Entwurf'. David Espinet has pointed out to me that Heidegger sometimes seems to commit to an ontological monism on the basis of his analysis of the event as 'unique', such as in the following passage from Heidegger, 'The Principle of Identity', pp. 36–7: 'The *belonging* together of man and Being in the manner of mutual challenge drives home to us with startling force that and how man is delivered over to the ownership of Being and Being is appropriate to the essence of man. Within the framework there prevails a strange ownership and a strange appropriation. We must experience simply this owning in which man and Being are delivered over to each other, that is, we must enter into what we call *the event of the appropriation*. The words event of appropriation, thought of in terms of the matter indicated, should now speak as a key term in the service of thinking. As such a key term, it can no more be translated than the Greek λόγος or the Chinese Tao. The term event of appropriation here no longer means what we would otherwise call a happening, an occurrence. It is now used as a *singulare tantum*. What it indicates happens only in the singular, no, not in any number, but uniquely. What we experience in the frame as the constellation of Being and man through the modern world of technology is a prelude to what is called the event of appropriation.' I agree that Heidegger oscillates between a monism of the event and a pluralism of the kind I believe he should hold and I, therefore, leave it open as to whether Heidegger's take on the event can fully be translated into a functional account. Yet, if Heidegger indeed thinks of the event as substantial (maybe even as tied to Hölderlin's poetry or to really bad things such as national socialism), he is subject to the error he himself calls 'ontotheology'. David Espinet also suggested that Heidegger might not be speaking in his own voice when talking about the 'casus' due to his general tendency to use Latin expressions only in a critical mode (Latin as the language of the forgetfulness of being). However, if this is generally true, this should not be taken seriously given the very absurdity of a fallen language. If Heidegger ever seriously thought that there are languages more apt for being in touch with 'being' (say German and Greek), he was just seriously misguided.

7. Cf. Gabriel, 'Is the World as Such Good?' This view is also available in a nascent form in Gabriel, *Der Mensch im Mythos*, § 5, pp. 104–15, and Gabriel, *Transcendental Ontology*, pp. 8–21.

8. Kant, *Critique of Pure Reason*, A 568/B 596; A 575/B 603.
9. This was the basic idea in Markus Gabriel, *An den Grenzen der Erkenntnistheorie*, where I still tried to defend a broadly Kantian approach to the relation between world and object.
10. Heidegger, 'The Age of World Picture', pp. 115–54.
11. Cf. Kant, *Critique of Pure Reason*, A 298/B 354.

Actuality and Possibility

The functional ontological difference between fields of sense and objects leaves room for events, that is, for configurations that cannot be anticipated from the standpoint of metaphysics. Facts do not generally fall within a unified field of anticipation, a transcendental frame. This entails that there are no metaphysical modalities determining what could generally be the case beyond the ontological insights into functional differences. In order to clearly see what this means and how this informs the concept of ontology and maybe of philosophy in general, it is time to move on to a discussion of the modalities, which is one of the most central battlegrounds of the history of the concepts of being, or rather existence. We now know that there cannot be a completely flat ontology, where a completely flat ontology would be an ontology only containing objects, as this would rule out essential conditions for any objects' actual existence, namely that there be a field of sense in which it appears. We also know that the ontological difference between fields of sense and objects is functional and not substantial. In this way, the ontology of fields of sense occupies a middle ground between ontotheology (hierarchical substantial metaphysical difference) and a completely flat ontology, an ontology without ontological difference.

As might already be obvious from various discussions in the preceding chapters, I reject the very idea of possible worlds as an attempt to regiment modal discourse. The literature usually assumes that the concept of a world can be used without further clarification, which is the first basic mistake in the very theoretical setup of possible worlds semantics and metaphysics.[1] The second major mistake is that it is hopelessly and viciously circular to define *possibility* as truth in some *possible* world or other. The idea of a possible world is utterly unclear and based on a whole array of unarticulated metaphysical assumptions. For this reason, it is necessary to redefine the modalities against the background of the conclusions so far established without assuming that there is a world, and that this world has modal alternatives that share the feature of the alleged actual world to be a closed totality or any complete account of what was, is, and will be the case.

Actualism is usually understood as the view that actuality and existence have the same meaning, or rather, that actuality is the modality of existence. I agree with this view to the extent that the fact that something appears in some field of sense can indeed be equated with actuality. Note, however, that actuality is as orthogonal to the reality/fiction and the mind-dependence/mind-independence distinction as existence: Faust is actual in *Faust*; Hamlet is actual in *Hamlet*. Everything exists in some field of sense or other apart from the world and associated nonsensical pseudo-objects such as an all-encompassing principle, rule, law of nature, structure or algorithm, which are all versions of the same illusion.

The fact that everything exists does not mean that there is a unified field of actuality ('reality') that encompasses everything that exists. *Actuality* is the fact that some object appears in some field of sense. Thus, everything is actual, but just not in the same field, which is why ontological pluralism is not subject to the usual problems of actualism associated with the claim that everything is actual in the same domain. Hamlet is not actual in the history of Denmark, whereas Lars von Trier is. However, Lars von Trier is not actual in *Hamlet*.

This immediately raises further issues regarding identity. In what sense is Denmark both an actual object (for instance in the European Union) and an actual object in *Hamlet*? Does 'Denmark' really or actually refer to the same object when appearing in the European Union and in *Hamlet*? Or what about a bottle that I look at one moment, then turn my head away from it and imagine it? Is the bottle looked at the same as the imagined bottle?

I argued that objects are bundles of senses held together by a governing sense. The identity of an object over different fields depends on the availability of a governing sense. Denmark in *Hamlet* is compatible with Denmark in the European Union because there is a governing sense relating the two, for example, European history. It is true of Denmark (the country in the European Union) that it appears in *Hamlet*. It is part of Denmark's history to have been represented in *Hamlet*, as much as it is part of the bottle's history to have been imagined or looked at. But, one might object, objects sometimes dissolve under field change. If I melt a plastic bottle in a big melting pot together with other plastic objects, it ceases to be the bottle; if I locate Denmark in China (as a province) and then write a play about it in which Chairman Mao resides over Denmark together with a prime minister by the name of Hamlet (or rather: 哈姆雷特), is this still Denmark in any sense? And what about Arnold Schwarzenegger? We know that it is possible for him to not have been elected the 38th governor of California or not have been chosen for the role of the terminator. But could he have been a female Swedish sex worker? Would *that* still have been Arnold Schwarzenegger, had he been born to the same parents and been baptised under the name of 'Arnold Schwarzenegger'? Or could he have been born as Marie Rotenegger to the neighbours of the Schwarzeneggers, and after an awesome decade as a sex worker decided to invest some of the incredible amounts of money he earned into body building and altering his secondary sex characteristics to make his body match his long-standing gender identity?

Kripke famously wants to fix the puzzles in modal variation from the standpoint of a theory of reference. As already pointed out above (see pp. 230–7) one defining feature of his methodology consists in appreciating the fact that we can use both good (true) and bad (at least partly false) descriptions in order to establish reference to objects whose identity, therefore, transcends our ways of fixing it. In this way, Kripke gives a far-reaching realist account of reference, where the relevant contrast of objectivity is that between the identity conditions projected by our descriptions and the actual identity conditions of the object referred to. Both sets of conditions might diverge to some degree even when we successfully refer, which is one way in which objects outrun our beliefs about them and are still capable of relating to our beliefs and motivate reflectively adjusted changes in them. His tool of rigid designation together with the associated semantic externalism suggests that the identity of at least some objects is determined by the object and not by the descriptions we use in order to refer to it.

However, this paradigmatically (and, for all that has been argued, only) works in contexts where we refer to an object that is both in itself determined independently of the senses *we* use in order to individuate it and determined as a natural kind. Yet, what is actual and what is possible is not generally determined by the individuation of natural kinds. It is, for instance, impossible for me to become the president of the United States or (even more clearly so) for me to become the next chairman of the Chinese Communist Party. Yet, presidents are not natural kinds, and I am not identical with the natural kinds associated with me (including my genes, my cells, my brain, the water I just drank, and so on). The modal variations in which I am involved by far transcend the modal variations of the object referred to by others when they mistakenly refer to me by bad descriptions. If they only referred to my human body in their environment by the bad descriptions of me they use, they hardly cover my identity at all.

As already said, Kripke implicitly draws on a bottom-up deter-mination of essence; the object is fixed and rigidly designated, and this is possible because it is not identical with its modes of presentation. However, this picture always relies on our semantic resources and seems to model modality on the basis of human fallible reference to spatiotemporal objects as a primordial fact. In my view, then, spatiotemporal location is the model for essence in Kripke. What else would be intended by the term 'natural kind'? What does 'nature' mean in this context if not whatever can be studied by the science of nature? His metaphysics is the Cartesian metaphysics of an external physical material world, on the one hand, and an internal mental fallible referring mind, on the other hand, trying to get a grip on the identity of those independent objects out there.

Traditional metaphysics is anchored in the misguided idea that the fact that our reference to how things are comes late in the history of how things are makes our reference somehow volatile, fallible and vulnerable. Objects are not generally, paradigmatically or primarily mindless physical extended natural kinds, as these things could not even exist on their own unaided by the facts in which they are involved. Not even the universe is so alethically cold that there are no facts about it, and the facts about the uni-verse are simply not identical with the totality of spatio-temporal individuals. The fact that pure water is H_2O is not itself H_2O. This is why we can know so many things about the universe: because it does not only consist of things, but contains the elements neces-sary for it to be at least locally knowable to us (that is, there are facts which are not themselves more physical stuff and there are knowers who are also not identical with more physical stuff).

In order to better understand what the account presented here adds to our understanding of identity over modal variation, let me now pin down the concepts of actuality and possibility and continue drawing consequences from my definitions.

Actuality is the fact that some object appears in some field of sense. *Possibility* is the governing sense of a field of sense regardless of what appears in the field. Possibility is an abstraction from actuality. Actuality is given first, and from actuality we can attempt to uncover its possibilities. For instance, someone is a Danish citizen, and some other person is a Danish citizen too. They can both be Danish citizens because the rules or laws of Danish citizenship allow for a plurality of Danish citizens. One counts as a Danish citizen (and actually is a Danish citizen) if one meets a number of descriptions defined by the relevant laws. Those descriptions all gravitate around the governing sense 'Danish citizenship'. Someone can, thus, have the identity of a Danish citizen and be a Danish citizen according to the law. If we abstract from the fact that the actual and living Danish citizens are Lars von Trier, Anders Moe Rasmussen and a few million other people I do not know, we grasp the concept of Danish citizenship defining a field of sense. In this sense it is true that what is actual is possible in that the actual always appears in a field of sense individuated by a governing sense around which other senses gravitate, as it were.

Thus, if we ask the question whether it is possible that Arnold Schwarzenegger could not have been elected as the 38th governor of California, we are abstracting from actuality and consider the relevant governing sense, in this case, the electoral laws of California. These laws do not entail that Arnold Schwarzenegger will become the 38th governor of California, but they determine a course of action that someone like Arnold Schwarzenegger in relevant respects could choose and happens to have chosen. The range of modal variation, thus, hinges on what is actually the case in a field of sense where the field of sense in its turn appears in another field of sense. Possibility is therefore always itself an actual object; it exists as objectively as the moon, but it is not a metaphysical category, that is to say, a universal concept defined over all fields of sense in one stroke. Possibility, like all other ontological concepts, is a thin and malleable concept co-determined by what is actually possible, that is, by what is the case.

Actuality and possibility are relations between a field and its objects. Actuality is a relation between a given object and the field in which it appears, whereas possibility is the relation between the governing sense of a field and the range of objects it covers. Possibility is defined as ways objects appear in a field; it characterises the form of appearance, whereas actuality consists in there being objects in a field that are not exclusively individuated by the possibility in question. Any actual table differs from tablehood by appearing in other fields too, by instantiating other possibilities.

At this point, the objection has been raised that after all there seems some kind of a hierarchy of forms of modality with logical possibility at the top, metaphysical possibility somewhere in the middle and actuality at the bottom.[2] If we want to figure out, say, whether it is possible that Arnold Schwarzenegger could not have accepted the role of the terminator, we first and foremost need to figure out whether this is logically possible (which it is). It also seems metaphysically possible in some sense, at least, in the sense in which we see no immediate obstacle to his deciding otherwise. Of course, someone might argue that this metaphysical possibility is really only epistemic in that complete insight into the fact might lead us to conclude that he never had any such choice, that he had to become the terminator. Here, a lot hinges on our notions of free will and of what would count as ascribing metaphysical possibilities to someone who is actually determined by his involvement in physical contexts. At the very least, it seems that what is actual has to be logically possible in some relevant sense. So, however the details of the hierarchy, is there not a structured field of modal notions such that we could have some kind of a priori grip on its structure?

But what is 'logical' or 'metaphysical' possibility supposed to mean? If 'metaphysical possibility' just means compatibility with the laws of nature in contradistinction with 'physical possibility', which accordingly might be understood as 'compatibility with the actual course of events in nature', it amounts to a local form of possibility in my sense. The laws of nature define a space of facts, things and events that can count as appearing in that space. We can regard them as the governing sense of the field of sense investigated by the natural sciences. 'Logical possibility' is traditionally intended to define the largest field of sense defining what can be actual at all. For nothing seems to be actual that would have to be described in such a way that the description violates some fundamental laws of logics. We could then think of the alleged hierarchy of modalities in terms of sets of laws where the set of laws of logics is somehow less restricted than the set of laws of nature.

However, this traditional picture understands logics as metaphysics in the sense of the discipline that somehow studies every-thing by giving an account of some minimal or most fundamental laws that everything has to obey in order to count as anything whatsoever. In other words, it is a world view. Yet, if I am right, no sense can be attached to the idea of there being such fundamen-tal laws. This is not to say that there might not be some fundamen-tal laws of thinking such that if we violate them we did not really think at all. There might be such laws, even though it is unclear how these laws of logics in a more traditional sense relate to suc-cessful attempts to develop paraconsistent formal systems. Many of the traditional candidates for the most fundamental logical law that can then serve as a clue to the most fundamental metaphysi-cal law have been abandoned or successfully questioned (such as the unrestricted applicability of the law of non-contradiction).[3] Whether some statement or overt assertion is contradictory or expresses a logically possible proposition depends on criteria of meaningfulness that the statement does not wear on its sleeve.[4] This is the rationale for Husserl's late project of a genealogy of logical concepts, as he insists on the point that making sense of a statement so as to be able to assess the truth value of the proposi-tion it expresses affects our understanding of logical laws.

Against this background, we can make sense of the idea of a defeasibility of logical theory without thereby undermining the idea of the unity and universality of our capacity for thinking logically, of reason itself. In other words, any contentful notion of 'logical possibility' that goes beyond the mere insistence that something or other has to be logically possible involves our grasp of particular fields of sense. There is no position from which we grasp everything by grasping the most fundamental laws it has to obey. This is one way of fleshing out what it means that there is no 'view from nowhere', without thereby threatening our self-understanding as rational animals who orient their claims in light of possible future revisions required by criteria of consistency and meaningfulness. These criteria need not be conceptualised in such a way that they consist of 'rails to infinity' laid out in advance and structured regardless of how we are able to make sense of them.[5]

The question: 'Is X possible?' is meaningless unless some field of sense defines the specific meaning of 'possibility'. My favourite example is the question, 'Is it possible that $2+2=1$?' If the field of sense in which our inquiry takes place is basic arithmetic, the answer is negative. Yet, if a child reasons that two drops of water added to drops of water become one drop of water, there is a perfectly legitimate sense in which the answer is positive. Now, one reaction to this would be to claim that the meaning of the symbols '2', '+', '=' and '1' is restricted to basic arithmetic so that there really is only one answer to the question. The water case just does not matter. Yet, this restriction results from our capacity to think within different fields of sense. It is constitutive of our understanding of arithmetical addition that it differs from addition in the sense in which we add drops of water to drops of water, even though the senses are relevantly related. Otherwise, basic arithmetic would not have any applicability in the realm of moderate sized dry goods, which it has given that it holds for the many fruits, chairs and tables that resist chemical fusion.

There is no overall set of *a priori* principles we can rely on in uncovering the constraints that define a local form of possibility. What we actually do is abstract away from given actual objects and relations among them in order to uncover the governing sense of the field in which they appear. This extrapolation allows us to make predictions, a capacity not rooted in some overall universal and necessary laws of what has to follow what in order for it to exist at all. Our concepts of the modalities are rooted in our understanding of *fundamental heuristics*, that is to say, in what it means for us to be able to predict future events on the basis of an insight into the governing sense of the field within which they appear.[6]

But does this not turn possibility into a purely epistemic concept, a mere abstraction, such that 'in itself' everything might be actual or even necessary? In order to see why this is not the case, let us consider Lars von Trier. He actually is a Danish citizen. Could he become a Spanish citizen? Is this possible? The answer is positive: He could become a Spanish citizen under the right conditions, and he could choose the relevant course of action to achieve this goal (move to Spain, and so on), whereas it is not possible for him to become the next chairman of the Communist Party of China, as this also involves much more than just meeting descriptions defined by the law or the party handbook. There is no way he could achieve this political goal, even if he found out that there is a sense in which at least not be illegal for him to be the chairman. If we want to know whether Lars von Trier could possibly become a Spanish citizen, it is of almost no interest to us that there is no contradiction involved in Lars von Trier being a Spanish citizen. The very idea of an overall logical possibility (determined by the law of non-contradiction, say) is flawed, as it is a mere chimera of frictionless abstraction gone metaphysical. There is no such thing as a ghostly logical space spread out by logical laws as a crystalline basic substance attached to every actual object. This is Husserl's main point most clearly spelled out in his *Formal and Transcendental Logic*. He simply points out that it is a condition for the applicability of any logical law or principle we might be able to formulate that it can be related to actual judgements. But actual judgements are not only subject to logical laws, but also to further conditions of what counts as meaningful, what has sense, and what is pure nonsense, a distinction that cannot be drawn on the level of a pure symbolism allegedly manipulating the most general variables. Yet, he points out that our understanding of any allegedly purely logical propositions always presupposes a prior understanding (a presupposition, in his sense) of what can possibly count as meaningful.

> *Formal-logical considerations* and theory, with their focusing on what is Objective, have nothing to say about that: but every one of their logical forms, with their *S*'s and *p*'s, with all the literal symbols occurring in the unity of a formal nexus, *tacitly presuppose* that, in this nexus, *S*, *p*, and so forth, have '*something to do with each other*' *materially*.[7]

From this consideration Husserl draws the conclusion that this is the reason why logic is unable to provide us with a universal ontology, as it has no means of guaranteeing that it quantifies over everything even though it seems to be quantifying over objects or propositions as such, or *überhaupt*, an illusion Husserl tries to undermine.[8] In particular, this implies that we cannot think of literally all objects at the same time or from nowhere by thinking about objects as such, or *überhaupt*.

In my view, then, for something to be possible is for it to be compatible with the governing sense of a field of sense. For it to be actual is to meet the descriptions associated with the governing sense of a field. Some descriptions are fairly open and vague and sometimes it is not even clear if some object meets them, which is particularly problematic in the human world, as this is part of the burden of freedom. Here I agree with Hegel's *Philosophy of Right*. Human freedom is grounded in the negativity of our capacity of abstraction, which is a fully objective fact about us.[9]

272 Fields of Sense

It only looks metaphysically mysterious if we presuppose that the physical world somehow crushes our abstraction from the outside as it were and turns it into an illusion. But this is the true illusion, a metaphysical overgeneralisation triggered by a misguided ontology. The very fact that I can consider different courses of action and inhabit different fields of sense is free will, and it need not be mirrored in my neurochemistry, which is just one field of sense I inhabit, albeit a very important one for my survival.[10] Even if (which I grant) we can only consider different courses of action if we have the relevant neurobiology (or are the relevant neurobiology in some sense), this will always only give us the actuality of thinking whose content is possibility. But that neither makes the content actual, nor does it undermine the sheer existence of possibility. If we want to know whether it exists, the question is not whether free will is unconditional or subject to prior conditions. It does not matter whether the brain generates thinking and therefore substantially contributes to the existence of thought acts whose content is possibility. Whether it is the brain, a Kantian logical I, or an immaterial soul is not the question, as has rightly been pointed out by many a critic of free will. In any event, the brain, a Kantian logical I, and an immaterial soul are equally subject to prior conditions. From this I do not draw the conclusion that there is no free will because there are conditions of our realisation of possible goals, but rather the conclusion that 'free will' cannot refer to the activity of carrying out plans out of nothing. Why would this be the concept of free will?

If we ask whether our neurobiology is free, there might be a sense in which this can have interesting ramifications. For instance, the information processing on the level of neurological connections might have to be interpreted as fully-fledged intentionality, and there certainly is an important contribution by the complexity of our brains to our capacity for abstraction. But neurobiological and intentional 'stuff' nevertheless belong to different fields of sense, which does not mean that they are separated and cannot interact. There is no reason to believe that no fields intersect or interact for the overall reason that there is nothing that holds for all fields (such as that they do or don't interact). This is one respect in which the ontology of fields of sense is not the new monadology.

Nevertheless, the question of how the potentially illusory impression of free will fits into the monistic framework of a causally closed and deterministic meaningless universe is a meaningless overgeneralised metaphysical question. The ontology of fields of sense can be used as a clue to some important questions in the philosophy of mind to the extent to which these questions can be formulated independent of the standard metaphysical assumptions associated with physicalism, monism, or dualism and their logical skeleton. But no account should rule out in advance that our actual decisions are just not made by our neurochemistry. When I steal a beer in a supermarket, and someone tells a police officer to catch me, they are not after my brain or my body, which can easily be seen by the case where a bottle of beer falls into my bag and it only looks as if I stole it intentionally. In both scenarios, my body does the same: it carries a bag with a beer in it, and the facts about how the beer got into my bag are not completely physical or neurochemical. For someone to steal a beer there has to be a very complex interaction of coordinated fields of sense *involving* the neurochemistry of the brain, the history of the production of beer, the economy of supermarkets, property laws and so on. Whether I can be free when stealing a beer given that there are laws of nature is an antiquated and ill-formulated question based on incoherent thought-experiments (such as Laplace's demon) unifying every-thing (including allegedly illusory concepts such as 'free will') into an all-encompassing domain.

Accordingly, we have to learn to separate whether everything in the universe is subject to deterministic laws (which is not completely settled) from whether I had a choice when stealing the beer. Crime is just not part of the universe; it cannot be fully covered and exhaustibly investigated even by our best natural scientific methods because it belongs to a different field of sense, although it certainly intersects with the universe in informative ways. Whether Faust had a choice to kill Gretchen's brother is not a question about the universe, as the 'medical' doctor Johann Georg Faust, who once was with some of his descriptions part of the universe (or still is such a part of the universe if it is identi-cal with all of space-time past, present and future), did not kill Gretchen's brother. That the question discussed in literary theory as to whether Faust had a choice might give rise to different inter-pretations of the play is certainly not at all reducible to whether Goethe's brain could have come up with a different plot.

From the standpoint of reference and knowledge, that is to say, epistemically, actuality determines possibility. We only grasp what is possible by grasping what is actual. We grasp what is possible by abstracting from certain features F^1 of what is actual and by unifying certain features F^2 into the structure of a fact. In other words, we are able to separate objects and fields of sense in a functional analysis. In principle, nothing stands in the way of a successful, truth-apt and true functional analysis. That our grasp of the concept of possibility presupposes our capacity of abstraction should, consequently, not mislead us into isolating *epistemic* from other, say *logical* or even *metaphysical*, modalities.

On the current standard picture, there is an unfortunate division of labour between epistemic and metaphysical modality. The idea behind this is familiar. To claim that it is possible that Angela Merkel is in Frankfurt right now might mean at least two things: I might not know her exact whereabouts and, for all I know, she might be in Frankfurt, or metaphysically nothing stands in the way of Angela Merkel right now being in Frankfurt. If she is in Frankfurt right now, it is possible that she is in Frankfurt. Otherwise, how could she actually be there? On the one hand, we predicate modalities, in particular possibility, out of a lack of information. On the other hand, we predicate modalities in order to entertain our 'sense of possibility' (*Möglichkeitssinn*), to invoke the famous idea at the beginning of Musil's *The Man Without Qualities*.[11] This is also Aristotle's sense of modality in his distinction between history and poetical narrative: whereas history investigates what actually took place, poetical narrative explores, 'a kind of thing that might happen'.[12] In addition to epistemic and metaphysical possibility, theorists often add logical and physical possibility to their list of the forms of possibility. Logical possibility is defined via compatibility with the 'laws of being true (*Gesetze des Wahrseins*)',[13] whereas physical possibility is compatibility with the laws of nature.

The crucial question at this point is how to account for this plurality. Is it just the case that there are a number of kinds of modalities, where the list happens to be exhausted by logical, metaphysical, physical and epistemic modalities, or is there a common root, a base or all-out concept of modality? And if there is, what is the relationship between the all-out concept and the other modalities?

My answer to this question should by now be obvious: there is a thin concept of the modalities in terms of the ontology of fields of sense, and the actually existing forms of modality are co-determined by the sheer factual existence of those forms. There is no *a priori* way of limiting the forms of modality; there is no particular reason why there should only be the forms of modality recognised and analysed by contemporary mainstream theory of modality. Ontological pluralism suggests a modal pluralism beyond existence that is modelled in the same terms as the pluralism associated with existence. If one considers modal variation, the question regarding in what sense we ought to conceive of the modal variation in question accordingly always arises. There is no clear-cut or straightforward answer to the puzzle of whether Arnold Schwarzenegger could have been a better actor. We first have to settle the field of sense in question.

This view does not amount to *modal relativism*, but only to *modal relationalism*. The difference between *relativism* and *relationalism* generally consists in the fact that relativism is usually a name for a situation of undecidability, which is what accounts for the contrast between relativism and absolutism. For a position to amount to relativism, the following constraints have to be met:

(R1) There is more than one relevant frame of reference or system of beliefs in a particular region of discourse.
(R2) Propositions in that region of discourse cannot be assessed independently of their relation to one of the manifold systems.
(R3) There is no independent fact of the matter as to which system to choose in order to increase the likelihood of truth for beliefs formed about the subject matter.

For example, an ethical relativist does not usually only claim that all ethical values are relative to a system of beliefs, as Moses (who was almost certainly not an ethical relativist) could perfectly well agree with this. He himself believes that his ethical values are relative to the ten commandments, whereas the conflicting values of another group are simply all-out false, even though relative to their system. If God decided that not to kill is ethically mandatory or good and, therefore, gave us his commandments, there is an independent fact of the matter regarding the right choice of system. Any system incompatible with the fact that God decreed that killing is bad is simply false, even though there might be a different imperative derived from the false belief that some relevant anti-gods decreed that one ought to kill.

Which form of modality is relevant for a particular question is a fact of the matter independent of the outcome to be observed after one has chosen a system. Our modal beliefs are relational; they relate an object to a field of sense, but that relationship is itself independent or absolute in that it is not relative to itself. The relation relevant for the determination of the right kind of modality is settled objectively – it is just an all-out fact. Let me illustrate the point with an example. Is it possible that the glass on my table disappears while I go downstairs to fetch the mail? Well, that depends. It might disappear because my wife took it in order to use it to drink water. In that sense, it is certainly possible that the glass disappears because the field of sense is the standard social situation of cohabitation. If I ask whether the glass might disappear in the sense of turning into another object, such as a unicorn or a rain shower, the answer is no. And it certainly cannot disappear just like that. However, as soon as the relevant form of modality is settled by a relation between a field of sense and the object in question, there is an absolute fact of the matter determining the range of modal variation. There is no additional relativity.[14]

Relativism is usually generally regarded as a contrast to realism. The motivation behind drawing a line between the two resides in the notion that realism assumes structures whose individuation is independent of any arbitrary decision. Relativism, on the contrary, postulates a hitherto hidden form of conceptual relativity of a class of facts to a particular kind system such that the facts are only individuated relative to the system. Condition (R3) is usually interpreted as involving commitments that are incompatible with realism in that the arbitrariness in the choice of a frame of reference is a result of lack of friction. However, it is not arbitrary which form of modality is at stake when assessing modal variations.[15] The object whose variation is under consideration appears in a field of sense in the first place and the field in which we pick it up, as it were, serves as the ontological equivalent of 'Kripkean rigidification'. The structure of the field containing the object is as objective as the object itself, and it defines what it is for the object to appear within it. Here I agree with Étienne Souriau when he affirms that 'every being initially finds itself in a given situation that does not depend on its refusal or acceptance. This is constitutive of existence. But there still remains something to do.'[16]

Modal relationalism claims objective, non-arbitrary modal relativity. In particular, it claims that actuality and possibility are relations between a field of sense and its objects. The actuality of a field f_1 is thus a conjunction of all relations R of appearing-in between f_1 and its objects: $f_1 Ro_1 f_1 Ro_2 \ldots f_1 Ro_n$. To predicate of an object that it is actual is to claim that there is a relation between the object and a field. This view is modal relationalism for actuality. It does not amount to relativism because it is not generally arbitrary which field we choose and what defines the relation of appearing-in in the case in question. There might be uncertainty regarding the field of sense that is relevant, but this is not generally due to the absence of an individuating fact of the matter.

But does this not entail a vicious infinite regress of the following form: If o_1 only exists as a relatum in the relation of $f_1 Ro_1$ and if this relation itself only exists if it appears as an object in some field of sense f_x, we seem to have triggered the following regress:

$$f_\infty R\{\ldots f_3 R[f_2 R(f_1 Ro_1)_2]_3\}_\infty$$

In words: the relation of actuality (appearing-in) between an object and a field itself appears in another field. This second order relation in turn appears in another field and so on *ad infinitum*. On this construal, there is an infinite nesting of actualities, such as: my hand is actual in the field of sense of my perception, which is actual in the field of sense of this phrase, which is actual in the field of sense of this book, which is actual in the field of sense of books you have read until page number XXX, and so on. Yet, I do not see why this regress is either somehow generally vicious or why it should amount to relativism in any troubling sense of the term. As a matter of fact, I do not commit to one infinite nesting of actualities, as this would then create an all-encompassing chain of being, which is impossible. There is no single or generally ontologically privileged nesting of fields. One chain starts with my hand and moves from there to this book and beyond, while another chain begins a long time ago, in a galaxy far, far away, and leads to the empire striking back, and so on. It is simply not the case that everything is connected. There is no force holding everything together. Han Solo was almost right about that in *A New Hope*, the opening movie of the classic *Star Wars* trilogy, when he maintained in response to young Luke Skywalker:

> Kid, I've flown from one side of this galaxy to the other. I've seen a lot of strange stuff, but I've never seen anything to make me believe there's one all-powerful force controlling everything. There's no mystical energy field that controls my destiny.

Had Han Solo lived in one of the galaxies we observe and written the lines just quoted, he would have been right in an ontological sense. However, in the world of the movie he is wrong, as there clearly is a force controlling everything, which is the force holding the movie together as a movie. The spectator clearly sees the force, which is the facts which individuate the movie (it is directed by George Lucas, Han Solo happens to be played by Harrison Ford, and so on). The movie exists in the field of sense of my watching it. This field of sense is not directed by George Lucas, as it involves me sitting on my couch without following Lucas' script. The chain just articulated in which Han Solo exists in *Star Wars* and *Star Wars* exists in my living room, and so on, did not hang together with your reading of these lines when I wrote them (in the room next to the living room where I watched *A New Hope* yesterday). There are infinitely many chains of infinity that do not hang together with the chains just mentioned. One more time, the world does not exist. The popular myth of the *Butterfly Effect* as a result of the connection of everything or the age-old idea of a *sympnoia panta*, a coordinated, pre-established harmony of everything, is just plain nonsense.

For this reason, the fact that actuality is always embedded in more and differently individuated actuality is not evidence for ontological anti-realism precisely because the structures of infinity are mostly individuated independently and antecedently to any theory decisions at all. I defend a new realist ontology insofar as I commit both to ontological realism and to ontological pluralism without inflating this into a metaphysical view of the fundamental nature of reality.

If anything, the vision resulting from the ontology developed here looks like a ∞-dimensional continuum of continua: you can start with any point (object) you like and then establish a relation between the point and a line to which it belongs (representing field-membership). The line then is part of a plain, which is part of a three-dimensional object, which is part of a four-dimensional object, and so on. Wherever you start and whatever figure you choose in order to represent the continuity of one object appearing in a field appearing in a further field, and so on, there will always be infinitely articulated structures leading you to the next object appearing in another field. And yet, the points of departure will already appear in a determinate setting or other. There is no absolute arbitrariness, as you will begin with some given object and discover in which fields of sense it appears and in which it does not. There is no reason to believe that we first have to fight our way through to the first object of investigation. To such sceptical freedom or maximal detachment we never attain. Friction is guaranteed by the facts whose grip one cannot escape, which might have been the idea behind Parmenides's ontological metaphor of the sphere and its necessity. However, by now almost needless to say, there is no all-encompassing sphere or any other particular shape of any kind (be it physical, metaphysical, mathematical, or logical).

Notes

1. According to David Lewis 'the world is a big physical object'. Lewis, *On the Plurality of Worlds*, p. 1.
2. Thanks to David Espinet and Umrao Sethi for raising this worry.
3. On this see Priest, *Beyond the Limits of Thought*, which also contains illuminating passages on earlier attempts to somehow restrict the law of non-contradiction. Actually, those attempts hark back at least to Neo-Platonism and they play a role throughout European medieval philosophy as well as in classical Indian philosophy. The best known example is probably Nagarjuna. More recently, Quine has famously argued that all allegedly fundamental logical laws are defeasible due to their applicability conditions.
4. This is, of course, also a prominent Wittgensteinian point. On this see Baetzel, *Wittgenstein and the Limits of Philosophy*.
5. For discussion of the Wittgensteinian metaphor of 'rails to infinity' see Wright, *Rails to Infinity*.
6. On the very idea of metaphysics as rooted in 'fundamental heuristics' see Hogrebe, *Prädikation und Genesis* and his *Archäologische Bedeutungspostuale*.
7. Husserl, *Formal and Transcendetal Logic*, p. 219.
8. See, for instance, Ibid. p. 200: 'It will become apparent, from aspect after aspect, that the chief reason why logic is incapable of satisfying the idea of a genuine theory of science – that is: incapable of actually sufficing as a norm for all sciences – is that its formal universalitites stand in need of the intentional criticism that prescribes the sense and limits of their fruitful application.'
9. Cf. Hegel, *Outlines of the Philosophy of Right*, § 4, p. 37: 'In the first place, anyone can discover in himself an ability to abstract from anything whatsoever, and likewise to determine himself, to posit

280 Fields of Sense

any content in himself by his own agency; and he will likewise have examples of the further determinations [of the will] within his self-consciousness.' See also, Hegel, *Encyclopaedia of the Philosophical Sciences*, § 382: 'The essence of freedom is therefore formally freedom, the absolute negativity of the concept as identity with itself. On account of this formal distinction, spirit can abstract from all that is external and even from its own externality, its determinate being it can endure the negation of its individual immediacy, the infinite pain, that is, survive affirmatively in this negativity and be identical for itself. This possibility is its abstract being-for-itself generality in itself.'

10. However, it is not the only factor important for my survival, as I might decide to kill myself precisely because of the deteriorating conditions of my neurochemistry. For a recent discussion of this old Nietzschean point see Frédéric Worms, 'Un temps pour vivre et un temps pour mourir?' See also his recent *Revivre*.

11. Musil, *The Man Without Qualities*, pp. 10–13.

12. Aristotle, *Poetics*, 1451a37–b26.

13. Gottlob Frege, 'The Thought', p. 289.

14. Dorothee Schmitt has rightly insisted that my argument only amounts to a critique of absolute or global modal relativism, but that my view is really a form of modal relativism in a different sense, where the facts of the matter that are independent of a given system of reference (loosely speaking) are not all-out, but themselves only relatively independent. They are not absolute, albeit sufficiently independent. Her view seems to be that (R3) is just not a condition good relativism ought to subscribe to. To this my reply is that we can and should, therefore, distinguish between relativism (as characterised if not defined by (R1)–(R3)) and relationalism or relativity. For a much more detailed discussion of the issue of relativism see Dorothee Schmitt's Bonn dissertation: *Das Selbstaufhebungsargument: Der Relativismus in der gegenwärtigen philosophischen Debatte*.

15. For a defence of non-global relativism against this charge of implicit arbitrariness see again Schmitt: *Das Selbstaufhebungsargument*.

16. Souriau, *Les différents modes d'existence*, p. 110 (translation mine): 'tout être se trouve initialement dans une situation donnée, qu'il ne dépend pas de lui de refuser ou d'accepter. Cela est constitutif de l'existence. Mais il reste encore quelque chose à faire.'

11

Modalities II: Necessity, Contingency and Logical Time

In the last chapter I argued that we should understand actuality and possibility as relations between a field and its objects. Necessity and contingency differ from these relations in that they are field-immanent relations between objects. Aristotle defined contingency as 'that which can be otherwise (ὃ ἐνδέχεται ἄλλως ἔχειν)',[1] and he opposed contingency to necessity. Accordingly, a necessity is something that cannot be otherwise. To assert that it is necessary that 7+5=12 is to assert that it could not be otherwise than that 7+5=12 (because 7, 5 and 12 stand in this relation whose concrete meaning is defined by basic arithmetic). On the contrary, it is contingent that I raise my left hand during a philosophy lecture. I am capable of doing that not because there is no general metaphysical or physical obstacle to raising hands, rather, the field of sense of a philosophy lecture does not dictate raising or not raising my left hand during a lecture. The indeterminacy of action is not psychophysical (to borrow Husserl's term), it does not tell us anything about the specific structure of our neurobiology or about some objective 'gappy' indeterminacy in nature. The relations between the objects in this particular philosophy lecture licence both my raising my left arm and my refraining from doing it. I could, if I wanted; it depends on the situation. Both, raising and not raising my hands are possible; it is contingent which one happens or is carried out. Yet, the reason for this contingency is not entirely grounded in the possibility function of the lecture field. If I did raise my hand, understanding why I did it involves understanding relations between objects within the field, such as me drawing attention to my left hand or my constant inadvertent play with my left hand, and so on. Contingency is not just a logical combination of possibilities, as the standard logical account would have it, where we understand contingency as the fact that some proposition is possibly true or possibly false. If we consider whether something is contingent, we need to inspect relations among objects in a given field, and there is no overall answer to the question whether something is contingent or not regardless of the actualities of a given field.

For instance, insofar as I am also a swarm of subatomic particles, that is, insofar as I also appear in the field of subatomic particles, I might be involved in necessities. There are true descriptions of me (descriptive parts of me, as it were) in which I have no choice, in which it could not be otherwise than that a certain number of things happen to me. The relationships between subatomic particles might be subject to deterministic laws of nature, depending on the right interpretation of all laws involved in individuating the particles and governing their behaviour over time. I take it that it is very much an open question what exactly it means for there to be necessity in some relevant laws of nature, and how exactly any such insight relates to the age-old, yet over-generalised metaphysical question of determinism versus free will. My main reason for rejecting the very setup of this 'conundrum' is that it is driven by the metaphysical idea of unifying everything by grounding it in a fundamental level. Then the problem might arise whether free will really exists, or whether it is not just an illusion. Of course, even if it is 'just an illusion', it has to exist in some sense, namely as an illusion, which is still worth investigating. Actually, the metaphysical determinist always owes herself an account of how the manifold illusions arise that she needs to ground in the first place. But in this very activity of explaining the illusion away, of breaking the spell, usually too many factors have to be reduced, including decisive elements in the very motivational framework of the reduction, such as the very will to know. If we really were trapped in the illusion of free will or the illusion of a self (in the sense of an autonomous agent), then the very insight into this illusion will have to be ascribed to the illusory self, unless we want to tell a story according to which the grounding level (the subatomic particles) at some point 'wished' to break the spell they have unwittingly created. Traditionally, the most famous story along those lines was introduced by Schopenhauer, and that story is still with us today. It says that our brains simply evolved for no particular reason in such a way that they became aware of the ultimate randomness of their evolution. They then started noticing that the 'world as representation' is an illusion grounded in some other more fundamental world, which for Schopenhauer, of course, is not the world of atomism, but 'the world as will'.

However, the form of explanation Schopenhauer prefers is typical when we try to make sense of the integration of the illusion of free will into a larger domain not containing elements of freedom. Schopenhauer arguably invented many of the premises used in contemporary arguments for free will as an illusion in his prize essay *On the Freedom of the Will*.[2] I am only referring to the very setup of the problem here as a prime example of metaphysical overgeneralisation. I will argue in this chapter that contingency and necessity are ontologically restricted in a similar way to existence, actuality and possibility. Once more, there are no all-out metaphysical properties or relations, but there is only restricted existence, which is similar to the view that there is no unrestricted quantification. Yet, this similarity is rather superficial, as I reject the very idea of existential quantification anyway, given that I dissolve the tie between existence and quantity and accordingly give up on discrete ontology.

Recently, Meillassoux suggested that the dividing line between classical metaphysics and post-metaphysical thinking hinges on the question of whether there is a necessary entity. Against the idea of a necessary entity he urges his view that the only necessity there is the necessity that there be no necessary entity.[3] In other words, he argues that everything there is contingent in that it might not have existed and might cease existing at any moment. His reasons for this view are broadly derived from early modern concerns with the relation between the fallibility of our empirical (inductive) knowledge and the very idea of the laws of nature, that is to say, of laws that govern everything without possible exception. Nothing can contravene the laws of nature. Yet, any evidence we derive via our natural sensory anchoring in nature is defeasible. The evidence is of necessary relations between natural objects, but the conditions of our information processing make the latter structurally contingent.[4] Necessity is, on that construal, always only the result of an interpretation of our evidence in light of the defeasibility of the claims. We cannot have access to necessity beyond our contingent and, therefore, fallible interpretations of evidence, so that we have reasons to reinterpret necessity in somewhat Humean terms as a function of justified expectations, rather than as a feature of expectation-transcendent facts. At the same time, we have to presuppose that the evidence itself is derived from a domain governed by necessity without us ever being in a position to observe nature unaided by our fallible instruments of information processing. Nature for us is always interpreted nature. This notion is the epistemological origin of the conceptual structures Meillassoux unites under the heading of 'correlationism'. However, his concept of correlationism, albeit intuitively directed at an enemy, is not sufficiently clear.[5] Yet, his epistemological conception of correlationism and its weaknesses is inextricably bound up with the discussion of necessity and contingency, which is why it is important to take a closer look at some of the threads of his argument.

At the outset of *After Finitude* he defines 'correlationism' as 'the idea according to which we only ever have access to the correlation between thinking and being, and never to either term considered apart from the other'.[6] In this quote, a lot depends on how we interpret the term 'correlation'. In my understanding, a correlation certainly is a kind of relation. For all we know from Meillassoux' discussion of the conundrum, correlationism is the view that there is a relation between thinking and being that could not be otherwise. For instance, let *sceptical representationalism* be the thesis according to which we can only refer to non-intentional objects, such as trees, by having a mental representation of them that is the immediate object of our beliefs. In this scenario, whenever we refer to trees we primarily refer to representations of trees and secondarily, if such there be, to trees. In particular, we would have referred to our mental representation of trees had there been no tree. We can draw a simple distinction here and say that mental representations have descriptive content and thereby are *as if of* some non-intentional object O. Mental representations are *as if of* O regardless of whether O. If the idea is to identify a phenomenon independently of its actual truth value, Meillassoux might be right. In particular, there seems to be some lowest common denominator shared by a Fata Morgana, hallucinated content, and a fully-fledged sensory episode. This lowest common denominator has to have some structure or other independently of its relations to the facts. In all cases, something appears to us and this appearance only has to be truth-apt in order for it to have descriptive content. We do not need to commit to some appearance or other being really of the object or scene it presents itself to be at least as if of. This is indeed the quintessence of the 'highest-common-factor'-model pithily laid out by McDowell and other disjunctivists' attack on mental representationalism to the extent to which it is likely to motivate sceptical representationalism.[7]

In essence, this also corresponds to Heidegger's basic argument for the distinction between *ontic* and *ontological truth*.[8] Ontic truth is run of the mill correspondence; it is a relevant relation between beliefs or belief-like descriptive sensory content and belief-independent facts. Ontic truth can only be achieved at least bivalently, that is, under conditions of truth-aptness: beliefs and belief-like descriptive sensory content (such as my impression as if of my flashcards over there on my desk) are fallible. They represent something as being a certain way; they represent something under a description. However, even if a description fails, it would still present itself to us as if representing something different from the fact that it presents it. Descriptive content is truth-apt; it can turn out true-or-false, which is why it can mislead us. Yet, the very presence of descriptive content is not truth-apt, but a sheer manifestation of itself, a manifestation Heidegger labels 'ontological truth'. On an interesting side note, the Chinese translation of phenomenology is 现象学 (xiànxiàngxué). The first character means 'now' or 'present', whereas the second means 'outward appearance', 'shape', or 'image'. The second character etymologically is the pictogram of an elephant, but I will refrain from philosophical speculation about how this relates to appearance. In any event, the idea is that a phenomenon in the phenomenological sense is something that is present in such a way that we need not question it, maybe such as an unmistakable shape in front of us (is this how the elephant got there?).[9] Be that as it may, ontological truth for Heidegger is notoriously monovalent; it does not contrast with ontological falsity, which is exactly why both Tugendhat and Derrida almost simultaneously pointed out that monovalent truth is impossible precisely because it does not contrast with anything.[10]

Now, one of the problems of even stating the view of sceptical representationalism in terms of correlationism is that actual mental representationalism is not even correlationist. If there were a correlation between an independent object (being) and an act of truth-apt thinking about it – however tight the correlation is – the object would be present in the relationship. Imagine that I can only hold my cup in a certain way, and that it is impossible for me to hold my cup in any other way. In this case, there is a correlation between the cup and my way of holding it. This does not mean at all that I only have access to the correlation between the cup and my hand, as I am precisely holding the cup and not both my hand and my cup. An analogous situation obtains for thinking and being in Meillassoux' formulation: if I can only grasp being (which, I suppose, refers to a domain at least partly consisting of ancestral facts and objects) by thinking about it, this does in no way entail that what I have access to is a correlation and not one or both of its relata. Correlationism as officially stated by Meillassoux is not at all the view that we are 'sealed off from the world',[11] that we never know things in themselves or are possibly not even able to think them or to define some overall minimal ways they have to be in order to be things in themselves. The epistemological puzzles Meillassoux associates with the subjectivist 'era of Berkeley'[12] are not well captured by his underdetermined concept of 'correlationism' for the simple reason that according to his definition we, of course, have access to being by thinking it. To claim that being when thought of is a relatum in a somehow epistemically necessary relation, a relation in which we stand whenever we refer to being, is not to claim that we cannot think of things in themselves. It just means that we can only think them or of them by thinking them or of them, which is not a very spectacular, let alone an idealist or sceptical position. To establish that there is a relation with particular features (such as a correlation) between two relata is already to have access to the relata independently of the relation: tRb. Neither t nor b is identical with R, and it is quite easy to refer to them independently of the relation. This is even easy for mental representationalism insofar as it claims that individual acts of thinking are beliefs or belief-like descriptive contents to the effect that they are as if of O, whereas O is precisely introduced as something that is potentially independent of that relation, namely in the case where we correctly represent O as being a certain way. In this case, it at least just so happens that our mental representation and what it is about relate to each other in a way sufficient for our mental representation to be true. The essentially sceptical worries Meillassoux addresses might be derived from mental representationalism and, in particular, from the early modern conception of a second-qualitative mentally constructed realm of appearances (the mesoscopic coloured life world) that somehow sits on top of (emerges from) a primary-qualitative realm of subatomic particles and events. However, correlationism as defined by Meillassoux does not entail the sceptical scenarios he sets out to undermine in favour of speculative thinking, that is, in favour of our capacity to grasp the absolute. Because, trivially, Meillassoux also does not believe that he thinks the absolute without even thinking it, he just believes that thinking the absolute is not thinking the relation between thinking and the absolute, but, well, thinking the absolute. But this is exactly what the correlationist says with the additional proviso (and this is where scepticism might enter the picture) that in thinking the absolute we do not know whether we successfully think it or are prone to some illusion. The correlationist only adds to every thought that there is a possible I think behind it and, therefore, a fallible thinker, which in itself does not entail that we cannot think the absolute. It only amounts to Kantian modesty and ultimately to a rejection of our capacity to grasp facts about things in themselves if we add the particularities of the Kantian story, such as the notion that we could not cognise things in space and time if space and time were primary qualities or actual objects such as normal spatio-temporal things.

The view that really bothers Meillassoux is, thus, not correlationism, as there are indefinitely many unproblematic (non-subjectivist and anti-sceptical) ways of cashing out the position that there is a correlation between thinking and being, that some conditions always have to be met when we successfully refer to some non-intentional object or other. What bothers him is the idea that our conditions of accessing maximally modally robust facts and objects embedded in them potentially or even actually distort those facts. Let it be noted in passing that the problem of objectivity that Meillassoux poses is not limited to ancestrality in his chronological sense, that is, to facts that already obtained when no one was around to refer to them. Also, it is not sufficient to add post-apocalyptic facts, as Ray Brassier does, that is, facts that will obtain when no one will be around anymore to refer to them.[13] Post-human, or rather post-intelligent, reference facts obtain even if and as long as we are around. A lot of facts about us are maximally modally robust. Remarkably, even if there are a lot of facts we make the case by having beliefs about them, for those facts it is not in turn the case that we make them the case by having beliefs about them because we have that very belief about their 'creation and maintenance'.[14] As Searle has rightly insisted repeatedly: the *ontological subjectivity* of minimally modally robust facts, such as some social facts, does not undermine their *epistemological objectivity*.[15] We might make some things the case by believing them, which is not itself something we make the case by believing it. This is exactly why ideology in the sense of the erroneous naturalisation of social facts is possible: we need not be aware of the maximally modally robust fact that some facts in which we are involved are less modally robust.[16] Imagine that politeness is a socially constructed fact. Politeness only exists because we have beliefs about it. Then it is true that politeness could not have existed unless someone had beliefs about it. This, in turn, entails that even if politeness would never have existed, it would have been true that had it existed it would have been socially constructed. That there once was a time where no one referred to anything, because no one was around to have any beliefs, and that there might sooner or later be a time in which no one will be around anymore to notice anything, is exciting from the perspective of zoontology. It is not particularly profound for either epistemology or ontology. There are human beings (however exactly we single them out from a non-human environment) and human beings have truth-apt thoughts. Those truth-apt thoughts are part of what there is such that there are facts about them. Some of the facts in which human beings and their thoughts are embedded are maximally modally robust, others are less robust to the extent that they are socially or otherwise constructed, that is to say, they would not have been the case had no one ever had some individuating beliefs concerning them.

In a similar context, Crispin Wright has introduced the concept of a 'cosmological role' that can serve as a system of measurement of the degree of modal robustness.

> Let the width of cosmological role of the subject matter of a discourse be measured by the extent to which citing the kinds of states of affairs with which it deals is potentially contributive to the explanation of things other than, or other than via, our being in attitudinal states which take such states of affairs as object. I suggest that the idea which the Best Explanation constraint is really in pursuit of is that some discourses have, in these terms, a subject matter of relatively wider cosmological role.[17]

Wright's point in this passage is that some facts can be explained without explicitly invoking any kind of attitude. If I explain why and how there is a supernova in some galaxy by assembling the evidence for this fact with the help of the relevant instruments and detectors together with the right kind of theory, the explanation for this fact does not invoke any of our attitudes or instruments. We need to invoke the instruments in explaining how we know of the fact, but not in explaining the fact. That we observe the supernova under certain 'earthly', broadly anthropological, and maybe even transcendental conditions is not at all part of the explanation why and how this supernova in that galaxy came about. Explanations of Supernovae at the beginning of the twenty-first century do not usually (or ever) involve our attitudes. This will change if we ever come into the position (which is quite unlikely) to intentionally or unintentionally cause supernovae. Then we would have to explain the thus caused supernovae by referring to someone's attitudes. But this is not the case for hitherto known supernovae.

On the contrary, if we explain why Charles fell in love with Odette, this explanation has to invoke all sorts of attitudes. Falling in love has a narrower cosmological role than supernovae for the simple reason that it is an event largely constituted by attitudes and mutual attitude-adjustment. This is why falling in love strikes us as almost metaphysical or transcendent, because we experience that we create facts that significantly go beyond mere events without being completely intentional and conscious. Falling in love is middle ground between a volcanic event, as it were, and the execution of a preconceived plan. Be that as it may, facts about falling in love can only be explained by accounting for mutual attitude-adjustment, which gives these facts a narrower cosmological role.

The problem with Wright's concept of the width of cosmological role is that it individuates the width of cosmological role via an analysis of conditions of assertibility. His overall methodology is anti-realist in nature in the sense that his explanation of the different kinds of forms of explanation proceeds in terms of an analysis of our understanding of relations between the range of states of affairs and attitudes (discourses). The concept of width of cosmological role is a concept with a very narrow cosmological role, because its system of measurement includes attitudes as one end of the line representing the actual width. More specifically, Wright introduces the concept in terms of an analysis of 'the subject matter of a discourse'. The concept is, thus, an element in a theory of assertibility-conditions for a discourse. It is an element in 'a description of a theory-building process', as Quine calls this level of observation.[18]

Let us call *anti-realism* in general any view according to which the fully explicit individuation of a structure involves facts about assertion. In particular, *ontological anti-realism* is the view that the fully explicit individuation of facts about the meaning of 'existence' involves facts about assertion.[19] Given my arguments to the effect that ontological pluralism describes a fact about the meaning of 'existence', the debate of ontological realism versus ontological anti-realism boils down to how the plurality of domains is generated, how the different fields are individuated. Here, Wright's account of the width of cosmological role is clearly anti-realist, because the individuation of different subject matters of discourse proceeds via different forms of *discourse*. Even though Wright does not explicitly talk about existence in the context of the introduction of his concept of the width of cosmological role, he individuates the plurality of domains with reference to the individuation of discourses.

Against this background, I replace Wright's concept with an ontological realist counterpart, namely the system of measurement of modally robust facts, where a maximally robust fact corresponds to the widest cosmological role. The difference is that understanding what a maximally modally robust fact is does not generally involve assessing *assertibility conditions*, but *out-and-out truth-conditions*. Grasping a maximally modally robust fact is grasping the absolute. Recall that this is one of Hegel's definitions of speculation, the vindication of our 'capacity to cognize absolute objects (*Fähigkeit, die absoluten Gegenstände zu erkennen*)'.[20] To grasp the fact that the supernova would have gone off had no one ever referred to this fact and individuated it via discourses appealing to supernovae in a holistic theory-context is to grasp the absolute. What I just stated in the last sentence only indirectly expresses a fact about grasping facts about supernovae. It is an effect of supernovae being involved in maximally modally robust facts that grasping them is grasping the absolute.

But what about the relation between maximally modally robust facts and less, nay, minimally modally robust facts? After all, how do we not need to privilege ancestrality and extinction over our own parochial existence and our forms of enchanting and colouring an itself colour- and meaningless universe of blind ancestrality *a parte ante* and increasingly semantic cold extinction *a parte post*?

In order to substantially address this crucial issue that arguably is the ontological touchstone for nihilism, it is important to introduce the concept of *logical time*.[21] Here we can begin with *logical presence* and revive the idea behind Kant's and subsequent discussions of judgement first. By a judgement I understand an asserted truth-apt thought.[22] Judgements differ from (Fregean) thoughts or propositions in that they are asserted thoughts or propositions taken to be true. They define logical presence as whatever is present to them. Let us use the moon as an example here. If I judge that the moon is over here as I am pointing to it, the moon is present to my thought. It is present in the specific way it is present when I assert truths about it. In particular, in so asserting truths about it, I am aware that I could be wrong. My conditions of referring to the moon, for instance, involve visual descriptive content (such as the moon seen from this perspective), and visual descriptive content is partial. It is as if of the moon to the extent that it could also be of some other meteorite that to me looks like the moon and happens to be approaching the earth in a von Trieresque scenario. It is accordingly, now true of the moon that I referred to it under some conditions or other motivating my judgement that the moon is over there right now.

However, I am at the same time aware that the moon was somewhere else before and that I might not have referred to it at this particular moment. I am able to distinguish between the moon in general and the particular, fairly parochial fact that I just happen to have referred to it. In this way, I become aware of a transition in logical moon phases, as it were: the moon turned from an object not referred to previously by that thought into an object now referred to by that thought. The moon's antecedent states are part of its explanatory gravity, that is to say, of the fact that the moon is not identical with the one parochial fact to have been referred to by me under my limited visual descriptions. The antecedent states are antecedent relative to logical presence. They are not antecedent in themselves, but become antecedent at the moment where they have been referred to. This is why logical time is logical: it is generally measured by the moment determined by a judgement, a *logos*. The antecedent facts form the *logical past*, a past that is only generated belatedly, after the fact, or *nachträglich*, as we say in German.[23]

Logical future, accordingly, is measured by thought's own facticity. A judgement is itself a fact insofar as it is something that is true of something. Any future successful reference to how things were at the moment of judgement will have to refer to the judgement too. From now on, it will have been true forever that I referred to the moon and judged that it was over there. Logical past is the idea of the origin of antecedent truth-conditions of judgements. As Anton Friedrich Koch has recently argued extensively in his seminal *Essay on Truth and Time*, there is a relation between the realist platitude about objectivity that we do not make everything the case by asserting it, and logical time, where the realist platitude is related to our concept of the past.[24] As he also adds – and here I still agree with him – we change the future by presently thinking about the past. We make it the case that we judged that p and, thereby, create a logical future whose structure is objective and will potentially be the logical past of a logical future. This just happens, as we were referring back to our first judgement about the moon on the previous pages. Logical presence in logical future becomes logical past.

There is hardly any better poetical representation of logical time than T.S. Eliot's *Burnt Norton*, the first of the *Four Quartets*. Eliot opens his poems literally quoting Heraclitus with the Greek words *ton logon* (τὸν λόγον), which is *logos* in the accusative. And the poem begins with a statement about time:

> Time present and time past
> Are both perhaps present in time future
> And time future contained in time past.
> If all time is eternally present
> All time is unredeemable.
> What might have been is an abstraction
> Remaining a perpetual possibility
> Only in a world of speculation.[25]

He then goes on to describe a garden full of echoes, where an echo refers to an objective look, that is, to what things are really like once they are sampled by our capacities to refer to them by various descriptions: 'for the roses / Had the look of flowers that are looked at. / There they were as our guests, accepted and accepting.'[26] This intertwinement of dimensions (or ecstasies) of time is logical in that it integrates thought and judgement into what there is. The poem talks about the way in which it itself generates meaning, which is why it presents itself as one more echo: 'My words echo / Thus, in your mind.'[27] The poem read is like the rose looked at; its presence is sampled by judgements, which does not diminish its degree of reality. Poetry has the capacity to talk about the creation of semantic meaning, or rather it draws the line between internalist and externalist factors in meaning. When we refer to objects involved in maximally modally robust facts, such as the moon, we have to refer to them under some description or other. Our visual anchoring in what there is also presents us with objects, in this case things, under some descriptions, such as 'the moon seen from here by me'. The descriptions disclosed to us in the case of true descriptions both refer to us and to the objects presented. They refer to us, because they would not be present in this particular way, had we not been involved as the samplers of that presence.[28] This respect is traditionally called 'the imagination' or 'the imaginary': we project images of how things are. This is the internal contribution to meaning. Yet, the objects have to stand in a relevant relation to the meaning thus projected. The relevance of the relation cannot generally be deferred to causality, which at least partially works in the case of reference to natural kinds. But referring to reference itself or thinking meaningfully about meaning is different, in that the difference between the internal and the external contribution is drawn within language itself due to our capacity to use it in self-referential contexts. Interestingly, Hegel already pointed out this fact clearly in a side remark about the fact that 'sense' is used both to refer to our senses and to semantic meaning.

'Sense' is this wonderful word which is used in two opposite meanings. On the one hand it means the organ of immediate apprehension, but on the other hand we mean by it the sense, the significance, the thought, the universal underlying the thing. And so sense is connected on the one hand with the immediate external aspect of existence, and on the other hand with its inner essence.[29]

What is really at stake in the most recent rejection of anti-realism as a default position concerns the truth-conditions of thought in general. How can thought possibly be about facts whose individuation is potentially utterly independent of any prior assumption regarding the nature of these facts? How, in other words, can thought accounting for itself guarantee that there is the possibility of a radical surprise by what there is if it somehow or other necessarily imposes its own formal conditions on what it refers to? These questions arise against the background of the notion that thought has a better prior grasp of its presuppositions (such as logical or other transcendental rules) than of antecedently existing objects or facts. It looks as if we know much better that for all X: X=X than that it is raining in London right now.

However, as Russell has pointed out, do we really know better that for all X: X=X than that it is raining? Logical generality seems to admit of no counterexample. Yet, what about the case where we say of the round square that it is at least the round square? Is it the case that the round square = the round square? On this basis one could argue that 'for all X: X=X' might just not be the logical law we believe it is. At least, we need an account that either restricts the apparently unrestricted quantifier 'for all X' or we need to make sense of the unrestricted claim that even round squares are identical to themselves. More generally, the minimal grain of truth in the (neo-)pragmatist conception of logical laws as deriving from linguistic practices is that there are non-logical restrictions on the applicability of logical laws such that we have to conceive of them as more malleable than we traditionally did. For, the idea of logical laws utterly or, in principle, alien to our capacity of grasping them is as inconceivable as the idea that logical laws are identical with what we happen to take them to be. To put it bluntly: we have to make sense of the idea that thought generally is fallible, capable of revising even its most cherished assumptions. One way of stating this point is to insist that there is no epistemological safe haven that might give rise to the paradoxical impression that we now have to grant that thought could possibly be maximally far away, shut off from any contact with what there really is, including its own nature.

There seems to be an asymmetry between different kinds of thought articulated by a difference in truth-conditions: some thoughts are about utterly independently individuated objects (often called natural kinds, which is twentieth-century language for essences) whereas other thoughts are about themselves. In its current return, speculative thought often presents itself as post- or trans-human in that it focuses on the 'big outside (*le grand dehors*)', as Meillassoux has called it.[30] However, there is no reason to cling to the idea of a transcendental asymmetry between thought in its self-directed articulation and thought in general, which includes thought about maximally modal robust facts. It is equally real and absolute that it is raining, and that Britney believes that it is raining. It is equally real and absolute that our galaxy formed before we were there to notice it and that we believe such. Our galaxy and our thoughts about that galaxy both exist, and we can refer to them. Yet, there is a logical temporal relation between the galaxy and our thoughts about it. We are aware that our thoughts logically present the galaxy to us as something that has existed in ancestral times, and that still largely exists without being fully explored. The *logical* past of the galaxy, however, is not identical with the *physical* past of the galaxy. It is introduced in order to account for the objectivity of our thoughts about the galaxy. Meillassoux confuses logical and physical past (strictly speaking, there might be no such thing as *physical past*, but that poses even more problems for Meillassoux). His point about ancestrality should never have been cast in terms of an actual stretch of time before the existence of intelligent beings within the universe, as the point is really about truth-conditions and not about time in the physical or rather common sense sense of 'time'. If anything, his point is about logical time, but then ancestrality is, of course, a synchronic category: it does not only refer to facts obtaining prior to say five million BC, but also to unnoticed facts obtaining right now.

Generally, our thoughts about the galaxy are not objective because the galaxy existed before we noticed. If that were the reason why our thoughts are objective, then we would have identified a potential threat to the objectivity of our second-order thoughts, as their objects (namely the thoughts thought about) are not thought of as having existed before we noticed anything. Moreover, the third-order thought encapsulated in the preceding sentence has an object (a second-order thought) encompassing thought that cannot go unnoticed. Some thought by now is noticed, and as we notice some thought we become aware of the fact that the realm of thoughts stretches out beyond any particular thought noticed. This raises the question of the reach and structure of thought itself, which is the traditional topic of the discipline of logics. In logics we are not immune to error; logics is itself objective, which is why there can be genuine and far-reaching disagreement both about its contents and about its form. There is no reason to believe that thinking about thinking generally is immune to error by virtue of not being objective, whereas our beliefs about galaxies, sets, or subatomic particles are fallible because they are about a specific kind of object, namely physical things or their primary qualities (whatever that really means).

I conclude from this discussion that objectivity has to be an individuating feature of thought and not of all its objects.[31] What makes thought objective is not that it is about this or that thing, but that it is about anything. The way thought is objective is informed by its very intentionality. The reason for this is not some transcendental fact of the matter, such as that intentionality is both re-, at- and pro-tentional, reaching out into different 'ecstasies of temporality', or what have you.[32] There rather is logical time associated with the truth-conditions of thought in general. Logical past is the idea of realist truth-conditions, logical presence is constituted by judgements, that is, by actual thoughts, whereas logical future is the realisation of the fact that actual thought has occurred and therefore becomes part of the logical past of a future thought about it. Logical future is associated with the contingency of judgement, with the fact that we are open to revision in the future, even where we stick to our judgements (that is believe) in the present.

At the same time we know that there are many thoughts no one will ever think of. We might go on with the same kind of beliefs to some extent regardless of whether or not they are true. This idea can be generalised into the picture of our overall extinction and even the end of thought-occurrences in the universe. Yet, even if no one will ever think about the thought expressed in these lines (well, you just did) or rather even if at some point or other no one might be around anywhere to think about the thought just expressed, it will from now on be eternally true that the thought once occurred. The occurrence of a thought is as real and objective as the coming into being of a galaxy, as a chemical reaction, or the very inflation of a physical universe.

I take it that this is the rationale behind Brassier's objection to Meillassoux's claim that by necessity there is no necessary entity according to which the fact that the thought itself claims necessity turns it into a necessary entity, so that the rejection of necessary entities in this form is self-undermining, or at least deserves further clarification.[33] Meillassoux indeed presents an all-encompassing universal thought, namely the thought that necessarily there is no necessary entity or necessarily, all entities exist contingently. Now, to be more precise one could object that the truth of the thought formulated by Meillassoux is necessary, not the thought itself, as it might never have occurred to anyone. The truth-conditions of Meillassoux's version of the necessity of contingency imply a necessary entity, namely the fact itself that by necessity nothing is a necessary entity. This fact itself exists and it is the object of Meillassoux's allegedly all-encompassing universal thought.

Now, I have argued in the first part of this book that existence is not a proper property. I have provided additional reasons against adverbial ontology. So it is trivially true according to the ontology of fields of sense that there is no necessary entity and that nothing exists necessarily. Entities are not characterised by necessity, even though they might stand in relations of necessity or contingency. The relation between an object and any of its fields in virtue of which it exists, that is, actuality, is not qualified for either necessity of contingency. What about modal variation here? Do we not justly say of many things, at least of cars and refrigerators that they might never have existed? Is that not contingent existence so that we can at the very least conceive of necessary existence given that we can conceive of contingent existence?

Of course, I do not intend to deny the truth that many things might not have existed. For the methodology accepted here largely distinguishes itself by dealing with ontology under the condition that it does not amount to revisionary metaphysics, that is, to ruling out in advance that things that seem to exist actually exist.[34] In other words, ontology should not in principle incline towards error theories that ascribe massive systematic error to some form of discourse or other that deals with objects whose existence is well documented. For instance, if some ontological consideration entails that nothing really moves, we should look for the odd guy out or fallacy in the consideration rather than accepting the marvellous truth that nothing moves. The same applies to a claim according to which, say, refrigerators necessarily had to come into existence, as they might not have. The issue, therefore, becomes what the meaning of modal variation in existence claims is, what we mean when we say that something might not have existed.

My answer to this is that necessary or contingent existence, like any other form of necessity or contingency, is a relation between objects in a given field in the following sense. Arnold Schwarzenegger exists beyond any reasonable doubt. There is a relation between him and all the fields in which he appears that make him actual. For example, he exists as the 38th governor of California. Now if we ask whether he might not have existed at all, we would probably determine the field at stake as that of his birth or of his conception. Could he not have existed in the sense that his mother might never have been impregnated? Is it contingent that his mother was impregnated? Here again, a lot depends on how we understand this question. Do we mean that she might never have been interested in having children or might have been biologically impaired? Or do we mean to ask whether the whole universe as a deterministic physical system might not have given its causal consent to her being impregnated? But if we come to the conclusion that Arnold Schwarzenegger might indeed not have existed, we establish a relationship between some object in some field of sense (between the person who became his mother and some physical or biochemical circumstances, or between the person who became his father and some physical or biochemical circumstances, and so on). Asserting contingent existence, thus, is not a predication in 'the out-and-out-sense'[35] introduced by Kripke in his discussion of the existence and reality of hallucinatory, fictional and perspectival objects. *Perspectival object* is my term for the kind of object we perceive when we say that there is a speck on the night sky, where we know that the speck really is a star and not a speck. Yet, we perceive a speck, even if there is a sense in which there really is no speck, but a perspectival object full understanding of which presents it as just one visual mode of presentation of a star among many. According to Kripke, to speak about the shape, size and colour of the speck in terms of predication is like describing a fictional character, whereas describing the star is describing it in an out-and-out-sense without qualifications such as 'from my perspective' or 'in the novel'. He draws an analogy between perspectival objects and fictional ones resulting in the position

> that, as in the case of fiction we discussed before, one can have two types of predication: the out-and-out-sense, and what is ascribed to it purely visually, analogously to predication according to the story. The distinction can also be applied to hallucinatory objects. 'Is hallucinatory,' 'was caused to be seen by such and such medical problems,' are out-and-out usages, whereas 'has a certain shape,' 'is coloured green,' are analogous to predication 'in the story.'[36]

However, there is no absolute out-and-out sense. 'Out-and-out' is just shorthand for some qualification of one field of sense or another. The star is a speck in the field of sense of human vision, and it is a star in some other field of sense (for instance in the galaxy to which it belongs). Yet, there is no field of sense that is ontologically absolutely privileged (one more way to state the no-world-view) so that it can substantiate a 'reference magnet'[37] of Kripke's concept of 'out-and-out' predication in ontology. There is a functional equivalent of a substantial idea of 'out-and-out' predication, but it does not seem to me that Kripke has this in mind. We can also frame this point by saying that no view from nowhere is available, which, however, does not lead to sceptical consequences, but only to a revision of the notion that there has to be maximally unrestricted quantification.[38]

Thus, whether some object or person might not have existed or some event might not have occurred is shorthand for a relationship between objects in a given field. It is not a question about existence or actuality full stop. It is, therefore, not the case that we refer to an individual by some random description or other, then have it as an independent object pole of our thoughts about it so that we can run modal variations on the individual. Whether Arnold Schwarzenegger might not have existed full stop or just like that is a meaningless and incomplete question. We first need to establish a field of sense, then make assumptions about its actuality (about the objects appearing in it), before we can begin to answer the question regarding the modal status of field-immanent relations between the manifold objects.

Something similar holds for necessary existence. I can rightly claim that it is necessary that there is exactly one natural positive integer between 1 and 3, namely 2. The number 2 thus necessarily exists in a sense, namely as the single natural positive integer between 1 and 3. This necessity is not a relationship between the field of natural numbers and the number 2 alone, but involves the numbers 1 and 3 given that the number 2 is the successor of the 1 and the predecessor of 3. If we isolate 2 from its environment and wonder whether IT might have existed, we do not come up with an insight into its necessary existence. Objects considered by themselves, that is, as individuals, neither necessarily nor contingently exist. Their existence or actuality consists in the fact that they appear in a given field, which is a relation that is not qualified for the necessity of contingency in that very field. Thus, from the ontological point of view defended here it is trivially true that there is no necessary individual, which is just the flipside of the equally trivial truth that there is no contingent entity. Here we can say that things merely are.[39]

Hence, there are at least the following three reasons to reject the idea of the overall necessity of contingency:

1. There is no overall modality just as much as there is no unrestricted universal quantifier corresponding to the intended use of 'every' or 'everything' in phrases such as 'every entity exists contingently' or 'everything is contingent' (an application of the no-world-view).
2. Necessity and contingency are field-immanent modalities that characterise relations between individuals in a given field. Thus, an individual or entity is neither necessary nor contingent. Its isolated existence or actuality is not a matter of modal variation (contingency) or invariance (necessity) at all.
3. Contingent existence, if anything, is a relationship between a field and an object in another field, where the original field is an object. Let F_1 be the default field of sense and O_1 be the object we want to qualify as necessarily or contingently existing. Then we need another field F_2, in which F_1 and O_1 are related in a suitable way for being assessed as standing either in necessary or contingent relation. Settling the contingency of such a relationship in another field differs from settling the contingency of that other field. Consequently, we can never be in any position to judge the overall contingency of everything, as this would presuppose the possibility of overviewing all fields and all objects as appearing in a field of sense that is, at the same time, capable of ruling out its own necessity.

In my contribution to *Mythology, Madness, and Laughter*, I argued against Meillassoux's thesis of the necessity of contingency with an opposing claim to the contingency of that very necessity.[40] The idea, derived from Schelling and Hegel, was that the conditions of asserting necessity are themselves always contingent. For instance, the conditions of asserting that $7+5=12$ imply a system of rules that settle the relevant meaning of the symbols employed by basic arithmetic. In this way, we rule out that '+' means just any form of addition, such as adding drops of water to drops of water. As a child in Antonioni's *Deserto Rosso* rightly points out: adding water drops is not regulated by basic arithmetic given that one drop of water added to another one does not add up to two drops of water, but to a bigger drop of water. The way in which the meaning of the relevant symbols is settled is not (at least not always) subject to this meaning, and it need never be. This is probably the idea behind Castoriadis' dictum that 'the activity of formalization is itself not formalizable'.[41] Necessity can only be stated under conditions that need not be subject to the rules that make the necessity intelligible. There is, thus, at least a potential divergence between the assertibility conditions of any necessity and the conditions of that necessity itself. What accounts for the assertibility of 7+5=12 contains information different from all the information needed to assess whether it is necessary that 7+5=12.[42]

Another way of putting this would be to say that there are *internal* and *external modalities* that correspond to Carnap's later distinction between internal and external questions; however, I reject his idea that external questions are somehow meaningless or not ordinary enough to be interesting from a scientific point of view.[43] Be that as it may, the insight articulated by Carnap is that there is a potential divergence between answering an internal and answering an external question. A response to an internal question, such as 'Does 7+5 equal 12?' is different from the response to an external question such as 'Are there really any numbers?' or 'How is it that there are numbers and water drops?' Notoriously, Carnap's main interest in drawing these distinctions was to prohibit traditional philosophical questions and replace them by futuristic scientific philosophy whose only business is to make explicit how exactly science gets it right. That kind of blatant positivism turned out to be false and untenable under the scrutiny of Quine, Davidson, Putnam and others who undermined the semantic ideas behind Carnap's way of drawing the line between metaphysical humbug and scientific sobriety.[44] Yet, despite the fact that Carnap thought he could define externality in such a way as to effectively deprive us of any meaningful manoeuvres in the external realm, he pointed out that there are meaning-stabilising assumptions for any ordered and rule-governed discourse that could possibly assess questions of necessity and contingency. Again, trivially a lot has to be taken for granted when we are able to claim that 7+5=12, or any serious mathematical truth for that matter, but there does not seem to be an overall discourse capable of rendering all of these conditions explicit, as this would involve speaking about almost all matters human.

Of course, from a logical point of view these assumptions will look ungrounded at some point or other, which led Quine to the abominable consequence that we have to take the existence of physical objects (in the narrow sense of theoretical entities postulated by physics) on faith in the same way in which he believed some Greeks took their pantheon on faith. He famously confesses his constructivist sins at the end of *Two Dogmas of Empiricism*:

> For my part I do, qua lay physicist, believe in physical objects and not in Homer's gods; and I consider it a scientific error to believe otherwise. But in point of epistemological footing the physical objects and the gods differ only in degree and not in kind. Both sorts of entities enter our conception only as cultural posits. The myth of physical objects is epistemologically superior to most in that it has proved more efficacious than other myths as a device for working a manageable structure into the flux of experience.[45]

Despite the pluralist tolerance sometimes derived from it, I disagree with almost everything in this passage, from the idea that Homer's gods are explanatory posits, hypotheses of some kind designed to explain natural phenomena, to the even worse idea of a 'flux of experience' that stands in need of structuring, an idea widely banned from contemporary epistemology (but still very much present in many 'mind sciences'). As if it were not already structured in one way or other even if we present it as a mere 'flux'. A flux is as structured as any other cloud. That we can read faces into clouds does not make them less structured in themselves. And what exactly is a 'cultural posit'? What makes a posit 'cultural'? Quine is rightly led to the insight that we need a somehow historical account of how exactly we come to ask internal questions, but this account need not amount to constructivism of any sort, and it particularly need not amount to the idea of a flux of experience causally triggered by the fact that our nerve ends reach out to oscillating colourless events or absolute processes in space-time. However, he is right in insisting that the assertibility conditions of a theory capable of observing relations and individuals in its domain of investigation potentially diverge from the laws discovered by the very set-up of the theory itself. In this way, he accounts for theory change and for the plurality of theories that compete for the right description of some phenomenon. There is always a level of observation from which a given decision to treat some individuals as primitive – an 'ideology',[46] as Quine intriguingly calls it – seems to be optional. Accordingly, any relation between individuals in a field including necessity and contingency is potentially up for grabs as we might revise our decision to treat some of the alleged primitive individuals as really primitive and not in need of replacement. In §6 of *Word and Object* on 'Posits and Truths' he comes to the following remarkable conclusion:

> Everything to which we concede existence is a posit from the standpoint of a description of the theory-building process, and simultaneously real from the standpoint of the theory that is being built.[47]

There is theory change and history in this undemanding sense precisely because we are in a position to revise our theories given that they are crystallisations of a theory-building process run by a program that differs from the actually built theory by not being committed to the results. The results can be revoked and the theory-building process might replace elements from its ideology by other elements for some reason or other.

My earlier objection against Meillassoux' version of the necessity of contingency *mutatis mutandis* originally was in line with Quine up to this point. However, I underestimated the misleading nature of the view insofar as it leans towards an anti-realist form of constructivism. Quine makes it look as if there could be no further reason to adjudicate between theories than building another theory, as only wholesale theories could be in touch with information provided from pre-theoretical sources (experience).

> The totality of our so-called knowledge or beliefs, from the most casual matters of geography and history to the profoundest laws of atomic physics or even of pure mathematics and logic, is a man-made fabric which impinges on experience only along the edges. Or, to change the figure, total science is like a field of force whose boundary conditions are experience.[48]

However, it is clearly wrong that it rains because Zeus decides that it should rain. It is, by the way, also clearly wrong that Homer (or rather the many poets responsible for the verses erroneously attributed to 'Homer') believed that whenever it rained, Zeus had to have decided so. It is just not an option at all to believe that it rains because Zeus decides so if we accept that we ought to believe what is true. Someone might construct some elaborate form of madness and regard this as just more 'man-made fabric', and still be utterly wrong for the trivial reason that he has constructed madness. Here I can agree with Latour's side remark that we need to learn to distinguish between good and bad constructions in light of whether they relate to how things are.[49] Quine was just not able to accommodate ontological pluralism into his view, which is why his ontological relativity is restricted to an analysis of 'ontological commitments' rather than of 'ontological truth'.[50]

Returning to the problem of the necessity of contingency, I would now say that there is a potential divergence between the assertibility conditions of any necessity (including any instance of necessary contingency) and the necessity itself. They are often governed by different laws, as in the simple case of a theory formulating laws of nature. The theory will always be subject to some laws that are not laws of nature; it will, for instance, be truth-apt and subject to rational theory-change according to rules that are not written down in the 'book of nature'. The formulation of a law of nature in terms of mathematical equations evidently makes use of mathematical laws, which is not the same as saying that the laws of nature themselves are subject to mathematical equations, only that we can express them with their help. Yet, this does not add up to a wholesale view according to which all necessity is contingent in that the relevant relationships for necessity have to appear in a field in which they turn out to be contingent upon parameters that make them contingent on a different level of observation. In other words, it is neither true that it is necessary that everything is contingent, nor is it true that the necessity of any given relationship is contingent in the next field up in the order of ontological nesting. What is necessary and what is contingent is, thus, subject to the gorilla argument, according to which questions of this kind are empirical (in a non-empiricist sense of the term). We need to find out for every observed necessity or contingency what its degrees of modal variations are in the fields in which they appear. There is no possible overall *a priori* verdict in either way.

Meillassoux is a classic metaphysician who presents us with an alternative world view. What he calls 'metaphysics' and rejects for interesting reasons is not 'metaphysics' in general, as metaphysics need not claim that there is a necessarily existing entity, but only that there is something or other (including sets of rules, modalities or laws) that holds everything together and unites it into a singular domain, the world. Meillassoux' own 'world formula', his shibboleth, is the necessity of contingency. His view that it is absolutely impossible that there be a necessary entity is a classical metaphysical move.

In a debate between Meillassoux and myself that took place at the École Normale Supérieure in Paris in April 2010, Meillassoux objected that my view undermines the universality of rationality and that it amounts to a problematic form of scepticism. As I understood his objection, his claim is that we need to be able to assume that there is an all-encompassing rational structure in order to avoid the idea of undermining facts we could not even be cognisant of. He still tends to believe that this fact can be interpreted in favour of mathematicism, which is a different question.[51] Yet, as Husserl shows, it is perfectly fine to be a universalist in logics, to believe in a universal formal *a priori*, and deny that this universal formal *a priori* is a most general domain to which everything (including clouds, cats and mats) belongs.

More important at this juncture is the age-old problem associated with any form of genuine (that is to say, non-internal) realism that the reality captured in thought might undermine any beliefs we build on the basis of our thoughts insofar as elements from reality might have to serve as counter-evidence to our beliefs that are, in principle, unavailable to thought. Reality might be different from what we take it to be in crucial, yet undetectable respects so that our entire belief system, or rather our various belief systems, might all be false together, however much we improve it with the goal of ideal inquiry in mind. This is one of the main motives behind Putnam's manifold objections against what he calls 'metaphysical realism'. Imagine, for instance, we reach the unification of physics, and the unified theory speaks in favour of physicalism about the universe in that it is able to explain all chemical and biological facts in terms of the finally discovered fundamental physical facts. Even in this scenario we might be wrong, though, as the unified theory might not be in a position to discover the really fundamental facts, such as the facts needed in order to turn space-time as a whole (with however many extra dimensions derivable from futuristic physics) into a holographic projection. The domain from which the projection could be inferred might be inaccessible to physics by any standard, as there might be physical limitations to physical discovery on a large scale, maybe similar to those associated with the very fact that we need physical instruments (observers) in order to trace the behaviour of elementary particles. In other words, we might be very wrong about almost everything due to some systematic distortion or other, even if arguments from future science are not generally able to demonstrate that we might be wrong about everything. As

David Chalmers has recently reminded us, even if physical reality is that of some intricate *Matrix*-scenario, there is a structural relationship between the elements of the appearances generated by an ultimate, yet, inaccessible physical reality and that reality itself.[52] But how do we rule out that there is a really inaccessible and completely unintelligible form of hyper-chaos (not at all like the tamed version we find in Meillassoux) beyond the grasp of the in principle best exercise of our theoretical and rational capacities? Meillassoux' brand of realism is indeed speculative in the sense that he believes that there is no gap between rationality and the structures responsible for the overall necessity of contingency. But how does he warrant this claim? All that he has established is that there are some absolute facts we can know in principle, but not that there are no facts we cannot know such that these facts in turn might somehow undermine a good deal of our knowledge claims, maybe even all our beliefs about the actual structure of reason itself? We would then still be rational, but that would mean something quite different from what we take it to mean at any given moment.

In the division of labour suggested by Putnam and subsequent discussions, Meillassoux' speculative realism is really a form of anti-realism, as he does not allow for even a potential divergence between what he takes to be the most suitable exercise of our rational capacities (blind mathematical meaningless rule-following) and how things fundamentally are. This is captured by his insistence on our capacity to grasp the absolute. This also explains Meillassoux's flirtation with Fichte and Hegel, who, in part, are anti-realists to the degree in which they actually argue that there cannot be any objects outside of the reach of rationality.

Yet, this traditional commitment to the 'unboundedness of the conceptual',[53] as McDowell nicely sums it up, passes exaggerated *a priori* verdicts on what can possibly exist, which is part of the motivation behind the move away from what would later be called German Idealism in the nineteenth century. As already mentioned, Timothy Williamson has objected to McDowell's updated version of the old Eleatic identity of thinking and being on similar grounds. He points out that we should not rule out in advance that there could be 'elusive objects'.[54] Elusive objects are objects that withdraw from any grasp of them, such as certain animals with a hitherto unknown neurochemistry that effectively hides them from any of our ways of detecting their presence.

[F]or all that McDowell has shown, there may be necessary limitations on all possible thinkers. We do not know whether there are elusive objects. It is unclear what would motivate the claim that there are none, if not some form of idealism. We should adopt no conception of philosophy that on methodological grounds excludes elusive objects.[55]

The German philosopher Wolfram Hogrebe has even argued that some typical philosophical objects – such as self-consciousness, the concept of concepts, conditions of possibility of various orders – are elusive, and David Lewis has suggested a similar diagnosis for the very concept of knowledge.[56] Hogrebe coins the term 'orphic reference' to account for the phenomenon of elusive theoretical objects such as some of those investigated by philosophy. Reference is orphic where the object referred to is made to withdraw by the very act of someone directing their attention to it, like Eurydice who returns to the netherworlds if Orpheus turns around in order to make sure that Eurydice is still following him. Further recently discussed candidates of orphic reference are rules and Wittgensteinian certainties, and various traditions have discussed the prospects of an elusive concept of the unconscious in various shapes.

An additional difficulty consists in the fact that we cannot even tell in advance which phenomena we believe to be confronted with actually are elusive or objects of orphic reference. Even if we knew for all objects that they would have to fall under some concept or other, including the concept of an 'elusive object', it would come very close to gerrymandering to insist that there is a sense in which an elusive object falls within the boundless sphere of the conceptual. I take it that part of the motivation behind the idea that we can secure access to the absolute (meaning to something that falls into the category of maximally modally robust facts) in principle and independent of any specific instantiation of the absolute is epistemological. It is designed to account for our capacity to refer to the absolute via adequate concept formation. Yet, elusive objects undermine this strategy, as they could be of an undetectable kind that maybe even undermines most of our beliefs, at least most of our cherished and relevant beliefs, about how things broadly are.

Elsewhere I offered an extensive analysis of the force of sceptical scenarios in order to question the anti-sceptical force of McDowell's vindication of thought's 'unproblematic openness to the world'.[57] McDowell's basic strategy is transcendental in the sense that he believes that there are *a priori* reasons that guarantee that we cannot be entirely off track with our beliefs regarding how things broadly are. Transcendental arguments employed against sceptical scenarios have a decisive shortcoming, as they can pass no verdict on contingent sceptical hypotheses of the elusive objects type. It is sufficient to invoke the movie *The Truman Show* here. From a transcendental point of view, Truman knows a lot, and we can even enumerate a lot of propositions that he is in a position to know on any construal: that there is water surrounding the place where he lives, that the person he takes to be his wife has a nose, that his house is bigger than his left hand, and so on. Yet, Truman clearly lives in a sceptical scenario, a scenario in conflict with most of our beliefs and easily inflatable into a deviant explanation of most of the more complicated beliefs we all share. What if everybody you know is either in the position of Truman or in the position of an actor employed by the company running the bigger version of the Truman Show we are right now in? Imagine we live in the following scenario: the laws of nature happen to be exactly as Aristotle described them: the earth is an element with a downward direction, fire has an upward direction, and ethereal heavenly bodies eternally run in circles above us. All modern descriptions are simply misguided interpretations spread on the planet by some agency from the realm beyond the directly observable. Some Aristotelian God might have introduced modern science from above in mysterious ways so as to delude us about the fact that Aristotle was right about the structure and size of the cosmos; behind the limits of the Aristotelian observable there is an agency that runs this as a show on hyperspace TV, a program only accessible far above the visible spheres. Of course, this is just a paranoid fantasy, of which we can develop infinitely many. However, from a transcendental point of view we have no reason to disbelieve any such paranoid fantasy as long as our overall structures of disclosure of an independent reality are in place. In *Having the World in View* McDowell suggests an interpretation of his enterprise along the lines of Kant's idea of the world as a regulative idea or a world view, as he writes.

> [T]he intentionality, the objective purport, of perceptual experience in general – whether potentially knowledge-yielding or not – depends [...] on having the world in view, in a sense that goes beyond glimpses

of the here and now. It would not be intelligible that the relevant episodes present themselves as glimpses of the here and now apart from their being related to a wider world view.[58]

However, we must not forget that the 'wider world view' is still fallible, and we can only account for this fallibility by not limiting the range of options of what can possibly be the case. Whatever our anti-sceptical strategy, it should not guarantee contingent knowledge claims, such as that there really is water or that people really have noses. Most of the things we now know about the universe would have sounded like paranoid fantasies to Aristotle, or even to scientists at the beginning of the twentieth century. Imagine you were to tell Aristotle that we are in an expanding universe with stars shooting away from us that came into existence through a Big Bang followed by inflation, that life on earth as we know it has developed over millions of years, that we think with our brains, or rather, that our brains think, that we can fly to the moon, that there are continents on the other side of any ocean he might have been aware of, and so on. What if you told Aristotle that we could watch wars with incredible weapons on television, that we could see moving pictures of people long dead, or that we could simply take an airplane from Beijing to New York City? On a side note, it is certainly an amusing fact that the modern Greek word for automobile, *autokinêton*, corresponds to Plato's definition of an animal as that which can move itself. As Louis C. K. sums this point up in his joke about people's air travel complaints:

> I had to sit on the runway for 40 minutes. 'Oh my god, really? What happened then, did you fly through the air like a bird, incredibly? Did you soar into the clouds, impossibly? Did you partake in the miracle of human flight and then land softly on giant tires that you couldn't even conceive how they f**king put air in them? ... You're sitting in a chair in the sky. You're like a Greek myth right now.'[59]

Meillassoux argues that there are limitations on the variation of conditions, in particular, the limitation that nothing can restrict the range of contingency by being a necessary entity. He then sets out to give an account of these conditions. Yet, this account is surely defeasible, and the question accordingly is how to make sense of the defeasibility of any contentful analysis of a concept? My idea is that for every object we give an account of (including philosophical concepts that are objects of philosophical investigation), we have to locate it in some field of sense or other. Doing so is always operationally opaque in that we cannot both refer to an object and all our conditions of referring to it in the same field. Thus, we have to acknowledge a potential divergence between the object as it appears to us and the object as it really appears in the field under its objective conditions.

At this point, the transcendental philosopher would certainly present his preferred version of the thesis that this potential divergence cannot occur in pure thinking about thought itself. If we refer to some concept, say 'necessity', we know quite well in which field we are, namely in the field of conceptual analysis or conceptual investigation in a broader yet to be determined sense. Here we are able to have an object in view together with our conditions of having it in view. We have the object and our view of it in view – or do we? Of course, McDowell has presented an original line of thought leading to a defence of the possibility of first-order empirical knowledge by perception that can do without such a 'sideways-on point of view'.[60] However, he only argues that we can know something to be such-and-so by perceiving it without thereby also having to guarantee sideways-on that we are in a position to know things to be such and so by perceiving them. And that just has to be correct in order to account for the most basic externalist evidence, meaning the fact that we can know that p by perceiving it without thereby knowing that we know it. There will always be explanatory space for reflective opacity in our vindication of our capacity for knowing by perceiving. McDowell surely does not deny that. Yet, how does *he* have perception in view? Certainly not by perceiving it, which would be a different stance, for instance, the stance of a naturalised epistemology in which we can literally perceive perception to the extent that it is nothing but the relevant physiology of our relevant neurobiological equipment. The age-old question for the first time clearly articulated in Plato's *Theaetetus*, therefore, remains in place: under which conditions is fallible knowledge of (perceptual) knowledge possible?[61]

All I claim is that there is a potential divergence between what we are really doing when we are giving an account of some central concept like that of 'knowledge' and what we thereby give an account of. The possibility of error and disagreement lies in the fact that the field of investigation might significantly differ from what we take it to be. The actual conditions of appearance of an object do not appear alongside the object, which is one of the reasons why we can be wrong about them even while we have the object in view.

This allows me to disagree with Meillassoux about the conditions of philosophical rationality. The first point of disagreement is that I do not believe that we can find shelter with mathematics in general or any privileged form of mathematically structured reasoning. There is no replacement for ordinary language by some enhanced instrument of articulation when it comes to philosophy, as every possible replacement offered so far in the form of any formal system just replaces one language with another one. Formal languages are just more languages that in philosophy every once in a while might help us to better understand the stakes of a distinction otherwise obfuscated by some parochial features of the natural language we happen to articulate the distinction in. But this is just a general feature of multilingualism in philosophy, for which one ought to make a general case. The fact that some claim reveals hidden premises when translated into another language such as a formal language or any old ordinary language is relevant to philosophical thinking and must not be underestimated in the name of the just cause of digesting the excesses of the linguistic turn of the first three quarters of the twentieth century.

It is important for philosophy to engage in an encounter with translation so that we increase the chance of becoming aware of lacunae in our arguments, or rather in our thought habits. This is where intuition really comes into play. When we disagree in philosophy, we have something in view whose conceptual structures we try to articulate in the right way. This presupposes that we have independent cognitively relevant contact with the philosophical concepts whose details we intend to bring out. Philosophical concepts like thought, existence, knowledge, or object, are just more objects about which we can disagree so that we can always only grasp them partially, under some conditions of appearing or other. Philosophical thought is finite, which is not to say that its finitude makes it impossible, problematic or merely phenomenal, as Meillassoux assumes in his critique of finitude. As with any other form of knowledge, it needs to reduce the complexity of its object by building a theory, which can either mean that the representation of the object is somehow less complex than the object itself, or that we at least translate some features of the object into another language. We need not move beyond finitude in order to grasp the absolute, as we can grasp, for instance, that the table over there looks like this from here, which is a partial (finite) grasp of the table, and not of its appearance. The partial (finite) grasp is an appearance of the table; it is directly of the table precisely because the table's appearances are ways the table is in itself. It and not its appearance appears in a particular way; it has properties, such as relational objective phenomenal properties, that make it available to truth-apt thought.[62]

The finitude of philosophy is not a condition that somehow contributes to undermining it. *Per se* it need not be an element in a sceptical diagnosis of any sort according to which we are screened off from our objects of investigation due to human finitude. Rather, reality itself is finite and incomplete, which is why it appears in manifold ways. If anything, manifold appearing is the absolute, or rather, an absolute, given that there is no such thing as *the absolute*, but only various facts whose obtaining is not brought into existence by our beliefs about them.

Notes

1. See, for instance, Aristotle, *Nicomachean Ethics*, 1139a8ff.
2. Schopenhauer, *On the Freedom of the Will*.
3. Meillassoux, *After Finitude*, p. 62. For an illuminating critical discussion of the argument in Meillassoux see Livingston, 'Realism and the Infinite'.
4. Cf. Rometsch, *Freiheit zur Wahrheit*.
5. In any event, many of the enemies to which he ascribes correlationism in his sense are not at all correlationists. Many of his historical claims are false. Yet, he made many of us aware of a threat that often is unperceived when accepting the obvious, namely that we cannot *access* what *we* cannot access.
6. Meillassoux, *After Finitude*, p. 5.
7. Cf. McDowell, 'Criteria, Defeasibility and Knowledge'. Husserl's account of evidence and the modal variation of judgements in terms of ways of thinking about their relation to truth also seems to be a disjunctivist account. See his illuminating argument that 'judgement (*Urteil*)' and 'assertion (*Behauptung*)' have to be distinguished in *Formal and Transcendental Logic*, § 79, p. 197. Husserl comes to the disjunctivist conclusion: '*In itself every judgement is already decided*; its predicate truth, or its predicate falsity, "*belongs*" to its

essence – though, as we have pointed out, it is not a constituent mark of any judgement as a judgement.'

8. Cf. Heidegger, *Kant and the Problem of Metaphysics*, § 2, p. 18: 'However, ontic knowledge by itself can never conform "to" objects, because without ontological knowledge it cannot have even a possible "to what" [Wonach] of the conformation.' Also note in addition, Heidegger, *Being and Time*, Part I, § 3.

9. Thanks to Wolfgang Kubin and Guofeng Su for somewhat clarifying this issue for me. If I understood correctly, the relation between the *xiàng* character (the elephant) and the meaning is strictly conventional so that almost any other character not already occupying too many functions at the same time could have served the job.

10. Tugendhat, *Der Wahrheitsbegriff bei Husserl und Heidegger*, in particular § 16. Notice that Adorno already spelled out this point in his *Zur Metakritik der Erkenntnistheorie*, in which one can also find one of the most acute repudiations of the threads of mental representationalism in phenomenological epistemology.

11. Cavell, *Claim of Reason*, p. 144.

12. This is a formulation used by Quentin Meillassoux in his Berlin lecture, *Iteration, Reiteration, Repetition: A Speculative Analysis of the Meaningless Sign*.

13. Brassier, *Nihil Unbound*, pp. 58–9.

14. Searle, *Making the Social World*, p. 3.

15. Searle, *Making the Social World*, p. 18: 'How can one and the same thing be both subjective and objective? The answer is that this distinction is profoundly ambiguous. There are at least two different senses of the objective/subjective distinction: an epistemic sense and an ontological sense. The epistemic sense has to do with knowledge. The ontological sense has to do with existence. Pains, tickles, and itches are ontologically subjective in the sense that they exist only as experienced by humans or animal subjects. In this sense they differ from mountains and volcanoes, which are ontologically objective, in the sense that their existence does not depend on anybody's subjective experiences. But in addition to that, there is an epistemic sense of the distinction. Some propositions can be known to be true independently of anybody's feelings or attitudes. For example, the statement that Vincent van Gough died in France is epistemically objective, because its truth or falsity can be ascertained independently of the attitudes and opinion of observers. But the statement "Van Gough was a better painter than Manet" is, as they say, a matter of subjective opinion. It is epistemically subjective. It is not a matter of

epistemically objective fact. Ontological objectivity and subjectivity have to do with the mode of existence of *entities*. Epistemic objectivity and subjectivity have to do with [*sic*] epistemic status of *claims*.'

16. Cf. Gabriel, 'Facts, Social Facts, and Sociology'.

17. Wright, *Truth and Objectivity*, p. 196.

18. Quine, *Word and Object*, p. 20.

19. In this precise sense Eli Hirsch's thesis of quantifier variance amounts to ontological anti-realism. He sums up the view as the doctrine that says 'that there is no uniquely best ontological language with which to describe the world' (Hirsch, *Quantifier Variance and Realism*, p. xii). He qualifies the doctrine in such a way as to rule out some crazy forms of anti-realism: 'What varies in quantifier variantism is only the language; everything else remains the same. An anti-realist conception in which varying the language somehow changes all of reality is an entirely different story' (Ibid., p. xvi). However, in my terminology this is ontological anti-realism, as Hirsch argues that a full grasp of the meaning of 'existence' involves grasp of language. The meaning of 'existence' (not just the meaning of the word) varies relative to languages. There might be a way of safeguarding most facts from co-variation with the quantifier, as Hirsch argues, but on the level of ontology, his methodology amounts to anti-realism. Elsewhere I have argued regarding similar manoeuvres in late Heidegger that ontological anti-realism in this sense ultimately affects our lower-level conception of independent facts as well so that we cannot coherently be higher-order ontological anti-realists while maintaining an independent coarse-grained structure of facts on the ancestral level. Cf. Gabriel, 'Ist die Kehre ein realistischer Entwurf'.

20. Hegel, *Encyclopedia of the Philosophical Sciences*, § 10, p. 38: 'The thinking operative in the philosophical manner of knowing needs to be understood in its necessity. Equally, its capacity to produce knowledge of the absolute objects needs to be justified.'

21. For a historical account of where I derive the concept from, see Gabriel, *Transcendental Ontology* and Gabriel, 'Aarhus Lectures'.

22. Cf. Gottlob Frege, 'The Thought', p. 329, where he draws a threefold distinction: 'Consequently we distinguish: 1) the grasp of a thought – thinking 2) the recognition of a thought as true – judging 3) the manifestation of this judgement – assertion.' In a footnote he adds: 'It seems to me that thought and judgment have not hitherto been adequately distinguished. Perhaps language is misleading. For we have no particular clause in the indicative sentence which cor-

responds to the assertion, that something is being asserted lies rather in the form of the indicative. We have the advantage in German that main and subordinate clauses are distinguished by the word-order. In this connexion it is noticeable that a subordinate clause can also contain an assertion and that often neither main nor subordinate clause express a complete thought by themselves but only the complex sentence does.' Husserl's above mentioned argument (see footnote 7) that we need to distinguish between judgement and assertion hinges on his idea that we should not only avoid psychologising the content of thought-episodes, but also the acts. To judge is not to assert, for him, as this would undermine our capacity to step back from an act of thinking while at the same time holding on to the content. It would take more space to assess the consequences and premises of this view, which is why I stick to the idea that to judge is (among other things) to assert.

23. Cf. Gabriel, 'Nachträgliche Notwendigkeit'.
24. Cf. Koch, *Versuch über Wahrheit und Zeit*, p. 54.
25. Eliot, *Burnt Norton*, v. 1–8.
26. Eliot, *Burnt Norton*, v. 30–2.
27. Eliot, *Burnt Norton*, v. 14–15.
28. I am implicitly drawing on Mark Johnston's to my mind convincing discussion of us as 'samplers of presence' rather than as its creators. See Johnston, *Saving God*, p. 132, pp. 132–4, p. 151, p. 152.
29. Hegel, *Aesthetics*, pp. 128–9.
30. Quentin Meillassoux expressed this at a presentation at a Speculative Realism conference on 27 April 2007 at Goldsmiths College. The transcript of his talk appears as Meillassoux, 'Speculative Realism'.
31. On this see also extensively Gabriel, *An den Grenzen der Erkenntnistheorie*; Gabriel, *Die Erkenntnis der Welt*; Markus Gabriel, 'Dissens und Gegenstand'.
32. Heidegger, *Being and Time*, Part II.3, § 65, p. 329.
33. Brassier, *Nihil Unbound*, pp. 85–94.
34. For a defence of common-sense (meaning: non-revisionary) ontology in a similar perspective see Hirsch, *Quantifier Variance and Realism*, pp. 96–123.
35. Kripke, *Reference and Existence*, p. 95.
36. Ibid.
37. Cf. Sider, 'Ontological Realism'.
38. For a defence of such an understanding of Thomas Nagel's famous account in his *The View from Nowhere* see my *An den Grenzen der Erkenntnistheorie*.

39. Cf. Simon Critchley's book on the poetry of Wallace Stevens, *Things Merely Are.*

40. Gabriel, 'The Mythological Being of Reflection'.

41. Castoriadis, 'The Logic of Magmas and the Question of Autonomy', p. 300. Hilary Putnam comes to a similar conclusion in his *Representation and Reality*, p. 118: 'What Gödel showed is so to speak, that we cannot fully formalize our own mathematical capacity *because it is part of that mathematical capacity that it can go beyond whatever it can formalize.* Similarly, my extension of Gödelian techniques to inductive logic showed that it is part of our notion of justification in general (not just of our notion of *mathematical* justification) that *reason can go beyond whatever reason can formalize.*'

42. This, of course, derives from a reading of Wittgenstein. For a subtle, non-relativistic discussion of the notion of 'arbitrariness' that is at stake here see Forster, *Wittgenstein and the Arbitrariness of Grammar.*

43. Cf. Carnap, 'Empiricism, Semantics and Ontology'.

44. Cf. Putnam, 'The Content and Appeal of "Naturalism"', p. 110.

45. Quine, 'Two Dogmas of Empiricism', p. 44.

46. Cf. Quine, 'Ontology and Ideology', pp. 11–15.

47. Quine, *Word and Object*, p. 22.

48. Quine, 'Two Dogmas of Empiricism', p. 42.

49. Latour, *An Inquiry into Modes of Existence*, pp. 142–3.

50. Quine, 'On What There Is', pp. 1–19.

51. Cf. Quentin Meillassoux' lecture, *Iteration, Reiteration, Repetition.*

52. Cf. Chalmers, *Constructing the World*, Fifteenth Excursus: The Structural Response to Skepticism, pp. 431–40.

53. McDowell, *Mind and World*, pp. 23–45.

54. Williamson, *The Philosophy of Philosophy*, pp. 16–17; 'Past the Linguistic Turn'.

55. Williamson, 'Past the Linguistic Turn', p. 110.

56. Cf. Hogrebe, *Orphische Bezüge*; Hogrebe, *Metaphysik und Mantik*; David Lewis, 'Elusive Knowledge'.

57. McDowell, *Mind and World*, p. 155: 'So languages and traditions can figure not as "*tertia*" that would threaten to make our grip on the world philosophically problematic, but as constitutive of our unproblematic openness to the world.'

58. McDowell, 'Sellars on Perceptual Experience', p. 7.

59. From the skit 'Everything's amazing and nobody's happy' which aired for the first time 1 October 2008 on *Late Night with Conan*

O'Brian and later appeared in his film *Hilarious* on the album of the same name with the title 'Cell phones and flying'.

60. McDowell, 'Intentionality as a Relation', pp. 63–5.

61. Cf. Plato, *Theaetetus*; Gabriel, *Die Erkenntnis der Welt*, § 2.1 pp. 45–63. See also McDowell's commentary on the *Theaetetus* in McDowell, *Plato: Theaetetus*.

62. On this see Umrao Sethi's Berkeley dissertation. Thanks to her for letting me read some of this material during my visiting professorship in Berkeley in Spring 2013 and also thanks for discussion of these aspects.

12

Forms of Knowledge: Epistemological Pluralism

Ontology is the systematic investigation into the meaning of 'existence' and related matters. Epistemology is the systematic investigation into the meaning of 'knowledge' and related matters, such as assertion, thought, belief, justification, reference, rationality and many other concepts. So far I have defended a new realist ontology that is in line with the recent return to speculative thought in that it assumes that there has to be unproblematic access to the meaning of 'existence' that is not distorted by our very attempt to make it explicit and defend it coherently against objections. This means that I have claimed knowledge; in particular, I have claimed to know various things, such as that the world does not exist, that there is a plurality of fields of sense, that to exist is to appear in a field of sense, and so on. The recent return to speculative thought so far has not focused on what it means to claim speculative knowledge in philosophy. In this and the following chapter I will give an account of knowledge that corresponds to ontological pluralism. I shall defend *epistemological pluralism*, by which I mean the view that there are different forms of knowledge, such as sociological knowledge, mathematical knowledge, sensory and epistemological knowledge. These forms of knowledge differ not just by being about different kinds of objects or different fields of sense, for that matter. They are individuated by more specific conditions, such as the condition that we cannot know anything by hearing it without using the sense or combination of senses needed for hearing that something is the case. This condition does not hold for the knowledge just articulated, as it does not claim to know by hearing it that we can only know something by hearing it under specific conditions. Across the cases I am interested in, 'knowledge' refers to propositional or factual knowledge, that is, to knowledge that something is true about something. I will not discuss the question whether there are non-, pre-, or sub-propositional forms of knowledge, such as practical know-how, or knowledge by acquaintance. Accepting a version of this would be a different form of pluralism about forms of knowledge – one I am not discussing here.

In epistemology we claim knowledge about knowledge. This has lead many epistemologists to assume that there has to be unified treatment of all instances of 'knowledge' and relevant cognates at least with respect to propositional factual knowledge.[1] In this context, phrases such as 'our knowledge of the world', or just 'knowledge of the world', are widespread and are used to characterise knowledge as such, knowledge in general. The background picture is one in which there is the world in the sense of the totality of facts to which we try to refer in such a way that we can successfully claim knowledge in general, ranging from knowledge about penguins to knowledge about up-quarks or knowledge about ancient Chinese warfare. However, Stanley Cavell, Michael Williams and to some extent Bernard Williams have rightly pointed out that the idea of knowledge as such might be overgeneralised.[2] Cavell and Michael Williams, in particular, have begun to question the idea that epistemology is about the relation between the world as such and knowledge as such. However, despite the correct observation that we should not look 'at the world as though it were another *object*',[3] Cavell continues referring to 'reality' or 'the world', only adding that we have to assume 'a relation to reality which is not that of knowing'.[4] He calls this the 'truth of skepticism'[5] and reads Heidegger and Wittgenstein as having responded to this truth by undermining the idea of a general relationship between knowledge and the world. I take it that Michael Williams' assault against 'epistemological realism' has a similar upshot: if 'knowledge' is not itself a unified natural kind about which we can come to know certain facts in epistemology, we might have space for manoeuvres that undermine scepticism in the schematic general form of the claim that we cannot know anything about the world precisely because the conditions of said knowledge somehow cannot be satisfied for whatever reasons the sceptic might have on offer.

At this point, it might be interesting to take a look at Descartes, who is often both credited with being the culprit of a dualism of knowledge (mind) and world and at the same time having invented radical doubt. However, both charges are inaccurate. In particular,

Descartes' very point in the *Meditations* is that radical doubt is a non-starter, as it can never achieve the relevant generality. Let me spell this out in the detail needed for the following arguments for epistemological pluralism.

Descartes' attempt to motivate radical, that is to say, universal or unrestricted doubt about every form of knowledge proceeds in three steps: *fallibility, dreaming* and *evil demon.* He first points out that in claiming knowledge we are fallible. A knowledge claim is governed by success conditions it does not necessarily meet. Conditions that are necessarily met are not conditions. A condition is precisely something that can or cannot be met. When we claim that there are conditions of something or other, we claim that a conditional's antecedence might be true or false. This is at least one of the differences between *conditions* and *conditionals*: we are able to formulate conditionals whose antecedents are necessarily true, whereas conditions for something are also conditionals, but with contingent truth values for their antecedents. That there is sufficient light for me to see the mug on my table is a condition for me seeing the mug on the table, which means that there might not be sufficient light. This condition evidently differs from the conditional: if a mug is a mug, then a buck is a buck, in that this conditional is necessarily true under some appropriate interpretation (fixing the meaning of 'mug' and 'buck' respectively, and so on). The conditional: if a mug is a mug, then a buck is a buck, or any old trite tautology like if p and p, then p, holds unconditionally, which is to say that the relation between the antecedent and the consequent is such that the antecedent and the consequent are necessarily true. Thus, even if conditions can be stated in the form of conditionals, it is important to distinguish between the two.

The fact that we are fallible hinges on a set of conditions that can be stated in the form of conditionals. Some of the conditions of knowing something might be unknown to us, which is one respect in which we are fallible: unbeknownst to me, someone has replaced my mug with a mug imitation made of some material unable to hold coffee. If I claim to know that there is a mug in front of me by seeing it, one sense in which I might be wrong is that I do not in fact see a mug, but a mug imitation, which I can find out by trying to pour coffee into it.

Now, Descartes' point about fallibility is that the chain of reasoning so far presented does not give us a unified account of our fallibility. We only have piecemeal conditions for concrete knowledge claims that might or might not be met. At best, this amounts to the justified suspicion that *every single* knowledge claim might be wrong by not meeting some condition or other. Yet, this does not entail that *all* our knowledge claims might *jointly* be wrong. This corresponds to the simple difference between knowing for every element in a certain set that it might have some property, which is not at all the same as knowing that every element in that set might have that property. If there is no additional reason to believe that *all* items in the set or the category are somehow likely to share the property, the contrast between entities in the set or category such that we have reasons to ascribe the property to them and those for which this does not hold, will remain operative. In the particular case at hand, the set or domain under investigation is that of human knowledge claims. Knowledge claims can be successful or fail. There is no purely conceptual reason to believe that all knowledge claims might fail in one stroke, as this would undermine the conceptual contrast invested in our access to the domain of human knowledge claims. Therefore, we need additional reasons, reasons that lead us beyond the mere concept of human knowledge claims in order to argue that there is a systematic reason to suspect *all* knowledge claims of falsehood or failure.

Say I know of every single individual who is a suspect in a murder case that he might have done it. Then I do not thereby come to know that they might all have done it together, which is an altogether different claim. Analogously, knowing about every single knowledge claim that it might go wrong for some specific reason or other that we can state in the form of conditionals with contingent antecedents is not to know something about *all* knowledge claims or even knowledge in general. On this level, there is no overall way things might have gone wrong, no principled or systematic reasoning that underpins any suspicion regarding knowledge in general. Fallibility alone does not generalise to any form of scepticism or radical doubt. It just means that there are all sorts of conditions of failure. There need not be a single source of fallibility or even a unifiable system of such sources. Not all knowledge claims fail for the same reason: the claim that it is raining in London right now might fail because I called the wrong person or checked the wrong weather channel. To claim that Smith loves Jones might fail because I did not consider the option that Smith only cunningly pretends to love Jones. There is no such thing as fallibility as such according to which we might just be wrong about everything full stop. The very concept of fallibility is piecemeal on this level of analysis, as it derives from the idea of highly specific conditionals that have to be formulated in order for there to be a relationship between some kind of knowledge claim and its condition or conditions.

This is why Descartes in the second step of his alleged argument for radical doubt introduces the age-old idea of sources of knowledge. If there is a finite and known set of sources of knowledge, there might be an option to think of these sources as sufficiently unified conditions for knowledge as such.[6] Most schematically, one might come up with the disastrous and still common idea that there are two sources of knowledge: the senses and pure thought, and accordingly, empirical and *a priori* knowledge. Descartes indeed makes use of a similar idea when he first introduces his dreaming argument. Contrary to appearances, the dreaming argument is not designed to undermine knowledge as such, or even to threaten knowledge of the external world.[7] All it does is introduce the idea of sources of knowledge. It seems that all our knowledge of the kind of objects that we can only know by standing in causal relationships with them, leading to the kind of information-processing resulting in a mental map of our surrounding, is acquired through the senses. And, indeed, as a matter of fact, we could not know anything about things at a spatio-temporal distance from our ectoderm without there being a causal chain from those things via our nerve endings to some relevant region of our brain. All Descartes makes use of at this point is the principle that the same effect can be triggered by different causes. For all I know, the car I bought might have been manufactured under all sorts of circumstances by all sorts of people in all sorts of factories. Of course, the application of this principle to knowledge claims based on sense-perception is questionable. I can buy a car without thereby acquiring a warrant to believe that it comes from this or that factory, but if I claim to know that it is raining on the basis of sense-perception on the spot, it seems integral to the knowledge claim that the causal source of the belief (that it is raining) is revealed in the information processed in the form of a knowledge claim.

Against this background, I actually doubt that the dreaming argument can really be formulated on the basis of an abstract consideration of causation. Yet, if it could (and Descartes at least assumes that it can for the sake of the argument), all it would show is that the nature of the sources of empirical knowledge might be very different from what we take them to be. Yet, in any event, the sources would still be subject to causal structures, an idea which has recently been explored by Chalmers' structuralist response to Matrix scepticism.[8] Dreaming scepticism might result in undermining one of the sources of knowledge to the extent that we become unable to read the right conditions of their consequents: I believe that I see a mug in front of me under the condition that the mug over there causes me to see it in whatever way this works. Yet, I might be wrong about that and about every other phenomenal item in my subjective visual field. In an actual dreaming scenario, what I see is really utterly different from what I believe to see, or, depending on further conditions of relevant causation to be specified, I might indeed not be seeing anything at all.

At this stage of the argument Descartes himself just presents his version of a structuralist response to dreaming scepticism. His version maintains that the very structure of appearance is subject to rules: the appearance as if of a glass still differs from the appearance *as if of* my hands appearing to be typing these lines, even if I am a handless and glassless brain in a vat or lying in my bed and dreaming as if of me typing these sentences. Descartes notoriously argues that we can even come to know many things about the structure of appearances regardless of how they are actually caused. I can know, for example, that there only seems to be one glass on the table, that it always seems to be over there when I appear to move my head slightly to the right. Even in an actual dream with all its ambiguities, there is some structure or other, the structure of appearance. I can know what this structure is, at least on the superficial level of the appearance of primary qualities, such as shape, size and secondary qualities, such as the greenness of the meadow appearing in my dream. Of course, phenomenal size here is not really size in the primary quality sense, just as the phenomenal size of the moon is such that I can cover the moon with my two hands, which is not a primary quality of the moon in the technical sense. But the fact that there is a form of geometry or algebra of phenomenal reality even in a Matrix or dreaming scenario is evidence that such scenarios do not amount to the relevant unification of doubt into radical doubt. This is not how we can acquire the concept of knowledge as such, by specifying its overall conditions in the form of sources. If we cannot formulate a radical doubt by specifying an overall condition which not being met undermines knowledge as such, this can be interpreted as evidence that there is no such thing as knowledge as such.

In the third step, Descartes brings in the evil demon, which is his ultimate attempt to unify the concept of knowledge by individuating the ultimate condition of knowledge: namely the condition that we have to be in a position to so much as *claim* knowledge, which presupposes some minimal rational stability. Here by 'minimal rational stability' I intend to convey the notion that there are some facts about belief formation that unify it. Traditionally from Plato and Aristotle at least to Frege and Russell, these facts are regarded as the topic of logics, the idea being that logical laws unify rationality insofar as they summon it to follow them.[9] In this case, 'logics' is roughly equivalent to 'theory of rationality' in the sense of an investigation into the ultimate condition of any possible knowledge claim. Aristotle famously presented the law of non-contradiction as the in itself unconditional ultimate condition, whereas other theorists have proposed other candidates. Be that as it may, the idea should be familiar: in order for us to be rational, some minimal standards have to be met, most narrowly the standards necessary for truth-apt thought.

In the context of a similar discussion, James Conant has proposed a distinction between *Cartesian* and *Kantian scepticism*, which neatly corresponds to the distinction between the dreaming and the evil demon stage of Descartes' own considerations.[10] According to Conant, the second variety of scepticism he calls 'Kantian' threatens to undermine not only the truth-conditions of our actual thoughts, but rather their 'objective purport',[11] meaning the truth-aptitude of our thoughts in such a way that our attempts at belief formation might not even crystallise into minimally structured appearances of reference. Kant sums this up in his reflection on the possibility of an appearance of thought which is even 'less than a dream',[12] a scenario in which the illusion of even so much as a stream of consciousness that is about nothing but itself would be generated completely at random. This scenario, which is the sceptical hypothesis of a 'hitherto unknown form of madness',[13] as Frege puts it in a similar context, is much more radical than the unmotivated idea of a unified internal world of a nicely structured stream of consciousness that just might happen not to refer to anything beyond itself.

Unfortunately, Chalmers, like many other contemporary epistemologists, does not sufficiently distinguish between the dreaming

and the evil genius scenario, which transpires from his clear identification of 'structures within the evil genius if in Descartes' scenario'.[14] Even if the upshot of Descartes' discussion is a version of
a structuralist response to the problem, the evil demon is designed
to correspond to a scenario more radical than the most global
scenarios Chalmers envisages in passages like this one:

> To get a fully skeptical scenario, one may need to move to one on
> which experiences are produced at random, and by huge coincidence
> produce the regular stream of experiences that I am having now. This
> scenario cannot be excluded with certainty, but (unlike the Matrix
> scenario) it is reasonable to hold that it is extremely unlikely.[15]

It need not bother us why Chalmers believes that 'the Matrix
scenario' is likelier than the scenario he gestures at in the passage,
as this turns on his vision of science as uncovering Matrix-like
noumenal structures. The decisive point is that he assumes exactly
what Descartes undermines with his whole train of thought,
namely the unifiability of belief formation into something like a
stream of experiences. In an evil demon scenario, we are not even
left with a stream of consciousness. At most we could cling to a
shrivelled version of the solipsism of the present moment given
that we could not even speak of the present moment. In such a scenario, we might never even be in a position to identify ourselves
as conscious of ourselves at the present moment, as there might
be temporal conditions for a successful self-identification via any
such description. Of course, if we were in such a scenario right
now, there would be no point in trying to argue for or against it,
or rather, we could not even attempt to do so. Any such attempt
presupposes at least the illusion of seamless and rational consciousness, which would not even be available in the most radical
evil demon scenario. But this just means that we cannot both be in
an evil demon scenario and refer to this fact in a context in which
we rationally consider whether we are in an evil demon scenario.
If we are in such a scenario, things are so bad that it does not even
matter anymore to us as rational creatures, as we do not satisfy
the minimal demands for rationality. This does not prove that we
are not in an evil demon scenario: we might be. But if we were, we
could not know it or ever access that very fact in any form open
to rational consideration. Thus, evil demon scepticism is not an
epistemological problem; there is no principled way of making use

of the 'possibility' that there might be an evil demon. Also, if there were an evil demon, he could not intend to deceive us systematically, as this would again stabilise our rationality, even if only for minimal stretches of time, so that some things must be true and epistemically accessible for subjects sometimes in order for us to be deceivable.

Descartes' point is that such a picture of us being trapped in some conditions of belief formation such as that something at least appears to us as if being such and so is only a stepping stone in an argument that cannot coherently be fleshed out. In the evil demon scenario, we are not even minimally rationally stable, which is to say that there are no facts about reason itself that determine it as being a certain way. This is why we could not find out whether we are in such a scenario, as there would be nothing to be found out.

Here is another way of putting this with the help of a thought experiment. Imagine all our beliefs about reason in the sense of belief formation structured and guided by generally truth-conducive laws of reasoning were false. In order to really imagine this, we need a unified account or scenario that undermines all facts about reason in one stroke and not just piecemeal. This is what the evil demon scenario is supposed to achieve. The evil demon breaks into every transition from one belief to the next and makes it look rational to us. It suggests thinking of the activity of putting thoughts together (Kantian synthesis) as potentially covering up breaches. In other words, the evil demon scenario is a radical madness scenario, where we cannot rely on any stable transitions whose stability consists in rational synthesis.[16] How do we know we are not in a kind of psychosis to such an extent that all our beliefs are formed by random association? It seems to us as if we believed that it is raining, but all the elements we need to put together in order to acquire and maintain the belief that it is raining or any other belief for that matter only randomly fall into place, say by the evil demon throwing a dice with an infinite amount of sides specifying which elements will be combined in the belief thus generated in us.

However, it is impossible that we are in such a scenario. For anything we have considered assumes that there are facts about reason, facts the evil demon uses in the general interest of his overall manipulation, even if these facts might not be accessible to those manipulated by the evil demon. To manipulate some train of thought by creating gaps and lacunae that make the believer metaphysically irrational to a degree of madness more radical than any actual mental disease ever diagnosed presupposes the availability of a norm undermined by the evil demon. But what, a possible objection goes, if there is no intention behind all of this? What about a scenario we can call 'on-off-solipsism'? Imagine you popped into being right now with the impression of having read some other sentences of this page a moment ago. There is no reason why you thus popped into being under the false and unjustified assumption that you have been around before. Say, randomness itself produced this solipsistic moment, and, oops, you were just turned off and are right now back, and on, and off, and on, still on, ... In the scenario of on-off-solipsism there would still be facts individuating it as a scenario, but as a matter of fact no one involved in it would count as a rational believer unless in the contingent instances where the on-moment is long enough for you to have followed the arguments on the last five pages. But we can always accelerate the scenario, so that you can always only make it to reading a sentence, a word, or maybe a syllable. Yet, none of this would, of course, really count as reading by any known standard.

Having said that, in this scenario you are still there, even if only for an infinitesimal moment, which is why Descartes' temporal qualification in the *cogito*-statement really matters.

> This alone is inseparable from me. I am–I exist: this is certain; but how long (*quamdiu; combien de temps*)? As long as I think; for perhaps it would even happen, if I should wholly cease to think, that I should at the same time altogether cease to be. I now admit nothing that is not necessarily true. I am therefore, precisely speaking, only a thinking thing, that is, a mind (*mens sive animus*), understanding, or reason, terms whose signification was before unknown to me. I am, however, a real thing, and really existent; but what thing? The answer was, a thinking thing.[17]

Even in the most radical scenario of an undetectable hitherto unknown form of madness, something is the case about reason; for instance, that it does not get sufficiently far enough off the ground in order to assess its situation as one in which it is misled. Therefore, there would strictly speaking be nothing misleading, and no one would be misled; there would only be spontaneous eruptions of arational momentary 'consciousness' (if any).

328 Fields of Sense

The evil demon is not capable of fully undermining reason, only of manipulating it into misguided conceptions of itself. Yet, he still manipulates reason and in this sense supports it. His manipulation keeps reason in existence, even if in an undesirable form. In any event, our self-description as reasonable would still be correct had we only been in a position to make it explicit, which is why the evil demon can never deprive us of that very truth and reduce us to mere existence.[18]

The unification of reason needed by scepticism in order to undermine the ultimate condition of knowledge – the highest common factor of all knowledge claims whether successful or not – does not support the idea that knowledge as such might be impossible. We are able to imagine a scenario in which no one is in a position to assess their very situation as being a certain way, but this scenario relies on us not even having most of the forms of knowledge we were trying to unify in the first place. This is why Descartes imagines an evil demon scenario without any bodies in it, that is, a form of metaphysical solipsism, as this would be a scenario of utter unification of knowledge as such by elimination of all the features that specify forms of knowledge. Yet, as long as there is a genuine plurality of forms of knowledge, we cannot unify them with reference to their ultimate condition of minimal rational stability and then set out to undermine it, as the procedure of undermining hinges on the possibility of elimination of the differences we are trying to account for. The unification of knowledge by reference to minimal rational stability as one of the conditions of knowledge does not suffice, as many other conditions of knowledge claims have to be met in order for actual knowledge to get off the ground. To know something about minimal rational stability in the epistemological form of philosophical reflection differs from the form of our animal knowledge of our immediate surrounding. To know that someone is cooking by smelling it, differs from knowing that 2+2=4 or from knowing that you are in any position to know anything in an evil demon scenario.

As Jens Rometsch argues in an as yet unpublished manuscript, this is why Descartes in the *Regulae* or even in his *Discourse on Method* presents such a random-looking regulative epistemology.[19] Instead of delivering a full-blown logics or theory of overall rationality, he offers guiding principles and provisional rules of belief formation. In line with Rometsch's argument, one could even venture to claim that Descartes thinks of science as a pluralistic enterprise of belief-formation and knowledge-acquisition, an enterprise that does not hinge on our capacity to unify reason into a *substantial* account of its most universal nature together with rules of specification leading from reason as such to the different sciences. Rather, he is justified in leaving the rules of specification open to substantial discovery for the simple reason that reason cannot be unified *a priori* with the intent of defining a concept of knowledge as such, as this would presuppose the possibility of the one stroke radical doubt he has ruled out in his meditations on that topic. In Rometsch' and my reading, Descartes never makes it to radical doubt, but rather shows that it cannot be systematically formulated. At most, there is an irrational suspicion that all our beliefs might be wrong for some unified reason, but this suspicion cannot be formulated by giving an account of the unification of our knowledge in light of an equally unified underminer (the evil demon).

However, even if this might be contested as a contentious exegesis of Descartes, the point itself is valid: if knowledge cannot be unified by specifying any alleged universal and substantial structure holding knowledge as such together, there correspondingly is no position from which to undermine knowledge in one stroke. Epistemological pluralism, therefore, is a bulwark against scepticism, at least to scepticism in its Cartesian form, but also against other forms of scepticism that overgeneralise other epistemic concepts, such as justification, which might be the failure of Agrippan style scepticism.[20] The fact that we have mathematical, sociological, literary and epistemological knowledge undermines the idea of an overall possible defeater of all these forms of knowledge. At least, it is unclear how such a defeater could be construed. Undermining knowledge forever remains a piecemeal activity and can only be achieved by knowing something about some form of knowledge, which demonstrates that it is mere pretence, that is, a set of maybe systematically related failed knowledge claims. But there is no position from which we can undermine knowledge as such by knowing, for instance, which ultimate condition would have to be undermined so as to block us from knowing anything whatsoever. Unexpectedly, the three stages by which Descartes proceeds in his investigation of the prospects of radical doubt or global scepticism lead to knowledge about knowledge; they can be used to delineate the contours of epistemological pluralism.

Another very widespread notion is that we cannot know

anything because it is a condition of knowledge-acquisition that it always relies on partial views of objects. What I have in mind here is a typical instance of the fallacy that some fact about our cognitive finitude entails that we cannot know anything, or that we only ever deal with appearances, partial manifestations, and never with the things in themselves. Typically, arguments from finitude to ignorance invoke visual perception unaided by any other sense or information processing. They present the following picture of visual perception: what we see is not the thing in itself, but only the partial glimpse of it revealed to us in a perspectivally distorted manner due to our own position in space and time. We never see the table as it is in itself for the trivial reason that we have to see it from over here from within our flesh. More atmospheric versions of this claim maintain that we are only acquainted with the table itself by varying the adumbrations radiating from the thing itself. This is what Husserl's method of eidetic variation ultimately boils down to in its local application to perceivable objects: we can know that there is a table in front of us by repeated confirmation of the presence of table-adumbrations. This can, for instance, be cashed out as a theory based on an inference to the best explanation (which is not what Husserl had in mind) or as a statistical account of knowledge of identity according to which it is likely that there is a table in front of us as the likelihood of a table is quite high given the many adumbrations as if of a full table we acquire by walking around it and coming back to it on various occasions.

Independently of the exegetical question of the nature of the classical phenomenological method of *epochê*-cum-eidetic-variation, the *fallacy from finitude to ignorance* has been justly attacked by Meillassoux (albeit for different reasons), and the misleading idea should be recognisable: we cannot know things in themselves because we cannot grasp them independently of perspectivally distorted manifestations of them. We never see the table as it is in itself, but always only the table seen from this particular visual perspective, involving some overall optical laws that might even only hold for human beings and their neurological equipment. There are two views we need to distinguish here that are often assimilated, namely *mental representationalism* on the one hand and *partial descriptivism* on the other hand, as I will call the second view.

The first view, mental representationalism, has been extremely effectively attacked. Here by 'mental representationalism' I spe-cifically refer to the position that we do not grasp things in themselves by virtue of representing them. This is often referred to as 'the representative' or 'the representational theory of percep-tion'. According to the basic idea of this theory, we do not have direct access to things in themselves. What we have direct access to according to this model are the representations, ideas, mental images, or whatever else is supposed to be the right substantial candidate. By virtue of having direct access to the representations and the fact that they represent something that typically is not itself a representation, we are supposed to have indirect access to the represented. Yet, from Fichte, Schelling, Hegel, Russell (at some point), Wittgenstein and beyond, the major objection against mental representationalism has always been that despite itself, it articulates conditions for an immediate openness to how things are on the level of our reference to representations. Representations – in an as yet innocent sense – are just more ways things are; they are part of what there is. If I represent Seattle as being a rainy city by believing that it is a rainy city or by forming a mental image of drizzly downtown Seattle, my representation just adds to the facts. Representations are just more facts. As the photographer Garry Winogrand is reported to have said about his own work: 'The photo is a thing in itself. And that's what still pho-tography is all about.' Against this background it is also clear that what he meant when he said that photography changes the facts: 'Photography is about finding out what can happen in the frame. When you put four edges around some facts, you change those facts.'21

A representation is as much involved in facts as any object or fact it represents. However, if mental representationalism is motivated by the idea of an asymmetry between representation and represented such that we can only know anything about the represented by knowing its representation, or we can only refer to the represented by referring to the representation of it, it either triggers a vicious infinite regress or has to block the regress by fiat. Mental representationalism embarks on the regress if it rec-ognises that a represented representation is as much a represented as any old represented. To be represented as such is not identical with being of a particular kind. If representations are themselves represented in the same way and under the same conditions as the things supposed to be represented in the first place, we embark on the regress of having to represent represented representations, and so on.

This is usually blocked by fiat, or rather by introducing some incredible metaphysical point of view, such as transcendental idealism or knowledge of our own sensations by acquaintance. These views want to make a case to the effect that representations are only of a certain class of things, usually spatiotemporal things at least standing in causal relations to our representations of them. This allows for introducing an epistemological asymmetry between our higher-order representations of our representations (what Kant calls 'concepts') and our first-order representations of ordinary objects (what Kant calls 'intuitions').[22] From a formal point of view there is no reason to privilege first-order representations over higher-order representations. They are both representations of something. This is why Kant tells a complicated substantial story that is supposed to explain the asymmetry in terms of the spatiotemporal character of what is represented by first-order representations. Russell and others have worked with the concept of 'knowledge by acquaintance' in order to give a less substantial account that still serves the same job, that is, the job of accounting for the epistemological asymmetry of representations and what is represented. On this construal we are acquainted with representations, but not necessarily with what they seem to represent.[23] To these moves Wittgenstein laconically remarked:

> 'Only intuition could have removed this doubt? – If intuition is an inner voice – how do I know *how* I am to follow it? And how do I know that it doesn't mislead me? For if it can guide me right, it can also guide me wrong.
> ((Intuition an unnecessary evasion.))'[24]

The second view, *partial descriptivism*, fares much better. Instead of claiming that we never grasp things in themselves by representing them (but, say, their representations), it claims that we partially grasp things in themselves by representing them as being a certain way. My name for representing things (or more generally objects) as being a certain way is 'description', where this is evidently not meant to suggest that we can only describe objects by overt linguistic behaviour.

Let us illustrate this with a slightly more unfamiliar example of *tonal* objects in order to avoid the standard privileging of visual objects and vision as access to objects and facts we generally deem independent of the fact that they are thus accessed. Learning Chinese certainly makes one aware of the role tonal objects play even for linguistic representation, a factor widely underestimated by occidental philosophers usually conversing in European languages, where tone almost equally matters, but tends to be mostly overlooked or reduced to accents. However, learning Chinese is impossible without creating tone awareness. For instance, the syllable 'hua' has very different meanings according to the relevant tone and associated character. If pronounced in the first tone and represented by the character 花 it means 'flower'. If pronounced in the fourth tone and represented by the character 话 it means 'words', 'language', 'speech', 'conversation', or 'dialect'. Yet, in the same tone but represented by another character, namely 画, it means 'to draw', 'picture' and also 'painting', as is nicely brought out by the pictogram itself. Now, an occidental foreigner who sets out to learn Chinese will easily mistake one tone for another and be confused even about the reference of some of the basic words in a conversation. Maybe he only knows the words for 'words' and 'flower', but is not aware of 'huà' as also meaning 'painting'. Now imagine you hear some hua-token. You are aware of some of the semantic differences related to it. This is why you will hear the hua-token under some description, for instance, as a huà-token expressing something in the context of someone talking about words or using the token in a context unfamiliar to you (as huà is part of more complex words such as diànhuà, 电话, which means 'telephone', literally: 'electric words' or 'electric conversation'). Tonal objects are represented under some description, which can be called a *sensory description*. The view is, of course, not that hearing a tone as a Mandarin syllable or as associated with a particular character is being aware of the tone as falling under the concept of a Mandarin syllable. Other animals have sensory descriptions, too, but might not have a second-order awareness of this fact, an awareness relating them to awareness of the relation of falling under a concept.

Let me clarify this point with recourse to the case of hallucinations. Imagine you right now hallucinate Mary, the mother of Jesus, wearing a golden crown and a blue dress. In this case, you are aware of a free-floating sensory description, you are aware *as if of* Mary, the mother of Jesus, wearing a golden crown and a blue dress. When we then claim that your awareness is hallucinatory, what we claim is that you are not aware of Mary, as she is not there for anyone to be aware of in this way, but that there nevertheless is a sensory description. I am not claiming that you are therefore aware *of* your sensory description rather than *of* Mary. Rather there is a sensory description as if of Mary, and if there is an object the description is of, we know that it is not Mary precisely because we are dealing with a hallucination. I take it that this is the minimal sense in which one has to agree with John Searle's recent defence of the view that hallucinations have no object, but only content.[25] In my reconstruction of this point, there might well be an object of hallucination (I currently believe that many, but not all, hallucinations are *of* the brain states triggering them), but the decisive point is that the content (the sensory description) is not of itself. The sensory description 'Mary, the mother of Jesus, wearing a golden crown and a blue dress' is not about the fact that it is a sensory description. It is not a form of self-representation. But this does not mean that the sensory description does not exist. It is there, as real as the moon or a volcano exploding in ancestral times and in ancestral distances (that is, so far away that due to the sheer physical limitations of our instruments, we will never register it). In a passage already quoted above Russell generally nicely sums up his view about the reality of 'phantoms and images' (including hallucinations) in the following way:

> The general correlations of your images are quite different from the correlations of what one chooses to call 'real' objects. But that is not to say images are unreal. It is only to say that they are not part of physics. Of course, I know that this belief in the physical world has established a sort of reign of terror. You have got to treat with disrespect whatever does not fit into the physical world. But that is really very unfair to the things that do not fit in. They are just as much there as the things that do. The physical world is a sort of governing aristocracy, which has somehow managed to cause everything else to be treated with disrespect. That sort of attitude is unworthy of a philosopher. We should treat with exactly equal respect the things that do not fit in with the physical world, and images are among them.[26]

Now the decisive point at this stage of reflection is that the sensory descriptions are not themselves partially described. They can be seen as partial descriptions of something, but this does not entail that they *are* partial. They are as complete as the number 7. They are just more objects whose intelligibility or availability to thought or intentional representation in an undemanding sense has to be accounted for. This means that partial descriptivism cannot be a global claim about all knowledge, as we cannot claim that the partial descriptions we have of objects are themselves only partial so that we have partial glimpses all the way up.

There is, thus, no reason to believe that we are partial because every object only appears to us under the conditions of partial descriptions, precisely because the appearances just are not always partial. There is a sense in which every description only partially describes an object, as for any object there are indefinitely many descriptions. Even the object that can only be described with one description could be described as the object that can be described with less than 200 descriptions. But this does not mean that our descriptions themselves are partial or finite in the sense of potentially distorting perspectives onto an in itself aperspectival reality.

On the contrary, the very fact that we can describe an object differently is evidence for there being an object. Epistemological pluralism is far from making any concessions to arbitrariness or even metaphysical agnosticism of the kind attacked by Meillassoux. That we can describe an event sociologically or physically as a revolution or as an event in space-time, and that we can say that it looks different on TV than from within due to different optical conditions is not evidence for the event not taking place or for it taking place only in our descriptions of it. We are not 'sealed off'[27] from objects, as the very objects introduced to explain how we are thus sealed off would themselves have to be sealed off from us by the same argument. If we were really sealed off, we could not have any warranted belief to the effect that we are thus sealed off. It would be an utterly transcendent (and, therefore, irrelevant) matter.

In epistemology we can know that there are different forms of knowledge. This corresponds to knowing that there are different senses, different ways in which objects appear. This is not yet to know which forms of knowledge there are or which are the different ways in which objects appear. In epistemology we can draw a principled distinction between epistemological and other forms of knowledge, and we can safeguard the actual plurality of forms of knowledge from our overgeneralised reductionist tendencies. In other words, epistemology and ontology protect the reality of knowledge and of what there is against the monistic fantasy of an all-encompassing entity, domain, rule, or principle without thereby providing us with far-reaching insights into the actual structure of the plurality of fields of forms of knowledge respectively. That is the business of other cognitive or epistemic activities, a business no less or more dignified than philosophical reflection, just something human beings do because they believe that knowledge is better than ignorance (which in some senses of better is certainly true).

Notes

1. Kripke, 'Nozick on Knowledge', pp. 210–11: 'It is very plausible that a unified account [of knowledge] is indeed desirable; prima facie it would seem that "*S* know that *p*" expresses one and the same relation between *S* and *p*, regardless of what proposition *p* is, or for that matter, who *S* is.'

2. Cavell, *Claim of Reason*; Williams, *Groundless Belief*; *Unnatural Doubts* and *Problems of Knowledge*; Williams, *Descartes*.

3. Cavell, *Claim of Reason*, p. 236.

4 Cavell, *Claim of Reason*, p. 54.

5. Cavell, *Claim of Reason*, p. 448.

6. For a critical discussion of scepticism based on sources of knowledge see Kern, *Quellen des Wissens*.

7. To be historically accurate, we ought to take into account that there is no exact equivalent for 'external world' in Descartes. He does not actually talk about the external world anywhere, but rather of 'externa' (Cf. AT VII 22), meaning external objects, which is not the same, as there might be external objects without them being collected into a unified world. In the Principles (II.21), Descartes defines the world as a 'universe of corporeal substance' that has no limits to its extension (AT VIII 52). See also, Gabriel, *Skeptizismus und Idealismus in der Antike*.

8. Cf. Chalmers, *Constructing the World*, Fifteenth Excursus: The Structural Response to Skepticism, pp. 431–40. Umrao Sethi pointed out in discussion of this material that there is, of course, a degree of difference between the sources and the appearances they yield that must not be exceeded in order for us to still speak of knowledge. Beyond merely causal or merely structural matches between how certain things are and how they appear to us, we require an epistemically relevant form of matching.

9. For a contemporary defence of such a conception of logics see Rödl, *Self-Consciousness*, and Rödl, *Categories of the Temporal*.

10. Conant, 'Varieties of Scepticism'.
11. Conant, 'Varieties of Scepticism', 100.
12. Kant, *Critique of Pure Reason*, A112.
13. Frege, *Basic Laws of Arithmetic*, p. xvi.
14. Chalmers, *Constructing the World*, p. 438.
15. Chalmers, *Constructing the World*, p. 438.
16. Derrida, 'Cogito and the History of Madness'.
17. Descartes, 'Meditations on First Philosophy', p. 18.
18. In a somewhat different context, Michael McKinsey argues against what he takes to be Davidson's insufficient idea of privileged access to ourselves as access to our mere existence. Rather, McKinsey argues that we have to think of ourselves as thinking, which presupposes access to ourselves under some description or other. According to McKinsey Davidson 'wishes to claim, apparently, that one could have privileged access to an episode of thought independently of having privileged access to any particular descriptions that the episode might satisfy. But then what would one have privileged access *to* in such a case? Perhaps one would be privileged to know only that the episode exists; given what Davidson says, there is no reason to suppose that the agent would have privileged access even to the fact that the episode is an episode of *thought*, as opposed to being, say, an episode of indigestion.' Michael McKinsey, 'Anti-Individualism and Privileged Access', p. 11. However, Descartes' anti-sceptical strategy need not rely on us actually having privileged access to the description as thinkers of this thought in order to work. All he needs is that we need to satisfy that description in order to count as deceived.
19. Rometsch, *Freiheit zur Wahrheit*.
20. For further discussion of this point see my *Skeptizismus und Idealismus*.
21. I was not able to verify that these are actual Winogrand quotes. Yet, they were presented as quotations in a Winogrand exhibition at San Francisco MOMA, which is what I am referring to here.
22. Kant, *Critique of Pure Reason*, B 133f.
23. Russell, 'Knowledge by Acquaintance and Knowledge by Description'.
24. Wittgenstein, *Philosophical Investigations*, p. 90.
25. Cf. John Searle's forthcoming book on perception with Oxford University Press.
26. Russell, *Logic and Knowledge*, p. 257. See also p. 274.
27. Cavell, *Claim of Reason*, p. 144.

13

Senses as Ways Things Are in Themselves

After explicitly responding to Russell's paradox with his own version of a type-theory, Frege famously concludes his *The Basic Laws of Arithmetic* with the following remark:

> The prime problem of arithmetic is the question, In what way are we to conceive logical objects, in particular, numbers? By what means are we justified in recognizing numbers as objects?[1]

Interestingly, the emphasis here is on the concept of grasping, of 'fassen'. Generally, Frege seems to use 'fassen' synonymously with 'erfassen', 'auffassen' and 'ergreifen'. In his discussion of 'psychological logic'[2] in the preface of the book, or 'psychologism' as we are by now used to saying, we find a similar emphasis, this time associated with 'ergreifen', 'to apprehend', which is here opposed to 'erzeugen', 'to produce' or 'to create'.

> If we want to get out of the subjective at all, we have to interpret (*auffassen*) knowing (*Erkennen*) as an activity, which does not produce that which is known, but which grasps (*ergreifen*) something already there (*das Vorhandene*).[3]

The discussion of psychologism in *The Basic Laws* displays an ambivalence inherent in the object of critique, an ambivalence, I believe, Frege was not fully aware of. For there are at least two forms of psychologism in the realm of thought: there is first a *psychologism about thought* in the sense of the propositional content of a thought, and there is second a *psychologism about thinking* in the sense of the activity of having or grasping thoughts. Both claims need to be distinguished even though they naturally overlap in various respects.

In the first part of this chapter, I want to show that Frege might have the resources to combat psychologism about thought, but that he himself is an overtly psychologistic thinker about thinking. Yet, psychologism about thinking cuts deeper than psychologism about thought, as it ultimately undermines the force of anti-psychologism about thought. This is manifest in Frege's emphasis in the above-quoted passages from *The Basic Laws* where he claims that not only what is grasped but also the grasping ought not to be thought of as merely 'psychological' in the psychologistic sense. Let me note here already that the relevant concept of 'psychology' in 'psychologism' is part and parcel of a typical philosophical fiction. The 'psychology' Frege is referring to does not coincide with the scientific discipline 'psychology'. This does not mean that no psychologist is prone to psychologism, but that is a different question. 'Psychologism' is a philosophical doctrine that can be stated independently of any particular conception of what psychology is. It is important not to confuse the psychology envisaged from a psychologistic or anti-psychologistic point of view with the scientific discipline we call 'psychology'. As Cavell once correctly noted in his typical aphoristic mode, we need 'to undo the psychologizing of psychology'.[4]

> We know of the efforts of such philosophers as Frege and Husserl to undo the 'psychologizing' of logic (like Kant's undoing Hume's psychologizing of knowledge): now, the shortest way I might describe such a book as the *Philosophical Investigations* is to say that it attempts to undo the psychologizing of psychology, to show the necessity controlling our application of psychological and behavioural categories; even, one could say, show the necessities in human action and passion themselves.[5]

Psychologism is the claim that certain apparently non-psychological entities under closer inspection, that is, under the scrutiny of conceptual analysis, turn out to actually be psychological entities. Here 'psychological' refers to 'mental' or 'subjective', and 'subjective' is understood as 'merely subjective'. The presupposition is that mental content is private or 'in the head', and that psychology studies what is 'private in the head'. However, this is not what the actual discipline psychology does – not even if we understand psychology as a natural science. As I will argue, psychology could not study the mind in the sense of the 'private in the head' for the simple reason that there is no such thing. If psychology studied the mind in this particular 'homuncularist'[6] sense, to borrow Mark Johnston's phrase, we should close all psychology departments immediately. Studying what is literally going on in my head, that is, brain-processes, is precisely not tantamount to studying private processes in the sense of objectively inaccessible mental contents. Such a view of what psychology does is at the very least highly contentious.

In this chapter I will also argue that something very close to Fregean 'senses', but senses without underlying psychologistic assumptions, are indeed ways things are in themselves. I have only recently discovered that Mark Johnston has defended a very similar set of claims on the epistemological end of the spectrum, defending the view that we are not 'producers' of modes of presentations, but rather 'samplers', as he puts it.[7] I approach this from an ontological point of view. I believe that objects really are identical with what is true about them. There are a number of things true about every object. In order to have a variety of truths about an object, we need a variety of senses, modes of presentation. There are no objects without senses, and no senses without a plurality of senses. If an object could not be presented at all, even as something that we cannot present to ourselves, nothing would be true of it, not even that it is an object that we cannot present to ourselves (maybe because we lack a proper medium for cognition, such as sonar). And if an object could only be presented in one way, it could not be thought of at all, given that thinking of an object is such that we can already present it in different ways, for example as O or as Not-Not-O or as 'If O then O' or as 'O is not Not-O.' In my view, this is an *ontological truth* and not just an *ontological commitment* of semantics.[8] Research into ontological truth is not tantamount to commitment-research.

Thinking itself *is* part of what there is, and thus it is not just *about* what there is. This conception of thinking is part of a response to the form of scepticism entailed by psychologism about thinking. Thinking has to be 'out there' as much as any other object we are able to refer to in such a way that we get it right or wrong. Given that we are often theorising about thinking and that there is substantial disagreement about its 'nature', we should avoid severing thinking in the sense of the activity of grasping thoughts from what there is.

Thinking is a sense, and we therefore have more than five

senses (there are other reasons as well). Emotions are also senses, a fact that the sceptic about other minds, say a behaviourist, misconstrues by already misunderstanding the concept of senses. In this context I maintain that the word 'sense' in 'Fregean senses' and in 'sense-organs' or in 'sensing' is not used equivocally, but that 'Fregean senses' and 'sense-organs' are indeed closely tied together, which I take to be a version of the claim that there is no non-conceptual given in sense experience, or that the conceptual is limitless or whatever contemporary enhanced version of Parmenides-cum-Kant-cum-Hegel you prefer. However, I see no reason to call this 'objective mind', as Johnston does.[9] Despite a little irony in his almost explicit profession of objective idealism, I think he succumbs to the standing classical temptation to be overly impressed by the fact that facts are intelligible or manifest. However, I think it is a quite natural affair that I can understand that I am in London even though I only ever grasp a finite amount of modes of presentations of London. This is how things are, and how things are is only surprisingly intelligible if we are implicitly tempted to deny their intelligibility.

Frege has provided far-reaching insights into the shortcomings of what has ever since been labelled 'psychologism'. As I already said, *psychologism* is the claim that certain apparently non-psychological entities, under closer inspection, that is, under the scrutiny of conceptual analysis, turn out to actually be psychological entities. I say 'psychological' here and not 'mental', as Frege does not deny that thinking is a mental process in some sense. What he does though is relegate the study of the activity of thinking to 'psychology' in the problematic psychologistic sense.[10]

Note that this general view might have some coherent local instantiations, and that Frege does not attempt to refute psychologism in an even more general form where it would consist in the discovery that some alleged utterly non-mental or inanimate fact is really related to minds. For example, psychologism in this very different sense about certain aspects of race and gender might be entailed by pointing out their socially constituted or historical nature. Where we formerly believed that certain social functions were necessary because we naturally associated them with female and male bodies respectively, we now know that we were wrong. One element in that discovery is psychologism about certain aspects of race and gender, but obviously not about all aspects of race and gender. No one has recently gone so far as to argue that the very fact that we have bodies is socially constituted or histori-cal. Even though one might be tempted to believe that gender, like sex, is a feature of the human animal body, it nevertheless turns out to be a psychological entity in the sense of something that would not have existed had no one ever had a belief about it. If we had no beliefs, we would still have bodies, but we would not have gender.

Again: psychologism as such need not be a general or even uni-versal thesis, for example, the thesis that everything is psychologi-cal or that at some ground level everything is really psychological. Frege can therefore not be seen as generally attacking psychology or even some extension of psychology into domains hitherto considered non-psychological. He is not defending a general anti-psychologistic stance, let alone an anti-psychological one.

Evidently, it is easy to prove that not every discourse is subject to psychologistic reduction: talking and thinking about oxygen is not, even though I have heard psychologistic thinkers, in this case highly decorated psychology professors, tell me that oxygen is nothing but a sum of sense impressions with the illusion that they refer to something external to the brain. This is at best 'a hitherto unknown form of madness',[11] to borrow from Frege again, and stands in need of therapy.

Frege is troubled by psychologism about thought itself, and arguably psychologism about oxygen is often the result of some-one's profound commitment to psychologism about thought itself, as certainly was the case with the psychology professor I have in mind. It is not quite correct that Frege's problem is psychologism about logics, even though this is the official doctrine, as it were. It is more precise to keep in mind that he is worried about psy-chologism about logics due to his conception of the relationship between thought itself and logics. His main focus is showing that psychologism about all aspects of thought is not and cannot be warranted. There is something about thought that is not psycho-logical in the psychologistic understanding of 'psychological'. The problem with psychologism remains even if one could defend a more pluralistic concept of logics, that is, a conception of logics that allows for a plurality of formal systems, without therein seeing a threat to rationality as such. Frege thinks that a very universal form of logics lies at the roots of rationality as such. But even if that is not true, his arguments against psychologism about all aspects of thought are still valid.

Frege's basic argument amounts to an interesting form of semantic externalism. What is external for Frege, though, are not natural kinds or the external world, but thought in the famous sense of the propositional content of a thought-episode in the standard meaning of the term. For him the externality of thought is still part of the thought itself in a different way than that that lake over there is part of my thought that water is H_2O. The shape Frege's argument takes famously hinges on the distinction between the truth-conditions of a thought and the conditions of someone taking a thought to be true, between the conditions of *Wahrheit* and the conditions of *Fürwahrhalten*, or in short between truth and belief. Frege argues that truth and belief have to be subject to different conditions or to different laws, as he puts it.

His starting point is the observation that truth and belief potentially differ. Not everything we take to be the case therefore is the case. Truth potentially outruns belief, and if Frege's critique of psychologism is true, he has shown the actual divergence of truth and belief for at least one particular belief about the very relationship between truth and belief. For, even if psychologism were true, the fact remains that it was true before someone acquired the then correct belief that it is indeed true. There will, thus, always be a sense in which the belief the psychologist holds about thinking is true regardless of any belief about it. If successful, Frege's argument against psychologism is an argument for realism. Some truths are necessarily independent of our beliefs; something is the case whether we recognise it or not. Something is the case anyway.

This is a presupposition the psychologistic thinker has to accept. For he argues that thought generally really is psychological, where this often is associated with the intention to study thought empirically. Now even if psychologism were true, this would not be the case because psychologism makes it so. Rather psychologism is also committed to realism about the realm of thought itself. The psychologistic thinker is a realist about thought. But if he is a realist about thought, he has to grant that he can either get thought right or get it wrong. Given that the psychologistic thinker finds himself in disagreement with the non-psychologistic thinker, he has to come up with some error theory for his opponent's discourse. All of this presupposes the potential divergence of the conditions of truth and the conditions of taking for true, between a thought and its apprehension, whatever the nature of the apprehension.

Therefore, Frege concludes, a general psychologism about thought itself is incoherent.

Even though I am inclined to believe that there is more than one coherent and convincing reconstruction of Frege's basic argument, or rather arguments, against psychologism, I believe that regardless of the reconstruction, Frege ultimately remains mired in psychologism. For Frege is a psychologistic theorist about grasping thoughts, which he implicitly holds in the passages where he talks about the relation between a thinker, a 'bearer of thinking (*Träger des Denkens*)',[12] and a thought. He is so busy limiting the scope of a general psychologism about thought itself that he neglects to fight shy of psychologism about thinking where it is necessary. This shortcoming generates a whole new territory of sceptical manoeuvres, manoeuvres of the type James Conant has described under the heading of the 'Kantian variety of skepticism'.[13] A general psychologism about thinking is as bad, nay, even worse, than a general psychologism about thought.

Whereas general psychologism about thought might threaten to enclose us in some immanent sphere of pure mental acts, general psychologism about thinking undermines our overall 'mindedness',[14] as Conant puts it. If we think of thinking in terms of a mental act and if we model mental acts along the lines characteristic of psychologism, we lose our sense for our capacity of grasping thoughts that significantly go beyond the sphere of 'the mental'. To grasp a thought is then seen as internalising a reality, of transforming it from something 'out there' into something 'in here'. But this opens up a potential gap between our acts of thinking and the fact that they are about something, which makes objective purport look mysterious in the characteristic sense of a 'Kantian skepticism', as Conant puts it.

Frege grants the terrain of 'mental representation' to the psychologistic thinker, just as he tends to grant the terrain of reference-free play with thoughts to poetry. Both moves are equally unwarranted. *Death in Venice* is really about Venice and about death, even though 'Gustav von Aschenbach' might not refer to a person who was once also an aggregate of elementary particles. Not all poetry is senses without reference, just as not all mental episodes are the objects of study of psychology. Frege in this context notoriously introduces the apparently harmless category of 'Vorstellung', sometimes simply translated as 'idea'. As is well known, he distinguishes between sense, reference and mental representation. Arguably, the latter concept is precisely the focus of Wittgenstein's quarrel with private language. Let me just note in passing that I take Wittgenstein not even primarily to be attacking sense-data conceptions of mental content, but psychologism about thinking, thereby also pointing out the crucial shortcoming in Frege's theory of thought. This is what Cavell apparently means when he sees Wittgenstein as undoing the psychologising of psychology.

Before I go into the details of the shortcomings of Frege's theory of thinking, I would like to prepare the ground for my own argument by highlighting one of the premises of Frege's complex argument against psychologism about thought. The premise I have in mind states that in order for a thought to be objective, its identity cannot wholly consist in the temporal fact that someone grasps it at some point in the history of minds, of 'Geister', as Frege himself says in a remarkable passage where he distinguishes between the categories 'mind (*Geist*)' and 'minds (*Geister*)'.[15] I call this *the objectivity condition*, which we can pin down thus:

> *The Objectivity Condition for Thought*: If a thought is to be objective, its identity cannot wholly consist in the temporal fact that someone grasps it at some point in the history of minds.

In order for the objectivity condition to be met, thoughts have to be modally robust entities in the following way. An entity is modally robust if it has modal properties anyway. Rocks are modally robust. There would have been rocks had no one ever believed such. Some thoughts are not modally robust; in particular, some thoughts are about thoughts. We also know that we have not exhausted the nature of thought itself. Thought itself has some modally robust properties we have not discovered yet, which is why there still is philosophy.

At least for some (Fregean) thoughts, it has to be the case that they would have been the thoughts they are had no one ever grasped them. Some thoughts meet the objectivity condition. Now there are two aspects of the objectivity condition: sense and reference. Reference guarantees that some aspect of thought is modally robust in the relevant meaning of the term. If a thought refers, what it refers to is sometimes a modally robust entity. Some thoughts thinking about thought itself are an exception to this rule, given that thought thinking about some stretch of the history of minds definitely is to the extent to which some thoughts about thoughts only exist if they are referred to. Sense, on the other hand, guarantees that there are many different thoughts. The senses of a thought constitute a thought as this rather than that thought. I agree with Johnston that we should understand modes of presentation as 'features' of the objects whose modes they are, which means that they individuate the objects.[16] I also agree with him that this holds independently of the specific nature of the objects, be they physical objects like electrons, or logical objects like modus ponens. Senses are the principle of identity and plurality of thoughts, whatever they happen to be about. If there were no senses, there would be no plurality of thoughts, but maybe just one monolithic lump, the true. In this sense, one could say that senses are properties of thoughts, given that properties are precisely those kinds of things that are introduced in order to explain the identity and plurality of objects of some kind or other. The introduction of senses in a theory of thought corresponds to the introduction of properties in a theory of objects for the simple reason that thoughts are just so many more objects.

At this point it is important to be explicit about the fact that there are many Fregean premises I do not share. For example, I believe that the substantial distinction between concepts and objects leads to nonsense, and that this nonsense is robust, that is, not somehow illuminating nonsense. In addition, I do not believe that Frege was aware of this. Robust nonsense as such first comes into view with Wittgenstein, and it more or less merely happens to Frege out of a certain intellectual honesty. Frege finds himself committed to this nonsense, and he is surprised by it. Against this background I drop the dualism of object and concept and replace it by its functional equivalent of objects appearing in fields of sense. For me whatever is an object can become the content of truth-apt thought because objects are not different from what is true about them. The formal theory of objects is grounded in the functional ontological difference between objects and fields. There are no substances metaphysically hidden behind their appearances, that is, behind whatever is true of them. Even if there were substances in that sense, this would be true about them. This is the quintessence of the formal theory of objects defended in this chapter.

When I think about a thought, I think about an object. So as to avoid confusion, one could distinguish between *things* and *objects*. Whereas an object is the more general category, things are spatiotemporally extended objects, that is, objects with particular properties. When I say that thoughts are objects, I am therefore neither implying nor yet ruling out that they are or could be things. Whether thoughts are things is another question. To some extent Frege himself would of course agree that thoughts or some aspect of thought is indeed an object, given that he takes truth values to be objects in his own technical sense of the term. But I think that his distinction between the 'features (*Merkmale*) of a concept' and 'the properties (*Eigenschaften*) of an object' is merely verbal and not substantive.[17] That it is a property of concepts that they do not necessarily have all the properties of the objects that fall under them is a true proposition, but this does not justify the introduction of a difference in category or type, as Frege believes. There is a functional equivalent of the distinction that does not classify certain entities in a substantial category distinction. Frege seems to hold on to a categorical distinction between objects and concepts (functions), even though he then also allows for a variety of functions. Yet, this is still a form of ontological monism to the extent to which concepts and functions exhaust what there is by being the most general categories.

Thoughts are objects, and for Frege they have at least the properties of being either determinately true or false, and also of being individuated by their senses. We can now raise the question of whether it is even coherent to think of thinking as something that would generally be studied by psychology, where 'psychology' refers to the in fact imaginary discipline psychologism uses as a base for its reduction. It is quite telling that in a footnote in *The Thought* Frege has to resort to the nonsense characteristic of his way of setting things up when he imagines the relation between thinking and its thoughts:

> The expression 'apprehend' is as metaphorical as 'content of consciousness'. The nature of language does not permit anything else. What I hold in my hand can certainly be regarded as the content of my hand but is all the same the content of my hand in quite a different way from the bones and muscles of which it is made and their tensions, and is much more extraneous to it than they are.[18]

In this passage Frege wrestles with psychologism about thinking. In my view, he comes close to the claim that sense is also a property of thinking and not just of thought, but seems to want to reject this claim on pains of psychologism about thought. In the main text, however, Frege explicitly acknowledges that there must be a conceptually relevant connection between a thinker and her thought.

> The apprehension of a thought presupposes someone who apprehends it, who thinks. He is the bearer of thinking but not of the thought. Although the thought does not belong to the contents of the thinker's consciousness yet something in his consciousness must be aimed at the thought. But this should not be confused with the thought itself.[19]

Yet, how can a thinker aim at a thought without looking in a particular direction, as it were? How can we even conceive of consciousness as a phenomenon below the threshold of true descriptions of it? In terms of the allegory of the telescope: how is it possible to dissociate the content of the mental image from the fact that the telescope points in a particular direction? From here, this is exactly what I get to see. It is not an accident that I see this from here and not that, because this is what I can see from here.[20]

If thinking really were actually entirely psychological in nature, for example a process in our brains (on the contemporary most widespread conception of psychology as psychophysics), we would wind up with a devastating form of scepticism. For we could never claim to have grasped a thought given that this would presuppose that some chunk of matter would have to get in touch with sense, a completely immaterial kind of substance made up of the properties of thoughts which are themselves completely immaterial.

Frege unfortunately resorts to another version of Cartesian dualism, not between extended and thinking substance, but rather between thoughts and thinking. If the former could not be bridged without God's help for conceptual reasons, no wonder the problem returns in a different disguise when we psychologise the act of thinking. Against Frege we therefore have to find a way to defend the idea that thinking does not generally stop short of its thoughts, just as thoughts do not generally stop short of the facts.

General psychologism about thinking is at least as devastating as psychologism about thought. Both create sceptical scenarios. In the latter scenario, belief and truth threaten to merge such that we could never have any false beliefs. To be true and to be recognised as true must not coincide. In the first scenario, however, it might even well be that we never really grasp a thought. Thinking might be the illusion of meat machines who believe themselves to be grasping thoughts, to be in touch with something beyond brain states. However, whatever appears to me as this rather than that thought might be an illusion. I might not even have thoughts. But if I had no thoughts, then what exactly am I doing right now? Thinking without thoughts is hardly thinking at all. Even though on this scenario I cannot rule out that there are Fregean thoughts because I cannot even ascertain that I am thinking, I also cannot evaluate that thought itself.

The argument so far presented is inspired by Sebastian Rödl's engagement with the requirements for the objectivity of thinking he derives from his engagement with Kant and Frege.[21] However, my own solution to the problem of psychologism significantly differs from his. For in my view, properties of objects, such as the property of being thought of, are modally robust in a quite general sense. In order to make things as clear as possible, let us rehearse a simple first-order example, the example of literal visual perspective. A visual perspective of a spatiotemporal object – say of the volcano Mount Vesuvius in the Gulf of Naples – in my view is not a Fregean 'Vorstellung', but rather a sense. It is objective and modally robust. Vesuvius would have looked the way it does from Naples at some point in the history of the universe, or the continent on which Italy is currently located, had no one ever seen it. And the way it looks right now is objective in that we can share the same view of Vesuvius from Naples and agree that this view differs from the view of Vesuvius you get in Sorrento, that is, from the other side of the Gulf. The introduction of the concept of perspective in modernity originally refers to an objective structure, describable in optical terms.[22] That Vesuvius looks such-and-so from Naples is not a function of my nervous system. Rather, my nervous system is suited to views of Vesuvius. I am capable of grasping that Vesuvius looks such-and-so from Naples, and my nervous system is part of that story. But the story involves a view of Vesuvius we can share. In other words, there is nothing inherently subjective in the concept of perspective in the sense of 'subjective' acquired by the term in the unfolding of the 'dialectic of perspectivism', as Conant calls it, in the Post-Kantian era.

Let me just mention in passing that the dialectic of perspectivism is not a particularly modern product. As I have argued elsewhere, it can be found in ancient philosophy, where over the centuries it became a powerful argumentative weapon culminating in Pyrrhonian scepticism.[23] I am saying this here just to dispel the possible impression that there is a characteristically modern downfall epitomised by Nietzsche. As Nietzsche himself was very well aware, his early and his middle selves are just following the outlines of Pyrrhonian and really already pre-Socratic scepticism.

Be that as it may, it is important to note that even spatiotemporal adumbrations in something like Husserl's sense cannot be reduced to Fregean 'Vorstellungen'. Perspectives are about something that is not identical with any particular perspective on it, and that also cannot be incompatible with the fact that there are perspectives on it such that these perspectives are genuinely about the object in question. This is the upshot of Husserl's theory of evidence.

Contrary to Frege, I am not inclined to regard this train of thought as a piece of semantics, or rather, not of semantics alone, as I maintain that modally robust perspectives and more generally modally robust senses are properties of the objects they are about. By this I mean that the fact that Vesuvius would have looked such-and-so even had no one ever noticed, is a property of Vesuvius and not a property of some external relationship to Vesuvius, such as my particular relation to Vesuvius at some point in my biography. How something looks is objective; it is 'out there', 'in reality', as it were, or more precisely – given that neither 'out there' nor 'in reality' have a well-defined meaning – how something looks is modally robust.

Objects only appear in fields of sense; there is no Fregean reference without Fregean sense, as he was well aware. Yet, this is not only the case because we make up the sense. A lot of sense is found and not constituted. What we find when we discover some new sense is a new property or some new properties of an object the sense is about. Objects only exist in fields of sense, and there is a nesting of fields of sense within each other, a nesting surreptitiously reified if we refer to it as the world. If I see an object, the perspective in which I see it as well as the fact that it has at this point in time been seen by me are properties of the object itself and not only of my relationship to it.

Frege treats sense and reference as an epistemological or semantic problem, which is why he creates a sceptical threat for his own position in the form of the hypothesis of a fully-fledged realm of sense without any reference, a hypothesis he interestingly associates with the 'inventions of legend and poetry'.[24] He commits to partial descriptivism and, at least, does not defend himself against the fallacy from finitude to ignorance one might see operative in the following passage:

> The sense of a proper name is grasped by everybody who is sufficiently familiar with the language or totality of designations to which it belongs; but this serves to illuminate only a single aspect of the *Bedeutung*, supposing it to have one. Comprehensive knowledge of the *Bedeutung* would require us to be able to say immediately whether any given sense attaches to it. To such knowledge we never attain.[25]

Now we can of course not only think about Vesuvius, for example, by looking at it, but we can also think about thoughts. If we do that, a thought appears to us in a particular manner. Thoughts also have modes of presentation. Otherwise, there would only be one thought, a monolithic thought lump, maybe the object Frege labels 'the true', or maybe a logical space encompassing two monolithic thought lumps, 'the true' and 'the false'. Thoughts in general come with a variety of modally robust properties we grasp when thinking them. A thought is like Vesuvius. It can be apprehended in manifold ways, which – in Frege's analysis – is an important condition of the possibility of the fact that thinking is a form of information processing. But again, the information we process cannot be generally created by the fact that we process it. That 5 is both the first prime number after 3 and the sum of 2 and 3, or that some thought carries information, are not facts created by our relationship to them, as Frege himself insists with his metaphor of 'grasping' or 'apprehending'. Thus, sense has to be there.

Frege's Kantian heritage blocks this option from his view. The main problem is that he divides the world up into the external world, which he explicitly defines as 'the whole of space and all that therein is',[26] and some realm of abstract objects, as this has later been called. As an intermediary he is happy to ontologically commit to 'Vorstellungen'. I disagree with all three ontological commitments, and I do not even believe that this very unfortunate trinity is in any way constitutive of the concept of sense or of reference.

Thinking is a legitimate part of what there is. It is a fact among other facts. If Britney thinks that it is raining in London, her thinking is as much a fact as that it is raining in London. Both facts are objects insofar as we can think about them. In epistemology, we often think of thought and its relation to objects as if the concept of an 'object' was primarily the concept of an object in a world without spectators. But whether there are spectators or not is much less exciting ontologically than one might think. The idea that we are epistemic aliens, that we inhabit the illusory situation of the fly in the fly-bottle, is hopelessly misguided. As Cavell has also emphasised, it is not the case that there are two big objects, the world and our knowledge, such that we can meaningfully ask how they relate to each other. Both objects are artefacts of philosophical discourse and neither even exist, which becomes clear if one tries to take a closer look at them.

I wholeheartedly agree with McDowell's famous dictum that 'thought does not stop short of the facts',[27] which of course is not intended to rule out fallibility, but only that a thought that is as a matter of fact true could have the modal property of being metaphysically possibly false. I am not sure if he would agree that thoughts are therefore not just about facts in such a way that they do not generally stop short of them, but that they are themselves facts. Thoughts are objects in themselves, just as tables, atoms, the earth, moon and fingernails are. A thing or object in itself is something that has at least some maximally modally robust properties, by which I mean properties it would have had 'anyway'. Every thought has such properties, such as the property of being a thought. *My* thought that p would have been *the* thought that p had no one ever been around or had no one, including me, ever noticed. Many thoughts, which are actually believed, written down or justified, turn out to have properties we did not notice before. For example, the property of Euclidean thoughts about space turned out to be geometrically local in a surprising way, that is, true only in a limited domain and not true of space in general. Nothing rules out that many past beliefs had maximally modal robust properties we will never make explicit for some reason or other. In particular, this holds for thought about thought. The very fact that we disagree in central disciplines of philosophy such as logics, ontology, or epistemology is evidence that thought has maximally modally robust properties we simply have not discovered yet. Or, in other words, there are many senses for which we have not developed a sense yet, which leads me to my final topic, to the relation between sense and sensing.

Aristotle has claimed that we have five senses, that is, five sense-organs that he introduced as media in which properties of material substances become manifest. In his view, thinking is not an additional sense, but distinguished from the senses in that it encompasses and organises the various sense impressions delivered to it by the five sense-organs. Thinking is, if a sense at all, the common sense, the synthesising activity of putting sense impressions from various sources together. Thinking is, he writes, 'a synthesis of thoughts as if they were one'.[28] He takes his text *On the Soul* to be an exercise in the philosophy of nature. It is a quasi-biological account of human sensing. It has always struck me: why one would accept these claims and actually believe that we only have five senses. I admit that I am as suspicious of the claim that we have five senses as I am of Aristotle's zoology. Weirdly enough, his theory of the senses is still widespread: many of us believe that they have five senses and that these are well distinguished and rooted in the structure of our brain or our body in general. But what is a 'sense', where this term refers to our sensory capacities?

It seems evident to many philosophers that our bodies are bare particulars consisting of bare particulars, and that somehow these bare particulars are able to download concepts either from a heaven of forms or from the external world. However, I follow Wittgenstein to a certain degree in rejecting the very idea of the world as a totality of objects in the first place. If anything, the world is rather a domain of facts, even though I also reject the idea that it is a *totality* of facts, which is the no-world-view. Objects have properties, and facts are whatever is true of an object. Objects are not independent of what is true of them. Hence, there are no bare particulars in the sense of ontological elementary particles. The fact that I am right now changing this sentence from the oral form in which it was originally presented to a written form is constitutive of the object I am. I would not be the object I am if I were not embedded in this fact. If a fact indeed is a true thought, and if thoughts are objects having senses as their properties, the very idea of the world as an atomistic universe consisting of bare particulars of any kind is incoherent.

A *sense* – when we talk about sensing – is a fallible relationship with potentially maximally modally robust facts. The fact that this sound is a chord in C major is modally robust. If I believe that I hear that this sound is a chord in C major I am in a fallible position just as when I believe to see an animal in the bushes. When I get things right, I sense a sense, and my sense enables me to grasp a fact. When I get things wrong, there is a fact that explains why and how I got things wrong, given that false belief is at least embedded in the fact that it is a false belief. For any false belief B[booh!] there is the possibility of the true belief B[yeah!] that B[booh!] is a false belief.

If a sense is defined by a fallible relationship with potentially maximally modally robust facts, thinking itself is a sense. It just so happens that the human animal has a well-developed sense of thinking. Thinking is the sense by which we grasp objects in the most distant regions of our environment. We can think of things long gone, of things yet to come, and of things so far away from us in time that we can never get into actual physical contact with them. Other animals also think, but their sense of thinking is just not developed in the way ours is. However, there are also senses we do not have at all, such as sonar, or senses that are weak in human beings. In addition, our economy of senses is to a certain degree individualised: some have better hearing and others better taste.

Let me add that I do not want to restrict our senses to six by adding thinking to the senses. Emotions are senses too. If I feel that someone likes me, I get in touch with a modally robust fact, and I might be right or wrong about it. As soon as I try to reconstruct this capacity, my sense of feeling sympathy, in terms of any of the five senses, I will wind up with familiar sceptical paradoxes. Of course, feeling that someone likes me is not a side effect of smelling, touching, tasting, hearing, and seeing a spatiotemporal object, but it is nevertheless a sense, namely a sense *sui generis*. When I made this point recently during a seminar in Beijing, Binghao Hu referred me to a nice Zhuangzi episode I was not aware of before:

> Travelling with Huizi over a bridge on the Hao River, Zhuangzi said, 'The fish is swimming at ease. This is how the fish enjoy themselves.' Huizi said, 'You are not a fish. How do you know the fish are enjoying themselves?' Zhuangzi said, 'You are not me. How do you know I don't know about the fish?' Huizi said, 'I am not you and certainly don't know about you, you are certainly not a fish and you will not know about the fish. That's for sure.' Zhuangzi said, 'Let's trace back to your original question. You said "How do you know the fish are enjoying themselves?" This question shows that you know I know about the fish. Since you know about me, why can't I know about the fish? I got to know it over a bridge on the Hao River.'[29]

By definition, all senses are world-involving in a twofold way: They are *in* the world and *of* the world. To be more precise, it is not exactly true that a sense is in the world and of the world. Rather, a sense is in some region of the world and of some region of the world. The world as a whole is never successfully referred to, and the idea of the world as a whole is incoherent. The world as a whole does not exist. But even if you believe that there is something like 'reality in its entirety' – and if you do please tell me how you justify that belief – seeing that it is snowing only concerns a very small portion of it. All we need is, thus, the view that senses are reality-involving: They are of a reality and in a reality.

Our senses are therefore not rooted in some inaccessible overall noumenal environment. They are themselves part of any environment we would want to identify as 'noumenal'. Our access to what there is belongs to what there is, which is why we explore things in themselves when we explore thought itself. Thinking about thought is thinking about things in themselves, and while thinking about thought we discover that there are many thoughts that are individuated by their senses. Otherwise, there could be a thought entirely individuated by the object it is about. But that it is about this rather than that object is constitutive of the thought itself, and that fact cannot be identical with the object. The thought that my left hand is not my right hand is true of my left hand but is not identical with my left hand. Many other things are true of my left hand. These thoughts are senses, modes of presentation of my left hand. The object itself is in no way independent of the manifold senses in which it can appear to thinkers. The object is not absolute in that way.

There are fields of sense, and we orient ourselves in these fields with the help of our manifold senses for what there is. Of course, we sometimes get it wrong. And yet, even if we get it wrong we do not thereby transcend 'the world', as it is still a fact about someone getting it wrong that he got it wrong and not right. The very idea of a general psychologism about thinking is thus metaphysically incoherent, because it undercuts the conditions of thinking being a fact among facts, and therefore of our fallible attitude with regard to thinking itself. If I am right about this, I could have been wrong; if I am wrong about this, I could have been right saying something else. Thus, I can at least be confident that you will not convince me in the debate to follow this sentence that we cannot be right or wrong when thinking about thinking itself. But, am I now suggesting that we have merely been thinking about thinking and not about things or objects in themselves all along? Only if you believe

356 Fields of Sense

that thinking hovers over the waters of the real. However, it does not; it belongs already to what one wants to avoid when thinking about thinking as happening in the special realm of 'the mind', a word we fortunately do not have a translation for in German. And why deprecate the reality of thinking by either relegating it to the physical or outsourcing it to another realm, a realm somehow coming late in the history of the universe – as if there only were dark meaningless extended spaces before animal thinking brought the light of the intellect to the universe, only to find out that there is no room for it in a cold, cold world?

Notes

1. Cf. Frege, *The Basic Laws of Arithmetic*, p. 143 (original pagination p. 265): 'Als Urproblem der Arithmetik kann man die Frage ansehen: wie fassen wir logische Gegenstände, insbesondere die Zahlen? Wodurch sind wir berechtigt, die Zahlen als Gegenstände anzuerkennen?'
2. Cf. Frege, *The Basic Laws of Arithmetic*, introduction, pp. v–xxvi. Nietzsche uses this expression in a similar sense: 'The psychological logic is this: *the feeling of power*, when it suddenly and overwhelmingly overruns a man – and this is the case in all great affects – makes him doubt his own person: he doesn't dare think of himself as the cause of this astonishing feeling – and so he posits a *stronger* person, a divinity, to explain it.' Nietzsche, *Writings from the Late Notebooks*, p. 261, originally KSA 13, 14[124]. See also: Nietzsche, *Human, all too Human: A Book for Free Spirits*, Aphorism 11 'The Wanderer and his Shadow', p. 306.
3. Cf. Frege, *The Basic Laws of Arithmetic*, p. xxiv.
4. Cavell, *Must We Mean What We Say?*, p. 91. Thanks to James Conant for referring me to this passage after a discussion of the paper underlying this chapter during a conference on skepticism and intentionality at Bonn University in October, 2012.
5. Ibid.
6. Johnston, 'Self-deception and the Nature of Mind', pp. 63–5 and pp. 79–86.
7. Johnston, *Saving God*, p. 132 and Johnston, 'Objective Mind and the Objectivity of Our Minds', p. 235.
8. Quine, *Word and Object*, p. 22.
9. Johnston, 'Objective Minds and the Objectivity of Our Minds', p. 256: 'But modes of presentation are not mental; they are objective,

in that they come with the objects themselves as the very features of those objects that make them available for demonstration, thought and talk. And they are individuated by the objects they present.'

10. Bill Brewer objected during a presentation of the paper underlying this chapter at the speaker series at King's College London that it would not be intelligible that someone discovered that thinking was psychological, as this would be trivial. In this sense, no one could be a psychologist about thinking in my sense. However, the very idea of thinking as a hidden subjective process taking place in our minds actually comes rather late in the history of the theories of the nature of thinking. See, for instance, Bruno Snell's analysis of mental vocabulary in Homer in Snell, *The Discovery of the Mind*. The idea of thinking as a subjective process to be studied by psychology is even foreign to Kant to the extent that he wants to insist that thinking is governed by non-psychological laws, as he believes that psychology only describes appearances of ourselves, that is to say, events governed by natural laws. It is, therefore, not trivial to claim that thinking is studied by psychology or rather that all aspects of thinking are studied by psychology, which is why psychologism about thinking is not trivially ruled out by my definition.

11. Frege, *Basic Laws of Arithmetic*, p. xvi.

12. Frege, 'The Thought', p. 299.

13. Conant, 'Varieties of Scepticism', pp. 97–136.

14. Conant, 'Varieties of Scepticism', p. 104.

15. Frege, 'The Thought', p. 308.

16. See Johnston, 'Objective Mind and the Objectivity of Our Minds', p. 235: 'All the modes of presentation of each existing thing, be they intellectual or sensory modes, all the possible ways of thinking and sensing each such thing, come into being with the things themselves, whether or not there are any individual minds to sample these modes of presentation, i.e. to access them in individual mental acts.' See also p. 245: '[W]e are to think of these modes of presentation as objective (if sometimes relational) features of the things themselves. This is the idea that each item that could be a topic of thought and talk has associated with it a host of standing ways, or manners, or modes, of presenting.' Finally see p. 247: 'But modes of presentation are not mental; they are objective, in that they come with the objects themselves as the very features of those objects that make them available for demonstration, thought and talk. And they are individuated by the objects they present.'

17. Frege, *Basic Laws of Arithmetic*, p. 11 (original pagination, p. xiv).

18. Frege, 'The Thought', p. 307, footnote 1: 'The expression "apprehend" is as metaphorical as "content of consciousness". The nature of language does not permit anything else. What I hold in my hand can certainly be regarded as the content of my hand but is all the same the content of my hand in quite a different way from the bones and muscles of which it is made and their tensions, and is much more extraneous to it than they are.'

19. Frege, 'The Thought', p. 308.

20. On a similar train of thought see Johnston, 'Objective Mind and the Objectivity of our Minds', p. 242f.

21. See in particular his 'Logical Form as a Relation to the Object'.

22. Cf. Conant, 'The Dialectic of Perspectivism, I'; 'The Dialectic of Perspectivism, II' and Bredekamp, *Das Fenster der Monade*.

23. See Gabriel, *Skeptizismus und Idealismus in der Antike* and Gabriel, *Antike und moderne Skepsis zur Einführung*.

24. Frege, *Foundations of Arithmetic*, § 14, p. 20.

25. Gottlob Frege, 'On Sinn and Bedeutung', p. 153. See also Frege, 'The Thought', p. 298: 'Accordingly, with a proper name, it depends on how whatever it refers to is presented. This can happen in different ways and every such way corresponds with a particular sense of a sentence containing a proper name.'

26. Frege, *Foundations of Arithmetic*, § 87, p. 99: 'The laws of number will not, as Baumann thinks, need to stand up to practical tests if they are to be applicable to the external world; for in the external world, in the whole of space and all that therein is, there are no concepts, no properties of concepts, no numbers. The laws of number, therefore, are not really applicable to external things; they are not laws of nature. They are, however, applicable to judgements holding good of things in the external world: they are laws of the laws of nature. They assert not connexions between phenomena, but connexions between judgements; and among judgements are included the laws of nature.'

27. McDowell, *Mind and World*, § 3, pp. 27–9.

28. Aristotle, *On the Soul*, 430a27f.

29. Zhuangzi, *Zhuangzi*, p. 283.

Bibliography

Albert, David, 'On the Origin of Everything: A Universe From Nothing by Lawrence M. Krauss', *New York Times* (25 March 2012), p. BR20.

Allen, Woody, *Love and Death*, Film, written and directed by Woody Allen (USA: Jack Rollins & Charles H. Joffe Productions, 1975).

Anscombe, Gertrude E. M., *Intention* (Cambridge, MA: Harvard University Press, 2000).

Aristotle, 'Metaphysics', in *The Complete Works of Aristotle: Revised Oxford Edition*, Vol. 2, ed. Jonathan Barnes, tr. W. D. Ross (Princeton: Princeton University Press, 1991).

Aristotle, 'Nicomachean Ethics', in *The Complete Works of Aristotle: Revised Oxford Edition*, Vol. 2, ed. Jonathan Barnes, tr. W. D. Ross (Princeton: Princeton University Press, 1991).

Aristotle, 'On the Soul', in *The Complete Works of Aristotle: Revised Oxford Edition*, Vol. 1, ed. Jonathan Barnes, tr. J. A. Smith (Princeton: Princeton University Press, 1991).

Aristotle, 'Physics', in *The Complete Works of Aristotle: Revised Oxford Edition*, Vol. 1, ed. Jonathan Barnes, tr. R. P. Hardie and R. K. Gaye (Princeton: Princeton University Press, 1991).

Armstrong, David M., *Sketch for a Systematic Metaphysics* (Oxford; New York: Clarendon Press, 2010).

Austin, John L., *Sense and Sensibilia* (London; Oxford; New York: Oxford University Press, 1962).

Badiou, Alain, *Logics of Worlds*, tr. Alberto Toscana (London; New York: Continuum, 2009).

Badiou, Alain, *Briefings on Existence: A Short Treatise on Transitory Ontology*, ed., tr. and intr. Norman Madarasz (Albany, NY: SUNY Press, 2006).

Badiou, Alain, *Being and Event*, tr. Oliver Feltham (London; New York: Continuum, 2005).

Badiou, Alain, *Theoretical Writings*, ed. and tr. Ray Brassier and Alberto Toscana (London; New York: Continuum, 2005).

Baetzel, Conrad, *Wittgenstein and the Limits of Philosophy* (Doctoral Dissertation at Bonn University, 2015).

Barnes, Jonathan, *The Ontological Argument* (London: Macmillan Press, 1972).

Benoist, Jocelyn, 'Alien Meaning and Alienated Meaning' (forthcoming).

Benoist, Jocelyn, *Éléments de Philosophie Realiste* (Paris: Librairie Philosophique J. Vrin, 2011).

Berto, Francesco, *There's Something About Gödel: The Complete Guide to the Incompleteness Theorem* (Oxford: Wiley-Blackwell, 2009).

Blumenberg, Hans, *Paradigms for a Metaphorology*, tr. Robert Savage (Ithaca, NY: Cornell University Press, 2010).

Blumenberg, Hans, *Höhlenausgänge* (Frankfurt am Main: Suhrkamp, 1996).

Blumenberg, Hans, *Work on Myth*, tr. R. M. Wallace (Cambridge, MA: MIT Press, 1990).

Boghossian, Paul, *Angst vor der Wahrheit: Ein Plädoyer gegen Relativismus und Konstruktivismus*, tr. Jens Rometsch (Berlin: Suhrkamp, 2013).

Boghossian, Paul, *Fear of Knowledge: Against Relativism and Constructivism* (Oxford: Oxford University Press, 2006).

Brandom, Robert, *Tales of the Mighty Dead: Historical Essays in the Metaphysics of Intentionality* (Cambridge, MA: Harvard University Press, 2002).

Brassier, Ray, *Nihil Unbound: Enlightenment and Extinction* (Basingstoke: Palgrave Macmillan, 2007).

Bredekamp, Horst, *Das Fenster der Monade: Gottfried Wilhelm Leibniz' Theater der Natur und Kunst*, 2nd edn (Berlin: Akademie Verlag, 2007).

Bryant, Levi R., *The Democracy of Objects*. Available online at http://hdl.handle.net/2027/spo.9750134.0001.001

Cantor, Georg, *Contributions to the Founding of the Theory of Transfinite Numbers*, tr. P. E. B. Jourdain (New York: Cosimo Books, 2007).

Cantor, Georg, *Briefe*, ed. Herbert Meschkowski and Winfried Nielsen (Berlin; Heidelberg: Springer, 1991).

Cantor, Georg, 'Mitteilungen zur Lehre vom Transfiniten', in Georg Cantor, *Gesammelte Abhandlungen mathematischen und philosophischen Inhalts*, ed. Ernst Zermelo (Berlin: Julius Springer, 1932), pp. 378–439.

Caplan, Ben, 'Ontological Superpluralism', *Philosophical Perspectives*, Vol. 25 (2011), pp. 79–114.

Carnap, Rudolf, *The Logical Structure of the World:* and *Pseudoproblems in Philosophy* (Peru, IL: Open Court 2003).

Carnap, Rudolf, 'Empiricism, Semantics and Ontology', in Rudolf Carnap, *Meaning and Necessity: A Study in Semantics and Modal Logic*, 2nd edn (Chicago: University of Chicago Press, 1956), pp. 205–21.

Castoriadis, Cornelius, 'The Logic of Magmas and the Question of Autonomy', in Cornelius Castoriadis, *The Castoriadis Reader*, ed. David A. Curtis (Oxford; New York: Oxford University Press, 1997), pp. 290–318.

Cavell, Stanley, *The Claim of Reason: Wittgenstein, Skepticism, Morality, and Tragedy* (New York; Oxford: Oxford University Press, 1999).

Cavell, Stanley, *Must We Mean What We Say? A Book of Essays* (Cambridge: Cambridge University Press, 1976).

Chalmers, David, *Constructing the World* (Oxford: Oxford University Press, 2012).

Chalmers, David, David Manley and Ryan Wasserman eds, *Metametaphysics: New Essays in the Foundations of Ontology* (New York: Oxford University Press, 2009).

C. K., Louis, *Hilarious*, Film, written and directed by Louis C. K. (USA: 2010).

Conant, James, 'The Dialectic of Perspectivism, II', *SATS – Nordic Journal of Philosophy*, Vol. 7, No. 1 (2006), pp. 6–57.

Conant, James, 'The Dialectic of Perspectivism, I', *SATS – Nordic Journal of Philosophy*, Vol. 6, No. 2 (2005), pp. 5–50.

Conant, James, 'Varieties of Scepticism', in *Wittgenstein and Scepticism*, ed. Denis McManus (Abingdon; New York: Routledge, 2004), pp. 97–136.

Conant, James, 'The Search for Logically Alien Thought: Descartes, Kant, Frege and the *Tractatus*', in 'The Philosophy of Hilary Putnam', *Philosophical Topics*, Vol. 20, No. 1 (1991), pp. 115–80.

Critchley, Simon, *Things Merely Are: Philosophy in the Poetry of Wallace Stevens* (London; New York: Routledge, 2005).

Deacon, Terrence, *Incomplete Nature: How Mind Emerged from Matter* (New York: Norton, 2012).

DeLanda, Manuel, *Intensive Science and Virtual Philosophy* (London: Continuum, 2002).

Derrida, Jacques, *The Animal That Therefore I Am*, tr. David Wills (New York: Fordham University Press, 2008).

Derrida, Jacques, 'Cogito and the History of Madness', in Jacques Derrida, *Writing and Difference* (London: Routledge, 2001), pp. 36–76.

Descartes, René, 'Meditations on First Philosophy', in *The Philosophical Writings of Descartes*, Vol. 2, ed. John Cottingham, Robert Stoothoff and Douglas Murdoch (Cambridge: Cambridge University Press, 1984–91), pp. 1–50.

Descartes, René, *Principles of Philosophy*, trans. V. R. Miller and R. P. Miller (Dordrecht: Reidel, 1983).

Dummett, Michael, *Frege: Philosophy of Language* (Cambridge: Harvard University Press, 1993).

Düsing, Klaus, 'Hegel und die klassische griechische Philosophie', in Dietmar Heidemann and Christian Krijnen eds, *Hegel und die Geschichte der Philosophie* (Darmstadt: Wissenschaftliche Buchgesellschaft, 2007), pp. 143–62.

Eliot, T. S., 'Burnt Norton', in T. S. Eliot, *Collected Poems 1909–1962* (New York: Harcourt Brace & World, 1963), pp. 175–81.

Engelhard, Kristina, 'Hegel über Kant: Die Einwände gegen den transzendentalen Idealismus', in Dietmar Heidemann and Christian Krijnen eds, *Hegel und die Geschichte der Philosophie* (Darmstadt: Wissenschaftliche Buchgesellschaft, 2007), pp. 191–216.

Fichte, Johann G., *The Science of Knowing: J. G. Fichte's 1804 Lectures on the Wissenschaftslehre*, tr. Walter E. Wright (Albany, NY: SUNY Press, 2005).

Forster, Michael, *Wittgenstein and the Arbitrariness of Grammar* (Princeton: Princeton University Press, 2005).

Frank, Manfred, *Auswege aus dem Deutschen Idealismus* (Frankfurt am Main: Suhrkamp, 2007).

Frege, Gottlob, 'On Sinn and Bedeutung', in *The Frege Reader*, ed. M. Beaney (Oxford: Blackwell Publishing, 1997), pp. 151–71.

Frege, Gottlob, 'Dialogue with Pünjer about Existence', in *Gottlob Frege: Posthumous Writings*, ed. Hans Hermes, Friedrich Kambartel and Friedrich Kaulbach, trans. Peter Long and Roger White (Oxford: Basil Blackwell, 1979), pp. 53–67.

Frege, Gottlob, *The Basic Laws of Arithmetic: Exposition of the System*, tr. Montgomery Furth (Berkeley: University of California Press, 1964).

Frege, Gottlob, *The Foundations of Arithmetic: A Logico-Mathematical Enquiry into the Concept of Number*, tr. J. L. Austin (New York: Harper, 1960).

Frege, Gottlob, 'The Thought: A Logical Inquiry', *Mind*, New Series, Vol. 65, No. 259 (July 1956), pp. 289–311.

Frege, Gottlob, 'On Concept and Object', *Mind*, Vol. 60, No. 238 (1951), pp. 168–80.

Frisk, Hjalmar, *Griechisches etymologisches Wörterbuch* (Heidelberg: C. Winter Verlag, 1960–72).

Gabriel, Markus ed., *Der Neue Realismus* (Berlin: Suhrkamp, 2014).

Gabriel, Markus, 'Existenz, realistisch gedacht', in Gabriel, Markus ed., *Der Neue Realismus*, pp. 171–89

Gabriel, Markus, 'Schelling's Ontology in the *Freedom Essay*', *SATS: Northern European Journal of Philosophy* Vol. 15, No. 1 (2014), pp. 75–98.

Gabriel, Markus, 'Ist die Kehre ein realistischer Entwurf', in David Espinet and Toni Hildebrandt eds, *Suchen Entwerfen Stiften: Randgänge zu Heideggers Entwurfsdenken* (München: Wilhelm Fink Verlag, 2014), pp. 87–106.

Gabriel, Markus, 'Facts, Social Facts, and Sociology', in Markus Gabriel and Werner Gephart eds, *The Normative Structure of Human Civilisation: Readings in John Searle's Social Ontology* (forthcoming, 2014).

Gabriel, Markus, *Warum es die Welt nicht gibt* (Berlin: Ullstein, 2013). English translation as *Why the World does not Exist* (London; New York: Polity Press, 2014).

Gabriel, Markus, 'Aarhus Lectures: Schelling and Contemporary Philosophy', *SATS: Northern European Journal of Philosophy*, Vol. 14, No. 1 (Nov. 2013), pp. 70–101.

Gabriel, Markus, 'Nachwort', in Paul Boghossian, *Angst vor der Wahrheit: Ein Plädoyer gegen Relativismus und Konstruktivismus*, tr. Jens Rometsch (Berlin: Suhrkamp, 2013), pp. 135–56.

Gabriel, Markus, 'Is the World as Such Good? The Question of Theodicy', in Vittorio Hösle ed., *Dimensions of Goodness* (Newcastle Upon Tyne: Cambridge Scholars Publishing, 2013), pp. 45–65.

Gabriel, Markus, 'Ist der Gottesbegriff des ontologischen Beweises konsistent?', in Thomas Buchheim, Friedric Hermanni, Axel Hutter and Christoph Schwöbel eds, *Gottesbeweise als Herausforderung für die moderne Vernunft* (Mohr Siebeck: Tübingen, 2012), pp. 99–119.

Gabriel, Markus, *Die Erkenntnis der Welt: Eine Einführung in die Erkenntnistheorie* (Freiburg: Karl Alber, 2012).

Gabriel, Markus, 'Dissens und Gegenstand – Vom Außenwelt zum Weltproblem', in Markus Gabriel ed., *Skeptizismus und Metaphysik* (Berlin: Akademie Verlag, 2012), pp. 73–92.

Gabriel, Markus, *Transcendental Ontology: Essays in German Idealism* (New York: Continuum, 2011).

Gabriel, Markus, *Skeptizismus und Idealismus in der Antike* (Frankfurt am Main: Suhrkamp, 2009).

Gabriel, Markus and Slavoj Žižek, *Mythology, Madness and Laughter: Subjectivity in German Idealism* (London: Continuum, 2009).

Gabriel, Markus, 'God's Transcendent Activity: Ontotheology in *Metaphysics* 12', *The Review of Metaphysics* (2009), pp. 385–414.

Gabriel, Markus, 'The Mythological Being of Reflection – an Essay on Hegel, Schelling, and the Contingency of Necessity', in Markus Gabriel and Slavoj Žižek, *Mythology, Madness and Laughter: Subjectivity in German Idealism* (London: Continuum, 2009), pp. 15–94.

Gabriel, Markus, 'Nachträgliche Notwendigkeit — Gott, Mensch und Urteil beim späten Schelling', *Philosophisches Jahrbuch* I (2009), pp. 21–41.

Gabriel, Markus, *An den Grenzen der Erkenntnistheorie: Die notwendige Endlichkeit des objektiven Wissens als Lektion des Skeptizismus* (Freiburg; München: Karl Alber, 2008).

Gabriel, Markus, *Antike und moderne Skepsis zu Einführung* (Hamburg: Junius, 2008).

Gabriel, Markus, *Das Absolute und die Welt in Schellings Freiheitsschrift* (Bonn: Bonn University Press, 2006).

Gabriel, Markus, *Der Mensch im Mythos: Untersuchungen über Ontotheologie, Anthropologie und Selbstbewußtseinsgeschichte in Schellings 'Philosophie der Mythologie'* (Berlin; New York: DeGruyter, 2006).

Garcia, Tristan, *Form and Object: A Treatise on Things*, tr. M. A. Ohm and Jon Cogburn (Edinburgh: Edinburgh University Press, 2014).

Goethe, Johann W. v., *Faust: Part One*, tr. David Lukes (Oxford; New York: Oxford University Press, 1987).

Goodman, Nelson, *Ways of Worldmaking* (Indianapolis: Hackett, 1978).

Goodman, Nelson, *The Structure of Appearance* (Cambridge, MA: Harvard University Press, 1951).

Grim, Patrick, *The Incomplete Universe* (Cambridge, MA: MIT Press, 1991).

Habermas, Jürgen, *Truth and Justification* (Cambridge, MA: The MIT Press, 2003).

Hampe, Michael, *Tunguska oder das Ende der Natur* (München: Carl Hanser, 2011).

Harman, Graham, 'On the Undermining of Objects: Grant, Bruno, and Radical Philosophy', in Levi R. Bryant, Nick Srnicek and Graham Harman eds, *The Speculative Turn: Continental Materialism and Realism* (Victoria, Australia: re.press, 2011), pp. 21–40.

Healy, Kevin, Luke McNally, Greame D. Ruxton, Natalie Cooper and Andrew L. Jackson: 'Metabolic Rate and Body Size are Linked with Perception of Temporal Information', *Animal Behaviour* Vol. 86 (2013), pp. 685–96.

Hegel, G. W. F., *Lectures on the Philosophy of World History: Vol. I. Manuscripts of the Introduction and the Lectures of 1822–23*, tr. and ed. by Robert F. Brown and Peter C. Hodgson (Oxford: Oxford University Press, 2011).

Hegel, G.W.F., *Encyclopedia of the Philosophical Sciences*, tr. Klaus Brinkmann and D. O. Dahlstrom (Cambridge: Cambridge University Press, 2010).

Hegel, G. W. F., *The Science of Logic*, tr. George Di Giovanni (Cambridge; New York: Cambridge University Press, 2010).

Hegel, G. W. F., *The Encyclopaedia Logic: Part 1 of the Encyclopaedia of Philosophical Sciences*, tr. T. F. Geraets, W. A. Suchting and H. S. Harris (Indianapolis: Hackett, 1991).

Hegel, G. W. F., *The Difference Between Fichte and Schelling's System of Philosophy*, tr. H. S. Harris and Walter Cerf (Albany, NY: SUNY Press, 1977).

Hegel, G. W. F., *Faith and Knowledge*, trans. W. Cerf and H. S. Harris (Albany, NY: State University of New York Press, 1977).

Hegel, G. W. F., *Hegel's Aesthetics: Lectures on Fine Art*, Vol. 1, tr. T. M. Knox (Oxford: Clarendon Press, 1975).

Hegel, G. W. F., *Outlines of the Philosophy of Right*, tr. H. B. Nisbet (Cambridge: Cambridge University Press, 1991).

Heidegger, Martin, *Das Argument gegen den Brauch (für das Ansichsein des Seienden)*, Jahresgabe der Martin-Heidegger-Gesellschaft 2013/2014.

Heidegger, Martin, *Introduction to Metaphysics*, trans. Gregory Freid and Richard Polt (New Haven, CT: Yale University Press, 2000).

Heidegger, Martin, *Aristotle's Metaphysics – 1–3: On the Essence and Actuality of Force*, trans. Walter Brogan and Peter Warnek (Indianapolis: Bloomington, 1995).

Heidegger, Martin, *The Basic Problems of Phenomenology*, tr. Albert Hofstadter (Indianapolis: Bloomington, 1982).

Heidegger, Martin, 'The Age of World Picture', in Martin Heidegger, *The Question Concerning Technology and Other Essays*, tr. William Lovitt (New York: Harper and Row, 1977), pp. 115–54.

Heidegger, Martin, 'Einblick in das was ist: Bremer Vorträge 1949', in *Gesamtausgabe*, Part III, Volume 79, ed. Petra Jaeger (Frankfurt am Main: Vittorio Klostermann Verlag, 2005), pp. 5–77. Partly translated as 'The Turning', in Martin Heidegger, *The Question Concerning Technology and Other Essays*, tr. William Lovitt (New York: Harper & Row, 1977), pp. 36–52.

Heidegger, Martin, 'The Question Concerning Technology', in Martin Heidegger, *The Question Concerning Technology and Other Essays*, tr. William Lovitt (New York: Harper & Row, 1977), pp. 3–35.

Heidegger, Martin, *Identity and Difference*, tr. Joan Stambaugh (New York: Harper & Row, 1969).

Heidegger, Martin, *What is Called Thinking?*, trans. F. D. Wieck and J. G. Gray (New York: Harper & Row, 1968).

Heidegger, Martin, *Kant and the Problem of Metaphysics*, tr. J. S. Churchill (Bloomington: Indiana University Press, 1962).

Henrich, Dieter, *Fichtes ursprüngliche Einsicht* (Frankfurt am Main: Klostermann, 1967).

Hindrichs, Gunnar, *Das Absolute und das Subjekt: Untersuchungen zum Verhältnis von Metaphysik und Nachmetaphysik* (Frankfurt am Main: Klostermann Verlag, 2008).

Hirsch, Eli, 'Against Revisionary Ontology', in Eli Hirsch, *Quantifier Variance and Realism: Essays in Metaontology* (New York: Oxford University Press, 2011), pp. 96–123.

Hirsch, Eli, *Quantifier Variance and Realism: Essays in Metaontology* (New York: Oxford University Press, 2011).

Hogrebe, Wolfram, 'Sein und Emphase — Schellings Theogonie als Anthropogenie', in Wolfram Hogrebe, *Die Wirklichkeit des Denkens: Vorträge der Gadamer-Professur* (Heidelberg: Universitäts Verlag, 2007), pp. 37–60.

Hogrebe, Wolfram, *Orphische Bezüge: Abschiedsvorlesung an der Friedrich-Schiller-Universität zu Jena am 5.2.1997* (Erlangen: Palm & Enke, 1997).

Hogrebe, Wolfram, *Metaphysik und Mantik: die Deutungsnatur des Menschen (Système Orphique de Iéna)* (Frankfurt am Main: Suhrkamp, 1992).

Hogrebe, Wolfram, *Prädikation und Genesis: Metaphysik als Fundamentalheuristik im Ausgang von Schellings »Die Weltalter«* (Frankfurt am Main: Suhrkamp, 1989).

Hogrebe, Wolfram, *Archäologische Bedeutungspostulate* (Freiburg/München: Alber 1977).

Holt, Jim, 'Physicists, Stop the Churlishness', *New York Times*, 10 June 2012, p. SR12.

Horgan, Terence, and Matjaz Potrc, 'Blobjectivism and Indirect Correspondence', *Facta Philosophica* 2 (2000), pp. 249–70.

Husserl, Edmund, *Formal and Transcendental Logic*, tr. Dorion Cairns (The Hague: Martin Nijhoff, 1969).

van Inwagen, Peter, 'Being, Existence and Ontological Commitment', in David Chalmers, David Manley and Ryan Wasserman eds, *Metametaphysics: New Essays in the Foundations of Ontology* (New York: Oxford University Press, 2009), pp. 472–506.

van Inwagen, Peter, *Metaphysics*, 3rd edn (Boulder: Westview Press, 2009).

van Inwagen, Peter, 'Meta-Ontology', in *Erkenntnis*, Vol. 48, No. 3 (1998), pp. 233–50.

Jacobi, Friedrich H., 'Concerning the Doctrine of Spinoza in Letters to Herr Moses Mendelssohn (1785)', in *The Main Philosophical Writings and the Novel Allwill*, ed. and tr. by George Di Giovanni (Montreal: McGill-Queen's University Press, 1995), pp. 173–252.

Jauernig, Anja, *How to Think about Things in Themselves – An Essay on Kant's Metaphysics and Theory of Cognition* (Oxford; New York: Oxford University Press, forthcoming).

Johnston, Mark, *Saving God: Religion after Idolatry* (Princeton: Princeton University Press, 2009).

Johnston, Mark, 'Objective Minds and the Objectivity of Our Minds', in *Philosophy and Phenomenological Research*, Vol. 75, No. 2 (September 2007), pp. 233–68.

Johnston, Mark, 'Self-deception and the Nature of Mind', in Brian P. McLaughlin and Amélie O. Rorty eds, *Perspectives on Self-deception* (Berkeley: University of California Press, 1988), pp. 63–91.

Kant, Immanuel, *Groundwork of the Metaphysics of Morals*, tr. Mary Gregor (Cambridge; New York: Cambridge University Press, 2011).

Kant, Immanuel, 'Anthropology from a Pragmatic Point of View', in Immanuel Kant, *Anthropology, History and Education*, ed. Günter Zöller and R. B. Louden, tr. R. B. Louden (Cambridge: Cambridge University Press, 2007), pp. 227–429.

Kant, Immanuel, *Prolegomena to Any Future Metaphysics: That Will be Able to Come Forward as Science*, tr. and ed. by Gary Hatfield (Cambridge; New York: Cambridge University Press, 2004).

Kant, Immanuel, *Critique of Pure Reason*, trans. Paul Guyer and A. W. Wood (Cambridge: Cambridge University Press, 2000).

Kern, Andrea, *Quellen des Wissens: Zum Begriff vernünftiger Erkenntnisfähigkeiten* (Frankfurt am Main: Suhrkamp, 2006).

Koch, Anton F., *Versuch über Wahrheit und Zeit* (Paderborn: Mentis, 2006).

Koch, Anton F., *Subjektivität in Raum und Zeit* (Frankfurt am Main: Klostermann, 1990).

Krauss, Lawrence, *A Universe from Nothing: Why there is Something rather than Nothing* (New York: Atria Books, 2013).

Krauss, Lawrence and Ross Andersen, 'Has Physics Made Philosophy and Religion Obsolete?', *The Atlantic*, 23 April 2012. Available online at http://www.theatlantic.com/technology/archive/2012/04/has-physics-made-philosophy-and-religion-obsolete/256203/.

Kreis, Guido, *Negative Dialektik des Unendlichen* (Habilitationsschrift, Bonn, 2014).

Kripke, Saul A., *Reference and Existence: The John Locke Lectures* (Oxford: Oxford University Press, 2013).

Kripke, Saul A., 'Nozick on Knowledge', in Saul Kripke, *Philosophical Troubles: Collected Papers Vol. 1* (Oxford: Oxford University Press, 2011), pp. 162–224.

Kripke, Saul A., 'Naming and Necessity', in Milton K. Munitz ed., *Identity and Individuation* (New York: New York University Press, 1971), pp. 135–64.

Langton, Rae, 'Elusive Knowledge of Things in Themselves', *Australasian Journal of Philosophy*, Vol. 82, No. 1 (March 2004), pp. 129–36.

Langton, Rae, *Kantian Humility: Our Ignorance of Things in Themselves* (Oxford: Oxford University Press, 1998).

Latour, Bruno, *An Inquiry into the Modes of Existence: An Anthropology of the Moderns*, trans. Catherine Porter (Cambridge, MA: Harvard University Press, 2013).

Leibniz, Georg Wilhelm, 'Meditations on Knowledge, Truth and Ideas', in Georg Wilhelm Leibniz, *Philosophical Essays*, tr. and ed. by Roger Ariew and Daniel Garber (Indianapolis: Hackett, 1989), pp. 23–7.

Lewis, David, *Papers in Metaphysics and Epistemology* (Cambridge: Cambridge University Press, 1999).

Lewis, David, 'Elusive Knowledge', *Australasian Journal of Philosophy*, Vol. 74, No. 4 (December 1996), pp. 549–67.

Lewis, David, *On the Plurality of Worlds* (Oxford: Oxford University Press, 1986).

Lewis, David, 'Putnam's Paradox', *Australasian Journal of Philosophy*, Vol. 62, No. 3 (September 1984), pp. 221–36.

Liddell, Henry G., Henry S. Jones and Robert Scott, *A Greek-English Lexicon*, 9th edn (Oxford: Oxford Clarendon Press, 2009).

Livingston, Paul M., 'Realism and the Infinite', *Speculations: A Journal of Speculative Realism*, IV (2013), pp. 99–107.

Luft, Eduardo, *Deflationary Ontology as Network Ontology* (forthcoming).

Luhmann, Niklas, 'Erkenntnis als Konstruktion', in Niklas Luhmann, *Aufsätze und Reden*, ed. Oliver Jahraus (Stuttgart: Reclam, 2001), pp. 218–42.

Mann, Thomas, *Death in Venice*, tr. M. H. Heim (New York: Ecco, 2004).

McDowell, John, *Plato: Theaetetus*, trans. John McDowell, paperback edition (Oxford: Oxford University Press, 2014).

McDowell, John, 'Sellars on Perceptual Experience', in John McDowell, *Having the World in View: Essays on Kant, Hegel and Sellars* (Cambridge, MA: Harvard University Press, 2009), pp. 3–22.

McDowell, John, 'Intentionality as a Relation', in John McDowell, *Having the World in View: Essays on Kant, Hegel and Sellars* (Cambridge, MA: Harvard University Press, 2009), pp. 44–65.

McDowell, John, 'The Disjunctive Conception of Experience as Material for a Transcendental Argument', in Haddock, Adrian/Macpherson, Fiona eds, *Disjunctivism. Perception, Action, Knowledge* (New York: Oxford University Press, 2008), pp. 376–89.

McDowell, John, 'Having the World in View: Sellars, Kant, and Intentionality', *The Journal of Philosophy* XCV/9 (1998), pp. 431–91.

McDowell, John, *Mind and World* (Cambridge, MA: Harvard University Press, 1996).

McDowell, John, 'Criteria, Defeasibility and Knowledge', *Proceedings of the British Academy*, Vol. 68 (1982), pp. 455–79.

McGinn, Colin, *Logical Properties: Identity, Existence, Predication, Necessary Truth* (New York: Oxford University Press, 2000).

McKinsey, Michael, 'Anti-Individualism and Privileged Access', *Analysis*, Vol. 51, No. 1 (1991), pp. 9–16.

Meillassoux, Quentin, *Iteration, Reiteration, Repetition: A Speculative Analysis of the Meaningless Sign*, Talk given at Freie Universität Berlin (20 April 2012).

Meillassoux, Quentin, *After Finitude: An Essay on the Necessity of Contingency* (London; New York: Continuum, 2008).

Meillassoux, Quentin, *Speculative Realism: Presentation by Quentin Meillassoux* in *Collapse*, Vol. III (Nov. 2007), pp. 408–35.

Meinong, Alexius, 'The Theory of Objects', in Roderick M. Chisholm ed., *Realism and the Background of Phenomenology*, trans. Isaac Levi, D. B. Terrell, R. M. Chisolm (Atascadero, CA: Ridgeview, 1960), pp. 76–117.

Meixner, Uwe, *Einführung in die Ontologie*, 2nd edn (Darmstadt: Wissenschaftliche Buchgesellschaft, 2011).

Melville, Herman, *Moby-Dick: or, The Whale* (London: Penguin Classics, 2013).

Metzinger, Thomas, *Ego-Tunnel: The Science of the Mind and the Myth of the Self* (New York: Basic Books, 2009).

Metzinger, Thomas, *Being No One: The Self-Model Theory of Subjectivity* (Cambridge, MA: University of Massachusetts Press, 2003).

Miller, Barry, '"Exists" and Existence', *The Review of Metaphysics*, Vol. 40, No. 2 (Dec. 1986), pp. 237–70.

Miller, Barry, 'In Defence of the Predicate "Exists"', *Mind*, Vol. 84, No. 335 (1975), pp. 338–54.

Moore, Adrian W., *The Infinite*, 2nd edn (London; New York: Routledge, 2001).

Moore, Adrian W., *Points of View* (Oxford; New York: Oxford University Press, 1997).

Moore, G. E., 'Proof of an External World', in G. E. Moore, *Philosophical Papers* (London/New York 1959), pp. 127–50.

Musil, Robert, *The Man Without Qualities: A Sort of Introduction and Pseudoreality Prevails*, Vol. 1, tr. Sophie Wilkings (New York: Random House, 1996).

Nietzsche, Friedrich, *Writings from the Late Notebooks*, ed. Rüdiger Bittner, tr. Kate Sturge (Cambridge: Cambridge University Press, 2003).

Nietzsche, Friedrich, *Human, all too Human: A Book for Free Spirits*, tr. R. J. Hollingdale (Cambridge: Cambridge University Press, 1996).

Nietzsche, Friedrich, *Beyond Good and Evil: Prelude to a Philosophy of the Future*, tr. Walter Kaufmann (New York: Vintage Books, 1989).

Orenstein, Alex, 'Is Existence What Existential Quantification Expresses?', in Robert B. Barrett and Roger F. Gibson eds, *Perspectives on Quine* (Oxford: Blackwell, 1990), pp. 245–70.

Plato, *Theaetetus*, tr. John McDowell, paperback edition (Oxford: Oxford University Press, 2014).

Plato, 'The Sophist', in *The Complete Works of Plato*, ed. John M. Cooper and D. S. Hutchinson, tr. N. P. White (Indianapolis: Hackett, 1997), pp. 235–93.

Prauss, Gerold, *Kant und das Problem der Dinge an sich* (Bonn: Bouvier, 1974).

Priest, Graham, *Beyond the Limits of Thought*, 2nd edn (Oxford: Oxford University Press, 2001).

Putnam, Hilary, 'The Content and Appeal of "Naturalism"', in Hilary Putnam, *Philosophy in an Age of Science: Physics, Mathematics and*

Skepticism, ed. Mario de Caro and David Macarthur (Cambridge, MA: Harvard University Press, 2012), pp. 109–25.

Putnam, Hilary, *Philosophy in an Age of Science: Physics, Mathematics and Skepticism* (Cambridge, MA: Harvard University Press, 2012).

Putnam, Hilary, *Ethics without Ontology* (Cambridge, MA: Harvard University Press, 2004).

Putnam, Hilary, 'Truth and Convention', in Hilary Putnam, *Realism with a Human Face*, ed. James Conant (Cambridge, MA: Harvard University Press, 1990), pp. 96–104.

Putnam, Hilary, *Reason, Truth and History* (Cambridge: Cambridge University Press, 1981).

Quine, W. V. O., *Word and Object* (Cambridge, MA: MIT Press, 2013).

Quine, W. V. O., 'On What There Is', in W. V. O. Quine, *From a Logical Point of View*, 2nd edn (Cambridge, MA: Harvard University Press, 1980), pp. 1–19.

Quine, W. V. O., 'Two Dogmas of Empiricism', in W. V. O. Quine, *From a Logical Point of View*, 2nd edn (Cambridge, MA: Harvard University Press, 1980), pp. 20–46.

Quine, W. V. O., 'Ontology and Ideology', *Philosophical Studies*, Vol. 2, No. 1 (1951).

Ramsey, Frank P., 'General Propositions and Causality', in Frank P. Ramsey, *The Foundations of Mathematics and other Logical Essays*, ed. R. B. Braithwaite (London: Routledge, 1931), pp. 237–55.

Rescher, Nicholas, *Process Metaphysics: An Introduction to Process Philosophy* (Albany, NY: SUNY Press, 1996).

Rödl, Sebastian, review of Joel Smith and Peter Sullivan eds, *Transcendental Philosophy and Naturalism* (Oxford: Oxford University Press, 2011), forthcoming in *European Journal of Philosophy*.

Rödl, Sebastian, *Categories of the Temporal: An Inquiry into the Forms of the Finite Intellect* (Cambridge, MA: Harvard University Press, 2012).

Rödl, Sebastian, *Self-Consciousness* (Cambridge, MA: Harvard University Press, 2007).

Rödl, Sebastian, 'Logical Form as a Relation to the Object', *Philosophical Topics*, Vol. 34, No. 1 & 2 (Spring and Fall 2006), pp. 345–69.

Rometsch, Jens, *Freiheit zur Wahrheit: Grundlagen der Erkenntnis am Beispiel von Descartes und Locke* (Habilitationsschrift, Bonn University 2014).

Ross, James F., *Portraying Analogy* (Cambridge: Cambridge University Press, 1981).

Russell, Bertrand, 'The Philosophy of Logical Atomism', in Bertrand

Russell, *Logic and Knowledge: Essays 1901–1950* (Nottingham: Spokesman, 2007), pp. 175–281.
Russell, Bertrand, *The Principles of Mathematics* (New York; London: W. W. Norton & Company, 1996).
Russell, Bertrand, *Introduction to Mathematical Philosophy* (New York: Dover, 1993).
Russell, Bertrand, *Basic Problems of Philosophy* (Oxford: Oxford University Press, 1951).
Russell, Bertrand, 'Knowledge by Acquaintance and Knowledge by Description', *Proceedings of the Aristotelian Society*, New Series, Vol. XI (1910–1911), pp. 108–28.
Ryle, Gilbert, 'Logical Atomism in Plato's Theaetetus', *Phronesis*, Vol. 35, No. 1 (1990), pp. 21–46.
Schafer, Karl, 'Kant's Conception of Cognition and our Knowledge of Things-in-Themselves' (forthcoming).
Schaffer, Jonathan, 'The Action of the Whole', *Proceedings of the Aristotelian Society Supplementary Volume* LXXXVII (2013), pp. 67–87.
Schaffer, Jonathan, 'Monism: The Priority of the Whole', *Philosophical Review*, Vol. 119, No. 1 (2010), pp. 31–76.
Schaffer, Jonathan, 'The Internal Relatedness of All Things', *Mind*, Vol. 119, No. 474 (2010), pp. 341–76.
Schaffer, Jonathan, 'Spacetime the One Substance', *Philosophical Studies*, Vol. 145 (2009), pp. 131–48.
Schelling, F. W. J., *Philosophical Investigations into the Essence of Human Freedom*, trans. Jeff Love and Johannes Schmidt (Albany, NY: SUNY, 2006).
Schelling, F. W. J., *Philosophischen Untersuchungen über das Wesen der menschlichen Freiheit und die damit zusammenhängenden Gegenstände*, in *Sämmtliche Werke*, Vol. VII, ed. K. F. A. Schelling (Stuttgart: Cotta, 1856–61).
von Schirach, Ferdinand, *Tabu* (München/Zürich: Piper Verlag, 2013).
Smith, Joel and Peter Sullivan eds, *Transcendental Philosophy and Naturalism* (Oxford: Oxford University Press, 2011).
Schmitt, Dorothee, *Das Selbstaufhebungsargument: Der Relativismus in der gegenwärtigen philosophischen Debatte* (Doctoral Dissertation at Bonn University, defended 2014).
Schmitz, Hermann, *System der Philosophie I* (Bonn: Bouvier, 1964).
Schnieder, Benjamin and Fabrice Correia eds, *Metaphysical Grounding: Understanding the Strcuture of Reality* (Cambridge: Cambridge University Press, 2012).

Schopenhauer, Arthur, *On the Freedom of the Will*, 2nd edn (Oxford: Blackwell, 1985).

Schrödinger, Erwin, *My View of the World* (Cambridge: Cambridge University Press, 1964).

Searle, John, *Making the Social World: The Structure of Human Civilization* (Oxford: Oxford University Press, 2010).

Searle, John, *The Rediscovery of the Mind* (Cambridge, MA: The MIT Press, 1994).

Searle, John, 'Minds, Brains and Programs', *Behavioral and Brain Sciences*, 1980, Vol. 3 (1980), pp. 417–57.

Seibt, Johanna, 'Pure Processes and Projective Metaphysics', *Philosophical Studies*, Vol. 101, No. 2 (2000), pp. 253–89.

Seibt, Johanna, *Properties as Processes: a Synoptic Study of Wilfred Sellars' Nominalism* (Atascadero, CA: Ridgeview, 1990).

Sellars, Wilfrid, 'Foundations for a Metaphysics of Pure Process', *Monist*, Vol. 64 (1981), pp. 3–90.

Sider, Theodore, *Writing the Book of the World* (Oxford: Clarendon Press, 2011).

Sider, Theodore, 'Ontological Realism', in David Chalmers, David Manley and Ryan Wasserman eds, *Metametaphysics: New Essays in the Foundations of Ontology* (New York: 2009), pp. 384–423.

Sider, Theodore, *Four-Dimensionalism: An Ontology of Persistence and Time* (Oxford: Clarendon Press, 2001).

Simon, Josef, *Kant: Die fremde Vernunft und die Sprache der Philosophie* (Berlin; New York: De Gruyter, 2003).

Simon, Josef, *Wahrheit als Freiheit: Zur Entwicklung der Wahrheitsfrage in der neueren Philosophie* (Berlin; New York: De Gruyter, 1978).

Snell, Bruno, *The Discovery of the Mind: The Greek Origins of European Thought*, 2nd edn (Tacoma, WA: Angelico Press, 2013).

Soames, Scott, *Philosophy of Language* (Princeton: Princeton University Press, 2010).

Sosa, Ernest, *A Virtue Epistemology: Apt Belief and Reflective Knowledge, Part I* (Oxford; New York: Oxford University Press, 2007).

Souriau, Étienne, *Les différents modes d'existence* (Paris: Presses Universitaires de France, 1943).

Strawson, Peter F., *Individuals: An Essay in Descriptive Metaphysics* (London; New York: Routledge, 2003).

Stuhlmann-Laeisz, Rainer, 'Freges Auseinandersetzung mit der Auffassung von "Existenz" als einem Prädikat der ersten Stufe und Kants Argumentation gegen den ontologischen Gottesbeweis', in

Christian Thiel ed., *Frege und die moderne Grundlagenforschung* (Meisenheim am Glan: Anton Hain, 1975), pp. 119–33.

Thanassas, Panagiotis, *Parmenides, Cosmos, and Being: A Philosophical Interpretation* (Milwaukee: Marquette University Press, 2007).

Theunissen, Michael, *Pindar – Menschenlos und Wende der Zeit* (München: C. H. Beck Verlag, 2000).

Thompson, Michael, *Life and Action: Elementary Structures of Practice and Practical Thought* (Cambridge, MA: Harvard University Press, 2008).

Thompson, Michael, 'The living individual and its kind', *Behavioral and Brain Sciences*, Vol. 21, No. 4 (1998), p. 591.

Tugendhat, Ernst, *Der Wahrheitsbegriff bei Husserl und Heidegger* (Berlin: De Gruyter, 1967).

Turner, Jason, 'Ontological Pluralism', *The Journal of Philosophy*, Vol. 107, No. 1 (2010), pp. 5–34.

Weber, Max, 'The "Objectivity" of Knowledge in Social Science and Social Policy', in Max Weber, *Collected Methodological Writings*, tr. H. H. Bruun, ed. H. H. Bruun and Sam Whimster (London; New York: Routledge, 2012).

Weber, Max, 'The Disenchantment of Modern Life', in *From Max Weber: Essays in Sociology*, tr. and ed. H. H. Gerth and C. Wright Mills (New York: Oxford University Press, 1946), pp. 129–56.

Williams, Bernard, *Ethics and the Limits of Philosophy* (London: Routledge, 2006).

Williams, Bernard, *Descartes: The Project of Pure Enquiry*, revised edition (London; New York: Routledge, 2005).

Williams, Michael, *Problems of Knowledge: A Critical Introduction to Epistemology* (Oxford: Oxford University Press, 2001).

Williams, Michael, *Groundless Belief: An Essay on the Possibility of Epistemology*, 2nd edn (Princeton: Princeton University Press, 1999).

Williams, Michael, *Unnatural Doubts: Epistemological Realism and the Basis of Skepticism* (Princeton: Princeton University Press, 1996).

Williamson, Timothy, *The Philosophy of Philosophy* (Oxford: Blackwell, 2007).

Williamson,Timothy, 'Past the Linguistic Turn', in B. Leiter, ed., *The Future for Philosophy* (Oxford: Oxford University Press, 2004), pp. 106–28.

Wittgenstein, Ludwig, *Philosophical Investigations*, tr. G. E. M. Anscombe, P. M. S. Hacker and Joachim Schulte, 4th edn (Chichester: Blackwell Publishing, 2009).

Worms, Frédéric, *Revivre: Éprouver nos blessures et nos ressources* (Paris: Flammarion, 2012).

Worms, Frédéric, 'Un temps pour vivre et un temps pour mourir?', *Annales d'histoire et de philosophie du vivant*, Vol. 4 (2001).

Wright, Crispin, *Rails to Infinity: Essays on Themes from Wittgenstein's* 'Philosophical Investigations' (Cambridge, MA: Harvard University Press, 2001).

Wright, Crispin, *Truth and Objectivity* (Cambridge, MA: Harvard University Press, 1994).

Žižek, Slavoj, *Less than Nothing: Hegel and the Shadow of Dialectical Materialism* (London; New York: Verso Books, 2012).

Žižek, Slavoj, *For They Know Not What They Do: Enjoyment as a Political Factor*, 2nd edn (London; New York: Verso Books, 2002).

Zhuangzi, *Zhuangzi*, trans. Wang Rongpei, Quin Xuqing and Sun Yongchang (Beijing: Foreign Language Press, 1999).

Index

absolute clarity, impossibility of, 24
actualism, 264
actuality, 5, 185n, 264, 267–8, 272, 277,
    278, 283, 297, 299, 300
    and Kant, 72, 73, 78, 111n
    determines possibility, 273–4, 276
    as relations between a field and its
        objects, 281
Adorno, Theodor, 313n
adverbial ontology, 102, 135–6, 138, 297
alteration, 242–3
analogy, 193, 194, 208n
ancestrality, 150, 199, 287, 290, 295
Anscombe, Elizabeth, 21–2
anthropocentric ontology *see* zoontology
anti-realism, 9, 10, 34, 41n, 99, 163, 223,
    289–90, 293, 306, 314n
antinomy, 56, 206, 239, 240, 242, 249
appearance, 18, 28n, 44, 85, 108n, 109n,
    158, 161, 162, 166, 167, 174, 175,
    183n, 184n, 226, 227, 241, 244,
    245, 268, 284, 285, 311, 312, 323,
    324
    in a field of sense, 158, 166, 187–8,
        190–1, 192, 213, 242, 246n
    vs reality, 1, 2, 3, 6–7, 26n, 168–9,
        171–2
Aristotle, 102
    and adverbial ontology, 138
    and analogy, 193, 194, 208n
    and categories, 220
    and contingency vs necessity, 281
    and domain ontology, 136, 138
    and *dynamis* vs *energeia*, 135,
        220
    and indeterminacy, 133n
    and individuals, 51, 52
    and mathematics vs physics, 136, 153n
    and metaphysics, 137–8
    and modality, 274

and ontotheology, 138
and senses, 352–3
arithmetic, 19, 122, 269–70, 281, 300,
    338
Atomzeitalter (Heidegger), 38
attention, foci of, 255–6
Austin, J. L., 4, 135, 172–3
awareness, topic-neutral, 217

Badiou, Alain, 115n, 133n
    and appearance, 184n
    and existence, 123–4, 133n
    and mathematicism, 222
    and multiplicity, 120, 122, 130–1,
        133n, 184, 196, 222
    and set-theoretical ontology, 116, 117,
        122, 123, 130, 131n
    and transfinite set theory, 221–2
Benoist, Jocelyn, 122
Berkeley, George, 75
Blumenberg, Hans, 23
Boghossian, Paul, 15, 44, 66n
Bryant, Levi, 260n
bulb-board, allegory of, 253–4
bundle theories, 230–1, 237

Cantor, Georg, 121–2, 132n, 222
Cantor's theorem, 116, 117, 221, 249n
Caplan, Ben, 25n, 70n, 106n
Carnap, Rudolf, 145–6, 146, 152, 155n,
    301
categories, 76, 86, 89, 106n, 107n, 111n,
    137, 149, 218, 219–20, 221, 231–2,
    248n, 339
Cavell, Stanley, 4, 319, 339, 345
Chalmers, David, 323, 325
Chinese Room Argument, 118
cogito (Descartes), 327
cognising *see* Erkennen
Conant, James, 324, 344